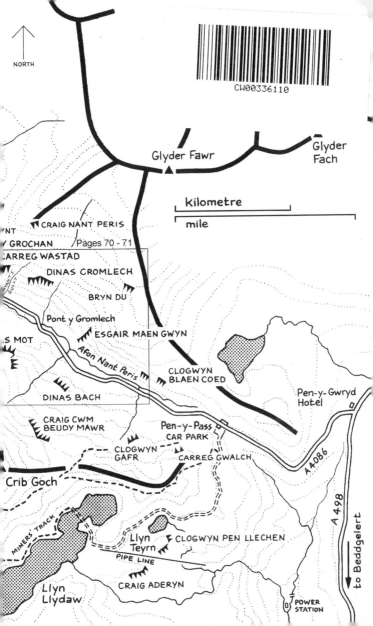

NORTH

CW00336110

Glyder Fawr

Glyder Fach

kilometre

mile

CRAIG NANT PERIS

NT

GROCHAN

CARREG WASTAD

Pages 70 - 71

DINAS CROMLECH

BRYN DU

Pont y Gromlech

ESGAIR MAEN GWYN

S MOT

Afon Nant Peris

CLOGWYN
BLAEN COED

Pen-y-Gwryd
Hotel

DINAS BACH

CRAIG CWM
BEUDY MAWR

Pen-y-Pass
CAR PARK

CLOGWYN
GAFR

CARREG GWALCH

A 4086

Crib Goch

MINERS TRACK

Llyn
Teyrn

CLOGWYN PEN LLECHEN

PIPE LINE

CRAIG ADERYN

A 498

to Beddgelert

Llyn
Llydaw

POWER
STATION

Spectrum (E3, page 55) Dinas Cromlech
Climber: Peter Robins   Photo: David Simmonite

Rift Wall (VS, page 38) Craig Ddu
Climber Stephen Coughlan · Photo David Simmonite

Climbers' Club Guides

Edited by Bob Moulton

Llanberis

by

Iwan Arfon Jones

with

Mike Bailey, Dai Lampard, Steve Mayers, Mark Richards and Jez Stephenson

Artwork

by

Simon Cardy, Don Sargeant

 Published by The Climbers' Club

A Climber's Guide to Snowdon and the Beddgelert District (1926)
by H R C Carr
Three Cliffs in Llanberis (1944)
by J E Q Barford
Llanberis Pass – First Edition (1950)
by P R J Harding
Llanberis North – First Edition (1961)
by D T Roscoe
Llanberis South – First Edition (1966)
by P Crew
Cwm Glas – Second Edition (1970)
by P Crew and I Roper
The Three Cliffs – Second Edition (1974)
by M P Hatton
Llanberis Pass – Second Edition (1978)
by G Milburn
Llanberis Pass – Third Edition (1981)
by G Milburn
Llanberis – First Edition (1987)
by P Williams
Llanberis Pass – Fourth Edition (1993)
by P Williams and I A Jones
Llanberis – Fifth Edition (2003)
by I A Jones

©The Climbers' Club 2003

Jones, Iwan Arfon   Llanberis   (Climbers' Club Guides)

British Library Cataloguing in Publication Data

A catalogue record for this book is available from the British Library

796.522

ISBN 0-901601-76-4

Front Cover: *Cemetery Gates* (E1, page 104), Dinas Cromlech
Climber: James Ibbertson
Photo: David Simmonite

Rear Cover: *Nexus* (E1, page 177), Dinas Mot
Climber: Sam Leary
Photo: Alan Leary

Typeset and prepared for printing by John Willson
Slide scanning by Redheads Digital, Sheffield
Produced by The Ernest Press, Glasgow, G46 6AQ
Distributed by Cordee, 3a De Montfort Street, Leicester, LE1 7HD

Contents

Maps and Diagrams

Photos: [1]Simon Cardy, [2]Don Sargeant, [3]Malcolm Griffith,
[4]Ken Wilson, [5]Ray Wood, [6]Iwan Arfon Jones

All photodiagrams prepared by Simon Cardy

All maps and photoplans by Don Sargeant

This book is dedicated to Paul Williams.

His encyclopedic knowledge of routes, descriptive dexterity, and a fondness for a well honed turn of phrase enabled him to produce a series of inspirational guidebooks.

His enthusiasm for climbing was a spur to many, whether reading his texts, gazing at his posters, attending his slide shows, or being at the receiving end of one of his barbs out at the crag.

Paul Williams (1946–1995)   Photo: Ian Smith

Climbers' Club Guides

The Climbers' Club

The publisher of this guidebook is The Climbers' Club, which was founded in 1898 from origins in Snowdonia and is now one of the foremost mountaineering clubs in Great Britain. Its objects are to encourage mountaineering and rock-climbing, and to promote the general interest of mountaineers and the mountain environment.

It is a truly national club with widespread membership, and currently owns huts in Cornwall, Pembrokeshire, Derbyshire, Snowdonia, and Argyll. Besides managing seven huts, The Climbers' Club produces an annual Journal and runs a full programme of climbing meets, dinners, and social events. Club members may also use the huts of other clubs through reciprocal arrangements. The club publishes climbing guidebooks (currently 20 in number) to cover most of Wales and Southern England. The club is a founder-member of, and is affiliated to, the British Mountaineering Council; it makes annual contributions to the Access and Conservation Trust, as well as to volunteer cliff and mountain rescue organizations. In 1999, the Climbers' Club Colin Kirkus Guidebook Fund was established as a means of distributing some of the profits earned from guidebooks to assist climbing-related projects that are in keeping with the aims of the club, though they need not be confined to the club's guidebook areas.

Currently, membership is around 1,300, and at present there are no limits on growth. Members of two years' standing may propose a competent candidate for membership and, provided that adequate support is obtained from other members, the Committee may elect him or her to full membership; there is no probationary period.

Climbing Style

The following policy statement on climbing style was agreed in principle at The Climbers' Club Annual General Meeting on 25th February 1990:

The Climbers' Club supports the tradition of using natural protection and is opposed to actions which are against the best interest of climbers and users of the crags. This applies particularly to irreversible acts which could affect the crags and their environs.

Such acts could include: the placing of bolts on mountain and natural crags; retrospective placing of bolts; chiselling, hammering, or altering the rock appearance or structure; excessive removal of vegetation and interference with trees, flowers, and fauna.

The Climbers' Club policy is that guidebooks are written to reflect the best style matched to the ethos and traditions of British climbing.

Ynys Ettws, the Climbers' Club hut in the Llanberis Pass   Photo: Ian Smith

Guidebook Disclaimer

This guide attempts to provide a definitive record of all existing climbs and is compiled from information from a variety of sources. The inclusion of any route does not imply that it remains in the condition described. Climbs can change unpredictably: rock can deteriorate and the existence and condition of *in-situ* protection can alter. All climbers must rely on their own ability and experience to gauge the difficulty and seriousness of any climb. Climbing is an inherently dangerous activity.

Neither The Climbers' Club nor the authors and editor of this guidebook accept any liability whatsoever for any injury or damage caused to climbers, third parties, or property arising from the use of it. Whilst the content of the guide is believed to be accurate, no responsibility is accepted for any error, omission, or mis-statement. Users must rely on their own judgement and are recommended to insure against injury to person and property and third party risks.

The inclusion in this guidebook of a crag or routes upon it does not mean that any member of the public has a right of access to the crag or the right to climb upon it.

Acknowledgements

Nearly all modern guidebooks depend upon their predecessors and this guide is no exception. The work of all authors and their editors of the various previous editions, eleven in total, has provided the starting-point for this book: Herbert Carr, John Barford, Peter Harding, Don Roscoe, Peter Crew, Ian Roper, Pete Hatton, Geoff Milburn and Paul Williams, and editors Geoffrey Winthrop Young, Nully Kretschmer, Wilfred Noyce, John Neill, Trevor Jones, Geoff Milburn again, and Ian Smith.

We would like to thank those who updated various sections for this book: Mike Bailey, Dai Lampard, Steve Mayers, Mark (Baggy) Richards and Jez Stephenson. We would also thank Barbara Jones of the Countryside Council for Wales for the Conservation Notes and Simon Panton for the Bouldering section.

Our thanks are also due to the following for contributing in a range of different ways (written contributions, pointing out corrections to the previous guidebooks, commenting on the text, answering queries, and climbing with Iwan): Damo Carroll, Norman Clacher, Nigel Coe, John, Cox, Martin Crook, John Darling, Nick Dixon, Martin Doyle, Dave Ferguson, Gary Gibson, Dave Green, Jon Green, Fred Hall, Owen Hayward, Graham Hoey, Dave Holmes, Gwion Hughes, Glenda Huxter, Toby Keep, Mark Katz, Paul Jenkinson, Barbara Jones (of the Snowdonia National Park Authority), Ken Latham, Pat Littlejohn, Gary Logan, Leigh McGinley, Tim Neill, Andy Newton, Simon Panton, Iain Peters, Clive Powell, Dave Powell, Mick Poynton, Mike Pycroft, Mark Reeves, Don Roscoe, Tony Schelmerdine, Chris Slinn, George Smith, Kevin Stephens, Louise Thomas, Mike (Twid) Turner, Michael Ward and Ray Wood. Our appreciation is also due to the instructors at Plas y Brenin for providing the Graded List and the star-ratings used in this guide, and also for their help with the pitch grades for the Severes and Hard Severes; particular thanks are due to Iain Peters for coordinating this contribution and to Tim Neill for delivering the goods.

Finally we would like to thank all those involved in the actual production of this book: Martin Brice, Nigel Coe, John Cox, Dave Ferguson, Mark Hounslea, John Willson and Mike Vetterlein for reading through the proofs at various stages; Joe Brown, Simon Cardy, Dave Ferguson, Malcolm Griffith, Will Hurford, Ron Kenyon, Alan Leary, Bill McKee, Mary Niklas, Don Sargeant, David Simmonite, Ian Smith, Don Roscoe, Martin Whitaker, Ken Wilson, and Ray Wood for the action and crag photos; Ian Smith for taking on the work of coordinating the action photos; Don Sargeant for the maps, and for taking and marking up the photoplans; and Simon Cardy for taking on all work on the photodiagrams; thanks also to Dave Basford, who provided crucial back-up every time Simon's computer went down! Particular thanks are due to Dave Ferguson, who has contributed to many of the stages mentioned above, from climbing with Iwan through to final checking of the lines on the photodiagrams. Finally many thanks to John Willson for the typesetting and ongoing support throughout the whole project.   IAJ, BM 2003

Introduction

The Llanberis Pass is one of the foremost areas for rock-climbing in Britain. To many, the variety of its climbing, with its history and the scenery, is unrivalled in mountain crag areas. A quick look at the number of guides to this area produced over the last 75 years will give you an inkling of its popularity. Climbing evolution and developments in rock-climbing have taken place here at a terrific pace.

The crags above the road between the Pen y Gwryd Hotel and Capel Curig, which have been described in previous editions of this guidebook, have been omitted from this edition. They will be described in the next edition of Ogwen and Carneddau. In the meantime details can be downloaded from the Climbers' Club website.

The two sides of the Llanberis Pass, though rather different in character, are fine complements to each other. On the north side the four main cliffs are situated low down on the hillside below the Esgair Felen ridge and the southern slopes of Glyder Fawr. They are steep, impressive, fast-drying (apart from Craig Ddu) and mostly have solid well-gardened rock, picked clean by the passage of countless climbers. Many of the lines are trade routes in what has become one of our most popular mountain outcrop areas. Here a climber at work can be watched keenly from the road by critical fellow climbers (some using binoculars!) amongst a horde of car-bound tourists. The other major crag is Esgair Maen Gwyn (Scimitar Ridge), where there are no easy climbs.

The south side of the Pass is a totally different proposition. Here the crags are generally bigger, more serious, and slower to dry out. The extensive cwms reach up to 1,000 metres to the Crib Coch ridge and the summit of Crib y Ddysgl, which together form the northern half of the famous Snowdon Horseshoe.

The Crags

In keeping with the practice in other Climbers' Club guides, the names that have been used for the crags in this edition are the correct Welsh names. In two particular cases, Diffwys Ddŵr and Diffwys Ddu (Craig y Rhaeadr and Cyrn Las respectively), these names have been used in preference to the names used up until now by climbers. We hope that climbers will bear with this usage and that future generations will learn to use the proper names.

Six-figure map references, which refer to Grid Square SH, are given for all crags. The most useful maps are the Landranger 115 (1:50,000) and the Explorer OL 17 (1:25,000).

The approaches to the crags are from a number of lay-bys on the A4086, the main ones being below Clogwyn y Grochan and Dinas Cromlech, or if they are full from the car-park in Nant Peris. The crags at the head of the Pass are best approached from the car-park at Pen y Pass. There is a bus service through the Pass. At the time of writing the parking arrangements are subject to review following the recent rejection of the Green Key park-and-ride proposals. The British Mountaineering Council can be contacted for details of any changes: phone 0870 445 4500, website www.thebmc.co.uk.

The Climbs

The climbs are described from left to right on each crag unless clearly stated to the contrary. Likewise left and right are always as you face the cliff unless indicated otherwise. This is the first edition of this guidebook to use metric measurements for climb and pitch lengths. Most of the lengths have been obtained by converting the previous lengths from feet to metres. No attempt has been made to round off the resultant metric lengths. The fact that lengths are given in odd numbers (e.g. 23 metres for 70 feet) should not be taken to indicate a level of accuracy that does not exist, as most of the lengths were originally estimated to the nearest 5 feet.

Every effort has been made to ensure that the routes in this guide are fairly and accurately graded, though this is very difficult when some of the newer routes are unrepeated. The standard adjectival grading-system has been used and it assumes that climbers are carrying a full rack of gear and wearing modern rock boots. The grades are as follows: Easy, Moderate, Difficult, Very Difficult, Severe, Hard Severe, Very Severe, Hard Very Severe, and the E grades. E grading is an open-ended system represented by the symbols E1, E2, E3, E4, E5, E6, E7, E8, E9, etc. The E grades give an overall impression of the difficulty of a climb, be it a desperate well-protected physical effort, or a thin and poorly protected 'mind game'. Numerical pitch grades are included in the text, starting at 3a and running through to 7a for the current hardest routes in the area. Three short climbs have been given bouldering V grades, as this reflects the way in which they have been climbed. V grades are also used in the Bouldering section.

The grading-system, if used properly, is very flexible and can cope with a wide variety of situations. That it still works is commendation enough of its early instigators. However, the British grading-system (or any system in fact) is open to abuse by those wishing to massage their egos whether by vastly overgrading the E-numbers and tech-grades or, curiously enough, in severely undergrading their routes — just to show others it was all far too easy. Misgrading is also the result of too much top-pope practice, the true grade for an on-sight lead being lost in a haze of familiarity.

Grade changes are almost inevitable in a guidebook, as new routes clean up and lose some of their edge, old established climbs take on a sheen, and others may lose a crucial hold or two. The grades in this guide are the consensus opinions of a great number of climbers with a vast amount of climbing-experience — not just in the Pass. However, what is certain is that someone out there will not agree with a particular grade given for a specific route. Be that as it may, guidebooks and grades are a guideline, which should be used with a certain degree of caution.

It is perhaps appropriate that in a guidebook with a climb named *Play Safe Be First* we take a look at the rather vexed question of first-ascent ethics and grades. There has been an increasing trend for new routes, particularly the harder ones for their time, to have been 'prepared' in some way. The preparation, usually on abseil, can take a number of forms: prior inspection of holds, brushing, cleaning and gardening, trying gear, practising moves, and pre-placement of gear through to top-roping. The use of any of these practices by a first ascensionist means that the first ascent is not an on-sight, ground-up ascent.

When a climb is prepared, what goes on is largely in the hands of the first ascensionist. There are, and never have been, hard and fast rules, merely an ethical reticence imposed by the circumstances of the history of British climbing and the traditions that have been established. At any one time this will be distilled into a perception of what is acceptable to the local activists, which at times various individuals have been prepared to challenge.

The best and purest form of first ascent is an on-sight, ground-up ascent. In the past, criticism has been made of the lack of information on first ascents in guidebooks. However, we have to rely almost entirely on the information as to the style and ethics as recorded by the first ascensionists, who should not hold back on recording the style of their ascents.

All the routes in this guidebook are meant to be graded for on-sight ascents, although this concept is quite hypothetical in some cases and where routes have had few if any repeats. Subsequent on-sight ascensionists may find such routes to be harder than the grade given. Conversely, they could be found to be easier than the grade given because estimating an on-sight grade can be difficult. A number of ascents are needed before the grade settles down.

Standards have increased and attitudes have changed gradually over the years, and we have now arrived at the stage where it should be assumed that there has been some form of preparation on the harder new routes unless an on-sight ascent has been specifically claimed. Such claims have been recorded in the First Ascents section. The fact that there are only a handful of routes described as having been climbed on-sight is not to say that all the other first ascents were not so climbed. In fact, the large majority of the first ascents prior to the 1970s were climbed on-sight (which almost certainly accounts for what by current standards may well seem to be an undue amount of aid being used on certain climbs), and in subsequent years this also applies to the easier routes. Likewise, details of preparation are those that are known (usually from the first ascensionists having recorded the details) are given in the First Ascents section.

Unfortunately, owing to lack of information and the large number of visiting climbers, it has not been possible in this guide to include daggers to indicate routes not known to have had second ascents in the same way as in the CC guides to the South West, Pembroke, and most recently Meirionnydd. This practice would have gone some way to alleviating the situation described above.

Fortunately, there seem to be few grading anomalies amongst the established routes, most of which have settled down to a certain level of acceptance. If a route is deemed to be 'high in the grade' it has only missed a higher grading by a whisker. A soft touch for the grade does not mean that the route is a path, merely that it is a little easier than others at that level. Owing to popular demand, a graded list is present once again. The graded list is bound to rekindle a few old arguments, and certain to ignite a sheaf of others: please don't take it too seriously!

A decision has been made to continue with the use of stars to indicate the quality of routes irrespective of their grades in this guidebook. This decision was not made lightly, because there is a growing body of opinion against the star-system on the grounds that it tends to concentrate traffic on the starred routes. The absence of stars does not mean that a climb is unsatisfactory, as poor climbs are specifically described as such. Most of the unstarred routes in this guidebook are well worth seeking out.

The star-ratings and the graded list in this book have been provided by the instructors at Plas y Brenin.

Bolts in traditional areas such as mountain crags and outcrops are regarded as unethical. Any climber caught placing one should be restrained from doing so if possible. The use of unnecessary pegs should also be frowned upon: try to use as little 'artificial aid' as possible.

All routes are described in their freest form. Wherever aid of any form is used, the minimum number of points of aid for each climb is given in brackets after the grade of the route, e.g. Very Severe (1 pt aid). The nature of the aid will be made clear in the route description. Many of the old routes now go free owing to steady use, a wide selection of nuts, cams, chalk, climbing-wall fitness, and most important of all a healthier attitude towards climbing ethics.

The word peg is used in three contexts: for runners, aid, and belays. The few pegs used for aid are clearly indicated. Peg belays are described as such. In all other cases the word 'peg' is used to indicate a peg runner. It is hoped that all pegs mentioned in the text will be left in place (if they haven't corroded). If any pegs are found to be missing, please record the fact as below.

Please either enter new-route descriptions and comments on the grades and descriptions in the Pete's Eats log book; or email them to info@petes-eats.co.uk; or send them to Pete, Pete's Eats, 40 High Street, Llanberis, LL55 4EU. Details of new routes will be found on the Pete's Eats website: www.petes-eats.co.uk. There are similar arrangements for new bouldering problems in the North Wales area.

Conservation Notes
by Barbara Jones

Before the construction of a road through Llanberis Pass in around 1830, the usual way to reach Llanberis was by a 'dreadful horse-path' or by boat up Llyn Padarn. This topographically imposed isolation maintained a near natural 'wilderness' in the valley and, until around 1700, eagles still soared above the hills of Snowdonia. With the construction of the road, access improved dramatically and by the end of the century climbers were exploring many of the cliffs and crags once considered to be the abode of demons. With over 100 years of climbing in the Llanberis Pass, now one of the most popular climbing areas in Britain, it is tempting to ask whether there is anything left to conserve?

Undeniably there is, and a little awareness will reward anyone with views of darting peregrine and diving chough, or meadow rue, starry saxifrage and insectivorous butterwort, with banks of bluebells and primroses on some ledges and descent gullies in spring. Climbing activities may have had an impact, but the occasional sight of a tiny oak or rowan tree starting to grow alongside a popular route gives hope that all is not lost.

Both sides of Llanberis Pass are part of the Eryri Mountains Site of Special Scientific Interest (SSSI) and Special Area of Conservation (SAC). These titles may not mean much to most people, but they identify an internationally important upland site, designated for its varied, and sometimes rare, upland plant and animal life and its geological and geomorphological features, reflecting the effects of glaciation on the complex of rock types in Snowdonia. The complex geology includes areas of base-rich rocks where the vegetation becomes herb-rich and, in the places where grazing sheep cannot reach, you can find a luxuriant cover of roseroot, ladies mantle, moss campion and numerous fern species amongst many others. Over much of the site, however, sheep grazing has produced a dominant cover of acidic grassland and abundant clubmosses, with heather only locally abundant on some of the steeper slopes.

The animal life of Snowdonia is varied ranging from a relict arctic-alpine invertebrate fauna including the rare Snowdon Rainbow Beetle through to nesting peregrines and chough, both of which have regular breeding-sites in the Pass. Feral goats can often be seen here, but their presence is not always welcome as they can damage the vegetation when their numbers are too high.

The main climbing cliffs on either side of the Pass are composed of solid tuffs of the Upper Rhyolitic Series, which are more acidic and tend to form dense, hard rocks, less conducive to vegetation growth and more conducive to climbing. We can therefore climb on most of the cliffs described in this guide, without causing further damage or disturbance to the fauna and flora, if a sense of awareness is coupled with a minimum impact philosophy in the form of no gardening and care in descent, especially avoiding wet gullies which are often the refuge for a luxuriant diversity of plant life. Avoiding too much trampling on any still-vegetated ledges and using trees as little as possible will also prevent further deterioration of the vegetation cover. Avoiding climbs close to nesting sites during the breeding season will protect the tenuous hold birds such as chough and peregrine have on these mountains.

Despite all these measures, however, there are some areas covered by this guide that are still relatively uncrowded and little used, where an increase in exploration and activity could result in damage and disturbance to the wildlife. Most notable in this respect is Cwm Glas, which, owing to the nature of the rocks in the cwm, supports a luxuriance of arctic-alpine and lower plants, including some very rare species. These plants are restricted essentially to the cliffs and steep rocky ground by sheep grazing. Needless to say, any gardening and cleaning in any new-route activity on these cliffs would severely deplete these uncommon plant communities and render the mountains a much poorer place as a result.

Remember these plants and birds are protected by law, and offences are prosecuted under the 1981 Wildlife and Countryside Act or the The Countryside and Rights of Way Act, 2000. Gardening or disturbance to wildlife could result in prosecution, so make yourself aware and if in doubt ask first. Our countryside has been affected for many years by far more damaging activities than climbing: activities such as agriculture, forestry, drainage, construction and pollution. However, because of the very nature of our sport which we undertake in some of the hitherto least affected areas, our impact is magnified, as these can be the refuges for plants and animals displaced from their more natural distribution by these widespread activities. There is also the added burden of possible climate change and the consequential results this may have for our upland species.

The mountains, plants and animals of Snowdonia yearly attract hundreds of botanists, naturalists, photographers and walkers who delight in the presence and diversity of wildlife found here; they have as much right to experience and enjoy it as we do, and they would be rightly concerned and angry at any wilful destruction. For these reasons, tread lightly, and, as the production of this guide is likely to stimulate new activity, if you intend to develop a new cliff, crag or bouldering area, please contact the Countryside Council for Wales (CCW) before you start so that advice can be given on the likelihood or known existence of any rare plants, sensitive vegetation communities, birds or other animals likely to be affected by climbing activities.

For information on the conservation interest of areas within the guide, contact the CCW Area office on 01248 672500.

The Cromlech Girdle (E2, page 107) Dinas Cromlech
Climber: Don Whillans (first ascent)   Photo: Joe Brown

Brant Direct (HVS, page 59)
and
Brant (VS, page 61)
Clogwyn y Grochan
Climbers unknown
Photo: Don Sargeant

Right Wall (E5, page 103) Dinas Cromlech
Climber: Catherine Destivelle
(International Women's Meet 1984)
Photo: Ian Smith

Historical

Climbing in Snowdonia started in earnest in the 1860s and 1870s when members of the then recently formed Alpine Club came to stay at the Pen y Gwryd Hotel, owned by Henry Owen. This venue became the social centre of Welsh climbing at that time, one of the most prominent regulars being C E Mathews. He founded the Society of Welsh Rabbits, an informal club that explored Snowdonia in winter. With the seemingly better snow conditions at that time it was an ideal centre for Alpine training. The rock remained for the future.

The earliest ascents in about 1879 are credited to R Pendlebury, and in 1884 the *Clogwyn y Person Arête* was ascended after the *Western Gully* start. E R Kidson, an enthusiastic pioneer, also climbed the Crib Goch gullies during this period.

The beginning of Welsh rock-climbing was marked by the formation of the Climbers' Club in August 1898 with a nucleus of P y G regulars headed by Matthews. The activities of the climbers were recorded in the journals, and traditions were soon established. Kidson led a party of CC members up *The Parson's Nose*; this route was supposedly climbed as long ago as the 1840s by the 'climbing parson'.

By this time Archer Thomson was firmly established as one of the leading Welsh climbers. His *Black Cleft* on Dinas Mot was, for some time, the hardest route in Wales. For the next 13 years he dominated Welsh climbing and when not on Lliwedd he ascended many of the gullies in this area with the Williams brothers, R F Blackwell, E R Turner, and M K Smith. The formidable *Great Gully* of Diffwys Ddu finally fell to Thomson in 1904 after two years of serious attempts. It was in this period that a large party of schoolmasters attacked the gullies of Diffwys Ddu and named the last in honour of their profession. Towards the end of the gully epoch, *Crib Goch Buttress* was ascended: first by the Abraham brothers and then by G W Reade, who put up his excellent buttress route. Thomson added several routes on Clogwyn y Ddysgl, including the fine *Gambit Climb*, just prior to his sudden death in 1912. It was he who led the migration out of the gullies and onto the open cliff faces in Eryri.

Geoffrey Winthrop Young was active in the area before the Great War and opened up Craig Cwm Beudy Mawr. George Mallory climbed during the war and added *The Black Gates*; but sadly the war took its toll of many that loved the hills.

Herbert Carr and Maurice Guinness were active in the post-war years, climbing a number of pleasing little routes, possibly the best being *Little Benjamin*. Their activity was in preparation for the Climbers' Club Guide to Snowdon in 1926. In it there was only a passing reference to the steep crags on the north side of Llanberis Pass. These were left for the next generation, which took advantage of developments in equipment and, in particular, rubber footwear.

Ivan Waller added the infamous *Fallen Block Crack* in 1927; he was one of the few remaining members of the leisured set so dominant before the Great War. A change took place in the 1930s: groups of young climbers, mainly from Liverpool and Manchester, began to make regular weekend visits to the hills. When not on the mountain crags, they would practise their art on their local outcrops – be it sandstone or grit. During 1930 the Bathursts became the first team to use artificial aids when they climbed *The Cracks*. However, it was Colin Kirkus who made a really significant advance with his classic *Direct Route* on Dinas Mot, and he followed it the next year with another masterpiece, *West Rib*.

In 1931, J Menlove Edwards made his debut with *Western Slabs* on Dinas Mot before moving across to the north side of the Pass, where he started his great period of exploration with *Holly Buttress* on Dinas Cromlech. During the next 10 years he dominated both sides of the Pass, putting up a host of excellent new routes including the classics, *Flying Buttress* and *Crackstone Rib*, as well as harder routes such as *Pharaoh's Wall* and *Shadow Wall*. His lines invariably involved fights with vegetation, overhangs and loose rock, much of which has now disappeared. The names of some of Edwards's routes show the extent of his lively imagination. Edwards did not have it all his own way, however, for in 1935 E Pentir Williams succeeded in climbing one of the three great Cromlech corners to give *Sabre Cut*. The same year, Jake Cooke and P L Roberts found the superb and impressive *Main Wall* on Diffwys Ddu, as well as other minor lines on the south side of the Pass.

By far the greatest step forward in the Pass was Arthur Birtwistle's remarkable ascent of *Diagonal* in 1938. The route was not repeated for ten years and even now demands respect. Edwards was very active during the war and added the fine routes of *Brant* and *Slape*. Both Edwards and John Barford had been responsible for many pre-war developments and the interim guide by Barford, reprinted from the CC journal, marked the end of the Edwards era. It is sad that Barford was killed in the Alps before completing his guide to Dinas Mot, but Arnold Carsten took over the work, and even climbed routes solo when short of a companion. His manuscript was eventually included in Harding's Pass guide.

The Second World War robbed us of many fine climbers, but in the post-war period another generation of 'tigers' was developing rapidly on the northern gritstone outcrops. In this group were the aforementioned Peter Harding and Tony Moulam, who, aided by an improved crack technique and modern protection, began to push the standards even higher. *Spectre* fell in 1947 and at the time was thought to be a grade harder than previous routes. Despite this, Harding soloed it in 1948. Another fine Harding route from 1947 was the imposing corner of *Ivy Sepulchre*, which was inspected and gardened from abseil on the day prior to its ascent (a practice more in keeping with the 1970s than the 1940s). In 1948 Harding opened up the rather forbidding-looking Craig Ddu, and then further up the Pass he sorted out *The Wastad Girdle* and *Kaisergebirge Wall*. On the first ascent of the latter, seven pegs were used and the climb was thought to be a good deal harder than the other routes on the cliff with the possible exception of *Spectre*. A year later *Unicorn* and *Lion* were discovered just in time to get into Harding's magnificent Llanberis Pass Guide, published in 1950, which soon became known as the 'Bumper Fun Book'.

Soon after the guide came out, a young climber appeared on the scene armed with the strength and technique to forge new routes in the most difficult conditions. Joe Brown reigned supreme in the Pass for nearly a quarter of a century. The first feature to attract Brown's attention was the commanding line of *Cenotaph Corner*. This compelling line had so far repelled all attempts; jamming and bridging up to the niche about three metres from the top, Brown hammered in a peg, in the process of which he dropped his hammer onto the head of Wilf White who was belaying. Fortunately, White was all right; unfortunately, Brown had no pegs left, so *Cenotaph Corner* won this first encounter with the 'Baron' – but not for long.

In 1951 Brown ascended *Hangover* and in the same year teamed up with Don Whillans for their first Pass route, the intimidating *Cemetery Gates*. Classic lines began to fall thick and fast. Inevitably *Cenotaph Corner* yielded to Brown in 1952 and then the following year, with Whillans, he added the strenuous *Surplomb*, whose single aid point was removed in 1959 by young southern sandstone ace Phil Gordon. In early 1953, Brown and Whillans turned their attention to the south side of the Pass, alternating leads on *Subsidiary Groove*. Six months later saw the ascent of Brown's super-classic *The Grooves*, which is still no pushover for its grade. Whillans powered his way up *Erosion Groove Direct* in 1955, a characteristically bold and serious lead. *Grond* and *The Thing*, both short vicious problems, also belong to this era, but the major route at the time was undoubtedly *The Cromlech Girdle*. Tales from this era are legion: *Surplomb* for many years was supposedly done wearing nailed boots during a snowstorm. Another story is of *Cobweb Crack*, which was apparently named after a spider, who spun its web above Brown's stance – ensuring that on that particular day there would be no flies on Brown.

After the initial onslaught by Brown and Whillans, other leaders such as Ron Moseley and later Hugh Banner took up the challenge and produced a variety of hard climbs. In particular Moseley's ascent of the intimidating *Left Wall*, using bootlace slings and Meccano nuts to overcome the crux, stands out, as does Banner's exposed masterpiece, *Overhanging Arête* on Diffwys Ddu.

As a result of long hard work, Don Roscoe produced the much-needed guide to Llanberis North in 1961, and this has formed the basis for all subsequent guides. At the time of publication it cleared up many rumours about the 'impossible' Brown and Whillans routes. Things quietened down somewhat in the Pass until Brown emerged once more to explore the wings of Dinas Mot. His ascent of *The Mole* initiated a wave of exploration and extensive gardening on the steep overhanging cliffs, which had remained in the shadows for so long.

May 1962 saw the first Pass route by that accomplished team of Pete Crew and Baz Ingle, when they produced *Trauma Grooves* on Diffwys Ddu. The early 1960s saw a host of high-grade routes by this forceful team when they were not up on Cloggy. Perhaps *Plexus* on Dinas Mot and *The Great Buttress* on Diffwys Ddu are the best of their routes. Also in this period *Epitaph*, the fierce left arête of *Cenotaph Corner*, was top-roped and assaulted in earnest by several teams until it was successfully led by Ron James using some aid. John Ewbank eventually climbed the route free in 1965.

The Llanberis South guide by Pete Crew came out in 1966 and was the last of the three guides to replace Harding's classic work. The prospect of the guide led to greater efforts in pioneering and developing the south side of the Pass. Martin Boysen made his mark with *Nexus* on Dinas Mot in 1963 and two of his finest efforts were *Black Spring* and *The Plexus Girdle* in 1965. *The Skull*, which he put up in 1966, still retains its reputation as one of the harder routes in the Pass, especially as it now goes completely free. The left wall of *Ivy Sepulchre* held out for a long time, despite many assaults, until *The Crucifix* fell to Lew Brown in 1966.

The Pass was quiet for a while with only a few filling-in routes being produced, but in 1969 Boysen and Dave Alcock created the excellent *Black Shadow* while Joe Brown and Crew teamed up together to add another hard route, '*T'ouse Wall*.

In 1970 the practice of soloing routes was at its height, leading exponents in the Pass being Alan McHardy and Cliff Phillips. Phillips fell over 65 metres while soloing on Dinas Mot and lived to tell the tale. Alan Rouse, trying to solo a new Extreme on sight, got up what is now the first hard pitch of *Ten Degrees North;* unfortunately it rained and he had to finish up *Plexus*. Another notable effort from this time was a solo ascent of *The Thing* by Eric Jones, but even this was capped by a tremendous on-sight solo ascent of *The Overhanging Arête* on Diffwys Ddu by McHardy. The consequence of a fall from such a route is only too obvious.

Although in the 1960s peg moves had been eliminated on some routes, in the 1970s there was a welcome and more thorough reappraisal of the aid situation. Ado Garlick set the trend in autumn 1970 with his superb free ascent of *Left Wall*. In 1974 Alec Sharp added several new lines on Dinas Mot. Of these, *Ten Degrees North* is probably the best and most popular. In the same year Pete Livesey brought a new approach to the Welsh scene and having inspected his line over several days he eventually led the *Right Wall* of Cenotaph Corner. It was a bold and committing lead, undoubtedly the hardest in Wales at that time, and it was one of the first climbs in Wales to merit an E5 grade. It was, astonishingly, soloed by Phil Davidson twice, in

1982 and 1983. Another major free ascent of this era was that of *The Skull* by Ray Evans and Hank Pasquill. Evans also created routes of his own such as the technical *Roll On* and the delectable *Superdirect*.

1975 saw the appearance of Gabriel Regan, a talented young climber from the Peak District who free-climbed *Spectrum* as well as *Hangover Direct*. In the same year, Rowland Edwards climbed *Resurrection*, a strenuous and technical line up the left wall of the Corner. It has rapidly become a classic route like its famous neighbours.

In addition to making the much-awaited second ascent of *Right Wall* in 1976, Ron Fawcett straightened out *Roll On* to give the sustained *Stroll On*. Livesey's contributions that year were *Memory Lane*, the immaculate *Foil*, and a hard start to *The Crucifix*. During the hot dry summer of 1976 a strong Lakeland team consisting of Ed Cleasby, John Eastham, and Rob Matheson came south and picked off a spectacular route, *Lubyanka* on Diffwys Ddu – done entirely on sight. Gordon Tinnings went one better when he made an amazing solo ascent (*in extremis* on the exposed top pitch) in 1980.

A 'Free the Pass' campaign was started by Geoff Milburn in 1977 to push modern free-climbing standards in North Wales and it soon brought a blitz on the aided routes when several young leaders set to work. In the forefront was Jim Moran who freed *The Toad* and *Jawbone* as well as adding several short but technical new routes of his own, such as *Quasar*. His finest achievement was, with Dave Hollows, to free *Black Mamba* of all its aid to give *Times Past*. Hollows excelled in freeing the roof pitch of *Sexus*. In July, Chris Hamper and Dave Roberts made the third and fourth ascents of *Right Wall*. Roberts then freed the frightening *Nexus Direct* on sight, and also beat Moran to free *Mole Direct*, but the latter added an independent start and finish two days later to give *The Molehill*. Competition for lines during the summer was keen and several teams were operating in the area. Sharp stormed up over the *Shadow Wall* overhang to give the powerful, frightening *Zangorilla*; Moran went for the fine arête of *Curfew*, while Roberts climbed the now classic *SS Special*. Later in the year four new routes appeared on the already overcrowded Wastad, including *Elidor*, which had in fact been done but not recorded many years before. Moran now picked off the much-tried groove of *Leftover* and before the winter set in added another hard route, *Runnymede*, up the obscure Groper Buttress. His final contribution for the 1978 guide, *Peeping Tom*, was completed during a spell of very bad weather after a potentially serious fall on the lethally loose first pitch.

It was now thought by some of the leading climbers that the Pass was sufficiently close to being worked out and that a new guide might not be needed again. However in May 1978 the new guide brought climbers flooding back to the valley not only to climb the old favourites and repeat the most recent routes but also to look at the spaces between the existing routes. Roberts and Paul Williams took a perverse delight in adding *First Amendment* solely to put the new guide out of date. This was followed by Moran's free ascent of *Crossbones*, which removed three points of aid in one fell swoop. Later in June, Fawcett solved the long-standing problem of *The Pump* to give a short but very hard test-piece. July brought Gary Gibson, a Peak District devotee, to the Llanberis new route scene; of his climbs in the Pass from this period, *Black and White* proved to be the best. Moran added a very hard route, *The Heretic*, to Craig Ddu in August, and in the same month Pete Whillance eliminated the two points of aid on *Groper*.

During 1979 more minor lines succumbed, but in addition several big routes were to appear. Williams first took Roberts up *Brute 33*, a vicious overhang, and then teamed up with Leigh McGinley for *Golgotha*, a rather serious climb to the left of *Ivy Sepulchre*. In the summer of 1979 two routes stood out from the rest, especially as they were well-known problems. Cleasby once again came south: this time for *Hindenburg* on Diffwys Ddu, which was eventually completed in two pushes after a mammoth cleaning session. The big news of the year, however, was the long-awaited ascent of *Lord of the Flies*, by Fawcett and Chris Gibb. Described as being considerably harder than its neighbour *Right Wall*, this creation set a new standard for the Pass at the time, although by the end of the 1980s, it was considered a hard man's trade route.

Early in 1980 Fawcett completed the often-tried problem of *Quantum Jump*, and he then packed in yet another super-route, *Precious*, on the right wall of the Corner after persuading a bystander to belay him. Over a period of some six weeks Fawcett was to bring new standards of difficulty to the Welsh crags. During this time, after teaming up with Williams, he well and truly blitzed the Cromlech, doing all the major unclimbed lines. *Hall of Warriors* was a particularly bold route up a friable wall involving the use of a tiny sapling but *Atomic Hot Rod*, a short brutal crack, was to provide what was then thought to be a 7a test-piece. Even with marked improvement in fitness and general rise in climbing standards it is still rated 6b. Fawcett's other Cromlech routes, *J R* and *True Grip*, were high-quality eliminates but *Ivory Madonna*, a new girdle, was a brilliant major addition to the central walls. At about this time, the grading system was extended to include E6. This was not only to cater for the hardest new routes, but also to allow for upgrading of some of the easier Extremes to avoid overcrowding in any one grade.

In the same year an exceptionally dry spring made it possible for Pat Littlejohn to add *Ghosts* and *Silent Spring* to Diffwys Ddŵr, a cliff which usually seeps and which has rarely been dry enough to merit much attention. A similar period of good weather in the following year enabled Steve Haston and McGinley, both climbing extremely well, to amaze the pundits with *The Red Ring*, their completely free ascent of the massive *Grinder* roof. Another ferocious piece of climbing around this time was the much-looked-at right arête of *Brant Direct*, which gave John Redhead some exciting moments. *Cockblock* was a powerful effort, hard move after hard move with little respite; it was soloed by a hyper-fit Phil Davidson in 1984.

On the Cromlech in 1981, Dave Atchison-Jones ascended his controversial excursion up and around *Left Wall* and *Epitaph* to the heckling of a team of locals who could not believe their eyes. *Tess of the d'Urbevilles*, as the 'route' was called, came in for much criticism. Paul Jenkinson ascended the actual line some seven years later. The best new route discovered in the Pass during 1982 was probably *A New Austerlitz*, on the East Wing of Dinas Mot by Gibson and Neil Harvey.

At the beginning of June 1983 Mark Lynden and John Silvester climbed *Rootorooni*, a counter-diagonal route to *The Thing*. Another activist on the scene at this time was Stuart Cathcart who, after a fine trio of routes on Ettws Isaf, shifted his attention to the smooth walls on the right of Diffwys Ddu. Before his ascents, Cathcart controversially placed three bolts (the first since Hamish MacInnes's use of bolts on the right wall of *Cenotaph Corner* back in the 1950s), an act which had the local activists on the verge of a coronary. Fortunately, within a couple of months the bolts were chopped and replaced with pegs by Nick Dixon and Andy Popp. They both led a combination of the provocatively named *New Era* and *Steel Appeal*, starting up the former and finishing via the latter to produce *Mild Steel* E6 – a particularly sterling effort from Popp who was leading E4 at that time. In the same area, Andy Sharp and John Harwood climbed *Hooded Crow* on little frequented Clogwyn y Ddysgl.

Clogwyn Gafr (Craig Fach), a small outcrop containing several aid routes, came under the scrutiny of various climbers. Dave Pycroft started the ball rolling with free ascents of *The Slash* and *Diapason*, and then Davidson was co-opted to free *Pulsar*, a fine crack. The 'holdless' groove just to the left gave Martin Crook and Pete Norton a good workout some months later when they freed *Pi*, now *Sacred Idol*.

Standards became so high that virtually anything seemed possible. Jerry Moffatt soloed half a dozen routes on the Cromlech including *Right Wall* and *Foil*, pronouncing it, 'an easy and outdated crag', while Andy Pollitt led *Quantum Jump*, *Cockblock*, *Venturi Effect*, *Mural*, *S S Special*, *C Minor*, and *Stroll On* – all in the same day. On a sadder note, the 1940s classic, *Nea*, suffered a major rockfall from its top pitch; as a result the route was upgraded to VS as the only alternative was to finish up *Spectre*.

In early 1985, Willy Todd added several short hard routes in the vicinity of Craig Ddu. This trend was repeated on Dinas Bach, where Bob Drury put up *Body Rock*, with its one mighty move, and on Little Buttress. The best of a crop of new additions on the latter was *Ryley Bosvil*, a technically precocious crack, from Redhead. Another interesting find was on the very traditional Carreg Gwalch, which yielded *Shadow of Youth*, a slanting crack, to Ray Wood and Lew Hardy. All new finds in the Pass were dwarfed, however, by the discovery of *Long Kesh* on Diffwys Ddu, a route of mind-blowing exposure between *The Skull* and *Lubyanka*. This was the first major find on this crag for about five years and a great effort from Steve Boydon and Simon Cardy.

A number of interesting discoveries took place in 1986. These were mainly on the smaller, more esoteric crags though they were nonetheless worthwhile. *Marlene on the Wall*, the prominent roof on Clogwyn Blaen Coed, went on sight to Trevor Hodgson. *The Nectarine Run* by Jon de Montjoye, on little known Clogwyn Gafr was one of the year's best finds. No less worthy, in the then obscure Cwm Glas Bach, was *Pretty Girls Make Graves*, a fierce finger-crack from Craig Smith. Smith was again active on the left arête of *Grond* with his sensational, *Rumblefish*, a lonely lead. Not to be left out, Dixon ascended *Grand*, the right arête, and then climbed the blank scoop right again, *Awesome*. A few weeks later, Dixon put up *Melancholony* and Crook found *Killerkranky* on Esgair Maen Gwyn, the first stirrings of development on these crags.

The publication of a new Llanberis guide in 1987 triggered off a wave of frenetic development with over 70 new routes recorded that year. Amongst the best of these were *The Bog of the Eternal Stench* on Craig Ddu, and *King Wad* and *Surgical Lust* on Esgair Maen Gwyn, three sensational finds for Paul Pritchard. Also on Esgair Maen Gwyn *The Kicker Conspiracy*, *Romany Soup* and *The Bells, The Bells, The Bells* from Crispin Waddy, plus *Mutiny on the Mouse Organ* and *The Tufty Club Rebellion* by Andy Popp, were all excellent, hard, sustained modern routes. Another addition, *The 39 Slaps*, gave Johnny Dawes a strenuous, technical and dynamic redpoint, which was superbly on-sighted by Popp. Dawes also added *Satsumo Wrestler*. On the walls and boulders of Cwm Glas Bach, many good routes were unearthed. These included the taxing off-width, *Fear of Infection*, from George Smith, *Rimsky Korsakov* and *Wagner's Ring* from Dawes, *Lasagne Verdi* from Pritchard, *Melon Transplant* and *Nick's Sexual Problem* (with its mighty move) from Dixon, and the sparkling *Weasels Rip My Flesh* from Steve Howe, to name but a few.

The development of Cwm Glas Bach continued throughout 1988, though at a much slower pace than in the previous year, Popp's first ascent solo of *King of Rumpy* being particularly noteworthy. Littlejohn, who had just moved into to the area, quickly made his mark, climbing the prominent thin crack/seam on the Equator Walls to produce the superb *Alchemy*. Other notable routes were *Outspan* by Al and Phil George, and *Red Giant* from Howe and Phil Baxter, both on Clogwyn Gafr, and *Vlad the Arête*, an excruciatingly hard micro-route from Dixon.

In 1989, Dai Lampard added five big routes to the south side of the Pass. On Plexus Buttress *The Smodge*, which runs up to the right of *The Windmill*, took one visit to the crag to complete, whereas *Perplexus*, a bold route through the overhangs near *The Red Ring*, took four. *Tales of the Riverbank*, on which leads were shared with Al George, was certainly an eliminate in line, but it was climbed on sight and the route breached some impressive ground on the East Wing of Dinas Mot. On Diffwys Ddu, the inverted V-groove between *The Grooves* and *The Prune* gave *Sunday School Outing*, but the plum find was *The Edge of Time* (on which Nigel Bonnett led the second pitch) a spectacular and airy expedition up the right arête of the crag. Elsewhere, on Clogwyn Tyllau, above Carreg Wastad, Owain Jones climbed his eponymous arête and Dave Holmes found *Unleashing the Wild Physique*, both powerful modern test-pieces. At the top of the Cromlech, the frightening and previously brutalized wall left of *Grond* yielded a short but serious pitch, *The Bastard Practice*, to Adam Wainwright.

There was little new activity in 1990 and 1991: Ed Stone tackled *The Roc-Nest Monster* on Esgair Maen Gwyn, and an almost unbelievable solo of *Lord of the Flies* by Dave Thomas on a sunny weekend afternoon nearly gave half the spectators a heart-attack. In 1992, with rumours of another guide imminent, frenetic activity resulted in four very hard routes. First, on Esgair Maen Gwyn, *The Trumpet Blowers*, a steep, uncompromising and oft-eyed line, fell to Wainwright; Cwm Glas Bach yielded the desperate rounded arête of *Melondrama* to Dixon; but those timeless walls of Dinas Cromlech still held the biggest prize of all. After solving the intricacies of the overhanging, square-cut arête above *Cenotaph Corner* to give *Overlord*, Steve Mayers, turned his attention to one of the recurring 'last great problems', the space left of *Lord of the Flies*. Pritchard had tried the line some years previously, but after reaching the Girdle ledge an escape was made up the upper part of *Lord of the Flies*. After thorough top-rope and abseil inspection, Mayers psyched himself up and succeeded in leading the aptly-named *Nightmayer*. Dixon created another desperately difficult micro-route with his *Beginners' Mind* in 1993, on the small crag above the Cromlech Bridge bends. Dixon then went on to produce *6B Melonoma* back at his old stomping-ground of Cwm Glas Bach.

Little activity of note took place in 1994, although John Tombs and Holmes found a new cliff to play with above the Grochan and Phil Targett found room to squeeze in *California Raisins* on Carreg Wastad. The best offering was probably Niel Gresham's *Grins Twins*. The following year, James Harrison saw some opportunities and good rock on the right-hand flank of Diffwys Ddŵr with routes such as *Rock Oil*. However, Rob Mirfin's *Microtrauma*, an evocative finger-searing addition pointed to future developments in the Cwm Glas Bach area. The emergence of a new force in the area came in 1996, with Tim Emmett and his ascents of *Gram -ve* and *'Totally Wired 9'*.

During 1997 Tony Schelmerdine and Norman Clacher developed a string of new lines in the Cwm Glas Bach area, with probably the best of these contributions being *Grazer* and *La Hain*. However, the powerful lines of *Grave Diggers,* led by both Gresham and Patch Hammond, coupled with Emmett's precarious *Down on My Knee* rather stole the limelight for that year. In recent years, routes have continued to trickle in slowly; this slow pace may be due to the fact that many of the locals were off developing the Pass's bouldering potential. Although most of the routes climbed in this period can be seen as fillers in, there have been enough exciting and adventurous contributions to keep the Pass in the forefront of mountain crag areas. These range from the strikingly difficult *Agua Caliente* by Mark Katz, to Leo

Houlding's enchantingly bold *A Sweet Encounter*. The latter was rather overshadowed by his later *Trauma*. The Mot also provided an arena for Hammond's *One Inch Punch* as well as Christian Klemmow's *The Dark Side*, the side of the Pass where most future developments are likely to take place. This has certainly been true regarding the majority of the routes climbed in the 2002 'sprint for print' led by Lampard. However, the most significant activity was on the light (north) side with the development of Bryn Du as a climbing venue by Damo Carroll and Dave Viggers, where *Geriatricks* was their best route.

'Crib Goch Buttress: The Pinnacle Pitch'
Reproduced from *A Climber's Guide to Snowdon and the
Beddgelert District* by H R C Carr (1926)
Reade's Route (VD,1908, page 140)
Climbers and photographer unknown

Nant Peris Area

Dinas
OS Ref 614 585

This isolated little outcrop sits forlornly on the lower slopes of Y Garn, above a wooded spur, almost due east of Nant Peris. The main feature is its central corner with an overhanging left wall. The corner has been climbed, as have the walls around to the left and right, some having been pegged in the 50s. The best, and probably hardest, two problems are the crack in the prow that forms the left arête of the central groove, and an exposed hand-traverse of the left wall.

Craig Ffynnon Peris   St Peris's Spring Crag   OS Ref 611 584

This tiny crag is almost buried in the trees about 200 metres down to the left of Dinas, on the left side of the flat wooded spur that dominates the village of Nant Peris. It is easily recognized by a small clean square-cut arête jutting out from the foliage, above the isolated white cottage at about 10 o'clock as you reach the 30mph signs at the bottom end of Nant Peris when approaching from Llanberis. After passing the Vaynol Arms on the right, take the first left turn and follow a track through a campsite; the track then gradually peters out as it rises. Many of the problems and variations that exist have been left for the itinerant boulderer to rediscover, so only the main routes are described. To the left of the prominent central arête (*Agua Caliente*, previously known as *Nick's Arête*), past an off-width crack, a rounded arête where the crag peters out gives:

★Nappy Brown and the Red Hot Pokers
9 metres   Hard Very Severe   5b   (25.5.88)

A mini-classic. Pull onto the front of the arête from the left (or start direct – much harder, 6a) and continue direct on sound rock to finish.

Autumn Acorns   9 metres   E3   6a
(9.92)

From the foot of the off-width, take a tenuous left-trending line up the wall, finishing direct (and right of *Nappy Brown*…).

Fists of Fury   9 metres   E2   5c
(1.6.88)

The painful off-width is painfully obvious.

Agua Caliente   12 metres   E8   7a
(28.3.98)

The prominent central arête presents an incredibly hard and serious challenge. Small gear arrives after the crux swing and is very hard to place. Climb the right-hand side of the arête until forced into a desperate swing around it (protection way out to the left). Rock up to the right and around the arête again to find easier climbing and eventually the top.

★Big Brother Is Belaying Me!   11 metres   E5 6b   (9.6.88)
A brilliant but heart-stopping little pitch. Starting just right of the arête, climb the flake and thin crack to a tied-off peg. Lunge right past this for good holds. Finish direct, passing two ancient pegs.

Four Horsemen of the Apocalypse   11 metres   E3 6a   (21.2.90)
Though short, this route requires a stable approach, being good value for its grade. Start in the obvious right-hand corner and climb it for 3 metres before moving out left, hands just above the overlap, to make a hard move up for an obvious flake (high peg). Alternatively, climb direct to the same point. Traverse left to a large foothold and pull up rightwards to finish at *in-situ* slings.

Times Laughin' Stocks   9 metres   E2 6a   (1.7.88)
Squeezed in between the direct start to the previous route and the corner, this serious micro-pitch is no laughin' matter. Using obvious holds (next to pockets), or just the pockets without the holds (harder), climb the wall, trending right to join the corner at the top.

The corner itself can be climbed direct at Hard Severe 4b.

Rediscovered   9 metres   E1 5b   (1.6.88)
A rather slight pitch up the right edge of the crag and then a corner.

Lime Street   9 metres   E1 6a   (29.6.94)
Follow a crack to a second crack, which leads to a break. Finish easily.

Craig Ddu   Black Crag   OS Ref 618 574

This is the most westerly of the cliffs on the north side of Llanberis Pass. Its black glint suggests a wet, unpleasant cliff but some of the rock is intrinsically jet black and rather smooth.

Mabinogion Area
At the left-hand side of Craig Ddu, just beyond the point where the descent path turns back along the foot of the crag, there is a clean isolated wall. It is clearly visible from the road and is split by a thin sloping crack, *Mabinogion*.

About 50 metres left of *Mabinogion* is a series of pinnacles. The first has a cave at its base, which provides the start of the next two routes.

Repellant   8 metres   Hard Very Severe 5b   (18.7.02)
Climb the broken right-hand wall to easy ground. A long reach left allows you to finish up the arête.

Spiritwalker 10 metres E2 5b (24.7.02)
Go up from the cave, move right to a ledge, swing right and layback the arête.

Further left is a larger, white pinnacle, which is home to two more routes.

The Uphill Gardener 8 metres Severe (25.7.02)
Follow the arête left of *Days of Speed* from start to finish.

Days of Speed 8 metres Hard Very Severe 5a (27.7.02)
Start below the white face, at a crack left of centre. Climb the centre of the pinnacle.

The next series of climbs is in the vicinity of *Mabinogion* itself.

Telegram Sam 12 metres E1 6a (4.85)
The wall left of the thin sloping crack of *Mabinogion* is just a little harder than the crack itself.

★★**Mabinogion** 14 metres E1 5c (2.5.85)
A little gem. Climb the crack to a good pocket (crux). Step left and continue up on pockets to a ledge. Finish up the thin crack in the short, overhanging headwall (good wire – difficult to place).

Stumpy the Dragonslayer 12 metres E2 5c (6.85)
Climb the wall right of *Mabinogion*.

Health and Efficiency 12 metres E2 6a (17.8.87)
The groove right of *Stumpy...* is a devious, oft-tried problem. Climb the groove to good pockets on the right wall. Finish direct.

Sound as a Trout 12 metres E2 5c (20.4.92)
Start at the obvious flake right of the groove of *Health and Efficiency*. Climb the centre of the flake to a small horizontal slot. Move left to the arête and ascend to a good flaky spike. Move right on good holds, place a runner in the top crack, and scuttle round to the right to belay.

Buoux in a Tin (Without a Tin-opener) 12 metres E5 6b (17.8.87)
Thirty metres around to the right of *Mabinogion* sits a huge flake whose front face presents a severely undercut wall. From a large flake, exacting climbing up a faint left-to-right diagonal weakness leads, hopefully, to a safe finish via a big groove. The direct start is **Saussuave** (6c).

Up and right of *Mabinogion*, about 300 metres above the left end of Craig Ddu, is a very steep rightward-leaning arête.

Gram -ve 9 metres E7 6c (10.3.96)
The leaning arête. Start on the blocks to the right. Acrobatic moves lead to the arête (peg), crux. Sustained, pumpy climbing leads to a rounded finish.

The Main Cliff

Drainage from the steep hillside above makes the cliff unusually slow to dry out. Boilerplate formation gives the crag a slabby appearance, but it is uniformly steep and in the central part, up which *Canol* forces a way, slightly overhanging. Many of the routes are better than their appearance would suggest, and there is a greater element of seriousness than on other cliffs on the north side of the Pass.

The obvious cleft of *Garlic Groove*, a wet vegetated gully, halves the cliff. Left of this lies the major section, bounded at its left end by *Short Tree Chimney*, which is topped by a tree. Just right of this, a boulder on the right edge of a watercourse at the foot of the cliff marks the start of *Crown of Thorns*. Left of *Garlic Groove* is a massive pinnacle. Between this and *Crown of Thorns* are *Zig-Zag* and *Canol*. The pinnacle provides the starts of *Black Wall* and *Scrog*. The main feature right of *Garlic Groove* is another flat-topped pedestal, the left side of which forms the obvious slab and vertical corner of *Rift Wall*. To the right, the cliff, still very steep, gives *The Heretic*, *The Bog of the Eternal Stench*, *Yellow Groove*, *Yellow Wall*, *Petite Fleur*, and several other short but entertaining routes.

The cliff is just above the 200-metre contour and is thus one of the lowest in the Pass. About 3 minutes from the road, it is mainly south-west-facing and receives ample sunshine from mid morning onwards during the summer months. Descent is down the easy hillside well to the left of the crag, or on the right down a gully just right of *Grooved Rib*.

Short Tree Chimney   50 metres   Severe   (11.4.49)

At the left-hand side of the main cliff proper, 3 metres left of a watercourse, is an obvious right-facing chimney capped by a tall tree. Start left of the chimney.

1 17m. Climb the chimney or its drier left wall to a ledge. The chimney is bridged by a large chockstone. Climb up and swing to the left, make a difficult mantelshelf and go back into the corner. Climb this to a large ledge and tree.

2 12m. Move left and climb the short wall to a belay. The easy-looking pitch above the belay is often climbed by mistake but is much harder.

3 21m. Scramble to the top, traversing first right, then left.

Variation

2a Very Severe. The wall directly behind the first stance may be climbed – lethal if wet.

★★Sea Panther   37 metres   E1   5b   (9.5.80)

Very fine climbing up the centre of the wall right of *Short Tree Chimney*, although it often seeps. Start a metre right of *Short Tree Chimney*. Climb steeply up the wall moving slightly left after a short way. Go up on small flakes past an awkward move at 8 metres to gain good holds and easier climbing (runner on the left). Traverse right at 18 metres to reach an obvious ledge below the steep upper wall. Ascend this on good holds via a hidden central crack until forced to move left. Cross a ramp and continue up to a good tree belay on the left. Scramble off left to finish.

★Crown of Thorns 41 metres Severe (30.1.49)
Pleasant if it's dry, but still serious for its grade. Start 12 metres right of *Short Tree Chimney*, where a boulder protrudes a metre out of the ground at the right-hand edge of the watercourse.
1 18m. Ascend direct to the right end of a grassy ledge at 8 metres. Climb the groove on the right, and then move back left to the top of the pedestal.
2 12m. Climb the wall on good holds to a sloping ledge, and then take a grassy groove until an entry can be made into a large scoop. Belays in the corner.
3 11m. Climb the flaky wall on the right. Step up and across the groove on the left, where difficult moves then bring the top within reach, or climb directly up the corner above the wall and back through the 'thorny crown' onto the grass. Belay well back.
Variation
1a Start 5 metres left of the boulder at the bottom of the watercourse and climb diagonally right to the grassy ledge 8 metres up the normal start.

Blackguard 60 metres Hard Very Severe (5.7.75)
A very good way up the cliff. Start immediately right of *Crown of Thorns*, at the foot of an indefinite crack.
1 18m. 4b. Follow the crack to join *Crown of Thorns* half-way up the groove on its first pitch. Continue as for *Crown of Thorns* to the pedestal stance.
2 15m. 5a. Traverse right for 6 metres. Climb a steep wall past a small quartzy area on good holds to reach ledges. Step up left to belay.
3 27m. 5a. Traverse right beneath an overhanging wall to a projecting block. Climb onto this from the right and surmount the bulge above to gain a slab. Climb this and finish up a short corner-crack.

Flying Trapeze 65 metres E1 (5.7.75)
An intimidating route with a bold top pitch. Start 8 metres right of the *Crown of Thorns* starting boulder, and just left of a clump of grass 6 metres up the crag.
1 21m. 4b. Climb the wall to a ledge at 8 metres. Step left and go up trending right, making for the foot of the right-slanting groove on *Zig-Zag*. Follow this for 3 metres to a small ledge. Nut and ancient peg belays.
2 17m. 4c. Continue up rightwards and move left to a shallow groove. Climb this to a large hanging block at the top. Traverse right below this to a sloping ledge and peg belays.
3 27m. 5a. Move back left and climb the crack in the left side of the block (scary). Go up the wall to just below the bulge. Traverse right for 5 metres to a sloping ledge, the last part on undercuts. Layback up to the left round the bulge to a precarious finish.

★Zig-Zag   64 metres   Very Severe   (17.6.52)
A very fine climb, not hard technically, but rather serious because of spaced
protection. Small wires are useful. Start under a prominent overhang 6 metres
up, and about 15 metres right of the *Crown of Thorns* starting boulder.
1 37m. 4b. Climb up leftwards to a grassy ledge at 6 metres. Go
diagonally right, steep, to another grassy ledge. Step left into a short
shallow groove and climb leftwards across an easy ramp-line to the foot of
a right-slanting groove 3 metres higher. Climb this groove to a grassy
stance. Care needed with belays.
2 27m. 4b. Continue diagonally right to a ledge and finish up the black
groove 6 metres right of the stance. Belay well back to the left.

China Girl   64 metres   E2   (7.83)
A direct line up the centre of the main face that crosses some very loose
rock. Start immediately right of *Zig-Zag*, below the overhang at 6 metres.
1 24m. 5c. Start up the quartz vein leading to a small overhang. Go over
this at the small hanging groove. Continue directly up the crack above to
easier but shattered rock. Belay on the ledge. Care needed to find belays.
2 40m. 5b. Climb the overhanging groove above the stance and then
easier rocks to the top. A poorly protected pitch.

★★Canol   69 metres   E1   (16.6.52)
A good route, steep and technically interesting. Start 12 metres left of the
slanting crack on the left side of the massive pinnacle, below a holly tree
on a grassy ledge.
1 24m. 4c. Climb steeply up to the holly tree. Bushwhack through the
grass and ascend diagonally leftwards to a sloping shelf, which leads left
to a blocky belay.
2 24m. 5b. Climb the short steep wall on the left behind the belay, using
an indefinite crack, to reach and then climb a rightward-sloping ramp.
From the top of this, turn the overhang on its left side (peg) and continue to
a ledge. Traverse easily right for 9 metres to an enormous block belay.
3 21m. 4b. Climb the obvious groove just left of the block, turning the
shattered overhang on the left to finish.
Variations
1a Direct Start 18m. Very Severe 4c. Start 8 metres left of the normal
start, 3 metres right of *Zig-Zag*. Climb the ledgy wall to the block belay at
the top of pitch 1, stepping right at 9 metres.
2a 24m. E1 5b. As for pitch 2 to the peg below the overhang; then
traverse right, using a fang of rock, to a good hold. Climb diagonally
down right, past a quartz hold, and round a corner to a detached block. A
shallow groove leads to flat holds, which are traversed to the right until it is
possible to climb up to trees.

★Jupiter   66 metres   E3   (21.7.82)
A bold and intimidating climb. Start as for *Canol*.
1 18m. 5a. Climb the wall and groove up to the holly. Go up the
shattered groove above (a bit grassy) to a peg belay. This is level with, but
8 metres right of, the blocky belay at the top of *Canol* pitch 1.

Rib and Slab (VD, page 37) Craig Ddu
Climber: Graham Sutton   Photo: David Simmonite

Bog of the Eternal Stench (E5, page 39) Craig Ddu
Climber: Patch Hammond   Photo: David Simmonite

2 21m. 5b. Step left and climb the overhanging wall via the remains of a dubious flake to the overhang. Move left round this and follow the steep quartzy crack diagonally left to a second roof. Boldly climb this, moving right and then left, to the traverse ledge of *Canol*. Move right to belay on the large block, as for *Canol*. An exposed pitch.

3 27m. 5a. Traverse back left for about 1½ metres, past *Canol*'s final groove, to a shallow scoop. Go up this using two good pockets to a ledge and finish direct.

The Despicable Act   67 metres   E2   (7.8.82)
A bold slabby lower section contrasts with the highly technical finale up an overhanging groove. Start at a small shattered spike 2½ metres right of *Canol*.

1 37m. 5b. Step left off the spike and climb steeply up the black streak to reach a large sloping niche at 9 metres. Pull rightwards around the overlap and ascend boldly on good sharp holds, first right and then left to a grassy ledge. Climb up over ledges to the foot of an overhanging groove. Go up this, exiting leftwards to the block belay on *Canol*.

2 30m. 5c. Move up leftwards from the top of the block. Traverse back right to beneath an overhanging groove. Make very hard moves past a peg to enter the groove, and climb it to finish. Scrambling remains.

Grey Wall   63 metres   E1   (25.3.57)
An interesting line. Start below the slanting crack with a tree at its foot on the left side of the massive pinnacle.

1 15m. 5a. The crack leads to a tree on the black slab. Continue up to a grassy ledge below an overhanging groove.

2 24m. 5c. Climb the groove to the small stance of *Black Wall* pitch 2. Follow *Black Wall* pitch 3 to the peg, and traverse 6 metres right to a stance below an overhanging crack.

3 24m. 4c. Climb the crack to below the overhang, and traverse right to good holds and the finish.

Variation

1a 15m. 5a. Step up onto a ledge just left of the tree. Pull boldly round the arête and go up to the tree at the top of the slanting crack.

★★Black Wall   64 metres   E1   (8.54)
A good route, but it is usually greasy and intimidating. Start below the wide crack on the right side of the massive pinnacle.

1 14m. 4c. Either traverse left and climb the arête; or, better, climb the arête from its base (poorly protected – thin line slings would help).

2 15m. 4a. Climb the steep wall on the left into a scoop. Go diagonally left to a small stance and good belays.

3 24m. 5c. Climb the steep crack to the overhang and swing out left (crux). Climb direct for 5 metres until it is possible to step right to a thin crack. Climb this for 3 metres (peg). A shallow groove on the left leads to the overhangs. Climb diagonally left across greasy slabs. Good stance and belays.

4 11m. Climb direct to the top.

Craig Ddu

1 Crown of Thorns	S	
2 Zig-Zag	VS	
3 Canol	E1	
4 Grey Wall	E1	
5 Black Wall	E1	
6 Scrog	E1	

7	Rib and Slab	VD	11	Yellow Groove	VS
8	Rift Wall	VS	12	Yellow Wall	E2
9	Orpheus	E2	13	Fever	HVS
10	The Heretic	E4	14	Petite Fleur	HS

Scrog   96 metres   E1   (17.7.55)
An interesting route with some good moves. Start as for *Black Wall*.
1 18m. 4b. Climb the wide crack on the right-hand side of the pinnacle.
2 27m. 5b. Step across and ascend the short overhanging crack on the
right. Go up the arête above for 5 metres; then traverse right to a good
tree belay in a large bay.
3 18m. 5a. Ascend the steep crack behind the tree, follow the groove
over an overhang and continue to a prickly holly stance.
4 24m. 5a. Move left for 2 metres to a groove leading back right to the
foot of an overhanging crack. Climb this and continue, bearing right to a
large block.
5 9m. 4a. Climb the pleasant finishing wall.
Variation
This gives a far better route and is worth E2 overall.
3a 27m. 5c. Climb the crack behind the tree; then step left to the foot of
an overhanging layback crack. Climb this with difficulty and belay on the
holly above. Continue up the groove of pitch 4.
4a 21m. 5b. Instead of moving back right, continue direct.

Sheep in Situ   95 metres   E1   (6.7.75)
A rambling expedition with a deceptively steep second pitch. Start at a
quartzy ramp about 3 metres right of the wide crack of *Scrog*.
1 12m. 4a. Climb the ramp to a sloping ledge on the right and a peg belay.
2 9m. 5b. Step down and move steeply right to a peg. Climb the groove
above on the right to an awkward finish on a grassy ledge.
3 15m. 4c. Step up left and follow the ledge until it is possible to climb
up to a large ledge with blocks (on the girdle).
4 15m. 4c. Climb the groove behind the blocks until a traverse left leads
to below the left end of a ledge with trees.
5 11m. 5a. Climb the vegetated groove behind the tree (past a peg) to a
rightward traverse which finishes over a large block to a holly tree belay.
6 24m. 5a. Traverse right to pitch 4 of *Scrog*, and follow this.
7 9m. 4a. Finish up the wall as for *Scrog*.

Garlic Groove   63 metres   Severe   (25.4.49)
Quite a pleasant climb above the initial slimy chimney. Start in the black
gully a few metres right of the massive pinnacle.
1 24m. 3c. The wet chimney leads to a grassy corner. Continue up this
with interest to the tall tree.
2 18m. 3b. The groove continues in a curving line. Climb the corner for
a metre or so, and then step into a subsidiary groove on the right. Ascend
this until a step is made to the edge. Go up to a large block and climb the
steep rib on the right to a holly tree.
3 21m. 3c. Scramble up the continuation of the gully. A short chimney
below a tree proves awkward. Finish in the same line.

Dill   66 metres   Hard Severe   (20.8.82)
Worth doing if you have climbed the other options. Start between *Garlic
Groove* and *Rib and Slab*.

1 27m. Climb the tapering slab, continue up the broken rib, and then traverse left to the tree on *Garlic Groove*.
2 18m. 4b. Above is an arête, which is gained direct or from the right. Climb this to rejoin *Garlic Groove*. Follow this to belay at a holly tree.
3 21m. Scramble up via a square-cut chimney to reach the final wall. Finish directly up this.

★★Rib and Slab   76 metres   Very Difficult   (29.10.48)
A popular beginners' climb. Start at the foot of the rib right of *Garlic Groove*.
1 30m. Climb the tricky rib, past a steepening near the top, to a broad terrace. Tree root belay.
2 46m. Climb the delightful slab to finish (the line is just left of centre). Care is needed with the final belay.

My Mum's Slabby Arête   12 metres   E3 6a   (6.87)
On the left, at the top of the central gully (the initial part of *Garlic Groove*), and left of the top pitch of *Rib and Slab*, is a pocketed arête with a tree to its right. The arête is hard to start, but gradually eases to a pleasant afternoon outing.

The Tickle   30 metres   Severe   (20.5.62)
This avoids the slab of *Rib and Slab* by taking the wall on the left. Start below the slab of *Rib and Slab*. In the gully is a slight bay with a roof about 2 metres up on the left.
1 18m. 3b. Climb the crack in the back of the bay, and move left under the roof round the corner into a niche. Go up to a block and climb a rib (or vegetation on its left) to belay at a holly tree.
2 12m. 3c. Climb the steep rocks behind (harder than it looks), keeping left of the finish of *Dill*.

Castor   54 metres   Very Severe   (8.6.67)
A rather disjointed and disappointing climb. Start from a quartz-topped boulder by the path, just left of the prominent rib, midway between *Rib and Slab* and the rusty metal.
1 15m. 4b. Mantelshelf onto a large block and continue up the wide crack to a large bay and tree belay.
2 15m. 4c. Traverse right through trees, over an arête, and then go up a crack and over the overhang above. Move left to belay.
3 24m. Finish up the right-hand side of the slabs.

Black Mike   21 metres   Hard Very Severe 5a   (28.4.87)
Really only a variation start to *Castor*, but with some good moves, and much more continuous than that route. Start to the right of *Castor* pitch 1. Climb the flaky groove and small overhang to a junction with *Castor* pitch 2.

★Carlos   28 metres   E1   (10.8.69)
A fierce little pitch, it takes the right-hand of three steep grooves. Start about 3½ metres left of the rusty metal.
1 17m. 5b. Climb the overhanging groove until an awkward move enables the right wall to be gained. From a precarious position, bold

climbing leads to a rest below the small roof on the right. Traverse right and then go up to a small stance. Tree belay.
2 11m. 5a. Swing into the groove on the left. Continue up the crack to finish. Belay on the slabs above.

Samson Too   15 metres   E3 6a   (27.4.91)
An awkward little pitch; deceptively steep. Start immediately right of the overhanging groove of *Carlos*. Climb the right-hand side of the arête to a large jug. Climb diagonally right to a good hold (crux); then boldly take the right wall of the corner to a tree belay – care needs to be taken with the rock on the top 2 metres. Abseil off.

Black Letter Day   21 metres   E1 5b   (29.4.87)
Short but tricky. Start behind the rusty metal remains of a fence. Gain a leftward-leaning ramp. Follow this awkwardly, and take the groove and crack above to the tree belay on *Samson Too*. Abseil off.

★The Black Pig   41 metres   E3   (9.5.81)
Another deceptively steep line, with absorbing climbing, between *Carlos* and *Rift Wall*. Start at a boss of rock about 1½ metres right of the rusty metal.
1 15m. 5c. Climb the black shattered wall keeping right of the groove. Make a hard pull over the bulge and step right to climb a 1-metre groove. Continue to a large ledge, and ascend a short wall to another ledge. Peg and nut belay on the right.
2 15m. 5b. Gain the top of the large flake above the stance. Ascend for about a metre, and then move left to the arête. Traverse back right and climb the bulging wall using an inverted spike. Pull strenuously into the scoop and climb it to a stance below a thin crack on the right.
3 11m. 6a. Climb the crack, which overhangs alarmingly, to a good hold. Exit left with difficulty.

★★Rift Wall   60 metres   Very Severe   (27.7.49)
A varied route up the large slabs and overhanging corner that form the left flank of the flat-topped pedestal. The hard section is only short but it packs a punch. Start in a bay at a rock step 8 metres right of the rusty metal.
1 21m. 4b. Go diagonally left on easy rock to a ledge. Climb up for a metre or so, and then traverse right on steep rock to gain the bottom of the slab. Climb this to a belay below the overhanging corner-crack.
2 27m. 5a. Fight your way up the overhanging corner, and then stroll up the easy slab to the top of a pedestal.
3 12m. 4a. Move up left to the foot of a steep corner. Swing sensationally onto the left arête on large flakes (very exposed). Finish easily.

Mas Gato Negro   64 metres   E4   (25.8.97)
Rather contrived but with some interest nevertheless. Start 6 metres right of *Rift Wall*, at two quartz bands.
1 21m. 5b. Go diagonally left up a shallow depression to a good flake runner. Continue up the flake and go up the slab to below a diamond-shaped wall.

2 43m. 6b. A crack in the wall leads diagonally up left; tackle this and then follow the easy slabs for 37 metres to the top.

★**Orpheus**   54 metres   E2   (13.6.67)
A juggy wall climb with rather spaced protection. Start as for *Mas Gato Negro*, at two quartz bands.
1 24m. 5b. Go diagonally left up a shallow depression to a good flake runner. Traverse 6 metres right across a slab to a small platform on the arête. Move boldly up on pockets, and then go slightly left to a small niche. Traverse right for about a metre and take the overhang at its weakest point to a slab and spike belay.
2 15m. 4c. Climb diagonally right up a short wall, and go easily up to a small bay on *Pedestal Route*. From the right-hand end of the bay, move right round a bulge and climb the arête to the top of the pedestal.
3 15m. 4c. Traverse right to a crack. Climb this and the overhang above to enter a groove. Finish up this.

Pedestal Route   64 metres   Very Difficult   (19.6.48)
A wandering route that reaches the top of the pedestal by a rising traverse from the short right-hand side, then descends to escape along a weakness in the slabs of *Rift Wall*. Start by scrambling 9 metres up into the grassy bay right of the pedestal.
1 18m. Traverse left and round the corner to a small bay. Climb the far corner to the top of the slab. The corner-crack of the grassy bay leads directly to the same point.
2 46m. Descend the slab by the corner to a small sapling, and traverse left out onto the far edge. The awkward slabs near the edge lead up to grass (this is the slab of *Rib and Slab*).

Slab and Groove   36 metres   Hard Very Severe   (30.5.86)
Start below the steep slab, above the start of *Pedestal Route*.
1 15m. 4a. Climb the middle of the slab.
2 21m. 5a. Follow the steep groove above, via some bold laybacking or less strenuosly by wide bridging (the rusty peg half-way up is useless).

★'**Totally Wired 9'**   21 metres   E8 6b   (25.7.96)
A ferocious route taking the leaning black wall left of *The Bog of the Eternal Stench*. Start slightly right of the faint groove below a left-trending break. Climb up and leftwards with a long reach to jugs at the base of a groove (a *Friend* ½ in a small slot is crucial). Continue direct on crimps to the safety of jugs and some slings. Carry on up, trending slightly right to finish left of the crack of *The Heretic*.

★★**The Bog of the Eternal Stench**   30 metres   E5 6b   (29.4.87)
A mighty pitch which forges its way directly up the leaning black wall crossed by *The Heretic*. Start by scrambling up to the first pitch of *Yellow Groove* to the large block at the top of the rock pyramid, and then descending the ramp on the other side for 5 metres. Climb straight up and then slightly left to reach groove on *The Heretic*, which is followed to the

break. A powerful move up and to the right gains a peg at the overlap and lands you below the crux. The headwall above gives a fitting finale.

★The Heretic   30 metres   E4 6a   (18.8.78)
A deceptively powerful pitch across the sombre black wall left of *Yellow Groove* with a problematical finish. Start just left of the large block above *Yellow Groove* pitch 1. Traverse left and climb the groove in the centre of the impending wall to a slanting crack. Sidle awkwardly left to a precarious finish. Scramble up for 9 metres to belay.

Black Power   21 metres   E2 5c   (22.6.96)
A good pitch taking the groove and roof left of pitch 2 of *Yellow Groove*. Follow *Yellow Groove* pitch 2 to where it moves right. Step left and follow the groove (quite awkward) to the roof. Pull up through the roof strenuously on the right, and finish up the wall just left of *Yellow Groove*.

★★Yellow Groove   36 metres   Very Severe   (17.7.55)
A steep and exposed line with good holds, which gives superb climbing up the left-hand side of the yellow wall. Start on the right-hand side of the obvious rock pyramid crowned by a large block, about 12 metres right of *Pedestal Route*.
1 15m. Scramble easily up to the block.
2 21m. 4b. From the block, climb a groove to an overhang, and move right to a ledge below a clean-cut groove. Ascend this, step left and continue up the wall to the top.

★Blackhead   30 metres   E3 6a   (10.5.81)
This powerful and independent line between *Yellow Groove* and *Yellow Wall* gives a superb and varied pitch. Start 3 metres right of and slightly lower than the start of *Yellow Groove* pitch 2, at a leftward-slanting weakness. Follow the leftward-slanting line up the wall, strenuous, to the foot of the clean-cut groove of *Yellow Groove*. Move right and climb the short left-facing groove (crux) to a sloping ledge. Surmount the large overhang on the left and finish up the crack, passing two hollies.

★★Yellow Wall   48 metres   E2   (16.7.62)
A fine sustained climb of interest and character. Start on the right-hand side of the rock pyramid at the foot of the steep wall, directly below the hanging groove of *Fever*.
1 27m. 5b. Climb the steep wall for 6 metres to a resting-place. Trend up leftwards to the base of a very shallow groove. Climb this to an overhang, which is turned on the right, and go up to a ledge and belay.
2 21m. 5b. Traverse left under an overhang to a sloping ledge (junction with *Blackhead*). A strenuous pull round the overhang leads to precarious climbing up a groove, which leads to the top.

Fever   41 metres   Hard Very Severe   (17.7.66)
An interesting climb with a technical groove. Start just right of *Yellow Wall*, below a hanging boss of rock and an overhanging chimney.

1 23m. 5a. Climb the steep crack and wall. Traverse left under the overhang to the foot of the obvious groove. Superb moves up the groove, past a peg at the top, lead to a step right along a flake. Climb the slab to a ledge behind a holly.
2 18m. 4c. Make a rising traverse left to a perched block. Climb a crack and traverse left from another holly to the top.

Petite Fleur   34 metres   Hard Severe 4b   (6.3.61)
Pleasant but short. Start as for *Fever*. Climb the steep crack and wall to the overhang. Move up right into the overhanging chimney. Climb this and the slabby continuation groove to a grassy bay and tree belay. Thirty metres of scrambling remains.

Grooved Rib   34 metres   Hard Very Severe 5a   (6.62)
A worthwhile pitch, slightly easier for the tall. Start 3 metres right of *Petite Fleur* at the foot of a steep rib. Climb the rib direct, avoiding rightward possibilities, to a steepening at 18 metres. A difficult stretch and a high step enable a ledge to be reached. Step left and climb a shiny slab into a groove. Finish at the same point as *Petite Fleur*.

Rolling Stone   30 metres   E1 5b   (9.5.81)
Better than it looks, although a little mossy. Start 3 metres right of *Grooved Rib*, at an obvious crack. Climb the crack and pull directly over the bulge onto the slab above. Go straight up to the roof and climb it into the narrow V-groove (crux). Follow this for 5 metres to a grassy terrace. Traverse 6 metres right on easy ground to a broken holly tree. Ascend direct for 6 metres to a tree belay.

Wounded Knee   30 metres   Hard Very Severe 5b   (9.5.81)
Start 3 metres right of *Rolling Stone*. Climb the arête and short slab to the bulge. Take this direct (crux) and traverse left to the slab and roof of *Rolling Stone*. Follow the short groove right of the roof to the grassy terrace. Traverse right to belay as for *Rolling Stone*.

The next two routes lie on the buttress above the stile on the path up to Craig Ddu from the Grochan lay-by.

The Rib Route   37 metres   Very Difficult   (7.02)
Much better than appearances would suggest, and an excellent way of approaching *Rib and Slab*. High in the grade. Start 5 metres up and right of the stile.
1 12m. Climb a leftward-trending ramp-line. At its top, make an airy step right and follow a staircase of holds to a ledge on the left.
2 25m. Step right onto the rib, surmount the bulge (crux), and weave your way up the cliff to ledges and the top.

Feeding Station   28 metres   Hard Very Severe   (30.3.03)
Fairly technical moves up a disjointed groove-system. Start 20 metres up to the right of the stile, at the base of an obvious groove.

1 20m. 5a. Bridge up the initial groove delicately past flakes to a rib, and follow this to a slabby area below the upper groove and a grassy area above.
2 8m. Climb the obvious crack in the pocketed rock above.

Girdle Traverses
The Black Belt   194 metres   Hard Severe   (14.7.49)
A traverse of the cliff from left to right with fine situations, bold and exposed although technically fairly straightforward. Absorbing and interesting, it is the best expedition of its standard on the north side of the Pass. It is worth waiting for a dry spell as many areas crossed seep badly and the climb will be found to be harder and more serious if at all wet. Start at the left-hand end of the cliff, around the corner from *Short Tree Chimney*.
1 21m. Climb the groove to a tree at 8 metres. Move right and climb *Short Tree Chimney* past the chockstone to a tree belay.
2 18m. 4a. Descend 1½ metres and traverse horizontally right on good holds to reach a ramp. Peg and nut belay on top of the pedestal (as for *Crown of Thorns*).
3 27m. 4b. Descend for about a metre and traverse horizontally right for 12 metres to the base of a rightward-slanting groove. Climb this (as for *Zig-Zag*) to a stance with poor belays on a small grassy ledge.
4 15m. 4b. Climb *Zig-Zag* for 5 metres to a narrow ledge. Traverse right along obvious ledges, descending slightly to the grassy ledge and block belay on *Canol*.
5 30m. 4a. From the right-hand end of the ledge, climb down 2 metres and go across a groove. Follow the ledge right and step down into the corner (peg). Move right to a good thread. Pull round onto a large ledge and cross a field to the tree belay at the top of *Garlic Groove* pitch 1.
6 11m. Walk right to belay at the foot of the large white slab of *Rib and Slab*.
7 21m. Climb easily up the right-hand edge of the slab to a small grassy ledge with a ramp descending rightwards. Good nut belay 3 metres up on the left.
8 12m. Descend the steep ramp and climb the slab to the top of the pedestal (*Pedestal Route* in reverse).
9 15m. Descend the steep corner-crack and scramble up to the large block belay on *Yellow Groove*. Care should be taken to protect the second on this pitch.
10 24m. 4c. From a grassy quartz niche 6 metres down the ramp, climb up; then make a descending rightward traverse across the wall on the obvious line to finish just right of *Grooved Rib* – an excellent pitch which although Very Severe is avoidable by scrambling down pitch 1 of *Yellow Groove*.

What a Jump   90 metres   Very Severe   (21.6.83)
An interesting, low-level girdle of the left-hand section of the crag. Not as long as *The Black Belt*, but the climbing is more continuous and equally good. Start below the right-hand side of the massive pinnacle, as for *Black Wall*.
1 15m. 4b. Traverse left and climb the arête to the top of the pinnacle.
2 24m. 4b. Traverse left along the prominent weakness to the block belay on *Canol*.

3 21m. 4b. Traverse left across to *Zig-Zag*. Continue left past some pieces of quartz at the foot of a rightward-slanting groove (*Zig-Zag*). Keep traversing more easily to the pedestal on *Crown of Thorns*. Peg and nut belay.
4 30m. 4a. Step down slightly and traverse across above the mantelshelf on *Short Tree Chimney*. Climb this to the tree (possible belay). Finish up the pitch 2 of *Short Tree Chimney*.

Hit the Basement   160 metres   Hard Very Severe   (21.6.83)
An intricate series of pitches split by some strolling. If the 5-metre crack on pitch 6 is bypassed the route becomes Very Severe. Start from the stile half-way up the path on the right-hand side of the crag.
1 43m. 4b. From the top of the stile, climb up to a grassy ledge at 15 metres. Make a steep move up the rib on the right, step left and ascend the broken wall to block belays 3 metres back.
2 23m. 4a. Scramble rightwards for 12 metres to reach a pock-marked wall. Move right into a crack and ascend pleasantly to block belays. Walk back 15 metres to the foot of the open rib that comes down from 6 metres right of *Orpheus*.
3 21m. 4c. Climb the rib and step left at the top onto a ledge. From the left-hand end of this, move steeply up to a sloping ledge and nut belays. Good spike 3 metres higher.
4 24m. 4a. Move round and descend the slab (below the crux corner of *Rift Wall*). Step across the gap and follow the sloping ledge round the corner to belay at the foot of *Rib and Slab*. Walk 9 metres left to belay on the tree at the top of *Garlic Groove*.
5 20m. 4c. Step up and climb to the top of the leaning corner-crack just left of *Garlic Groove*. Pull straight over onto a grassy ledge below a short overhanging crack.
6 8m. 5a. The crack yields quickly to bold laybacking. Flake and nut belays 3 metres back.
7 21m. 4b. Climb the shallow groove on the right, and finish up the smart little wall above.

Little Buttress
OS Ref 619 573

Between Craig Ddu and Clogwyn y Grochan, and about 100 metres from the latter, is a small buttress capped by a steep yellow wall, with hollies on its right-hand side. With new rock getting scarcer, it now boasts several desperate micro-routes.

Down on the left side of the crag, the twin cracks of *Bell Fruit* and *Tom's Plums* rise up to merge at 9 metres. The crack just to the left has also been climbed.

Pokey Little Puppy   9 metres   E5 6b   (28.6.94)
Tackles the seam in the hanging slab.

Bell Fruit   9 metres   E4 6b   (3.85)
The left-hand crack proves a desperate struggle with a finger-severing jam at half height.

Tom's Plums   9 metres   E3 6b   (3.85)
Climb the right-hand crack with extreme difficulty (low crux). Scramble up the slab to finish.

Too Late to Hesitate   15 metres   E4 6b   (22.2.90)
From just left of *Little Groover*, climb the obvious flake system to a set of good holds (tiny wires to the left and right). Move up and right to a good hold on the arête (crux), and finish up *Little Groover*.

★**Little Groover**   18 metres   E1 5b   (5.84)
Climb the slanting groove left of the peg-scarred crack of *Ryley Bosvil* with a hard move at 5 metres (awkward to protect with small wires) to a ledge. Continue in the same line and finish easily to the right (or direct – precarious) up the slab.

★**Ryley Bosvil**   15 metres   E5 6c   (7.7.85)
The obvious, much tried peg-scarred crack left of the Y-shaped crack of *Little Buttress Climb* is an extremely technical proposition. Climb the crack, passing the peg. Sustained, precarious, and a very sensational effort.

Little Buttress Climb   38 metres   Severe   (23.4.49)
Start left of the holly trees at the foot of the wide Y-shaped crack.
1 17m. Strenuously ascend the crack, taking its right fork.
2 12m. Climb up over shattered blocks to the foot of the final wall. Belay on a large block.
3 9m. From the top of the block, move out onto the steep yellow wall, by a large shallow niche. The crack above is taken on good holds.

The Three Cliffs   36 metres   E1   (10.3.85)
Start 5 metres right of and above the foot of the Y-shaped crack, below a dogleg-shaped groove.
1 15m. 5b. Climb the wall, via layaways, to a steep finish. Block belay.
2 12m. 5a. Take the thin crack behind the belay to easier ground below the final wall.
3 9m. *Little Buttress Climb* pitch 3.

Drws y Gwynt Area

The location of the various crags in this area is shown on the map on page 240.

Above the right-hand section of Craig Ddu are three prominent boulders consisting of a square one sandwiched between two thin ones. Just below these is a small buttress with a clean pillar that has a narrow overhanging face split by a crack.

Overhanging Deckchair   15 metres   E2 5c   (26.4.85)
This is certainly no picnic. Reach the crack using loose flakes. Barbarous jamming up this leads to a welcome finishing bucket. Painful.

About half-way along the path from the right-hand end of Craig Ddu to Drws y Gwynt, and 12 metres above it, is a crag with a deep V-groove/corner in its right arête . Below the left arête of the groove/corner is a curving overlap with a scooped wall to its right above a quartz marker.

Sheepslayer   27 metres   E3 5c   (6.82)
A deceptively steep pitch. Follow the curving groove to the right. Pull over the roof and move onto the arête. Climb this, past a large rock scar, to the top.

Root Canal   30 metres   E1 5b   (4.5.03)
A fine route tackling the obvious clean-cut corner to the right of *Sheepslayer*. Start directly below the corner at the arête. Pull up using a dubious jammed flake and make an awkward move to gain the ledge. Climb the excellent corner-crack to the top.

The deep V-groove/corner in the right arête to the right of the main corner of *Root Canal* gives a short Very Severe 4c.

Drws y Gwynt   Door (of) the Wind   OS Ref 621 574

This steep little crag, standing out from the hillside above and to the left of Clogwyn y Grochan, is well worth a visit. The rock is on the whole very clean, sound and rough. The cliff, rising in two tiers, is like a miniature Dinas Cromlech, consisting of large blocks and corners. The most conspicuous feature, towards the left-hand side, is the steep right-angled corner of *Little Sepulchre*. On its right retaining wall lies a thin finger-crack, and then a wide crack that rises from the top of a pillar. To the right again a large holly marks the groove of *Holly Gate*, beyond which a number of side walls, gradually diminishing in height, give several short problems of varying difficulty.

A Touch of Class   24 metres   E1 5b   (8.9.91)
Excellent holds, perfect rock and good protection where it matters combine to give a worthy outing. Unfortunately, the route is a little dirty at present but should improve and get slightly easier as it cleans up. Start left of the arête left of *Little Sepulchre*, under an obvious V-groove. Pull into the V-groove and climb it to a step up and right onto an uncomfortable ledge. Ascend the wall, direct at first; then move right to better holds. Go up left to a fairly wide crack and follow it to the top.

Demi Sec Dame   24 metres   E3 6a   (16.6.84)
The arête left of *Little Sepulchre*. Move left across the arête on underclings (fangs) to gain a shallow groove. Go up and climb the crack, which trends

left and then right to a prominent ledge on the arête. Take the final wall, via a crack just left of the arête, on superb finger-locks.

Little Sepulchre   24 metres   Very Severe   4b   (30.8.48)
A superb little climb, reminiscent of *Curving Crack* on Cloggy. Start below the clean-cut corner. Scramble up to tall spikes and traverse into the corner. Climb the excellent corner-crack with surprising ease.

Too Hard for Jim Perrin   24 metres   E1   5c   (7.78)
A classic test of finger-jamming. Start as for *Little Sepulchre*. Climb the thin crack between *Little Sepulchre* and *Cracked Wall*; hardest at the start.

Cracked Wall   30 metres   Very Difficult   (30.8.48)
A fine route on perfect rock. Go up to the spikes as for *Little Sepulchre*. Climb the wall to the overhanging crack (this point can also be reached by cracks on the right). The crack is tricky to enter but holds are large where it is steepest. Finish up a short wall.

Holly Gate   44 metres   Very Difficult   (30.8.48)
A good interesting line, though artificial in its lower part. Start below and to the left of the large holly tree.
1 24m. Climb the slabs delicately and go into the corner below the tree. Ascend a strenuous flake crackcrack on the right to a stance.
2 20m. Go up a little on the right, and then traverse back into the groove behind the tree. Climb the groove and ascend a crack in the wall to finish.

Reluctant   57 metres   Hard Severe   (14.9.58)
This takes the outside edge of the buttress right of *Holly Gate*, but escapes to the left for belays. Start just right of *Holly Gate*.
1 15m. 3a. Go up from the lowest corner of the buttress, keeping as much as possible to its crest. At 12 metres, traverse left along a grassy ledge to belay on *Holly Gate*.
2 12m. 4a. Return to 2 metres left of the ridge and climb awkwardly past a protruding chockstone at 9 metres to gain a large ledge (belay top left).
3 15m. Traverse back down along the ledge and continue in the original line to a large grassy ledge sloping down to the left (where the other climbs end). Belay at the foot of a crack.
4 9m. 4a. Climb the crack on good holds (strenuous) to another grassy terrace.
5 6m. 3b. Ascend the left-hand crack to finish; the chimney on the right is poor.

Leesled   32 metres   Severe   (16.12.51)
Rather dirty and unpleasantly vegetated. Start beneath a rowan tree high on the right, beyond the wall that meets the cliff.
1 6m. Go up the broken wall to a large ledge and belays.
2 26m. Climb the mossy slab to gain a ledge on the right with difficulty. Awkward steps up left lead to twin cracks. Ascend to the large holly and exit left or up the right-hand corner.

Some 60 metres left of the top of *Little Sepulchre* is a crag characterized by a gravestone-shaped wall facing up the Pass and forming the left wall of a corner; this is *Tombstone Wall*. The right-hand side of the crag is rounded and concave; beneath it is a good bivouac site, formed by a leaning flake. The wide corner-crack is Very Difficult.

Round the corner to the left are two overhanging pillars, the left one being a detached pinnacle split by a crack giving:

Masochist's Mambo   18 metres   E3 6a   (3.5.85)
No pain, no gain! Climb the fiercely overhanging finger-to-hand crack to a small ledge. Boulder the summit block and step across the gap to belay.

Barry Bush   12 metres   E5 6a   (8.01)
The prominent arête left of *Tombstone Wall*. Start left of *Tombstone Wall* and trend left with a committing move to gain the arête. Follow this on its right for a few metres, and then swing around to its left as the angle eases.

Tombstone Wall   12 metres   E4 5c   (3.5.85)
Go directly up the wall, just left of centre, on pockets and flakes. A superb and bold undertaking devoid of protection.

Fred   18 metres   E3 6a   (4.7.87)
The prominent scoop 15 metres right of *Tombstone Wall* is tenuous, strenuous, and quite bold. A sustained section protected by small wires leads up to the base of the bulge. Pull up on a poor pocket, and make hard precarious moves to gain the slab above. Belay 3 metres up and left.

Wyatt Earp   15 metres   E5 6b   (7.7.01)
A good, bold route that tackles the arête to the right of *Fred*, with a low peg at the start and hard climbing above.

The following routes are on the upper tier of the crag, above and behind *Little Sepulchre*. The main part consists of a wall seamed with cracks and divided by a huge blocky chimney. About 25 metres down and left of the chimney is a wedge-shaped grey wall which gives:

Play Safe, Be First   18 metres   E4 6a   (5.87)
Hard starting-moves precede bold but easier climbing to a juggy break, and the first protection, at 9 metres. The easier cracks above are something of an anticlimax.

Left of the blocky chimney are two thin cracks.

Featherlight   15 metres   E1 5b   (10.84)
Climb the left-hand crack; this is similar to (but easier than) *Foil* on the Cromlech.

Barnstormer   15 metres   E1 5b   (10.84)
A niche undercuts the right-hand crack; escaping from this provides the crux.

Chopping Block   15 metres   E2 5c   (5.87)
The benign-looking right arête of the *Barnstormer* wall does not yield
easily. Climb the arête, using holds and runners on either side until it is
possible to swing left into a fist-crack. Fight this to reach the break and the
lurking 'chopping block' – this should be treated circumspectly. Having
negotiated this, amble up the easy crack to finish.

Three large cracks break the wall to the right of the huge blocky chimney.

Ghost Dog   11 metres   Hard Very Severe 5a   (7.99)
Start right of the chimney and left of *Left-Hand Crack*. Climb to the top of
an obvious pinnacle via a wide crack, and then follow a thin crack in the
wall above, finishing near the arête on the left.

Left-Hand Crack   11 metres   Hard Very Severe 5a   (10.84)
An awkward V-chimney leads to an off-width struggle.

New Form   11 metres   E1 5c   (10.84)
Start just right of the last route. Climb the wall using thin shallow cracks.

Right-Hand Crack   9 metres   Very Severe 5a   (10.84)
The off-width right of *New Form* gives a struggle.

Unison   9 metres   Hard Severe 4b   (10.84)
On the right-hand edge of the crag and just right of the last route is a
short jamming crack. Climb this with pleasure.

Drws y Gwynt Uchaf   OS Ref 623 575
This cliff is the uppermost area of rock before reaching the rotting columns of
Craig Nant Peris. The best approach is from the Mabinogion Area, left of Craig
Ddu, heading up the steep gully on the left to a ridge and gaining the sheep
pens above. All the routes are located near the holly tree on the buttress.

No Fixed Abode   24 metres   Very Severe   (8.8.94)
Start 7 metres down and left of the holly at the toe of the buttress.
1 10m. 5a. Climb up rightwards using a crack and step left to a ledge
below the rib. Use the crack on the left to gain the top of the pinnacle flake
and climb direct to the terrace.
2 14m. 5a. Go up to the smoothish wall above and climb the clean-cut
corner on its right-hand side.

Strangling the Turtle   32 metres   E3   (8.8.94)
Start from the wide ledge up and to the right of the holly, at a steep crack
on the left-hand side.
1 10m. 5c. Climb the crack to the terrace.
2 10m. 5c. Go up and climb the hand/finger-crack splitting the wall
behind the belay.
3 12m. 6a. Stroll across to the right-hand side of the wall on the top tier.
Climb the wide rightward-facing crack, and continue up the thinner crack
in the wall above.

Sickle (HVS, page 57) Clogwyn y Grochan
Climber: Duncan Davey   Photo: Ron Kenyon

NORTH SIDE OF THE PASS ~ WEST

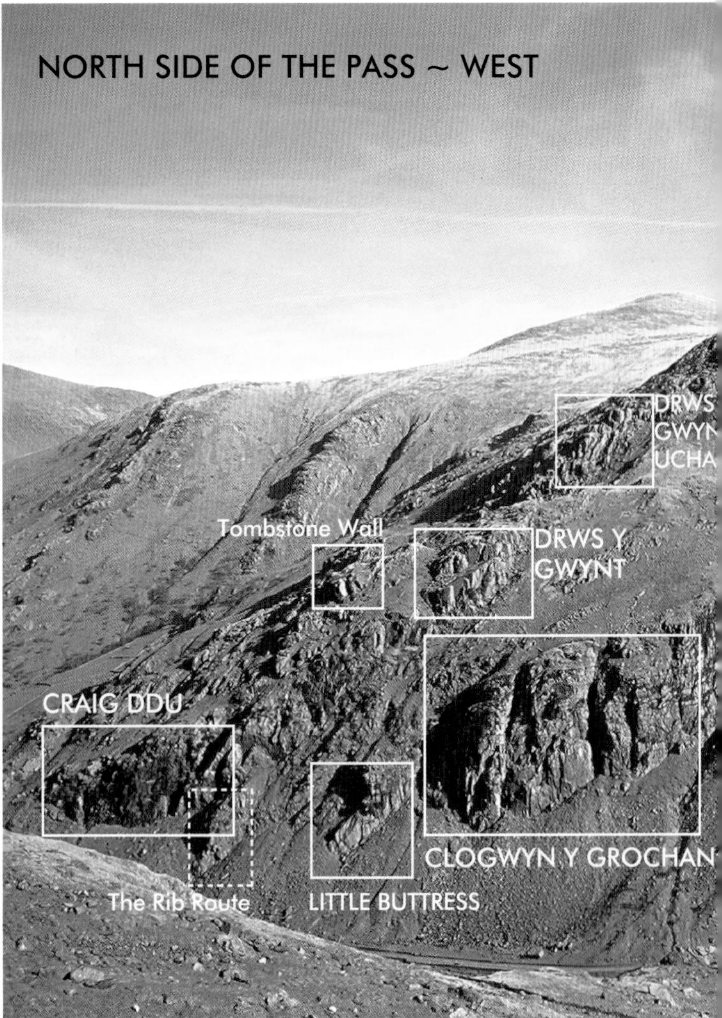

DRWS
GWYN
UCHA

Tombstone Wall

DRWS Y
GWYNT

CRAIG DDU

CLOGWYN Y GROCHAN

The Rib Route   LITTLE BUTTRESS

Esgair Felen

Glyder Fawr →

CRAIG NANT PERIS

CARREG WASTAD UCHAF

CLOGWYN TULLAU

CARREG WASTED FACH

Bryant's Gully

The Gorse Course

CARREG WASTAD

Wind (HVS, page64) Clogwyn y Grochan
Climber: Dave Viggers   Photo: Simon Cardy

First of the Ninth   26 metres   E1   (8.8.94)

Good rock and fine views. Start about 3 metres to the right of *Strangling the Turtle*, on a rock platform at the foot of a crack.

1 10m. 5b. Climb the crack to the top of the pinnacle. Step onto the flying arête and go up onto the terrace.

2 16m. 5b. Take the heathery off-width crack in the top tier of rock, left of the top pitch of *Strangling the Turtle*, and then the finger-crack above.

Clogwyn y Grochan   Cauldron Cliff   OS Ref 622 573

This popular crag lies a short way up the valley from Craig Ddu, just over 100 metres from the road. It has three buttresses, all extremely steep in the lower half, and divided by two fierce gullies. The rock is sound and gives good protection but, unfortunately, the upper sections are more broken and vegetated, although the angle eases.

Several prominent features make route-finding easy. The rightward-curving line of *Nea* splits the left-hand buttress, Goats' Buttress. Right of *Nea* is the dome-shaped block of *Spectre*, whilst to the left is the series of walls and ribs of *Phantom Rib*, *Hazel Groove* and *Delphos*. To the right is *Goats' Gully* and then Central Buttress, starting with a steep wall with a curving line of overhangs. *S S Special* accepts the challenge of the steep wall direct, whilst *Sickle* traverses under the overhangs after starting from an immense flake down on the right. Abutting this flake is the clean-cut V-groove of *Brant Direct*, with the improbable line of *Cockblock* on its right arête. A little further along is the severely overhanging groove of *Surplomb*, about 6 metres before you come to the broad groove of *Hangover*. *Stroll On* takes the steep wall between the grooves. The next smooth wall is taken by *Kaisergebirge Wall* and some hard crack climbs; it is topped by a broad grassy ledge, Lords.

Then comes the impressive Central Gully with a tall tree on the right marking Long Tree Buttress. The right wall of Central Gully gives *Fear and Loathing*, *N'Gombo* and *Ochre Groove*. *Slime Wall* and *Broad Walk* take a damp wall and corner on the right. The East Wing lies to the right of *Broad Walk*. Above the Gardens (a 'vegetable plot' about 12 metres up) is an imposing overhanging wall with *Perygl* and *Jawbone*. The last obvious features are the short chimney of *Fa* and the gully that defines the right-hand limit of the crag proper.

Clogwyn y Grochan lies around the 250-metre contour, about 5 minutes from the road. It faces south to south-west, and can receive a lot of sun from fairly early in the morning to late evening in the summer – almost too much for some.

Descent is via the steep and tricky gully on the western side of the crag, left of *Delphos*. A finger-stone marks the initial chimney at the top of the gully. Many of the routes finish half-way up the crag. It is left to the climber on

Clogwyn y Grochan

1	Delphos	HVS	5	Spectrum	E2
2	Phantom Rib	VS	6	SS Special	E2
3	Nea	VS	7	Sickle	HVS
4	Spectre	HVS	8	Brant Direct	HVS

9 Slape Direct	E2	13 Kaiserbirge Wall	HVS
10 Brant	VS	14 Long Tree Gate	VS
11 Surplomb	E2	15 Ochre Groove	E1
12 Hangover	E1	16 Perygl	E4

finishing these routes to decide whether to continue up another route or to abseil. Usually the options are obvious. Two much-used abseil points are the embedded blocks above pitch 2 of *Nea*/pitch 4 of *Spectre* and the holly trees above pitch 2 of *Hangover*. The latter can be gained from the left end of Lords by climbing down (in preference to adding to the unsightly abseil tat above *Wind*). As always when abseiling, care should be taken to ensure that the anchor is sound, that parties below are not endangered and that the ropes reach the ground. Please also take care when abseiling from trees to minimize damage to the tree itself.

At the foot of the descent gully, on its right and above a couple of rock steps, is a clean, smooth, short oval wall reached by an easy scramble. It gives three routes.

Bog-trotting   9 metres   E4 6a   (20.8.89)
The wall and crack left of centre is too hard for most bog-trotters.

The Yuppification of Deiniolen   9 metres   E4 6b   (20.8.89)
The central wall and crackline is a technical little teaser.

Grochanspiel   9 metres   E1 5b   (20.8.89)
The easiest line on the right side of the wall is available for those who wish to play.

Goats' Buttress
At the foot of the main crag proper is:

Delphos   85 metres   Hard Very Severe   (13.4.49)
A sustained and varied route. The wide crack on the first pitch (harder now that several old and misused trees have gone) gives an amusing problem. Start on the left-hand side of Goats' Buttress, below an obvious corner (well down and right of the three previous routes).
1 38m. 5a. Climb the corner to a damp scoop. Traverse left from a small tree to a good ledge. Climb the difficult thin crack to the overhang, and climb diagonally right into the corner. Struggle up the wide and awkward crack to a stance. This pitch can be split.
2 29m. 4a. Cross the wall on the right to a shattered ledge. Climb up and step left into a clean-cut groove. Continue up, via a large flake, to a broad ledge. Scramble up to below an overhanging red wall.
3 18m. 4a. The pleasant overhanging wall has good holds. Scramble up to finish.

Last of the Summer, Whine   77 metres   Hard Very Severe   (9.69)
A slight eliminate but with some nice moves, worth doing.
1 18m. 4b. As for *Hazel Groove Direct Start*.
2 17m. 5a. Step left and climb a small groove. Move left onto the rib and go round to a crack. Climb this and continue direct to the yew tree.
3 24m. 5a. Climb the fine crack in the wall on the right of the vegetated gully of *Hazel Groove* to a difficult exit. Belay on a higher ledge.

4 18m. 5a. Go up to the oak tree. Climb the wall behind the tree, trending slightly left, and go up using a slot to a move right and the top.

Hazel Groove   82 metres   Hard Severe   (17.2.35)
Quite a good route for its grade, but it deteriorates towards the top. Start 8 metres left of the lowest point of Goats' Buttress and scramble up the gully for 12 metres to a large grassy ledge below a corner.
1 17m. 4b. Climb the corner on good holds. At 6 metres, where it divides, traverse left along a narrow ledge; then swing down to a small sloping platform below the overhang. Step across to a tree and climb 3 metres to a ledge (junction with *Phantom Rib*).
2 20m. 4a. Climb the groove until it splits. Follow the left-hand crack until a step out left leads onto the nose, and go straight up to the large yew tree above. Alternatively, the harder right-hand crack leads to the same point.
3 15m. A vegetated gully leads to a ledge on the left rib.
4 15m. Climb the wall and traverse past an oak to a holly.
5 15m. Finish up the steep wall on good holds.
Direct Start   18 metres   Very Severe 4b
This takes the clean-cut V-groove that runs up to enter *Hazel Groove* from the left. Start just left of the normal start. Go up into the corner. Step right and swing up to a sloping platform. Continue up the groove and awkward crack to the stance at the top of pitch 1.

★★Phantom Rib   74 metres   Very Severe   (9.4.49)
An excellent and exposed route. The crux consists of an exhilarating rib with small holds. Small wires on this section help to reduce the stress of a quite committing lead. Start at the foot of the small gully leading up to the large grassy corner of *Hazel Groove*.
1 12m. 4b. Climb parallel cracks in the left wall of the gully (awkward). Step right and climb past a tree to belay at the top of *Hazel Groove* pitch 1.
2 12m. 4c. Ascend the groove for a short distance, traverse steeply right and pull up onto a ledge on the rib. An exciting section up the rib on small holds (crux) gains a stance just above in a corner.
3 18m. 4b. Climb the corner behind the tree (runner), and then move up and follow small ledges rightwards below two hanging grooves to a short groove in the arête. Climb this and step right into another groove. A couple of moves lead to the foot of a large sloping ledge. Good nuts in the wall behind.
4 14m. 4a. Move right along the ledge and climb the corner. Traverse 3 metres back left along a narrower ledge. Ascend for 3 metres to a spike and nut belay directly above the previous stance.
5 18m. Climb easily to an oak tree, and go diagonally right to a corner which leads to the top.

★Wang   21 metres   E3 6b   (6.80)
An excellent and very technical little test-piece. It takes the groove just left of the cornet-shaped groove on the dome of rock forming the headwall of *Hazel Groove* (*Phantom Rib* traverses below this wall at the start of its third

pitch). Start in the aspen coppice just above the second stance of *Phantom Rib*, below and left of the wall. Climb the awkward smooth groove to a bulge capped by a jug. From the jug, gain the groove above with difficulty and reach the arête on the right to finish.

★★Nea   75 metres   Very Severe   (10.9.41)
A very fine climb, which only just merits its grade. The present pitch 3 (borrowed from *Spectre*) feels a little more daunting than the climbing below, but those who persevere will find it has reasonable holds and protection, is well positioned, and offers the reward of reaching the top of the crag. The route takes the obvious curving line up Goats' Buttress. Start as for *Hazel Groove*, on the grassy ledge.
1 20m. 4b. From the grassy corner, climb the groove until it divides. Take the left-hand branch for 5 metres, and then delicately step right round the rib to reach a crack, which quickly leads to a constricted stance.
2 23m. 4a. Follow the slabby corner-crack until a small chimney leads to a comfortable ledge with several large embedded blocks. Care is required with loose stones on the ledge. The rock scar left after the original pitch 3 fell down can be seen above.
3 20m. 4b. Swing out onto a ledge on the steep left wall and move up a short corner. Make an exposed step left to gain the start of a shallow bottomless groove. Climb this on improving holds to a large ledge.
4 12m. Finish up the steep wall behind. Belay well back. From here, the descent gully is reached by moving to the left to reach the path below the chimney with the finger-stone above it.

God Told Me to Do It   18 metres   E5 6a   (14.7.93)
A good route, which takes the vertical seam on the right-hand side of the overhanging wall left of the pitch 2 of *Nea*. Start from a belay above pitch 1 of *Nea* and climb the seam, which is both technical and sustained, to reach a rounded finish. Finish easily up and left to belay on a tree.

The Revenge   37 metres   E2 5c   (29.8.87)
A reasonable eliminate, which just about merits a mention in this already overcrowded part of the crag. Start as for *Hazel Groove* or, more appropriately, up the first crack of *The Vendetta*. Climb the chimney as for *The Vendetta* and continue directly up the wall above to an obvious flake. Pull up and stand on the ledge by the holly (*Friend 1*). Traverse rightwards and ascend to a flake. Step up onto this and use a pocket to reach a good hold. Stand on this hold to gain two small flakes, step right and then trend leftwards up the slab to belay at a flake on *Nea*.

The Vendetta   46 metres   E1   (18.8.79)
In essence, a variation on *Spectre*, the best of several hereabouts. Start just left of *Spectre*.
1 12m. 5a. Climb the crack nearest the arête in the wall left of *Spectre* pitch 1.
2 32m. 5b. From the back of the ledge, ascend the chimney just right of *Nea* and exit on good holds. Move slightly right and pull over the

overhang into a crack, which leads awkwardly to easier ground. Climb the short slab to gain the slab below the crack taken by pitch 4 of *Spectre*.

★★★**Spectre**   90 metres   Hard Very Severe   (4.5.47)
A fierce, though well-protected, classic. The crack on pitch 4 gives food for thought on first acquaintance. Start at the lowest point of Goats' Buttress.
1 20m. 4c. Climb the thin crack or a slab to a good ledge on the right. Continue up easier rock on the right to a holly tree belay below a steep groove.
2 20m. 5a. Climb the steep groove with difficulty to a ledge below a butterfly-shaped overhang. A delicate move round the arête to the left leads to a short but tricky slab. Cross this, high or low, and then climb a groove to a belay. The slab can be avoided by a rather savage pull up the wall just right of the butterfly-shaped overhang.
3 9m. Climb easily across the slab to the foot of a steep wide crack.
4 9m. 5a. The crack is best started by laybacking. Steep jamming soon leads to the stance at the top of *Nea* pitch 2.
5 20m. 4b. *Nea* pitch 3.
6 12m. *Nea* pitch 4.

F B Madonna   66 metres   E5   (27.6.81)
A ferocious, finger-wrecking eliminate, which now sadly sports a chipped hold at the start. Start below the hanging rib right of *Spectre*.
1 12m. 6b. Climb the boulder-problem wall and overhang right of *Spectre* pitch 1. Hard!
2 24m. 6a. From the *Hazel Groove/Nea* starting-ledge, climb a thin crack just right of *Phantom Rib* to reach another crack above a grassy ledge on the right. Follow a curving flake and the continuation crack above.
3 30m. 6b. Move up to climb the cornet-shaped groove in the domed headwall above the traverse on *Phantom Rib* and right of the groove of *Wang*. Exit left over the bulge and follow a crack to a loose finish.

★★**Spectrum**   44 metres   E2   (4.10.65)
An exposed and strenuous route up an attractive piece of rock. Care is needed with protection on the first pitch, though the second pitch is one of the best of its standard in the Pass. Start 3 metres right of the chimney right of *Spectre* (and 12 metres left of Goats' Gully), below some shattered overhangs.
1 14m. 5b. Boldly climb the innocuous looking overhangs from the left. Pull directly into a shallow groove with good handholds, which quickly lead to a ledge.
2 30m. 5c. Move right onto the wall and climb thin cracks to the overhang. Pull round this to better holds and follow the crack diagonally right to a ledge. Move back left and pull over the left side of the overhang. Climb a groove to a ledge. Move right to a crack at the end of the ledge and climb it to belay above pitch 3 of *Spectre*.
Variation Start   E3
Start 3 metres right of the normal route.
1a 12m. 6a. Climb straight up via a shallow groove to reach a deeper crack, climb this and step left to the belay of the normal route.

Spectrological Arête   30 metres   E3 5c   (8.82)
The arête right of *Spectrum*. Bold for its grade. Start at the base of the
obvious arête, down and left of some blocks. Climb directly up the arête to
the overhang and a junction with *Spectrum* pitch 2. Step left and pull over
the left side of the overhang to the groove and ledge as for *Spectrum*, and
continue as for that route to the belay on *Spectre*.

'C' Minor   23 metres   E2 5c   (17.8.77)
High in its grade. Start just left of *Goats' Gully*, just right of some blocks
and below a crack in the steep gully wall. Climb the crack to reach slabs
and a runner on the flake. Move back left on undercuts and layaways to
the arête and a junction with *Spectrum* pitch 2. Step left and pull over the
left side of the overhang to the groove and ledge as for the previous two
routes and continue to the belay on *Spectre*.

★Pus   21 metres   E4 6b   (1979)
An exceptionally perplexing groove problem, which sees many failures. Follow
'C' Minor to the runner on the flake. Move left as for *'C' Minor* for a short way
and ascend the 'holdless' groove above to the belay above pitch 3 of *Spectre*.

Strapiombo Direct   40 metres   E2   (17.5.78)
A fine way of tackling this part of the cliff, a tidier version of the parent route.
1 23m. 5c. Climb the crack as for *'C' Minor*. After 8 metres step right
and go up behind the flake. Continue to hollies.
2 17m. 5b. *Strapiombo* pitch 2.

Strapiombo   29 metres   Hard Very Severe   (6.57)
A short difficult climb of great character; worth doing despite its repulsive start.
1 12m. 4b. *Goats' Gully* pitch 1.
2 17m. 5b. Step left to below the large overhang and climb it with
difficulty. Climb the crack to the belay above pitch 4 of *Spectre*.

Goats' Gully   76 metres   Very Severe   (15.7.49)
A vile route if wet, and it usually is. The grade is debatable and depends
on your attitude to slimy rock. Start below the gully.
1 12m. 4b. Back up the initial deep chimney and pull round the
overhang. Belay on the tree above.
2 18m. 4a. Climb easily to another tree at the foot of an open chimney,
which slants up left to the embedded block stance of *Nea*.
3 46m. Loose and dirty scrambling to finish.

Central Buttress
The Scapegoat   36 metres   E1   (23.7.82)
A wandering route, taking in the most amenable rock available.
1 21m. 5b. Climb the crack left of *S S Special* to a ledge. Traverse left
and continue diagonally left towards the roof. Step across into a groove,
and then climb it into a cave, often wet. Go left onto the arête and make a
hard move onto the triangular slab above. Climb this to its apex and belay
in the gully.

2 15m. 5a. Step down and climb the groove in the left wall of the gully. Exit left onto the large ledge, and move up to follow the crackline diagonally back right to a sloping ledge. Climb the wall, stepping left onto the arête, and continue up this to the stance at the top of *Nea* pitch 2.

Cunning Stunts   24 metres   E3 5c   (19.8.83)
A filler-in. Start as for *The Scapegoat*. Climb the crack left of *S S Special* to a ledge. Move up left to the obvious groove and exit direct to join the final moves of *Sickle* pitch 2.

★★**S S Special**   46 metres   E2 5b   (20.7.77)
A steep and popular eliminate running directly up the *Sickle* wall. Start on the left of *Sickle*. Climb the right-hand crack of the wall to a wide ledge. Go up the steep thin right-hand crack to join *Sickle* at the roof (a couple of hard moves into and moving up a shallow groove in the wall make this, the crux, feel hard). Make exposed moves rightwards round the roof using a flake to reach easier climbing above. Belay in a short corner above slabs.

★**Sickle**   57 metres   Hard Very Severe   (30.8.53)
A worthwhile and technical route that crosses the slabby wall beneath the overhangs: hard for its grade. Start at a huge flake about 10 metres right of *Goats' Gully*.
1 21m. 5a. Climb the flake by the crack on its right or left side. From its top, step left onto the wall and climb the thin crack to a ledge. Continue to a niche, and traverse right past some blocks to a sloping stance.
2 18m. 5b. Step down and make a hard starting move to cross the steep wall on the left with difficulty to a groove. Climb this to the overhang. Pass this delicately on the left; then climb the slab to a stance and belay in a small corner on the right.
3 18m. 4c. Climb across slabs on the left and follow a short steep crack in the left wall of Goats' Gully to the embedded block stance of *Nea*.
Variation
2a 5a. From the stance, climb up and traverse under the roof on undercuts and sidepulls to join the normal route at the top of the groove.

★**Venturi Effect**   37 metres   E5 6a   (23.5.80)
A thrilling pitch with some heart-stopping moves up the groove above the threatening *Sickle* flake. Start as for *Sickle* and climb the left-hand side of the *Sickle* flake. Painfully wide bridging up the groove above the flake leads to the overlap. Step right and climb the short, hard overhanging groove (in the left arête of the *Brant* groove). Continue direct in a fine position to finish up a thin flake.

★★★**Brant Direct**   23 metres   Hard Very Severe 5a   (24.4.49)
A popular and well-protected exercise in bridging and jamming. Climb the obvious, slightly overhanging, clean-cut chimney/groove past a couple of awkward sections to a long ledge and belay on the right.

Clogwyn y Grochan
Central Buttress

1	'C' Minor	E2
2	Strapiombo	HVS
3	SS Special	E2
4	Sickle	HVS
5	Brant Direct	HVS
6	Cockblock	E5
7	Slape Direct	E2
8	Brant	VS
9	Surplomb	E2
10	Slape	VS
11	Stroll On	E3
12	Hangover	E1
13	Leftover	E3
14	Quasar	E3
15	Mural (with Dr Start)	E4
16	Karwendel Wall	HVS
17	Kaiserbirge Wall	HVS
18	Wind	HVS

★★★Cockblock   23 metres   E5 6b   (25.8.80)
A fierce technical pitch often attempted and sometimes completed. Start below the right arête of *Brant Direct*. Boulder up to a ledge at 3 metres. Continue with difficulty past a small pillar and a good nut. Make a long reach up and right, and then pull up (all very tiring and technical) to an easing at 15 metres. Belay thankfully on the long ledge above.

Dried Voices   23 metres   E5 6b   (6.85)
Yet another ferocious test-piece, which takes the obvious eliminate line between *Cockblock* and *The Pump*. Start under the hanging groove parellel to the line of *The Pump*. Climb the wall, with considerable difficulty, directly up into the hanging groove. Finish up *Cockblock*. The first protection, *RP2* and *RP1*, can be placed by a traverse right from *Cockblock*.

★The Pump   21 metres   E4 6b   (5.6.78)
Aptly named, it tackles the leftward-slanting, undercut, hanging groove and the prominent crackline starting 8 metres right of *Brant Direct*. Climb the wall on the right and stride left into the top of the groove. Continue up the crack on good holds, stepping right at the top. Easier climbing soon leads to the *Brant* ledge.
Variations
The initial groove has been climbed direct to the foot of the crack – hard 6b. It is also possible to exit from the crack direct. This used to be done in ignorance of the normal finish. It is harder and very prickly.

Plus 4   21 metres   E4 6a   (1979)
Boldly climb the wall between *The Pump* and *Slape Direct*.

★★Slape Direct   21 metres   E2 5c   (23.9.54)
A classic little problem, quite high in the grade. Start about 5 metres down and left of the *Brant* sentry-box, at a leftward-slanting crack 2 metres right of *The Pump*. Reach the crack from the right and ascend to a small quartz ledge on the right. Some technical moves and an enigmatic pull round the bulge gain a crack and better holds. Continue easily to a holly belay.

★First Amendment   45 metres   E2   (10.5.78)
A problem wall and groove lead to an intimidating second pitch, which is serious for its first few moves. If only the first pitch is climbed, it gives a well-protected but strenuous E1. Start 3 metres right of *Slape Direct*.
1 21m. 5c. Climb the thin crack to the *Brant* traverse. Continue up the corner to the tree.
2 24m. 5b. Behind the tree is a large flake. From the top of this, climb boldly up the smooth wall; then continue up the superb, well-protected hanging groove above.
Variation
Between *First Amendment* and the first pitch of *Corruption* is a testing eliminate pitch, **Horizontal Departure** (E4 5c). Runners in *Corruption* can be used. The route moves left onto, and then continues up, the arête overlooking *First Amendment*.

★★Brant   113 metres   Very Severe   (5.8.40)
A fine, traditional, and devious route with steep wall and slab climbing.
Start about 16 metres right of the *Brant Direct* groove, on top of blocks
and below a sentry-box niche.
1 21m. 4c. Move up into the niche. A delicate traverse left leads to a
good jug. Pull up on this and continue left along a ledge; from its left-hand
end, climb up to hollies. Go up a little corner on the left and swing left
round a pinnacle to a ledge and belays.
2 15m. 4c. Continue the traverse, stepping down for a short way to enter
a short V-chimney. Climb this awkwardly to a ledge on the right.
3 43m. 4a. From the right-hand end of the ledge, an ascending traverse
left up the wall leads to a slab (possible belay). Climb the overlap and
slabs to an obvious corner. Follow this for a metre or so and move right to
ledges. Go up the ledges and easy slabs to a large yew tree. (The crux
pitch if wet – leaders often get gripped.)
4 34m. 4a. Follow the main nose of the buttress behind the yew.

Corruption   45 metres   E3   (29.4.66)
A technical and exhausting route. Much harder since the demise of the tree
that once sprouted out of the crack above the sentry-box. Start as for *Brant*,
below the sentry-box.
1 15m. 6a. Bridge up the *Brant* sentry-box and climb the crack to an
overlap, where a hard move gains quartz holds on the right. Climb the
short wall to a grassy bay and tree belay (on *Slape*).
2 30m. 5c. Finger-jam the corner-crack to a small ledge, and then
bridge up the corner to a large block on the left. Pass this and continue up
the dirty corner to another ledge. Either finish up *Slape*, or step round the
arête on the right to abseil off the tree at the top of pitch 2 of *Hangover*.

★★Surplomb   39 metres   E2   (1.3.53)
This strenuous and impressive route has a bold first pitch. Start as for
Brant.
1 24m. 6a. Climb into the sentry-box at 3 metres. Make hard moves
right to a finger-jug (crux). Go boldly up on well-spaced holds, trending
right to the *Slape* traverse ledge. Climb the short overhanging V-chimney
(good protection) to a belay.
2 15m. 5b. Bridge up the chimney until a swing onto the left arête can
be made. Continue up a shattered crack to a stance.

Pus in Boots   40 metres   E3 6a   (1979)
A superdirect version of *Surplomb*, at the very top end of its grade. Start
just right of *Surplomb*, above some cruel blocks. Ascend direct to the
finger-jug on the *Surplomb* traverse. Follow *Surplomb* to the *Slape* traverse
ledge. Climb the difficult groove on the left, stepping right at the top onto
the belay ledge of *Surplomb*. Finish directly up the chimney.
★Right-Hand Finish   15 metres   E4 6a
An intimidating pitch. From the belay ledge on *Surplomb*, move right
round the arête. Climb the wall just to its right (bold).

Slape 111 metres Very Severe (8.8.40)

A devious, but worthy, companion to *Brant*. Start at a large groove about 9 metres right of *Brant*.

1 24m. 4c. Climb the groove for a short way and step right onto a ledge (spike runner). Swing back round the corner on the left and make an awkward traverse under a bulge on good holds to a ledge. Traverse left along the ledge past a large tree to a junction with *Brant* at the pulpit.

2 8m. 5a. Step left off the top of the flake onto a steep wall (crux). Climb a crack and overhanging blocks to the belay above pitch 2 of *Brant*.

3 21m. An easy chimney on the right leads to a large triangular grassy ledge. Belay in the far corner.

4 24m. 4b. The crack in the centre of the wall leads to a tiny ledge. Traverse for a short way and climb the yellow overhang on dubious holds. Climb mossy quartz slabs to the ancient yew tree.

5 34m. Climb up behind the yew, keeping right of the edge, to a shattered ledge. Trend right past a large yew to finish.

★Roll On 46 metres E3 (14.9.71)

A fine steep route based on the crackline between *Surplomb* and *Hangover*; little climbed since the creation of *Stroll On*, but worth an ascent if you've done *Stroll On* before. Start as for *Slape*.

1 26m. 5c. Start up the groove and step right to the ledge below the first groove of *Hangover*. Climb a pinnacle and the crack in the wall above to the overhang. Traverse left under the overhang to *Surplomb* pitch 1 belay.

2 20m. 5c. Step right, round the arête, to a steep wall; then traverse right to the continuation of the pitch 1 crackline and follow it with difficulty.

★★★Stroll On 40 metres E3 6a (5.5.76)

The logical line for *Roll On* is one of the most popular hard crack pitches in the Pass giving superbly sustained climbing with one very difficult move. Climb the crack of *Roll On* direct. The crux is pulling round the roof, but above there is little respite and the climbing is harder now with the demise of a good undercut.

★★Hangover 66 metres E1 (18.5.51)

An exposed route of considerable character; the second pitch has seen many epics. Start as for *Slape*.

1 21m. 5a. Climb the groove for a metre or so and step right to a ledge at the foot of another groove. Climb this and continue to a small ledge. Care is needed with belays here.

2 24m. 5b. Move right round the arête to a shallow groove in the wall. Step right and up to an incut hold to gain a traverse-line leading back left to the main groove, which is steep and hard to start; bridge up to holly trees. (The traverse can be gained direct from the shallow groove, avoiding the step right and bumping the grade up to E2 5c.) Abseil off hollies or:

3 9m. Climb the wall by its left edge.

4 12m. Traverse left; then go up on good holds to a large ledge and yew trees (*Ledge Way*).

★Leftover   48 metres   E3   (9.9.77)
A fine technical exercise. Start 8 metres right of *Hangover*.
1 24m. 5c. Climb the crack for 6 metres into a scoop, and move out left
over the roof into another crack. Climb this for 5 metres to a resting place.
Move left and go up to belay as for *Hangover* pitch 1.
2 24m. 6a. The steep stubborn corner behind the belay is mean and
fingery even by today's standards. Finish via the main upper groove of
Hangover pitch 2.

★★Quasar   37 metres   E3 6a   (12.6.77)
A fine steep eliminate at the upper limit of its grade, with an obdurate crux
that has slowed many teams. Start just right of *Leftover*. Ascend the strenuous
groove to the overhang. Pull out right to a good flake and resting ledge.
Follow the thin crack above the flake to reach a ledge on the left. Climb the
wall to a ledge on *Kaisergebirge Wall*. Finish up the groove as for that route.

Quantum Jump   37 metres   E5 6b   (10.79)
An exceptionally fierce and technical pitch, which is rarely flashed on sight.
It takes the short but fierce crack to the right of *Quasar*. Start as for
Karwendel Wall. Climb up, traverse leftwards as soon as possible and
move up to the steep crack, or gain the crack direct (6b). The crack leads
strenuously yet precariously to the end of the *Kaisergebirge Wall* ledge.
Finish up the wall to the right of the groove of that route.

★Mural   34 metres   E4 6a   (8.5.77)
A tricky wall leads to a 'pumpy' crack. Low in the grade. Start as for
Karwendel Wall. Take a diagonal line left up open rock to the overhang
and move right to cross *Kaisergebirge Wall* or, more easily, start up
Karwendel Wall and climb the strenuous crack past one very technical pod
to reach a ledge above all difficulties. Finish easily up to Lords.
Variation
Scavenger's Daughter Finish   E4 6a
A very strenuous finish, and a 'must' for those who find the lower section
easy. At the top of the crack, traverse right for about 2½ metres, and go
over the small roof. Finger jams thren lead up the short crack.

★Karwendel Wall   34 metres   Hard Very Severe 5b   (1.8.58)
A short but interesting wall, which gives good climbing. Start at a small
spike left of *Kaisergebirge Wall*. Climb the shallow groove right of the spike
to join the *Kaisergebirge Wall* traverse. From the sloping platform, climb
up bearing slightly left until a difficult move right to a sharp hidden hold
enables the obvious rising traverse-line to be followed rightwards to easy
ground. Ascend to Lords.

Al Fresco   27 metres   E4 6a   (4.90)
A steep and strenuous eliminate, which is escapable. Start just left of the
start of *Kaisergebirge Wall*. Climb the pocketed wall and disjointed cracks
to a finger-pumping finale up the thin crack of the *Scavenger's Daughter
Finish* (to *Mural*).

★★Kaisergebirge Wall   36 metres   Hard Very Severe   (28.8.48)
A good climb, that gradually increases in both difficulty and exposure.
Protection is good where it matters. Much fallen off. Start 9 metres left of
Central Gully.
1 30m. 5b. Follow the rising traverse-line steeply leftwards to a good
ledge. Move left again to the foot of a steep shallow groove. Climb this
(crux) to a good ledge. You can abseil off the tree (at the top of *Hangover*
pitch 2) from here.
2 6m. The short wall on the right leads to Lords.

★★Wind   27 metres   Hard Very Severe 5b   (26.5.77)
A stiff little test-piece, and at the top of its grade. Start as for *Kaisergebirge
Wall.* Ascend the steep thin crack to the final part of *Babel* pitch 1. Finish
on Lords.

Advert   27 metres   E3 5c   (31.7.78)
A very serious pitch, which starts just right of *Wind.* Ascend the wall past some
flakes to the flared crack. Climb this with difficulty. Slabs then lead to Lords.

Babel   90 metres   Hard Very Severe   (27.7.49)
An interesting route with some good climbing, though often overlooked. It has
a serious third pitch and a fine top pitch. Start 3 metres left of *Central Gully.*
1 27m. 4c. Climb steeply up just right of a ledge on good holds to reach
a line of holds at 5 metres. From its right-hand end, make an awkward
move onto a ledge (this can be avoided by scrambling up the gully on the
right). Move up onto a second ledge; then traverse easily left to climb a
shallow flaky groove 2½ metres right of the corner (for purists), or more
easily climb the corner itself, to Lords. Belay just behind the tree.
2 15m. 5a. Walk 6 metres left. A problem start up the middle of three
small grooves leads to an easier finish up the left one. Block belay.
3 18m. 5a. Ascend the wall behind the block belay. This is hard and
poorly protected initially but gradually eases to a small oak tree. Thread
and nut belays 6 metres higher.
4 30m. 4c. Climb diagonally right over a rock scar and climb a short
open corner at the back of a broad ledge, finishing on juggy holds in
superb bubbly rock. Cross the ledge and climb directly up the wall behind
the corner, trending right to finish.
Variation   Hard Very Severe 5a
3a 12m. Step right and climb the obvious steep, dirty crack.

Second Wind   30 metres   E4 6a   (1991)
Bold and a little loose. Start at the top of *Wind.* Climb up for 8 metres with
poor protection (crux) and traverse right for 5 metres. Continue direct with
slightly less difficulty. Abseil off.

Ledge Way   105 metres   Very Difficult   (20.1.35)
A rather rambling route, with more than its share of water and walking.
Start at the foot of *Central Gully.*

1 34m. Climb the right-hand corner of the gully. Chimney up through the waterfall to the cave; then traverse out across the left wall to the large grassy ledge of Lords. Walk along Lords.
2 21m. Beyond the little tower where the ledge narrows a steep short wall leads back right to a pile of large blocks. Step off the blocks and traverse left to a slab. Continue to a yew tree.
3 14m. Climb up over awkward ledges behind the second yew tree to a large grassy ledge.
4 18m. Continue up the ledge to the right, and then go back left.
5 18m. Climb the steep wall, avoiding shrubs by keeping right.

Central Gully   63 metres   Hard Severe   (23.7.49)
A somewhat wet and greasy outing that masochists refer to as 'a traditional climb' – perhaps best done as a superb ice climb.
1 21m. Climb the bed of the gully to where *Ledge Way* traverses out onto Lords.
2 27m. 4a. Descend and cross over right to the Long Tree. Climb a groove slanting steeply up between two perched blocks, and then follow a series of steps leading back into the gully bed above the overhang (crux).
3 15m. 3b. Climb up and out over the roof to the easier upper section of the gully.
Variations
Left-Hand Variation   78 metres   Very Severe
Start from Lords, above pitch 1 of the normal route.
2a 9m. From a point overlooking the gully, climb a steep crack (hard to start) to good holds and a traverse across into the gully. Climb this for a short way to a stance.
3a 24m. Go up the gully and then steeply back across it into the left-hand crack. Climb this to where it comes back out into the gully, with a bit of a swing over the top.
4a 15m. Ascend the left wall to a large yew tree. Belays above.
5a 30m. Climb the steep pock-marked left wall of the gully, just right of the yew tree; then move right for a metre or so and climb steeply on better holds. Continue among some loose blocks by a holly and up a long open crack to the top.
Superdirect Variation   Hard Very Severe
2b 24m. 5b. When completely dry, a direct line through the overhang gives a spectacular and unusual pitch on good holds. Well-protected.

Long Tree Buttress
N'Gombo   55 metres   E1   (22.7.55)
An exposed, and rather worrying, diagonal line up the steep right wall of *Central Gully*. The highlight is to climb over a huge precarious flake that has stood the test of time – so far. Start just right of the foot of *Central Gully*.
1 15m. 4c. Climb the short steep crack below the Long Tree, often greasy. Continue in the same line until a traverse right over some large blocks leads to a grassy ledge and block belays at the foot of a vertical corner.

2 40m. 5a. Climb the corner with difficulty to a step round onto the left wall. A series of ledges leads diagonally left to the foot of a huge flake. Wedge the crack on its right-hand side to a ledge, and breathe a sigh of relief. Swing out left over the void and pull up (hard) to a small cave. Move a short way right and finish on good holds. Belay in a corner 8 metres back.

Long Tree Gate   65 metres   Very Severe   (20.4.35)
A good route, although somewhat contrived. Start at the foot of the buttress, right of *N'Gombo*, below and right of the Long Tree.
1 15m. 4c. Gain the ledge on the arête using widely spaced holds. Make a tricky move up left on a hidden hold and continue up to the Long Tree.
2 8m. Climb a short corner to the *N'Gombo/Ochre Groove* grassy ledge.
3 12m. Traverse round the arête to the right on poor rock (exposed). Climb to a small stance and thread belay.
4 18m. 4a. Ascend the interesting crack to a tree belay.
5 12m. Climb steeply up to grassy ledges.
Variation
1a 15m. 4a. Start more easily by climbing the slanting rake left of the toe of the buttress to join the parent route.

Fear and Loathing   63 metres   E1   (7.8.82)
A route to get the pulse racing. It takes the shattered wall below *N'Gombo* and is well named. Start just around the corner from *Long Tree Gate*.
1 23m. 5a. Climb the strenuous wall to the ledge on the arête of *Long Tree Gate*. Follow this to to the grassy ledge. Belay on a block left of the *N'Gombo* corner.
2 40m. 5a. Move up and left to the foot of a shattered wall. Climb this on juggy but suspect holds to a poor thread (or cam). Swing out right and layback up to join *N'Gombo* at a peg. Climb the corner above, pulling out onto *Ochre Groove*. Move back left to the foot of a lichenous groove. Ascend this delicately, exiting right at the top.

Toots Direction   21 metres   E3 6a   (24.6.89)
Short and steep. Takes the wall and groove left of *Ochre Groove* direct. Start below the centre of the wall. Climb flakes and continue to a spike. Step right and go directly up to the roof. Pull over this moving rightwards and finish straight up to belay as for *Ochre Groove*.

★Ochre Groove   65 metres   E1   (16.5.54)
A fine route which merits its grade thanks to a potentially ankle-snapping crux in the lower part of its initial groove – the peg having long gone. Start 6 metres right of *Long Tree Gate*, at an obvious V-groove capped by an overhang.
1 24m. 5b. Climb the technical V-groove (take care placing protection here). Move out right at the overhang to a ledge. Go back left between the overhangs to a grassy ledge and block belays (junction with *N'Gombo*).
2 29m. 4c. Climb the corner as for *N'Gombo* and continue up the corner-crack. Exit right to a tree belay above pitch 4 of *Long Tree Gate*.
3 12m. Ascend steep rock to grassy ledges (*Long Tree Gate* pitch 5).

Gizzard Puke   27 metres   E1 5b   (1982)
The name is very apt. Climb the wall between *Ochre Groove* and *Slime Wall* to a convenient abseil tree.

Slime Wall   60 metres   Very Severe   (18.11.61)
A serious route of its grade, for which it needs to be dry, which it seldom is. Start at a large flake about 8 metres right of *Ochre Groove*.
1 27m. 4c. Climb the crack to the top of the pinnacle. Step awkwardly left onto the wall. Climb diagonally left to the foot of a steep crack and climb it to a good ledge.
2 18m. 4a. From the right-hand end of the ledge, trend right for 5 metres; then climb the slab direct.
3 15m. Easy ledges lead up left; then break back right from a corner and traverse under the overhangs. Finish up a little wall.

Broad Walk   87 metres   Very Severe   (7.11.54)
Another route that is often wet, but is pleasant when dry. Start 8 metres right of *Slime Wall*, in a prominent damp black corner.
1 29m. 4c. Climb the corner to a sloping ledge on the right. Continue up the corner to a stance. Or traverse right and then climb a groove to the stance.
2 17m. 4c. Climb the tree to reach holds above. Follow the corner, traverse left and take the left wall to a stance and belay.
3 18m. 4a. Climb the corner for 8 metres, and then step right and ascend a grassy rake.
4 12m. Traverse left and go up a groove to a grassy ledge.
5 11m. The groove above has large but doubtful holds.

The East Wing
Perygl   93 metres   E4   (7.10.65)
A serious climb through the shattered overhangs right of *Broad Walk*, with a technical and strenuous crux. Much of the loose rock which once gave this climb a fearsome reputation has disappeared, but the route still demands respect. Protection is reasonable.
1 29m. 4c. *Broad Walk* pitch 1.
2 9m. Walk right along a ledge to the Gardens.
3 37m. 6a. Climb the wall to a small overhang and continue into an overhanging groove. Fight up the difficult groove; some care is needed in handling suspect holds on its right wall. Move right from the top of the groove into a good crack leading to a large ledge.
4 18m. Move round the corner on the left and go up easy rock.

The wall to the right of *Perygl* is taken by **The Worst Route I've Ever Done** (91 metres Extremely Severe 7.02) in three pitches, a frighteningly horrible route just to the left of the gully and crossing the overhangs at the top. No further details are available, which is probably just as well.

Scrambler's Gate   65 metres   Severe   (20.4.35)
Jungle-bashing leads to better climbing up some steep rock. Start to the
right of *Broad Walk*, at a chimney.
1 12m. Climb the short easy chimney to a holly tree rake.
2 9m. Ascend a short wall on good holds, and then go through heather
to a ledge and the sturdy trees of the Gardens.
3 11m. Traverse the ledge to the left, round a corner to an oak tree and
continue to a holly.
4 24m. Descend 3 metres and traverse across *Broad Walk* to the foot of a
little crack. Climb this to a stance. Step left onto a rake and go up this for 5
metres. Move right onto a reddish slab. Traverse left on a narrow ledge
below a steep wall to an oak tree.
5 9m. A weakness in the wall behind the tree leads to a little corner on
the right. Climb this awkwardly to a heathery ledge; scramble up to a
good stance.

Jawbone   48 metres   E3   (18.8.68)
The easiest line through the large overhangs is rather loose, rarely
repeated, and not recommended. Start below the big tree.
1 18m. 4b. Climb the obvious crack to the tree.
2 30m. 5c. Go up right on suspect rock to the overhang, aiming for the
prominent undercut groove which can be seen above it. Pull round the
overhang and ascend the tricky groove. Exit right and climb to a ledge and
tree belay. Abseil off to avoid the horrific jungle, which awaits a victim.

Fa   60 metres   Severe   (24.4.49)
An unsafe route on unstable rock. Start 15 metres left of the gully that
bounds the crag on its right. Follow the obvious chimney. Frequent belays.

Fatha   78 metres   Very Severe   (8.7.49)
A steep climb on vegetation, good and also bad rock, up the buttress
between the chimney of *Fa* and the bounding gully. Start at the obvious
break in the overhang 6 metres left of the gully.
1 12m. Go diagonally up the steep wall by a rib and groove to a small
stance and low belay.
2 24m. 3c. Step down and traverse right to a small slab. Climb this, and
then go round the corner, where a line of flakes leads to the rib above.
This breaks up at 15 metres, and vegetation followed by a 5-metre
traverse left leads to a platform with poor belays.
3 24m. 4b. The vegetable groove is quitted, via a mantelshelf, and the
wall climbed to some rotten flakes. Belay 6 metres to the right, below the
overhangs.
4 18m. 4a. Traverse back to the flakes. Gain the groove above and climb its
left wall to a good belay. Twenty-five metres of scrambling leads to the finish.

To the right of the gully bounding the Grochan on the right is a rocky ridge,
which consists of two buttresses. The lower buttress, which is distinguished by
a prominent corner and a red wall on its right, is best gained by traversing in
from the right of the Grochan along sheep tracks.

Drama Queen   23 metres   Hard Severe 4b   (25.9.02)
Go left up an easy ramp to flakes below a steep corner. Go steeply up this (good cracks) to finish up a big flake.

Control Freak   23 metres   E1 5b   (25.9.02)
Climb the attractive crack in the steep wall right of *Drama Queen*. Harder than it looks towards the top.

The upper buttress has a tapering face with a holly just above the base and a prominent boulder on a ledge just below the top.

Ground Zero   27 metres   E1 5b   (11.9.02)
Start at the lowest point of the buttress, at a groove just left of the holly. Climb the groove to an overhang, and barn-door rightwards to good holds. Gain good jugs above and then go swiftly up leftwards to good finger holds and so to the left end of the heathery ledge. The bold-looking wall above is easier and better protected than it looks, so climb it just right of the arête to the ledge with the big boulder. Blocks and flakes lead to the top.

The Gorse Course   24 metres   Very Severe 4c   (21.7.94)
Just right of the holly is a heathery crack. Climb to the right end of the heathery ledge. The obvious corner above gives good climbing to the big boulder. Go round this on the right, and then flakes and blocks lead to a belay on the crest of the ridge.

Girdle Traverses
Divertimento   66 metres   E2   (4.81)
A pleasant girdle, taking in some of the steep lower walls of the cliff below the first two pitches of *Sunset Boulevard*. Start as for *Kaisergebirge Wall*.
1 30m. 5c. Follow *Kaisergebirge Wall* for 9 metres; then drop down and traverse left under steep walls into *Quasar* at the flake. Swing across into *Leftover* and follow it to the *Hangover* stance.
2 9m. 5c. Traverse left into *Roll On* and continue to the *Surplomb* stance.
3 6m. 4c. Traverse left around into *Corruption*.
4 21m. 5c. Finish up *Corruption*. Originally the route finished across the wall on the left at 6b, but this was thought to be out of character with the rest of the route.

Sunset Boulevard   111 metres   Hard Very Severe   (22.7.54)
A very worthwhile girdle, which links differing sections of some of the best routes on the cliff. Start as for *Kaisergebirge Wall*.
1 37m. 5a. Follow *Kaisergebirge Wall* to the foot of its crux groove. Continue traversing left and stride across the final groove of *Hangover*. Traverse round into a V-chimney and go up to a good belay (care should be taken to avoid rope drag).
2 12m. Go round the block on the left and ascend to grass; then cross to the block belay above *Slape* pitch 3.
3 21m. Go down the grassy ledge to a short chimney. Descend this to a good ledge (*Slape* pitch 3 in reverse).

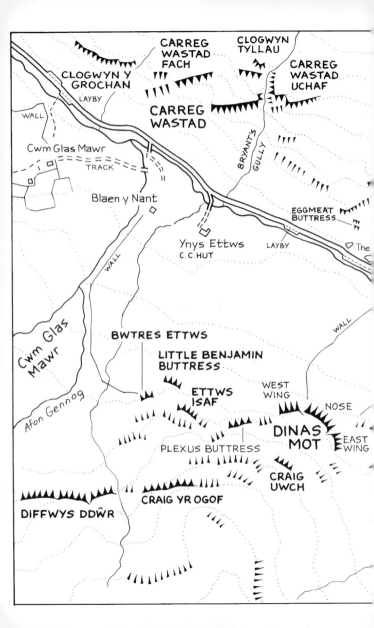

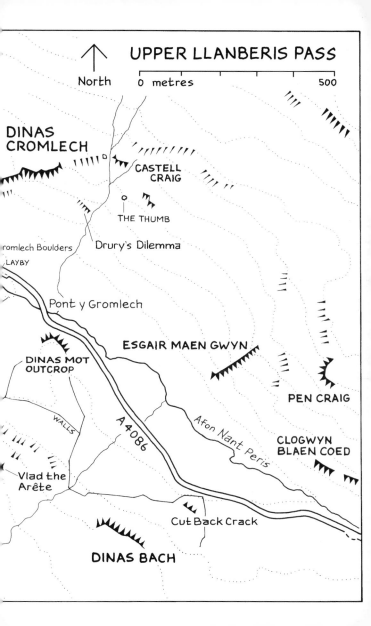

4 8m. 5a. Descend the crack and short difficult wall of *Slape* pitch 2.
5 21m. 5a. Cross to the foot of *Brant's* V-chimney. Step down left and continue the traverse left under the overhangs on awkward undercut holds. Ascend to a niche and flake belays on *Sickle*.
6 12m. Go diagonally left up the slab to a flake on the edge of Goats' Gully. Most parties finish here, but you can descend slightly and go left to reach the crack of *Spectre* pitch 4. After the crack, an alternative finish can be made by crossing *Phantom Rib* and *Hazel Groove*.

Bluebell Traverse   220 metres   Severe   (5.5.35)
A somewhat outdated girdle traverse of the cliff, with plenty of walking and endless variations. Follow *Scrambler's Gate*, but on pitch 4 keep traversing across *Broad Walk* to the block belay of *N'Gombo/Ochre Groove*, on the grassy ledge. Cross into *Central Gully* and go up to Lords; then descend to a large triangular grassy ledge 12 metres away. Continue along a rocky gangway leading out left. After 3 metres, climb a slab to a small tree, and then meander across slabs, crossing *Goats' Gully* to the embedded block stance on *Nea*. Descend *Nea* cross *Hazel Groove* high or low.

Carreg Wastad Fach   OS Ref 624 571

This is the broken yellowish crag left of the gully bounding Carreg Wastad on the west. The right-hand side has a short scooped wall of orange rock and quartz below grey bulges.

The first three routes lie on the buttress some 100 metres down and to the left of Carreg Wastad Fach. The buttress has an overhanging base and a holly tree up on its right side.

Dave's Route   24 metres   Hard Severe   (14.9.02)
Start in the grassy gully on the left, level with the bulges in the middle of the crag. Pull up right on quartz holds to a flake, and then go up into a V-groove. Head up to the crest of the ridge (the rock here is better than it looks).

Ground Pepper   27 metres   E2 5c   (14.9.02)
Start on the right of the overhanging base of the crag. Climb a quartz rib to place high runners in a crack. Stride down left and lean left to a flat handhold on the smooth wall. Crank up and left to a rest and flake runner (this is a serious section). Head up slightly left to the band of overhangs. From the right end of these, follow a crackline to the top.

Havago   24 metres   Very Severe 4c   (9.95)
Start as for *Ground Pepper*. Climb up and then right to follow a prow. Finish up the right-hand side of the summit block.

The remaining climbs are on the main crag.

Boston Spa Climb   44 metres   Severe   (14.6.58)
Total obscurity? Start at the left-hand end of the slab.
1 18m. Move up; then step right and continue up again to a small stance
and peg belay below an overhang.
2 15m. Traverse leftwards to the corner and go up a groove in this to
steep grass below a rib.
3 11m. Climb the pleasant rib.

Question Mark   48 metres   Very Severe   (28.5.55)
An interesting but neglected climb. Start below a slab at the lowest part of
the buttress.
1 24m. 4c. Climb the rib on the right; then follow a diagonal rightward
line over a series of small ledges to reach the overhangs. Step down and
move right under the overhangs to a stance and spike belay. A poorly
protected pitch with some poor rock.
2 24m. 4c. Move right onto the slab and go pleasantly round the
overhangs to large detached blocks. Continue on the same line for 3
metres, step left and climb a slab with a small overhang. Finish up a
heathery rib.

Days of the Weak   48 metres   E2   (24.9.02)
1 24m. 5b Start right of *Question Mark*, below the left end of the
overhangs. Go up a big flake and the lovely pocketed wall above to
another overhang. Hard moves lead to the left end of the upper
overhangs; then go strenuously up right to a good stance in a niche
(*Friday Night Beaver* crosses here).
2. 24m. 4c. Teeter up the continuation ramp to a quartz ledge, and climb
the bulging rib above.

Friday Night Beaver   36 metres   E2   (6.87)
A much neglected offering. Start below a crack running up to the
overhang.
1 12m. 5c. Battle up the vicious crack to better holds, and continue to a
belay (cams) below the prominent large overhang.
2 24m. 5b. Step right and climb direct to a tricky mantelshelf. Climb the
groove above before stepping out left onto the final straightforward arête.
Descend by scrambling down diagonally rightwards.

Carreg Wastad   Flat Crag   OS Ref 625 571

This crag, with its fine yew trees, lies a few hundred metres up the valley from
Clogwyn y Grochan and is opposite Ynys Ettws, the Climbers' Club hut. It stands
well out from the hillside and consists mainly of solid rock, which can, however,
be very unstable in places where the rock has an organ-pipe structure.

At the left-hand end of the crag are the fluted slabs of *Skylon* and *Wrinkle*. Right of these are the overhanging corner of *Gryphon* and the groove of *Unicorn*, with the roof of *Brute 33* in between. *Overhanging Chimney* and *The Crevice* both stand out well. The slabby rib just to the right of the latter is *Crackstone Rib*. In the centre of the cliff is a large corner, *Erosion Groove*, which runs the full height of the crag. On the right is a steep face, topped by the large slanting overhang of *Shadow Wall*; the rib of *Trilon* leads up to the right-hand end of this. The upper part of a scoop containing a line of yews is part of *Dead Entrance*, and *Yew Link* connects the first two yews. Right of the scoop lie the tower of *Old Holborn* and the obvious upper groove of *Bole Way*. *Main Scoop Route* takes the line of the huge scoop in the right-hand side of the cliff. At the right-hand end is a fine prow of rock supported by *Red Rock*, a triangular buttress of reddish rock whose summit is an earthy ledge.

The height of the crag, around 350 metres above sea-level at its base, and its south to south-westerly aspect, make it an open spot, receiving the sun almost all day on one facet or another in the summer months. Each side of the cliff has an easy descent gully.

Skylon   61 metres   Hard Severe   (13.4.52)
A popular and well-protected route: quite hard for its grade. Start at the left-hand end of the cliff, below a small overhang at 5 metres.
1 37m. 4b. Climb easily up to a ledge below a small overhang. Move up right and climb a crack until it is possible to make a difficult step left onto the overhang; then move up to a ledge. Climb diagonally right to a terrace. Belay behind the large flake at its upper left edge.
2 24m. 3c. The wall above the flake leads, via a bulge at 9 metres, to a stance. Scramble to the top.

★★Wrinkle   71 metres   Very Difficult   (5.47)
A very popular climb, which finishes up the fluted, slabby walls right of *Skylon*. The rock in some sections has been polished to a high gloss. Protection is well spaced on pitch 3. Start as for *Skylon*.
1 24m. Move right up slabby steps, and then work back left to below the *Skylon* overhang. Make an exposed traverse right to a slightly descending gangway. Follow this for 5 metres to the right to a comfortable ledge with nut and thread belays in a ragged crack.
2 20m. Climb the wide corner-crack at the right end of the ledge. Make an awkward move to gain a ledge. Traverse this rightwards for 3 metres to a shallow groove slanting back left. Climb this and then a wrinkled slab to a good ledge.
3 27m. Take a short crack on the right to the top of a small pedestal. Ascend the slabby grooves above with care to a ledge. Finish up the broken corner on the right. The rock at times is suspect. Belay well back.

Sun Valley   60 metres   Hard Very Severe   (9.9.77)
A worthwhile trip with some diverting climbing; the protection on the first pitch is spaced. Start just right of *Wrinkle*, to the left of a shallow scoop of dark shattered rock (often wet).

1 21m. 5a. Climb easily to a large sloping ledge. Traverse right just above the lip of the cave/scoop to a small niche. Climb direct to the ledge at the end of *Wrinkle* pitch 1.
2 21m. 4c. Climb the ragged crack for approximately 5 metres to a good sloping ledge on the left. From its left end, make some difficult moves up the wall and then follow an easy crack, moving right to a grassy bay below a steep crack with a huge pinnacle on the left.
3 18m. 4c. Climb the thin crack to a quartz ledge. Ascend the overhang on good holds and finish up a slab.

California Raisins   61 metres   E2   (19.8.94)
Even more of an eliminate than its neighbours but still with some good moves. Start as for *Sun Valley*.
1 37m. 5b. As for *Sun Valley* to the large sloping ledge. From the pockets (cams) go straight up the shallow groove to gain the gangway on *Wrinkle* pitch 1 (both bold and precarious). Continue direct up the wall, moving right at the top, to belay as for *Sun Valley* below the steep crack.
2 24m. 4c. Climb the slab left of *Sun Valley*; then traverse left under the bulge, move up, step right through the bulge and continue straight up.

First Test   61 metres   Very Severe   (6.8.77)
A good direct line, quite stiff for the grade. It is based on the obvious large corner above the traverse on *Wrinkle*. Some care is needed with the rock on pitch 2. Start 10 metres right of *Wrinkle*, at a short corner.
1 21m. 4c. Climb the corner and make for the steep broken white wall. Climb the wall keeping right of the ledge at the end of pitch 1 of *Wrinkle*, eventually moving slightly left to reach the ledge traversed by pitch 2 of *Wrinkle*. Step up and across left to belay in a groove some 5 metres below a small tree. A good sustained pitch.
2 40m. 4c. Climb the groove above the belay to easy ground. Get into the big corner on the left with difficulty and continue to the overhang above. Move 3 metres right and up a second corner for 2 metres. Make an exposed step out left onto the arête and finish up slabs.

Gryphon   64 metres   Hard Very Severe   (5.8.54)
A reasonable route with a perplexing and strenuous crux. Start at a pedestal 6 metres left of *Unicorn*, where a prominent overhanging corner starting 10 metres up runs up to the left end of an overhang.
1 11m. 4c. Follow a gangway up left until a direct ascent can be made to a step right onto the sloping floor of the corner.
2 18m. 5b. Climb the crack in the corner to the top of the flake on the right. Move left to the top of the corner by very trying moves. Continue to the holly tree in the corner above.
3 35m. 4c. Go diagonally right to a spike runner on the rib adjacent to *Unicorn* (possible stance). Continue up the rib, zigzagging to avoid difficulties.

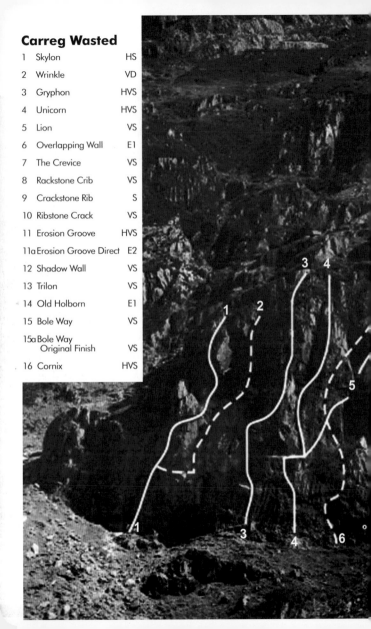

Carreg Wasted

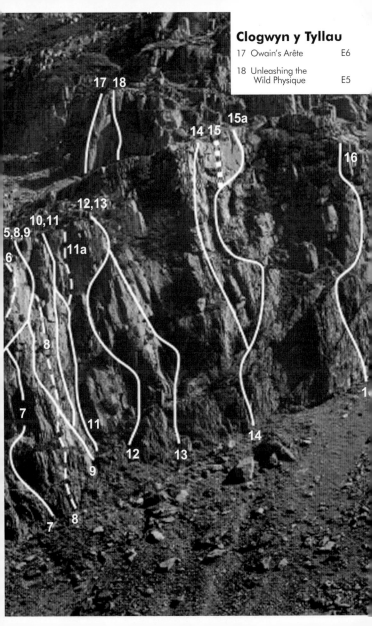

Clogwyn y Tyllau

17 Owain's Arête   E6

18 Unleashing the
    Wild Physique   E5

★Brute 33   54 metres   E3   (12.5.79)
An exhausting and thrilling line through the big overhangs just left of the
long groove of *Unicorn* – worthy of the attention of any aspirant jug-thug.
Start at the foot of a white groove below the overhangs.
1 12m. 5b. Climb the groove and trend right to belay as for *Unicorn*.
Delicate and poorly protected.
2 12m. 6a. Attack the overhang by the obvious crack to belay on some
flakes 6 metres higher. Strenuous but well-protected.
3 30m. 4c. Finish direct up the rib of *Gryphon* pitch 3.

Unicorn Direct   59 metres   Hard Very Severe   (26.5.51)
A more sustained line than the original route. A forceful approach is
required.
1 15m. 4b. *Unicorn* pitch 1.
2 20m. 5a. From the left-hand end of the ledge, climb the overhanging
crack with difficulty. Go through trees as for *Unicorn*.
3 24m. 5a. Climb the groove, awkward at 9 metres. Ascend to the final
chimney splitting the overhang. Doubtful rock. The groove has become
unpleasantly vegetated and the slabby right wall of the groove provides a
good alternative at the same standard.

★Unicorn   60 metres   Hard Very Severe   (17.4.49)
Quite a good route, with a fierce little groove on its second pitch. Start below
the obvious groove, just right of the conspicuous overhang 15 metres up.
1 15m. 4b. Zigzag up the wall to avoid difficulties, and then go over
cracked blocks to a good ledge.
2 15m. 5b. Climb the V-groove behind the stance and make a difficult
move up and left (crux) to enter the main groove. Carry on through trees
to belay below an overhang.
3 30m. 4b. Take the groove on the right for a short way, and then
traverse delicately right to a small ledge on the far rib. Climb the delightful
rib in a fine airy position.

★Elidor   58 metres   E1   (21.6.64)
Some steep moves up the blank-looking groove above the *Lion* traverse
lead to an easier finish up the top rib of *Unicorn*. Poorly protected.
1 15m. 4b. *Unicorn* pitch 1.
2 43m. 5b. Step right onto the black slab, and climb diagonally right
and then straight up to the foot of the blank little groove. Bridge up this
and exit left at the top. Continue boldly up to a rightward traverse. Follow
this and finish up the rib. A good pitch.

★Lion   84 metres   Very Severe   (26.6.49)
An old classic, taking a rising traverse from left to right, which is both
technical and interesting despite having a contrived finish.
1 15m. 4b. *Unicorn* pitch 1.
2 24m. 4c. From the foot of the V-groove on *Unicorn*, step right onto a
black slab. Cross this diagonally rightwards to the overlap and traverse
right to the chimney of *Overhanging Chimney*. Climb this, via the large

chockstone, and then cross the right wall to a stance and belay. A fine pitch.
3 27m. Ascend the slab on the right, step across the short chimney and swing up onto *Crackstone Rib*. Follow this to belay at a sloping stance.
4 18m. 4a. Traverse into the upper part of *Ribstone Crack*. Ascend to a tree, from which a huge flake leads to the top.

★★Overlapping Wall   75 metres   E1   (7.48)
A fine open climb with a fairly bold crux that is much harder than the rest of the route. Protection below the crux is quite good, but above it is well spaced, and the climbing is balancy. Start directly below the chimney of *Overhanging Chimney*, just left of a large overhang.
1 27m. 4c. Go up for 6 metres, and then traverse right on good holds to a ledge. Climb the steep wall, moving left and then right, to a large quartz ledge. From its left-hand end, a shallow groove leads to a stance below the large chockstone of *Overhanging Chimney*.
2 21m. 5b. Climb the groove and then gain its left rib. Move left and climb the overlap at its weakest point (crux). From a good nut, traverse left a short way; then go up and follow a groove back right to a ledge. Move right to belay in the corner. Serious.
3 27m. 4c. Make a rising traverse across the right wall and go up onto the rib. Finish up this in an exhilarating position.
Variation
★★Overhanging Chimney
This makes the whole route an excellent VS.
2a 15m. Very Severe 4c. Ascend the groove direct, and climb the chimney as for *Lion* and continue as for that route.

Jayway   71 metres   E3   (5.75)
The vicious little wall on the second pitch should not be underestimated.
1 27m. 4c. *Overlapping Wall* pitch 1.
2 14m. 5c. Climb the incredibly awkward, thin, jagged crack in the right wall of *Overhanging Chimney* to belay as for *Lion* pitch 2.
3 30m. 4b. Move right and finish direct.

Overhanging Buttress   72 metres   E4   (23.4.02)
The prow between *Jayway* and *The Crevice*. Start at the groove 7 metres right of *Overlapping Wall*.
1 24m. 4c. Climb the groove and its left rib to belay below the prow.
2 18m. 5c. Climb the right side of the arête on small incuts to the bulging prow. Pull through this and continue up the face above to belay at a huge spike.
3 30m. 4b. Pass the bulging rock above on the left and continue easily to the top.

The Crevice   77 metres   Very Severe   (5.47)
A pleasant route for the slim, but a fiendish problem for those of above average girth. It is the right-hand of the two chimneys. Start directly below the rib of *Crackstone Rib*.

1 30m. Ascend the leftward-slanting rake to a tree. Traverse delicately right onto a slab, and go up to a stance at the foot of the chimney.
2 15m. 4c. Climb the strenuous chimney (folk often get stuck here for hours) to a slab. Ascend this to a good crevasse stance.
3 12m. 4a. Climb up and swing round onto *Crackstone Rib*. Follow this to the sloping ledge at the top of pitch 1.
4 20m. 4a. *Crackstone Rib* pitch 2.

Rackstone Crib   57 metres   Very Severe   (2.4.58)
An inferior but more direct variation on *Crackstone Rib*. Start 6 metres right of *The Crevice*.
1 21m. 4b. Ascend a short wall and step left to the foot of a cracked corner. Follow this to a ledge, and climb a shallow groove until forced onto the rib on the right to reach a stance (junction with *Crackstone Rib*).
2 21m. 4b. Climb the easy groove on the right of the arête of *Crackstone Rib*, then ascend a short wall on the right and continue to belay at the top of *Crackstone Rib* pitch 1.
3 15m. 4a. Finish up the corner-crack.

Slipstone Slab   66 metres   Very Severe   (19.11.89)
A wandering route that covers little new ground; protection is sparse. Start midway between the arête of *Crackstone Rib* and *Erosion Groove*, below a patch of grass at 6 metres.
1 18m. 4c. Take a thin wet crack to the grass. Step left into a shallow niche, and continue up a faint rib to the traverse-line of *Crackstone Rib*. Move left to belay in the depression.
2 30m. 4c. From the right end of the ledge, climb an awkward shallow groove, and continue to a holly. Climb steeply up a thin crack behind the holly to reach another ledge. Make an exposed traverse right below the overlap into *Ribstone Crack*. Follow this and belay on the right.
3 18m. 4a. The wide crack behind the belay.

★★★**Crackstone Rib**   54 metres   Severe   (14.7.35)
One of the great Welsh classics. It has a very fine exposed arête pitch that is especially photogenic. Start at the foot of *Erosion Groove*.
1 34m. 3b. Climb a short crack to a ledge. Follow the well-worn traverse leftwards to the arête, passing a depression (good runners). Step round boldly and follow the arête in an exposed position to reach a ledge. A short wall leads to a better, sloping ledge.
2 20m. 4a. Climb the easy groove on the right to a corner. Continue up to a traverse-line on the left wall. Follow this to finish up a short steep crack.
Direct Start
Rottish Monk   Hard Very Severe
1a 15m. 5a. This takes the blunt rib that bounds the alcove of *The Crevice*. Start below the arête of *Crackstone Rib* and climb fairly directly up the lower rocks to gain and climb the arête (tricky) to meet the parent route.

Central Gully (HS, page 65)
Clogwyn y Grochan
Climber: Dave Ferguson
Photo: Ferguson col.

Esgair Felen

CRAIG NANT PERIS

DINAS
CROMLECH

CARREG WASTAD
UCHAF

Bryant's Gully

Corky

EGGMEAT
BUTTRESS

The
Cromle
Boulde

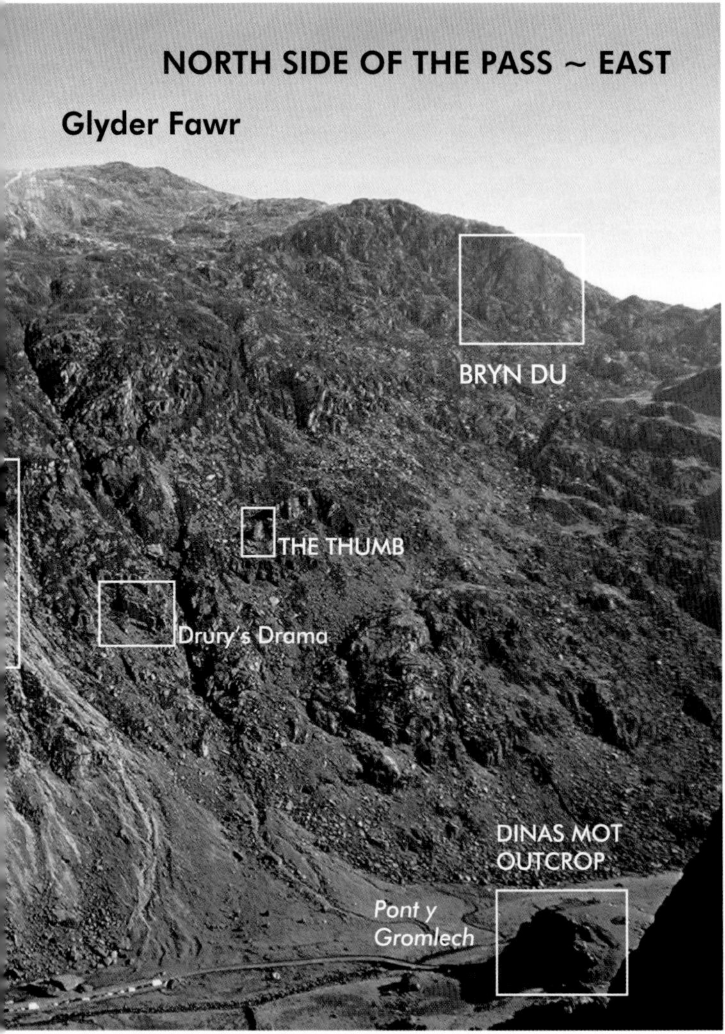
NORTH SIDE OF THE PASS ~ EAST
Glyder Fawr
BRYN DU
THE THUMB
Drury's Drama
DINAS MOT
OUTCROP
Pont y
Gromlech

Wrinkle (VD, page 74) Carreg Wastad
Climber: Ian Dunbar   Photo: David Simmonite

★★Ribstone Crack 52 metres Very Severe (22.3.51)

A steep, exposed and well-protected crackline just left of *Erosion Groove*.
Hard for its grade. Start at the foot of *Erosion Groove*.

1 34m. 4c. Climb the obvious crack direct to the belay above pitch 1 of
Crackstone Rib. Sustained, with a difficult move near the top.

2 18m. 4a. Traverse back right for a metre or so, and go up to a tree on
the left. Finish via a huge flake.

Erosion Groove 53 metres Hard Very Severe (26.4.53)

A popular but rather disappointing route with some suspect rock. It is the
obvious groove cleaving the cliff from top to bottom. Start at the foot of the
groove, below two holly trees.

1 15m. Scramble up past the first holly, and step left into a crack that
leads to a stance and belay on a huge flake.

2 20m. 5a. The main corner-groove on the left is hard to start and leads
to a small overhang after 14 metres. Pass this on the left (crux) and follow
the overhanging groove above to a stance.

3 18m. 4a. Climb the corner with a wide upper crack, as for *Ribstone
Crack*.

★★Erosion Groove Direct 20 metres E2 5c (17.8.55)

A strenuous and technical problem; in the past it had a notorious
reputation as a 'chop route'. Although tamed somewhat by modern
protection, it is still no pushover. From the belay above *Erosion Groove*
pitch 2, step right and enter the groove with difficulty. Finish more easily up
the wide overhanging crack.

★Twisted Sister 50 metres E3 (4.7.83)

An excellent eliminate between *Erosion Groove* and *Shadow Wall*,
sustained and strenuous. Start from the first holly on *Shadow Wall*.

1 27m. 5c. Climb the awkward slab up leftwards towards the obvious
crack. Pull left through the bulge to gain the crack and move up to a
finger-slot and good *Friend* placement. Swing precariously left and mantel
up using a spike. Rejoin the lower line and move left to belay below
Erosion Groove Direct.

2 23m. 5c. Follow *Erosion Groove Direct* past its crux. Move right across
the wall, and finish up the superb airy crack.

★★Shadow Wall 47 metres Very Severe (14.7.35)

A scrappy start leads to an exciting crucial traverse under the large
diagonal overhang. Start by scrambling up to the foot of the groove that
leads up to the left end of the overhang.

1 27m. 4a. Climb the groove to a holly tree (possible stance) and
continue up to a belay under the huge overhang.

2 20m. 4c. A series of three ledges leads up rightwards under the
overhang. From the top ledge, a hard move right gains a short groove.
Climb this to a tree belay.

3 8m. Climb easily to a good ledge.

★Yellow Crack   30 metres   Hard Very Severe 5b   (1958)
Start from the holly tree on *Shadow Wall* pitch 1. Step right to the foot of a
steep corner-crack and climb it fairly easily for 6 metres. The crack soon
bulges, leans left and becomes a 'real pig'. Jam up awkwardly to a large
ledge. Make a long step right into a groove (on *Zangorilla*) and take this
for a few moves until a swing up left leads to a narrow ledge and the
crucial traverse of *Shadow Wall*. Follow that route to its tree belay.

★★Zangorilla   49 metres   E4   (2.7.77)
An intimidating and impressive route, which blasts its way directly through
the large capping overhang above the *Shadow Wall* traverse. Bolder and
more strenuous since the rattling block came off the top pitch. Start 3
metres right of *Shadow Wall*, beside a huge flake.
1 34m. 6a. Gain the steep groove above and climb it and the wall
above to the ledge on *Trilon*. Step across left into the steep, smooth,
leaning groove about 2½ metres right of *Yellow Crack*. If you can start it,
climb the fingery and technical groove to reach good holds. Move up left
to belay on the ledges of *Shadow Wall*.
2 15m. 6a. Spacewalk boldly and strenuously out left on undercuts
across the overhang, with an awkward move to get established on the airy
wall above. Finish direct in a sensational position, with only imaginary
protection.

Trilon   63 metres   Very Severe   (24.4.48)
A poor start does not detract from the fine airy rib above. Start below and
to the right of the large overhang of *Shadow Wall*, at the lowest point of
the buttress.
1 21m. 4a. Climb the wall on good holds to a large perched block.
Traverse right to a pleasant yew tree ledge.
2 34m. 5a. Climb the crack to a large spike; then go diagonally left on
good flakes to the overhang. Step left onto a sloping ledge, and make a
fierce move up into a niche. After a few steep moves up the groove,
ascend the delightful rib to a holly tree belay.
3 8m. *Shadow Wall* pitch 3.

Goldcrest   37 metres   E1 5b   (6.65)
A good, sustained route that takes the obvious groove right of *Trilon*. Start
from the yew tree ledge above pitch 1 of *Trilon*. Climb the slab to the
overhang. Pull over this via a thin crack. Follow the crack and groove
above to a tree belay above *Trilon*.

Quasimodo   37 metres   E1 5b   (1964)
A strenuous pitch through the overhangs right of *Goldcrest*. Obscure but
worth finding. Start from the yew tree ledge above pitch 1 of *Trilon*. Climb
the crack a short way right of *Trilon* to the niche in the large overhangs.
Ascend these with difficulty to a small ledge. Step right and jam the
corner-crack.

Yew Link   14 metres   Hard Very Severe 5b   (1.6.53)
A short awkward pitch between the yew trees of *Trilon* and the upper yews
of *Dead Entrance*. Start from the yew tree ledge of *Trilon*. Climb the wall
behind the yews to a small holly in a groove. Swing out right and climb a
mossy wall to a peg in a niche. From a peg above, pull up to the yew trees
of *Dead Entrance*.

★★**Old Holborn**   81 metres   E1   (5.63)
A superbly exposed and enjoyable finale up the steep tower between *Trilon*
and *Bole Way* more than compensates for the scruffy lower pitches.
1 27m. 4c. *Bole Way* pitch 1.
2 9m. 4a. From the left end of the ledge, climb the short groove. Move
left and pass a large detached flake with care to reach a grassy ledge and
ash tree belay (the first bole) below the tower.
3 27m. 5b. Excellent sustained climbing up the steep groove behind the
tree leads to a step right. Move up past a loose block to a peg below the
large roof. Reach up to a good handhold under the roof and make a bold
swing out left to a hidden ledge. Go back onto the steep arête and climb
up to small ledges. Poor belays.
4 18m. 4c. Climb the steep slabby face, trending right to finish. A fine
exposed pitch.

★**Bole Way**   72 metres   Very Severe   (12.5.51)
This route takes the cliff at its highest point. In recent years, pitch 2 had
become overgrown with ivy. This has been cleaned and the route is once
again worthwhile, particularly when climbed as described with the Direct
Finish, which gives an interesting route with an exposed, well-protected and
photogenic climax on good rock. Start at a small rib with a gully/groove on
either side, about 30 metres right of *Trilon* and 9 metres left of *Dead Entrance*.
1 27m. 4c. Climb the groove on the right side of the rib, swing left onto
the rib, and from its top move awkwardly right onto a slanting rake. Follow
this and ascend to a cosy stance amidst hollies.
2 37m. 4c. Climb the wall behind the hollies, or step off the tree (both
hard), and go up the groove. Step right onto a rib and climb up to reach a
prominent block. Move left under the overhang to reach an open groove
(the first bole is the ash tree down to the left). Climb the steep and
interesting groove to belay on a large holly (the second bole). Beware of
rope drag on this pitch.
3 18m. 4c. Move up and traverse right below the overhang onto a
slanting rake. Traverse back left to gain an airy niche above the overhang.
Climb the fine crack to the top on good holds and jams.
Variations
The Original Finish
3a 20m. 4b. Continue the traverse right below the overhang by
following a long rake easily to a break in the steep headwall. Belay at a
tree in a bay.
4a 14m. 4b. Climb the break above, trending slightly left to a steep
finish.

Left-Hand Finish   21 metres   Hard Very Severe
Start from the second tree in the main groove.
3b 9m. 5a. Traverse left across the steep wall to the third stance on *Old Holborn*.
4b 12m. 5b. Climb the groove left of *Old Holborn* pitch 4.

Dead Entrance   106 metres   Very Difficult   (20.4.35)
A jungle-bashing saga, which contains some pieces of rock. Some parts of this route may now be unclimbable due to vegetation. Start below the grassy fault that defines the left side of Red Rock.
1 32m. Ascend the obvious gangway, continue up an interesting chimney, and then scramble to a ledge on the summit of Red Rock.
2 30m. Follow the grass left, and descend an awkward grassy scoop until a traverse can be made to two large loose spikes. Either ascend to a derelict block, go down by an ash tree and a greasy groove to the tree of Green Park, a large vegetated area of the crag. Or descend from the spikes and cross a little rock bay to the edge, beyond which a jump or descent can be made to Green Park.
3 44m. Traverse left to a yew tree. Climb a little slab on the right and follow trees to the top, via numerous belays.

Main Scoop Route   77 metres   Hard Severe   (7.5.35)
A pleasant route, less vegetated than *Dead Entrance*. The groove on pitch 3 can be rather stubborn if damp.
1 32m. *Dead Entrance* pitch 1.
2 12m. Climb diagonally left up an easy gangway to a stance.
3 12m. 4b. Descend 3 metres left to a ledge in the Great Scoop. Go over a small square block and climb the groove (crux) to hollies.
4 9m. Climb two short chimneys to a good ledge.
5 12m. 4a. Ascend the final wall to a strenuous pull over the last bulge. This pitch is aptly called the Hard Court.
Variation
Koala Finish   Hard Very Severe
An entertaining pitch. The hard section is quite short and reasonably protected.
3a 37m. 5b. Move up the wall on the right to the small overhang. Step right and then down into a groove; then move right again to a difficult mantelshelf onto a sloping ledge. Climb to a good thread runner, step left and continue until forced left again. Climb direct to a large pinnacle belay. Protection is well spaced above the crux.

Peeping Tom   72 metres   E3   (28.10.77)
The loose left arête of Red Rock leads to a fierce crack pitch. Start at the foot of Red Rock, just left of *Cornix*.
1 24m. 5b. Go steeply up the wall via obvious flakes, and then traverse left to a ramp sloping right. Follow this until a traverse left can be made to the exposed arête. Climb this to the summit of Red Rock. A very serious pitch.
2 27m. 5c. Go easily up to the big overhang. Climb this and the steep groove/crack above(hard), passing an old peg, to the hollies of *Halan*.
3 21m. Follow *Halan* to the second tree and finish steeply.

Cornix 71 metres Hard Very Severe (6.7.53)
Once past the chossy initial pitch (which can be avoided by scrambling in from the right) you gain some superb climbing above. Start under Red Rock, below an obvious groove.
1 23m. 4b. Climb the groove for a short way, and then go diagonally left until a traverse right can be made up a prominent rake to the obvious groove. Ascend the left wall of the groove and exit on the left. Belay on the summit of Red Rock.
2 30m. 4c. Traverse right to a shallow open corner. Bridge up this, with a tricky exit at the top, to gain the holly tree belay of *Halan* pitch 2. An excellent pitch.
3 18m. 4a. Climb up to a tree as for *Halan*. Traverse right onto the steep wall and ascend to the top.

The Red Rock has been girdled by following the obvious diagonal fault from left to right: **Fester** (Severe/Very Severe 27.7.69). The grade is variable, depending on your attitude to handling loose rock.

The Castle 63 metres Very Severe (28.4.63)
A poor route with some loose rock, which meanders up the arête of the tower-like buttress on the extreme right of the crag. Start at the foot of the grassy slope bounding Red Rock on the right.
1 15m. 4b. Climb up on the right of the damp break to a spike below the bulge; step right and climb the steep crack to a small stance. Holly tree belay.
2 14m. 4c. Descend a little and go left to the foot of an open groove on the front of the tower. Climb the groove to the top of a pedestal. Stance on the right.
3 34m. 4b. The wall above is undercut, so swing right into a shallow groove. Step up, and then move left onto the arête, where good holds lead to a ledge (junction with *Halan*). Move up right to an obvious traverse-line leading round the arête (possible belay). The short crack and wall above lead to a detached flake; pull up to the right on huge holds, in a fine position, to the final slab. Trend left to finish on the arête.

Halan 45 metres Hard Severe (26.4.49)
A devious route that spirals up the tower-like buttress on the right of the cliff. Fairly vegetated, but it contains some interesting rock and positions. Start up grass on the right of the crag to a quartz ledge about half-way up the buttress.
1 15m. 4b. Climb over a block on the left and go up into a groove. Here, an obvious line traverses the buttress. Pull up with difficulty onto the sloping ledge above to the left. Follow this to a niche below the overhang.
2 9m. Continue traversing under the overhang to a holly.
3 21m. 4b. Climb to a tree, and then pull onto the wall above to another tree. From this, regain the wall, go right to a sloping ledge, and traverse for a short way until a steep and exposed mantelshelf leads to the top.

Girdle Traverses
The New Girdle   200 metres   Very Severe   (3.7.53)
A good expedition, continually interesting, which takes a high line across
the cliff face. At the time of writing, pitch 7 is badly affected by ivy (despite
the clean-up to *Bole Way*). Much better than *The Old Girdle* and
recommended on weekdays. Start at the left end of the cliff.
1 24m. *Wrinkle* pitch 1.
2 27m. Go right to the far arête and climb it on good holds.
3 14m. Descend a groove to the lower of two hollies, and then abseil 9
metres to a good ledge (*Unicorn* pitch 2 in reverse).
4 & 5 51m. 4c. *Lion* pitches 2 and 3.
6 21m. 4c. Traverse right into the upper part of *Ribstone Crack* and
continue across *Erosion Groove* at the level of the belay. Step down under
the overhang to follow the series of three ledges rightwards under the roof
as for *Shadow Wall* pitch 2. Belay at the tree.
7 21m. Traverse right using trees and walk for 6 metres to more trees
(junction with *Dead Entrance*). From the far end of the ledge, work out right
round the corner, and go under an overhang to *Bole Way*, arriving below the
steep groove half-way up its second pitch (8 metres below the second bole).
8 21m. Descend slightly right, go over the derelict block of *Dead
Entrance*, and cross a fluted slab below an overhang. Climb up and
ascend the scoop of *Main Scoop Route* to the evergreen ledge and belay
as for that route.
9 & 10 21m. 4a. *Main Scoop Route* pitches 4 and 5.

The Old Girdle   244 metres   Very Severe   (12.6.48)
Mainly Severe in standard, but with a much harder crux. Follow *The New
Girdle* and make the abseil. Stroll under *Lion* and *The Crevice* to the arête.
A steep wall leads to the foot of the crack of *Ribstone Crack*. Traverse
across *Erosion Groove* to the holly tree on *Shadow Wall* pitch 1. Climb the
steep crack with a bulge (crux); then traverse right below the rib of *Trilon*
and descend to the yew trees. Follow *Bole Way* until the *Dead Entrance*
traverse can be reversed to the summit of Red Rock. One can finish here
or make another mediocre pitch.

Clogwyn Tyllau (Arêteland)
Cliff (of) Holes OS Ref 626 572

Just above Carreg Wastad is a small compact buttress with the obvious
rightward-slanting crack of *Ampyx* at its centre and the impressive
square-cut overhanging *Owain's Arête* at its left end.

Indoor Bowling Here I Come   12 metres   E5 6c   (6.89)
A striking micro-route, which gives a finger-wrecking problem. Follow the
path up and left of *Owain's Arête* to an obvious white wall with incipient

cracks. A boulder-problem start (protected by a sideways *RP3* in an obvious crack) leads to a mantel and easier climbing above. Move slightly left at the top. Belay well back.

Back to Trivia   12 metres   E3 6b   (29.5.89)
Aptly named, it takes a crozzly crack in the left side of *Owain's Arête*. Start 3 metres left of that route. The crack on the left side of the pillar front will feel anything but trivial during an ascent. A difficult exit left at 8 metres precedes a mediocre rambling finish.

At the left end of the main crag lies the much tried:

★★**Owain's Arête**   24 metres   E6 6b   (4.8.89)
This exacting pitch accepts the obvious challenge of the overhanging arête, giving some alarming moves in dramatic situations. Start below an obvious pillar and some stacked pegs at about 5 metres. Climb the pillar to the pegs, pass these, via a long stretch for a pocket (crux), and rock over onto a ledge. Gain a niche, stand in the niche, and exit precariously left. Move right and ascend the groove above on sidepulls to a huge jug. An easy arête leads up to the final spike belay.

★**Unleashing the Wild Physique**   24 metres   E5 6b   (7.87)
A powerful route up the overhanging corner-groove right of *Owain's Arête*, requiring a strong streak of perseverance. Start right of the arête, above a wide crack. Aggressively layback the overhanging groove, past two pegs, to reach an equally steep headwall; power up this.

Ampyx   33 metres   Very Severe   (24.3.63)
A pleasant little climb, though lacking the charisma and quality of its harder neighbours. Start below the central, slanting crack.
1 11m. 4a. First climb the wall; then follow the crack to reach a good ledge and a thread belay.
2 11m. 4c. Move right along the ledge until small flakes lead up the steep wall. An awkward move leads to a wide crack beside a huge perched block.
3 11m. 4b. Go through the tree and climb the overhanging crack.

Queer   21 metres   E4   (10.88)
Down on the right end of the crag a perfect white groove provides a frustrating little problem.
1 9m. 6b. The contortionate white groove has good micronut protection, which is hard to place (the trick is not to pull on it). Step left to belay in the gully.
2 12m. Step up and climb the thin crack above the cave, moving left to a block belay – a mundane pitch.

About 30 metres right of *Queer*, the crag is bounded on the right by three prominent pinnacles. Beware the awkward slippery approach.

No More Queensway Sales   11 metres   Hard Very Severe 5a (1991)
The left-hand arête of the first pinnacle is unremarkable.

Penal Colony   11 metres   E2 5b   (1991)
The right-hand arête of the first pinnacle has its moments.

Stand Prow'd   9 metres   E3 6a   (1991)
This is the best of this bunch of routes. The obvious sharp arête on the
second pinnacle is started from the right, and the crux is gaining the
obvious flat ledge. Finish more easily.

Bang Utot   12 metres   Hard Very Severe 5a   (21.10.88)
Tackles the corner-crack on the east wall of the third (uppermost) pinnacle.
Climb the crack for 9 metres, stepping left onto the headwall to finish.

The next route is on a prominent flat-topped block with a leaning arête,
easily seen from the road, overlooking Bryant's Gully and approximately
level with the upper part of Carreg Wastad Uchaf. To reach it, scramble to
the top of Clogwyn Tyllau, and continue for a further 50 or 60 metres
diagonally up rightwards, over grass and lichenous rock, to reach a grassy
slope overlooking Bryant's Gully. The flat-topped block does not appear
until you are almost upon it.

★★**Jem**   9 metres   E6 6b   (2.8.95)
Gain the arête from the right and climb it (2 pegs).

Carreg Wastad Uchaf   OS Ref 626 571

This lies above and to the right of Carreg Wastad and right of Bryant's Gully,
the deep winding gully running up the hillside. The crag consists of a
smooth, shallow, scooped cwm with a steep right wall above heather
terraces and broken rock. From Bryant's Gully, a subsidiary gully runs up
rightwards to scree (opposite the east end of Carreg Wastad). A steep path
breaks out left across rock and heather, and leads into a small cwm. On the
left wall of the cwm stands a large holly tree below twin cracks, the right one
containing numerous beards of grass and heather.

The Bearded Crack   31 metres   Hard Severe   (24.2.63)
Start 3 metres right of the holly, and 12 metres right of a shattered yellow
wall with three pinnacles in front of it.
1 8m. 4b. Climb the crack to a stance on top of the flake.
2 23m. Move left and climb the wall between the cracks on good holds,
moving into the left-hand crack near the top. Pleasant.

Pholidomya   27 metres   Very Difficult   (23.3.63)
The rib right of *The Bearded Crack*. Start as for that route. Climb the rib,
steeply at first, and then go slightly right on good holds to a grassy ledge.
Ascend the crack to the overhang, and then traverse left and finish up the
nose.

For Carreg Wastad Uchaf proper, follow the path left under the three pinnacles, after which the path turns right and runs up into the cwm. The routes are not immediately obvious from below.

Ensis 52 metres Hard Severe (23.2.63)
The obvious undercut, mossy cracks on the left of the wall. Start at the foot of a gully 12 metres left of the large rowan tree of *Little Whizzer*.
1 14m. 4b. Traverse right with difficulty above the overhang, and pull into the groove above. Continue on good holds until an awkward step can be made to a grassy ledge on the right. Belays on the right.
2 23m. Step left across the groove and go up on good holds to a ledge on the arête. Traverse left and climb a V-groove, pulling out left onto a quartz-streaked slab, which leads to a grassy bay.
3 15m. Climb the steep chimney on the right, moving left up a pleasant slab at the top.

Punk Puffins on Rock 37 metres E3 5c (5.90)
A surprisingly good pitch, approached via a steep scramble, taking a direct line up the centre of the scooped wall, through *Solen*. Start in the centre of the wall and boldly climb the beautiful slab to gain the ramp of *Solen*. Continue up, moving first right and then back left, to an interesting finish.

Solen 49 metres Very Severe (23.3.63)
The wall between *Ensis* and *Little Whizzer*. Start just left of the latter, below an obvious groove slanting left.
1 23m. 4c. Climb a short wall into the groove, go up this and exit left to a heather clump. Climb the slab to a mossy line leading right. This is followed to a short crack below and right of the first stance of *Ensis*. Ascend the crack and the difficult steep wall to a quartz shelf. Peg belay.
2 14m. Traverse the shelf until it peters out and continue steeply across a corner to the grassy bay on *Ensis*.
3 12m. Climb the corner on the left of the chimney.

Little Whizzer 45 metres Hard Very Severe (15.4.56)
A reasonable route. Start below a large rowan tree growing from a crack about 3 metres up.
1 9m. 4c. Climb up, bearing right to a spike belay.
2 18m. 5a. Step up to a small quartz ledge, traverse this for about 5 metres, and then move back at a higher level and go up the overhanging wall on small holds. Stance and belay on the left.
3 18m. Traverse left to a conspicuous V-groove, and then go up on fingerholds just to the right. Step round the corner and finish on a slab.

Craig Nant Peris   St Peris's Vale Crag OS Ref 626 575

This is the fine-looking but very broken crag, which forms the gable end of the Esgair Felen ridge. It is well worth a visit, for the scenery and position are superb, 600 metres above the valley floor. The tall organ-pipe sills of felstone are a unique sight, but much of the rock is unfortunately very rotten although it is climbable if handled with care.

The usual approach is by **Bryant's Gully** (Moderate 1899), one of the longest and finest gully scrambles of its type in Wales. The crag is about 60 metres high and consists of three main buttresses. The West Buttress is defined on the left by very light greenish-coloured rock. On its right are the twin gullies of *Tweedledum* and *Tweedledee* divided by a gaunt subsidiary buttress, which is taken by *The Rattle*. The Central Buttress has a gendarme on its right edge overlooking the upper part of Bryant's Gully. The East Buttress is very broken but gives good scrambling.

West Buttress Arête   60 metres   Difficult   (25.7.35)
Start at the foot of the twin gullies, at an obvious traverse-line beneath bulging rock.
1 18m. Traverse round into a groove and go up to a stance on the left. No secure belays.
2 12m. Climb the chimney to another stance.
3 18m. Either traverse 6 metres left and then go up a groove to a large quartz platform, or continue direct on poorer rock to the platform.
4 12m. Go steeply up the edge, and then scramble to the top.

Tweedledum   55 metres   Difficult   (25.7.35)
The left of the twin gullies. There is one small chimney pitch below the chockstone at 37 metres. The final section is interesting if climbed direct.

The Rattle   61 metres   Very Difficult   (25.7.35)
Start at the foot of the buttress dividing the two gullies.
1 34m. Scramble up the centre to a ledge below an overhang; then cross into the groove on the left at 21 metres, or continue up the rib on the right. Take the groove or the left-hand rib to the ledge below the large overhang.
2 27m. Climb diagonally to the right corner and climb up on the edge, move back to the left after a metre or so and ascend direct to finish.

Tweedledee   60 metres   Difficult   (25.7.35)
The right-hand gully is moderately grassy. Jammed blocks form a cave at the top.

Central Buttress Arête   33 metres   Very Difficult   (25.7.35)
Care is needed with the rock. Start by scrambling up for 45 metres on the left of the broad shallow gully, and then take a rib on its right to a large flake at the foot of the buttress proper – a ledge runs round to the right.
1 12m. Climb the groove on the right to a ledge below the gendarme.

2 21m. Go up to the gendarme. Step delicately across left and up behind the gendarme to easier rock. Fifteen metres of scrambling remains.

Eggmeat Buttress Area   OS Ref 628 568

Above and behind the Cromlech Boulders, a wide, low-relief ridge runs down the hillside to terminate in an overhanging wall that rises from scree-slopes. This is Eggmeat Buttress.

Way up and to the left of the overhanging wall, Dinas Cromlech throws down a long narrow ridge towards Ynys Ettws. The lower end of this ridge tapers sharply to a junction with the stream well above and to the left of the Cromlech Boulders. Eighteen metres right of this lower ridge are the two slabby grooves taken by *Cromlech Grooves*.

Corky   40 metres   E1 5b   (22.10.78)
The short wall and groove in the arête of the buttress a few metres left of *Cromlech Grooves*, on the other side of the stream. Climb directly up the short wall to the foot of the groove. A hard start leads to easier climbing up the groove (large tape runner around a pinnacle on the left). Undercut right across the top of the groove to gain a sloping ledge (tricky). Finish up the shallow leaning corner (trickier) or sneak off rightwards round the arête.

In the holly-filled alcove round behind *Corky*, what feels like an HVS jungle-bashing approach gives access to:

Honking by the Pool   14 metres   E3 5b   (1.1.89)
Allegedly a route of great character-building(?) potential, taking (or rather dismantling) the prominent corner. Climb the corner with difficulty, taking care to leave the holds in place as you pass.

Cromlech Grooves   30 metres   Severe 3c   (29.9.51)
Worth doing when you are tired of the slog up to Dinas Cromlech. Go up the right-hand groove to a small overhang. Step delicately round the corner into the left-hand groove and continue on doubtful rock. Scramble up the ridge towards Dinas Cromlech.

A small rounded, globe-like subsidiary buttress just above and beyond this (8 metres to the right across scree from the start of *Cromlech Grooves*) gives the first of a series of ferocious micro-routes:

Sheepcat   9 metres   E5 6b   (21.4.87)
Tackle the left-to-right crack splitting the front face of the globe. Protection is difficult to arrange and the climbing is fierce.

Eggmeat Buttress
OS Ref 628 568

The overhanging wall of the main section is breached by short, striking twin corners, which in turn are separated by the sharp, overhanging *Eggmeat Arête*. Around and up on the lower left side of the ridge is a short overhanging white wall containing a capped central groove.

Animal Locomotion   14 metres   E7 6b   (23.4.87)
A bold route, said to be 'choppier than the Bay of Biscay'. Climb the central groove, a flake, and then a wall up the overhanging black shield left of *Eggmeat Arête*. With sustained, strenuous and technical climbing above a nasty landing (and only one skyhook for protection), it seems unlikely to become a trade route.

Birdseye   11 metres   Very Severe 5a   (24.4.87)
The corner just left of *Eggmeat Arête* proves to be a trifle tricky.

★Eggmeat Arête   9 metres   E3 6a   (17.2.87)
A classic problem up the superb little overhanging arête reserves its contortionate crux to the very last move (which is protected by a crucial cam).

Ringsnack   9 metres   E2 5c   (24.2.87)
The steep, wet, dripping corner right of *Eggmeat Arête* merits its awful name.

Milk Cow   9 metres   E4 6b   (28.2.87)
Tackle the grooved arête 3 metres right of *Eggmeat Arête* direct. Looks a doddle, doesn't it?

Pork Trout   9 metres   Very Severe 5a   (21.2.87)
The slim groove and wall just right again are less beefy, and thus more amenable, than the neighbouring routes.

Dinas Cromlech   Fortress Cromlech   OS Ref 629 569

This imposing cliff, the showpiece of the Pass, stands starkly on the hillside 180 metres above Pont y Gromlech looking out over the upper reaches of the valley like some grim medieval castle. Its massive rhyolite walls and pillars, steep and exposed, are furnished with sound and often abundant holds giving probably the finest and most exposed top-grade climbing on either side of the Pass. There are also several first-class easier routes, which are enhanced by their dramatic surroundings. Modern protection has made all but the hardest climbs relatively enjoyable and safe. The rock, although seemingly brittle, is generally reliable but caution should be exercised when climbing on the East Wing (to the right of *Cemetery Gates*), as the rock tends to be a little more friable in this area.

The dominant feature of the Cromlech is its magnificent open-book corner whose central line is taken by *Cenotaph Corner*, perhaps the most famous Welsh rock climb. To the left lies the West Wing, the first feature of which is the corner of *Sabre Cut*. This rises from the Forest, a once vegetated, but now barren sloping ledge lying 25 metres up the face. To the left, past the cracks of *Dives* and *Holly Buttress*, the cliff rapidly diminishes in height. It is cut by three right-facing corners (*Pharaoh's Wall*, *Pharaoh's Passage*, and *Parchment Passage*) and finally by the overhanging groove of *The Thing* before broken rocks appear. To the right of *Cenotaph Corner*, past the prominent crack in its right wall, *Cemetery Gates*, lies another corner, *Ivy Sepulchre*, at the start of the East Wing. Further over, beyond the shattered crack of *Jericho Wall*, the cliff becomes less steep, deteriorating into vegetated rock with a large heathery ledge, the Heath, at about one-third height. Next comes the castellated *Flying Buttress*, which leans drunkenly against the base of the cliff and marks the end of the East Wing. Just to the right of this is *Castle Gully*, with three short routes high up on its right wall, and then the descent gully, isolated pinnacles and scree. Above *Cenotaph Corner* sits the Valley, a series of large grassy ledges traversing the face of the cliff, the starting-point for all routes on the smaller upper cliff.

The cliff lies above the 350-metre contour. Its structure is such that some faces receive early morning sunlight, while other walls only receive full sun in the afternoon. This allows you to seek the sun in the spring and follow the shadows in high summer. Its height and openness can make it quite a breezy place to climb.

Descents: for all the routes finishing at the top of the crag, scramble up and around the top of the cliff to find the steep but easy descent gully which curves round its right-hand side. The gullies on the left-hand side of the cliff are hard to find and follow, particularly at dusk, and are best avoided. For climbs finishing on the Valley it is usual to abseil down the wall just right of *Cenotaph Corner*; great care should be taken to avoid knocking stones down during this operation. For those who do not fancy the abseil or one of the shorter routes above, an escape is possible via *Tributary Crack*, the easy diagonal flake, which splits the short wall above and left of *Cenotaph Corner*.

The West Wing
Millwood's Wall   30 metres   Severe   (5.53)
Left of the overhung chimney/niche of *The Thing* is a large heather ledge, from which rise three corners/grooves (the right-hand one being the top part of *Vanishing Point*). Start between the left and central corners. Climb the centre of the wall, past a small grassy ledge at half height, trending right.

Vanishing Point   34 metres   E1 5b   (14.10.77)
A scrappy start leads to a few good moves up the final groove. Start as for *The Thing*, at the foot of a corner (often wet). Ascend the corner to a heathery ledge. Finish up the slim groove in the wall above.

1	The Thing	E2
2	Parchment Passage	VD
3	Pharaoh's Passage	VS
4	Pharaoh's Wall	VS
5	Noah's Warning	VS
6	Holly Buttress	VS
7	Dives/Better Things	HS
8	Sabre Cut	VS
9	Spiral Stairs	VD
10	Foil	E3
11	Memory Lane	E3
12	Left Wall	E2
13	Cenotaph Corner	E1
14	Right Wall	E5
15	Cemetery Gates	E1
16	Ivy Sepulchre	E1
17	Horseman's Route	HS
18	Jericho Wall	E2
19	Sexton's Route	S

Dinas Cromlech

for greater detail of the central area, see also page 112b,c

24 Ivy Sepulchre Crack   VD
25 Rumblefish   E7
26 Grond   E2
27 The Mystery   E1
28 The Monster   E2

CG The Cromelch Girdle   E2
F   The Forest
V   The Valley

20 Atomic Hot Rod   E5
21 Flying Buttress   VD
22 Tributary Crack   D
23 Overlord   E7

★★The Thing   38 metres   E2   (11.2.56)

A fierce and technical climb, which still sees its share of epics. Start at the left-hand end of the crag, beyond *Parchment Passage*, where an overhanging crack slants up to the right to merge into an overhanging groove/niche.

1 24m. 5c. Follow the rightward-slanting crack, past a couple of very thin moves and strenuous pulls, into the niche. Jam up to inverted flakes and use these to gain a foothold on the left. Continue up, trending right past a sapling, and after 6 metres move right round the arête to the tree of *Parchment Passage*.

2 14m. 4c. Move back left to rejoin the crack, which leads more easily to the top.

Variation

1a 38m. 5c. It is possible to climb directly over a bulge into the finishing crack, thus avoiding the rightward excursion onto *Parchment Passage*. Slightly harder but better.

Rootorooni   41 metres   E3   (5.6.83)

A steep and surprising route, with a bold second pitch. Start to the right of *The Thing*, by some jagged boulders.

1 18m. 5c. Climb the shallow groove to the roof and move left to pull over it. Continue up to the curling roof. Move right and hand-traverse back left to reach a small ledge. Go up to belay on *The Thing*.

2 23m. 5c. Follow *The Thing* for 5 metres to a small chockstone. Traverse left across the wall to a large spike and pocket. Trend slightly rightwards along a line of pockets and finish up a groove in the middle of the wall.

★★Cobweb Crack   33 metres   Very Severe   (2.9.51)

A very good climb, which is stiff for its grade. Start below and a metre or so left of the start of *Parchment Passage*, at the foot of a short crack.

1 12m. 4a. Climb the crack on good holds and traverse left to a stance.

2 21m. 5a. Above is a pocketed T-shaped crack, undercut at the start. Climb this strenuously past a tricky section at 6 metres. Continue up on improving jams and move left to a junction with *Parchment Passage*; finish up this.

Parchment Passage   38 metres   Very Difficult   (27.3.33)

An interesting route tackling the leftmost of the three right-facing corners in this part of the crag. The top section is very polished. Start below the corner.

1 27m. Scramble up to a tree, and then ascend leftwards until an exposed high step on polished holds gains a gangway running back up into an awkward corner stance.

2 11m. Ascend to the left-hand of two short cracks. Step right when it becomes difficult to a steep finish.

Scarab   42 metres   Hard Very Severe   (9.5.82)

A surprisingly worthwhile eliminate, whose second pitch is a more direct version of *Pharaoh's Passage*. Start just right of the foot of *Parchment Passage*, below a tree.

1 15m. 5b. Climb past the tree and follow the slim groove above, stepping right to a belay on *Pharaoh's Passage*.
2 27m. 5a. Go up and move right to good pockets, and then climb up and slightly left to the top of a flake. Continue directly up the centre of the wall to finish.

Pharaoh's Passage   39 metres   Very Severe   (27.3.33)
A wandering route taking the central right-facing corner and the wall to its right. Start at the foot of the corner.
1 15m. 4c. Surmount the overhang with difficulty until a strenuous pull out leftwards leads to a holly tree ledge.
2 24m. 4c. Ascend the wall behind the first holly, and from its top, traverse right to the skyline and finish up the airy rib.
Variation
2a The Original Finish 21m. Ascend the Moderate chimney.

Scroll   12 metres   Hard Severe 3c   (27.5.89)
Useful as an extra pitch to *Pharaoh's Passage* or *Wall*. Start from the terrace on which these routes finish. Climb the obvious corner for 5 metres, finishing up the crack above past a couple of loose chockstones.

Speedfreak   43 metres   E1 5b   (7.72)
A serious arête with some good climbing. Start 5 metres right of *Pharaoh's Passage*, above a sharp flake. The first 8 metres are strenuous but a good spike soon arrives. Finish more easily up the arête above.

★Pharaoh's Wall   34 metres   Very Severe   (17.4.33)
Steep and enjoyable. Start below the right-hand of the three right-facing corners, at the foot of a short wall.
1 8m. Climb easily up the edge of the wall to a sloping platform and thread belays below the corner.
2 26m. 4c. Trend diagonally up the wall just right of the corner-crack to a series of potholes; then continue directly up the wall by steep but straightforward climbing. A good pitch.
Variation
2a 26m. 4c. Go diagonally up the wall, and traverse back left into the corner at the level of a large pothole. Finish up the corner-crack, which has widened into a chimney.

★★★Noah's Warning   67 metres   Very Severe   (3.9.51)
A fine sustained route of some character and high in its grade. It follows the obvious pockmarked crack right of *Pharaoh's Wall*. Start below the crack.
1 40m. 4c. Ascend the crack on good holds to the large pothole on *Pharaoh's Wall*. Continue up the wall past several bulges to an overhang. Turn this on the left to a ledge.
2 27m. 5a. Climb the chimney/crack splitting the steep wall above to reach an overhanging flake. Move round this to the right, and go straight up before moving left to a thin crack. At the top of this, exit left with difficulty onto a slab and a belay.

Rameses Wall   60 metres   E1   (6.10.57)
Although an artificial line, it has some interesting moves and a sting in its
tail. Start as for *Noah's Warning*.
1 30m. 5a. A high step onto the right wall gains a rising traverse, which
leads to the arête. Climb the wall round the arête, left of the *Holly Buttress*
crack, and scramble up over broken ground to belay by a holly tree.
2 18m. 4c. Step down onto the right wall and climb the obvious steep
groove trending up to the arête. Step left and go straight up to belay on
Spiral Stairs.
3 12m. 5b. Climb the short wall just left of the arête on the right, a
testing little problem. Finish easily.

The Nubian   54 metres   E1   (22.10.78)
A pleasant eliminate taking the arête left of *Holly Buttress* direct. Start 1½
metres left of the arête.
1 30m. 5b. Climb diagonally right to join the arête at the overlap. Pull
round left strenuously to good holds (crux). Follow the arête, and its little
continuation, to belay half-way up *Holly Buttress* at the tree. Good positions.
2 24m. 4c. Step left and follow the arête direct.

Holly Buttress   51 metres   Very Severe   (13.10.31)
A steep and direct climb. Start at the foot of the steep polished crack
leading up to hollies around the corner to the right of *Rameses Wall*.
1 30m. 4c. Struggle up the crack (much harder since the demise of the
holly tree) to reach a possible stance. It is better to continue easily in the
same line to a holly tree belay.
2 21m. 4b. Climb the steep corner-crack.
Variation
2a 26m. 4b. From the foot of the crack, traverse right across the steep
wall to reach a slab. Follow this back up left to the top.

Zimbabwe   60 metres   E1   (24.4.79)
A rambling route taking the arête right of *Holly Buttress*. Start just right of
Holly Buttress.
1 21m. 4b. Climb the narrow wall, with a steep finish, to a prickly stance
by some holly bushes below a short steep wall.
2 30m. 5c. Scramble up about 3 metres, and then ascend the wall to a
prominent pocket. A hard traverse right to the arête (crux) is followed by
exposed moves, rapidly easing, and a stroll up to the final belay of *Spiral
Stairs*.
3 9m. 4c. Finish up the short finger-crack above the stance.

★★★Dives/Better Things   60 metres   Hard Severe   (13.5.33)
A great classic climb, whose highlight is the excellent airy corner-crack of
the aptly named *Better Things* finish. Start a short way right of *Holly
Buttress*, where a steep corner-crack rises up to the black diagonal
overhang that leads to the Forest.

1 24m. 4a. Go up the strenuous crack on good holds. Continue diagonally right (often wet) below the overhang on curious pumice-like rock. Belay on the Forest at the foot of the slab.
2 12m. Climb the short crack leftwards as for *Spiral Stairs* and belay above it, below the steep V-shaped corner-crack.
3 24m. 4b. Finish up the corner-crack in a fine position.
Variation   Hard Very Severe   5a
The right-hand arête has also been climbed. This gives a very contrived pitch.

★★Sabre Cut   55 metres   Very Severe   (1935)
An excellent route, with a fine top pitch: the first of the big corners on the Cromlech to be conquered. Start at a vertical corner 3 metres right of *Dives*.
1 32m. 4c. Climb the corner until it divides. Step out right and ascend the wall to the Forest. Climb easily to a good belay on its upper right edge.
2 23m. 4b. Traverse left and ascend the enjoyable, wide corner-crack to the top.

★Curfew   67 metres   E1   (19.7.77)
A popular eliminate with an exposed finish. Protection is adequate where it matters. Start 5 metres right of *Sabre Cut* at a rib to the right of the black overhang
1 30m. 5a. (*Sabre Cut Direct*) Climb the rib to a gangway leading rightwards; from the end of this, step right into a steep corner, which leads to *Spiral Stairs*, and thus to the Forest.
2 37m. 5b. Climb the steep wall just right of the tree on *Spiral Stairs* (poorly protected). Ascend the left arête, past a ledge, to a horizontal break. Traverse this rightwards until the wall above bulges. A few hard moves around the bulge lead to superb juggy climbing up the top arête.

★★Foil   24 metres   E3 6a   (1.7.76)
A sparkling and superbly sustained pitch up the finger-crack in the wall right of *Sabre Cut*; exceptionally good protection. Start as for pitch 2 of *Epitaph*. Start up *Epitaph*, and then follow the thin crack, which becomes mean at 15 metres (possible escape left into *Sabre Cut* at this point). Continue to a semi rest at a pocket. Strenuous moves above lead to a precarious exit. Traverse off leftwards to a belay at the top of *Sabre Cut* (and a view of your second).

Cenotaph Corner Area

The Cromlech walls, the focal point of Welsh climbing, are probably unmatched in Britain for their unique concentration of hard, high-quality and atmospheric mountain routes. Well over a dozen fine Extremes ascend or cross these hallowed walls, each offering steep crack or pocket climbing mainly on impeccable rock – an irresistible magnet, which draws climbers back time and time again.

★Epitaph   67 metres   E3   (8.10.62)
The original way up the left arête of *Cenotaph Corner*. Although now
superseded by *Foil* and *Memory Lane*, it is still a very worthwhile route. Some
suspect rock and spaced protection make this a bold lead. Start as for *Curfew*.
1 37m. 5a. Climb *Curfew* pitch 1 and then continue up through the
Forest to belay on its upper right edge.
2 30m. 5c. Move left and climb a thin crack until a reachy move right
gains a ledge on the arête. Climb the arête, trending slightly left on two
friable flakes. Step up and then make a long reach, and a pull on a small
flake leads to easier climbing and, thankfully, the top. (The crack behind
the stance is Hard Severe.)

Corridors of Power   30 metres   E4 6a   (22.10.88)
A harder and more direct way of doing *Memory Lane*, adding a small
amount of new climbing to the Cromlech's considerable repertoire. From
The Forest, climb the crack and groove right of *Foil* to the overhang, pull
boldly onto the arête and follow pockets up to the ledge (junction with
Memory Lane). Finish up the arête above, as for *Epitaph* and *Memory Lane*.

★★Spiral Stairs   53 metres   Very Difficult   (6.12.31)
An exposed and highly polished trade route. Not recommended for
complete novices, as the traverse on pitch 1 is quite serious to second.
Start by scrambling (roping up if preferred) leftwards from the screes below
Cemetery Gates up polished ledges, and continuing along the narrow
path to nut belays just up on the left, by a short crack.
1 21m. Pull up the crack onto the obvious leftward traverse-line. Follow
this, descending slightly for 15 metres, until a rib leads up to the Forest. An
exposed pitch, which is apt to terrify nervous seconds (care needed to
avoid runners lifting out).
2 21m. Move across left into the prominent short crack. Climb this to a
ledge on the left. Trend up leftwards on good holds via an easy slab to a
poor stance and spike belays.
3 12m. Climb a chimney/groove to easy slabs.

★★Memory Lane   46 metres   E3 5c   (7.76)
A fine open and exhilarating route, serious and sustained. Start below the
left arête of *Cenotaph Corner*, at the belay below *Spiral Stairs*. A crack runs
up to the Forest. Climb the crack to a ledge on the arête. Move right onto
the left wall of the *Corner*. Ascend diagonally leftwards to the ledge on
Epitaph (crux, runners in *Left Wall* will be found necessary by most
leaders). Finish up the arête as for *Epitaph*, a testing pitch.

★Tess of the d'Urbevilles   46 metres   E6 6b   (7.8.89)
A scintillating and bold pitch. Start between *Memory Lane* and *Left Wall*.
Climb directly up the wall and do the crux of *Memory Lane*. Break right
and follow a rising crack via a hard move to reach *Left Wall* (runners). Step
back left and go up to small ledges and several reasonable *RPs*. From the
centre of the final ledge, boldly run it out straight up the wall to the top
(with minimal protection).

★★**Left Wall**   40 metres   E2 5c   (6.5.56)

A brilliant route at the top end of its grade. Still a contender for the most popular, most fallen off, and finest Extreme pitch in North Wales. It takes the crack that splits the left wall of *Cenotaph Corner*. Start on the large sloping ledge below *Cenotaph Corner*. Climb diagonally left to stand on a flaky ledge below the crack proper. Follow this on good holds, past an awkward section where it slants up rightwards, to a good resting-place below the fork. The thin left-hand branch gives 6 metres of sustained climbing before a series of large dubious holds leads left to the arête. Finish easily.

★★**True Grip**   40 metres   E5 6a   (19.4.80)

In essence, a superb direct version of *Left Wall*. Start as for *Left Wall*. Climb up for about 5 metres and pull out rightwards. Go directly up the wall to join *Resurrection* at a faded thread runner. Step left, and after a long reach for a pocket, gain *The Girdle* ledge. The leftward-curving flake above is climbed with your feet on it. Where the flake disappears, make a reachy move for a pocket and gain *Left Wall*. Continue up *Left Wall* to finish direct where that route moves left.

★★★**Resurrection**   44 metres   E4 6a   (1975)

A magnificent pitch of undeniable quality, sustained and strenuous, with a fingery crux at the top. Start just left of *Cenotaph Corner*. Climb up leftwards for 5 metres, and then go directly up past a faded thread runner to *The Girdle* ledge. Move right to a flat rib of rock. Ascend the left side of this (past two pegs) with a hard move to reach better holds. Move across to join *Left Wall* where the crack splits. Follow the right-hand fork with difficulty, very sustained for 9 metres, to a good spike and runner. The crack now closes. Make a long reach left to sharp finger-holds and finish up a shallow groove.
Variations
The Right-Hand Finish   Harder but better protected and more popular than the original. From where the crack closes, continue in the same line on small face-holds. Make a massive reach for a flat hold (6b for the short) and finish direct.
Redhead's Finish   From the spike go straight up the wall between the left and right-hand finishes – solid 6b.

★**J R**   43 metres   E5 6b   (12.4.80)

A fierce eliminate up the wall to the right of *Resurrection*, which has seen some long falls. Unfortunately it is possible to step into *Cenotaph Corner* for a rest at 24 metres. Only the purist will resist this temptation. Follow *Resurrection* for 3 metres, and then climb direct to *The Girdle* ledge. Follow *Resurrection* to the pegs and step right. A difficult pull on a rounded hold gains sharp finger-jugs. Climb up to a flake runner; then move right and upwards until a layback on a small edge and a pinch-grip move lead to the ledge below the crux of *Resurrection*. Follow the *Resurrection* *Right-Hand Finish*.

★★★**Cenotaph Corner**   37 metres   E1 5c   (24.8.52)
Perhaps the most famous of British rock-climbs and the focal point of the
Llanberis Pass: immaculate climbing with good protection. Although the
passage of countless feet has polished its holds to a high sheen, to lead
this route for the first time is both a thrilling and satisfying experience. Start
at the foot of the huge right-angled corner. Ascend to a difficult but
well-protected move at 8 metres. Continue more easily using a crack on
the left to a widening of the corner-crack. Struggle up this with an
awkward move into a shallow niche at 30 metres just past a chockstone
(the Pudding Stone). Bridge delicately up to gain thin jams, and exit via a
good hold to a tree belay over on the right.

★★**Nightmayer**   40 metres   E8 6c   (16.6.92)
A formidable test of nerve and stamina, which makes the most of the
baffling blank section of the wall between *Cenotaph Corner* and *Lord of
the Flies*. Both ascents to date have relied upon a top-rope inspection, and
an on-sight ascent will be a fantastic achievement. Follow *Lord of the Flies*
to the finger-traverse ledge. Pull straight up and continue direct on pockets,
moving right to gain the large pocket on *Lord of the Flies* (thread runner).
Crank up and left on a two-finger pocket, and then continue direct to *The
Girdle* ledge; move right for a rest. Move back, and ascend past a good
wire just above *The Girdle* ledge. A reasonable small wire protects the
sharp dynamic crux about half-way up. More tenuous climbing on small
pockets leads to a point 2 metres from the top. Move left and finish up the
last piece of the wall. A heart-stopping lead.

★★★**Lord of the Flies**   40 metres   E6 6a   (26.6.79)
A stunning route of great difficulty and quality between *Cenotaph Corner*
and *Right Wall*, which (unlike *Right Wall*) has lost little of its reputation.
Since the disappearance of, first, the peg and, more recently, the crucial
nut placement that once protected the crux, the route is now a much more
serious proposition. Start 3½ metres right of the *Corner*, below thin vertical
cracks. Climb the cracks until they run out, and then go directly up to a
thin ledge. Finger-traverse right along this with a hard move up at its end
to gain a large pocket. Continue up on reasonable holds for a short way,
until a short but fierce and fingery section leads up left to another pocket
(runner in the pocket and also good nut out to the right). Step right and
ascend to better holds and *The Girdle* ledge. A few moves up the wall gain
a finger-ledge leading right to the base of a shallow groove and
improving holds. Finish up the groove past a large nut placement.

The House of God (40 metres E6 6a 6.89) provides a more serious and
sustained way of doing *Lord of the Flies,* though it is not as classic a line as
the original, and rather contrived. It starts up *Lord of the Flies* and then
follows *Nightmayer* to *The Girdle* ledge, before moving right to finish up *Lord
of the Flies*.

★★★**Right Wall**   46 metres   E5   6a   (15.6.74)

Although it has lost its awesome reputation through many ascents, this brilliant climb is still a big lead. It is low in the grade but should not be underestimated. The original way up the wall, it is a route-finding masterpiece, the holds only coming to light at close quarters. Start at the right-hand end of a grassy ledge at a short wall and short corner below some old bolts. Ascend the short wall to a ledge. Climb the corner, breaking out left up the diagonal crack. Move back right and continue up the wall on pockets to a narrow ledge and so to a good rest on the right. Step up onto a prominent foothold and climb leftwards to a large broken pocket, or move left a short way and ascend direct. From the top of the pocket, step left and climb up on small pockets to a line of holds rising rightwards to *The Girdle* ledge. Traverse right until directly below a shallow pocket, the Porthole, 6 metres above. Start up the wall just to its right; then step into it and make the crux moves up to reach a series of good holds, which lead rightwards past a good spike. Traverse along these to finish up a thin crack.

★**Precious**   40 metres   E5   6b   (13.1.80)

A scary start and thrilling finish make this route a memorable outing. Unfortunately the line is very escapable. Start 5 metres right of *Right Wall*, below an inverted V-slot. Go straight up through the V-slot. Continue via a shallow scoop, and then go slightly up left to a resting-ledge (on *Right Wall*). Climb to good runners 3 metres higher. Ascend rightwards to a large pocket and so to another pocket. Move left a short way and pull up onto *The Girdle* ledge (often dirty). Follow *Right Wall*, past the Porthole, to where it traverses right. Finish direct to a small tree by superb pockety climbing.

Variations

The Original Start (6a) gained the shallow scoop above the inverted V-slot by a horizontal traverse from the diagonal crack on *Right Wall*.

An alternative from *The Girdle* ledge climbs up between *Right Wall* and *Cemetery Gates* to the rightwards traverse of the former at a similar standard.

★★**Ivory Madonna**   80 metres   E5   (18.4.80)

A majestic, rising right-to-left girdle of the *Cenotaph Corner* walls in two demanding pitches, with a particularly intense crux. Start as for *Cemetery Gates*.

1 43m. 6b. Climb *Cemetery Gates* to the first good resting-ledge. Traverse easily left to join *Lord of the Flies*. An adrenalin-pumping 6-metre sequence of 'brick edge' climbing enables you to gain the sanctuary of *Cenotaph Corner*. Ascend 5 metres to belay.

2 37m. 6a. A hard move left just below an overlap on the left wall gains two good pockets. Continue left to a flake runner, step down 1½ metres, and move across to join *Left Wall* where the crack forks. Climb boldly left along a line of rising pockets to join *Epitaph* at a perched block 5 metres from the top; finish easily.

★★★Cemetery Gates   52 metres   E1   (30.9.51)
The exhilarating and exposed crackline in the right arête of *Cenotaph Corner* is an impressive line. Most of the route is furnished with large holds but, although low in the grade, the climbing is still quite strenuous and this is not the place to bump up your lead grade. A hard move up into the crack proper at 12 metres is fairly serious but above protection is excellent. Start by carefully descending from the top of a huge flake right of *Cenotaph Corner* to a tree belay below the right arête.
1 34m.   5b.   Climb up first right and then left to the foot of the chimney/crack. Enter this boldly and follow it past an awkward section to a good ledge at 18 metres. Continue up the crack to belay on *The Girdle* ledge, the last few moves being the crux.
2 18m.   4c.   From the right-hand end of the ledge, climb the wide crack for 5 metres. Step round the arête to the right and go up to reach a series of Thank God holds, which lead airily to the top.

The Grim Jim   52 metres   E2   (26.3.81)
An obvious line, whose first pitch takes the arête and wall between *Cemetery Gates* and *The Crucifix*. Start as for *Cemetery Gates*.
1 40m.   5b.   Follow *Cemetery Gates* to the ledge at 18 metres. Move right round the arête, go up on dubious holds, and then step back left to a ledge on the arête. Ascend for a metre or so, and then go strenuously over the bulge, using a layaway hold in a pocket. Trend left up to the ledge and belay of *Cemetery Gates*.
2 12m.   5b.   Follow the crack behind the stance to join the last few moves of *Right Wall*. A superbly exposed pitch.
The Direct Start   18 metres   E4 5c
Climb *Cemetery Gates* to the chimney/crack. Move boldly up the bulge on the right on disposable holds to rejoin *Cemetery Gates* at the first ledge.

The East Wing
The Crucifix   64 metres   E2   (17.5.66)
A bold outing at the upper limit of its grade, which runs up a groove in the centre of the wall left of *Ivy Sepulchre*. The climbing is not too hard but friable rock and well-spaced protection combine to give a high grip factor.
1 24m.   4a.   *Ivy Sepulchre* pitch 1.
2 40m.   5b.   Traverse out leftwards and ascend steeply to a flake runner. Continue for 3 metres to a small ledge, and then trend up left to a shallow groove. Climb this boldly to a shallow niche (junction with *The Girdle*). Surmount the bulge, move left and climb the wall to Thank God holds to finish.

★Crucifix Direct   46 metres   E4 5c   (5.76)
A menacing version of the parent route, with some friable rock. Start from a ledge and tree belay below the centre of the wall. Boldly climb straight up to join *The Crucifix* at the flake runner after 18 metres of climbing and finish up that route.

Golgotha 40 metres E4 5c (25.6.79)

This route takes a surprisingly independent line between *The Crucifix* and *Ivy Sepulchre*, and is very serious, as the peg can only be clipped after the crux. The name means 'Place of the Skull'. Start at the foot of the *Ivy Sepulchre* corner. Climb the crack just left of the corner. Trend left under the overlap and step down to a resting-ledge. Pull rightwards over the bulge using a pocket to reach a hidden flake on the white wall. Stand on this with difficulty to reach the peg; then finish boldly up the wall just to its right.

★★**Ivy Sepulchre** 58 metres E1 (29.8.47)

An interesting and varied climb up the large corner right of *Cenotaph Corner*. Start well below the corner, on a grassy ledge.

1 24m. 4a. Climb vegetated rock and continue up left via a crack leading to trees. Traverse right along a ledge and go up over two rock steps to belay at the foot of the corner.

2 34m. 5b. Climb the corner, awkward at first, but soon easing, to a large overhung niche. Climb out of this with difficulty to better holds. Finish up the corner without further problems to an oak tree belay just below the top.

★**Hall of Warriors** 40 metres E5 6a (11.4.80)

A riveting route that has its harrowing moments and one very hard move. Start just right of the belay at the end of pitch 1 of *Ivy Sepulchre*. Climb the wall, with an awkward move left to a ledge at 8 metres. Continue up until it is possible to pull out onto the centre of a large ledge (on *The Girdle*) – all very serious so far. Step up left to a pocket. Go straight up with a telescopic reach for a jug (crux), and so to a sapling and grass ledge. Move 2 metres right, and then go up to finish via a crack.

Jericho Wall 76 metres E2 (28.9.52)

A steep and nerve-racking route on friable rock with only moderate protection. It follows the shattered chimney/crack up the edge of the wall right of *Ivy Sepulchre*. Start below the wall, at a 5-metre triangular buttress.

1 24m. 5a. Climb the left-hand side of the buttress and go up to a small wet overhang. Move right and climb a smooth white corner/groove on small holds to below another overhang. Go left to a ledge running out from the foot of the corner of *Ivy Sepulchre*.

2 20m. 5a. Traverse down right across the ledge to a damp scoop. Climb this, and the wall above, to a step left to an overhung niche. Step up and trend right with difficulty to a large ledge (dubious belay).

3 32m. 4c. Traverse 5 metres left and ascend to a holly tree. Traverse back right and go up to a scoop; continue up until it is possible to traverse left to a small pinnacle. Finish direct to the Valley.

Wardance 27 metres E1 5b (1982)

A poor route on doubtful rock up the arête just right of *Jericho Wall*. Follow *Jericho Wall* pitch 2 for about 5 metres. Step right and climb the arête, via an obvious groove, to belay at a good ledge on the right. Scramble off rightwards to finish.

Horseman's Route   108 metres   Hard Severe   (20.10.40)
A rambling expedition, with its share of bad rock and vegetation, but
somewhat redeemed by its imposing final chimney. Start as for *Ivy Sepulchre*.
1 23m. Scramble up to a ledge and climb a steep crack to a dead tree.
Move down to the right until a dirty chimney leads to another vegetated ledge.
Climb a chimney to the ledge running out from the foot of *Ivy Sepulchre*.
2 24m. Follow the ledge down along to the right as for *Jericho Wall*,
stepping low across the damp scoop. Go round the arête and up a broken
wall to a poor stance.
3 20m. Continue up a narrow rake to the foot of a chimney. Climb this
and move along the ledge above to belay between two cracks in the wall.
4 17m. Ascend the wall between the cracks of *Sexton's Route* and *Neb's
Crawl*. Walk up right through vegetation to a grassy ledge below a
prominent corner, the Haven.
5 24m. 4b. The initial corner proves awkward to the overhung chimney.
Climb the chimney until a step out right near the top.

Sexton's Route   65 metres   Severe   (17.6.33)
A botanical excursion, this vague and tedious route rambles up through
the most vegetated part of the cliff. Start on the rake at the foot of the
left-facing gully 9 metres right of *Ivy Sepulchre*.
1 18m. Climb the overhanging chimney to a large spike. Move delicately
left with difficulty to a good stance and belay.
2 24m. Scramble up to the grassy slopes of the Heath on the right and
continue via a heathery glacis and broken rock to a short wall.
3 23m. Ascend the left-hand crack, with an awkward exit onto a large
ledge with trees. Walk left and climb a steep wall above the tree to the
Valley, or finish up the right-angled corner immediately behind the trees –
much harder.

Pegasus   27 metres   Hard Very Severe 5a   (15.7.78)
A worthwhile little route. Start below the last pitch of *Horseman's Route*. Move
right and climb the obvious arête, with one hard move over the overlap.
Variation Start
The steep shattered wall below the arête has been climbed at E2 5b –
lethally loose.

Neb's Crawl   69 metres   Difficult   (2.2.33)
Another rambling route for the botanist, its acres of vegetation almost
dwarfing the amount of rock encountered. It takes a diagonal line from
right to left crossing the Heath and ending in the Valley. Start in the gully
immediately left of *Flying Buttress*, or at a vegetated crack, Crockett Crack,
a few metres left. Wander vaguely up, via the right-hand crack in a short
wall at about 34 metres. Scramble up rightwards, and then ascend
another wall to a sloping ledge and belay. Move round to the left and so
to the Valley. Variations are legion.

★★★**The Cromlech Girdle**   236 metres   E2   (1.4.56)
A historic expedition of great character. Cruising the airy walls of *Cenotaph Corner* gives a real adrenalin surge but its other pitches are not without interest. Although a popular way of doing it is starting at the Forest and finishing up *Cemetery Gates* (pitches 6 and 7), it is worth doing in its entirety. Either way, it is best done on weekdays to prevent traffic jams around *Cenotaph Corner*.

1 27m. *Parchment Passage* pitch 1.
2 15m. 5a. Climb up above the holly stump, and then traverse right, reversing *Cobweb Crack* for 2½ metres. Continue right round the arête to belay in *Pharaoh's Passage*.
3 12m. 4c. Climb down and round the next arête to a belay on *Pharaoh's Wall*.
4 18m. Traverse the wall diagonally rightwards to a belay on *Holly Buttress*.
5 34m. Make a descending traverse right to join *Dives*. Climb this to The Forest and so to a stance on the left edge of the wall of *Cenotaph Corner*.
6 30m. 5b. Step right onto a small ledge, go up for 2 metres and traverse right to *Left Wall*, which is climbed to a good flake and nut runner. Descend 3 metres and then make several hard moves to a horizontal break leading more easily into the *Corner*. Climb up to a hanging stance where the crack widens. A serious pitch to second.
7 30m. 5b. Climb the *Corner* to a good thread runner around the Pudding Stone. Descend to the start of a narrow rising ledge running across the right wall. Go along this using pockets in the wall above. A hard move gains the wider ledge leading across to the *Cemetery Gates* belay. Quite a serious pitch for both members of the party.
8 14m. 5a. Traverse right round the arête. Descend slightly on brittle rock, and then move across to *Ivy Sepulchre*.
9 15m. A descending traverse along ledges leads to the heathery terrace on *Jericho Wall*.
10 & 11 41m. 4b. *Horseman's Route* pitches 4 and 5.

Flying Buttress Area
★★★**Flying Buttress**   87 metres   Very Difficult   (18.12.31)
A steep and classic route, on sound but rather polished rock, with a remarkable degree of exposure, the finest V Diff in the Pass. Start at the foot of the buttress forming the right edge of the East Wing.

1 18m. Go straight up the centre of the buttress on large well-worn holds.
2 18m. Continue up the centre of the buttress to the pinnacles on its summit.
3 6m. Climb over the pinnacles to belay on the left wall of the gully.
4 15m. Ascend the large rock steps on the left wall, and then step round the corner across a little groove (or reach this point from below – harder) to a leftwards traverse-line and so to the pinnacle ledge.
5 15m. Climb the steep wall behind the flake to a rightward-slanting gangway. Follow this to belay on a ledge below a chimney.
6 15m. Climb the chimney, which is difficult to start.

Variation
Kamikaze Finish   Very Severe
6a 18m. 4c. Climb the slabby wall above the last stance of *Flying Buttress* to an overhang. Move left and finish direct – a fine little pitch although high in the grade.

Castle Gully   60 metres   Difficult   (1892)
The first climb to be done on the Cromlech. It is the gully right of *Flying Buttress*, starting at a big cave. Easy climbing, and a little chossy, save for the thrutch up the last 3 metres.

René   30 metres   Very Severe 4c   (14.10.48)
A short but steep route of surprising difficulty. Start on the right wall of *Castle Gully* at about the same level as the summit of *Flying Buttress*. Climb a groove to a tree. Traverse left to a perched block. Climb the nose between the grooves and move left into a square-cut corner. Climb this awkwardly to an easy finish.

The Puerile Ticker   30 metres   Very Severe 4c   (7.10.78)
A pleasant climb. As for *René* to the tree. Follow the obvious groove to the right of *René*.

The Quaker   30 metres   Hard Very Severe 5a   (13.10.78)
Slight but interesting. As for *René* to the tree. Climb the rib on the right to a ledge at 6 metres below the groove of *The Puerile Ticker*. Climb a slab, and then layback diagonally rightwards on a dubious flake to a small ledge below an overhang. Go up, moving left under the overhang, and pull up onto the arête. Move right and finish direct.

Crampon Route   30 metres   Very Severe 4b   (1.10.89)
Takes the ridge of the pinnacle to the left of *Notanda*. Start just left of the ridge, on a small ledge. Climb the wall and ridge delicately for about 24 metres. Traverse below the final crack of *Notanda* and ascend a heathery groove with difficulty to finish.

Notanda   34 metres   Hard Severe   (7.9.52)
Right of *Castle Gully* lies the obvious descent gully with a prominent pinnacle on its right wall. Start at the foot of this.
1 17m. Climb the corner to a small ledge and high flake belay.
2 17m. 4a. Step up above the belay, and then move awkwardly round the arête to the left to gain the foot of a difficult heathery crack; climb this.

Climbs in and above the Valley
Tributary Crack   12 metres   Difficult   (21.10.39)
The normal escape route. Start a metre or so left of *Cenotaph Corner Finish*. Pleasantly climb the diagonal crack.

★Misty Wall   18 metres   E2 5b   (15.5.79)
A serious little pitch up the wall left of *Cenotaph Corner Finish*. Start just right of *Tributary Crack*. Go straight up the wall to a small sapling. Step right and continue to reach the short finishing crack.

Cenotaph Corner Finish   15 metres   Severe 3b   (21.10.39)
An enjoyable pitch with its crux in the initial moves. The line of *Cenotaph Corner* continues above The Valley as another large right-angled corner; start below this. Climb strenuously up the corner for 6 metres, and then break out left and traverse steeply to the left edge, or better still finish directly up the corner at Very Severe 4b.

★★Overlord   17 metres   E7 6c   (6.92)
The painfully obvious sharp arête just behind and left of the tree belay at the top of *Cenotaph Corner* requires razor-honed climbing skills, and is still awaiting a repeat. Pull directly onto the arête, using a suspect flake; this enables you to reach a poor peg and small wire runner. An intricate sequence leads to a second peg (hard to clip) and then a slight shake-out. A further hard move and a slap for jugs gives an exciting finish.

Gruel   17 metres   Hard Very Severe 5b   (22.10.78)
The finishing crack is particularly stubborn. Start in the corner to the left of *Ivy Sepulchre Crack*. Climb the corner-crack, and then struggle up the wide overhanging continuation crack to the left.

Ivy Sepulchre Crack   15 metres   Very Difficult
Steep, strenuous and on perfect rock; good value for its grade. The Pass equivalent of *Monolith Crack*. Start from the Valley, at the foot of the obvious crack/chimney splitting the wall above and left of the finish of *Ivy Sepulchre*. Enter the crack and battle to the top.

★★Rumblefish   15 metres   E7 6b   (18.6.86)
The left arête of *Grond* gives a lonely and vicious lead. Pull onto the arête from the right, and make hard moves past two *Rock 1s* with a long stretch up for a peg (which may prevent a crater). Arrange *RP* protection behind some suspect flakes. Difficult moves up to the overlap precede a swing left on side-pulls to reach the 'safety' of a Thank God hold. Finish more easily.

★★The Bastard Practice   15 metres   E7 6c   (7.8.89)
Immediately right of *Rumblefish*, the peg-protected overhanging rib (so cruelly cleaned and equipped in the mid-80s) gives a short but mighty pitch. Climb the wall, rib and groove with more than a little difficulty, passing three pegs en route. The first peg is unfortunately rather dubious.

★★★Grond   15 metres   E2 5b   (9.58)
An explosive enough test-piece to put a smile on the face of even the most jaded of gritstone addicts. Right of *Ivy Sepulchre Crack* is a clean-cut, overhanging, right-angled corner-crack. Climb the crack with either difficulty or ease. Superbly butch.

Grand   14 metres   E5 6c   (21.6.86)
The sharp right arête is climbed dynamically past two tied-off pegs and an
in-situ wire to where the angle eases (the crux is at 6 metres). Exit left or right.

The Mystery   21 metres   E1 5b   (9.8.65)
The obvious corner 12 metres right of *Grand*. Climb the technical corner,
passing an old sling.

★★The Monster   21 metres   E2 5c   (1972)
A very good crack pitch: technical, strenuous and insecure. Start at the foot
of *The Mystery*. Gain the crack by a rightward traverse on jams. Difficult
moves now lead to an exposed and precarious finish where the crack
widens. Exit just left of a perched block. A brute of a route.

Joshua's Traverse   36 metres   Hard Very Severe   (23.10.65)
A boulder-problem wall leads to an eminently forgettable middle section
and a fine finish up *Horseman's Route*. Useful as a finish to *Jericho Wall*.
Start in the Valley, from the block belay at the top of *Jericho Wall* and
below *The Monster*.
1 18m. 5b. Move down to the right and ascend the fierce little wall below
the right arête of *The Monster* to a ledge. Walk along this round the corner
to the right and along another ledge to belay at an impending crack.
2 18m. 4b. Continue traversing right below overhangs (good worm's eye
view of *Atomic Hot Rod*), to finish up the final corner of *Horseman's Route*.

Awesome   15 metres   E4 6a   (6.8.86)
The poorly protected overhanging groove between *Gross Encounters* and
The Monster is usually very dirty and may need a light cleaning by abseil.
Start from the long ledge on *Joshua's Traverse*. Struggle up the overhanging
groove, a truly awesome experience. Two *RP3s* and an *in-situ RURP* protect.

Gross Encounters   21 metres   E2 5b   (15.7.78)
This takes a direct line up through the crack just left of *Atomic Hot Rod*. Climb
the initial wall to a ledge below the impending crack – rather loose. Glorious
jamming up the perfect hand-crack leads all too quickly to an easy finish.

Atomic Hot Rod   21 metres   E5 6b   (11.4.80)
A ferocious finger-ripping test-piece slices the crag as if with a scalpel. The
advent of camming devices has made this a much easier lead nowadays,
but the crack still manages to slow down most would-be suitors. Start on the
Haven below the final pitch of *Horseman's Route*. Follow *Horseman's Route*
up the corner; then move left to the foot of the undercut and overhanging
finger-crack, the ascent of which proves to be somewhat trying.

Valley Crossings   150 metres   Very Difficult   (6.12.31)
A rather vegetated girdle of the cliff, that nevertheless takes in some
impressive scenery. Start from the top of *Spiral Stairs* and step across the
top of *Sabre Cut* to hollies. Continue up over large blocks, across a wide
chimney and then airily across to a delicate step down and so to the Valley
proper above *Cenotaph Corner*. Ramble up and across above *Ivy*

Sepulchre round the corner to below The Monster. Descend the sloping ledge. Either climb or abseil down to some trees, and then scramble across rightwards to finish up Flying Buttress.

Castell Graig (The Thumb) Castle Rock OS Ref 632 569

About 200 metres right of Dinas Cromlech, and on a level with its base, is a blunt needle of rock. This isolated monolith has five ways up it. On the long side is the superb **Thumb Crack** (Hard Very Severe 5a). Opposite this, on the short side, is a wide crack, **The Thumb** (Hard Severe 18.1.59), also the descent other than by abseil. The arête 3 metres right of the wide crack gives the fingery **Thumbling with My Wicklows** (11 metres E3 6a 6.84). **King Kipper** (11 metres E1 5b 1980) is the left arête on the short side, stepping in from the right. **Dead Presidents** (11 metres E5 6b 9.97) is a good little route, past two *in-situ* RPs, up the front face of the Thumb.

★**Never a Dull Moment**   18 metres   E3 5c   (11.10.86)
A fine pitch. Fifty metres right of The Thumb is a slender buttress reminiscent of Trevallen Pillar (in Pembroke). Pull up leftwards on a hollow flake to gain a crack. Move back right (crux) to a hold. Climb boldly up the right arête to the top.

Midway between the foot of Dinas Cromlech and Castell Craig, and at a slightly lower level, is a prominent white wall:

Drury's Drama   15 metres   Hard Very Severe 5b   (9.85)
A pleasant diversion if you've done everything else. Climb the central dog-leg groove. The walls have been inspected but have not succumbed yet.

A little hidden crag lies on the hillside up and right of Dinas Cromlech. It has the following route:

Raiders of the Lost Sac   24 metres   E1 5b   (5.93)
The obvious central line. The first section tackles a rather bold pocketed wall leading to a groove. Follow this to an overhang, and then pull through it to gain a crack leading to the top.

Esgair Maen Gwyn Area

Esgair Maen Gwyn (Scimitar Ridge)
                              White Rock Spur OS Ref 635 564
Further up towards Pen y Pass from Dinas Cromlech, a striking slabby ridge running up the hillside for around 150 metres has a rounded left flank and

an extremely steep east face plastered with hard routes. This is **Scimitar Ridge** (107 metres Severe), whose crest gives a rambling but quite testing traditional climb for its grade in marked contrast to some of the sterner contributions lurking down to the right. Once something of a climbing backwater, the crag now boasts some of the best single-pitch climbing in the Pass and is much larger close up than it would appear to be from a distance. Catching the morning sun (when it chooses to appear) and receiving little drainage, the east face is quick drying — by local standards. The rock is blocky and should be treated carefully although most of the climbs are sound. Some of the harder routes have *in-situ* peg protection, so it is probably advisable to check the state of the pegs prior to an ascent. On approach, the first route you come to is **Artemis** (46 metres Very Difficult 6.79), the tree-filled groove at the bottom left end of the crag. It provides a quick way up to the top.

Approach along the valley bottom before striking up screes to the base of the crag at about 270 metres (some 15 minutes from Pont y Gromlech). Unusually for the Pass, this is a south-east facing cliff, and it receives sunshine early in the morning; in the afternoon this allows you to benefit from shade on hot summer days. To descend, go up almost to the top of the ridge, traverse right and cautiously descend the gully that runs up under the east face.

★The Roc-Nest Monster   24 metres   E4 6a   (7.8.90)
To the right of *Artemis*, this takes the line of scoops in the wall left of the flying arête of *King Wad*. Climb 3 metres up *King Wad* (runners), and then span left on undercuts to a peg. Climb directly up on blind layaway holds (passing a further three pegs) to finish up either the groove or the arête left of *King Wad*.

★★★King Wad   30 metres   E6 6b   (18.6.87)
A classic, with superb moves and stunning positions up a detached flake, bulging wall and amazing flying arête. Start right of *Artemis*, and just left of the arête. Layback the hovering flake and climb the groove above to a thread. Continue up and right to a niche (wire); then bridge up to the base of a groove (peg). Now swing right onto the arête in a sensational position and bridge thin air for 8 metres, passing a peg, to a dynamic finish.

★Surgical Lust   30 metres   E7 6b   (27.5.87)
One of the most strenuous routes in the Pass. Up and right of *King Wad* is the large groove taken by *Chreon*. This fine, severely overhanging test-piece, which is 'massively serious', tackles a line based on the crack in the impending wall left of *Chreon's* blunt left arête. Follow the line of the crack (two pegs), climbing the wall either side of the crack as necessary. The climbing is extremely serious up to the first peg: it is also still quite possible to deck it from 21 metres.

Crackstone Rib (S, page 80) Carreg Wastad
Climbers: unknown   Photo: Martin Whitaker

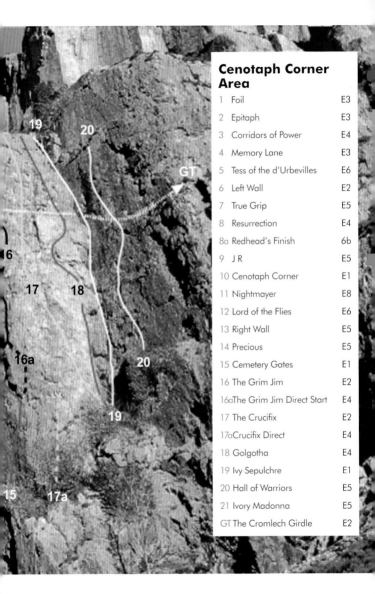

Left Wall (E2, page 101) Dinas Cromlech
Climber: Jill Blackburn   Photo: David Simmonite

★★★Tufty Club Rebellion   27 metres   E5 6b   (24.5.87)

Another excellent pitch based on the blunt arête left of *Chreon*, now harder since the demise of a hold. Start an 8 metres down and left of *Chreon*, at a tottering flake. Climb up and left to good holds on a dubious flake. Pull up slightly rightwards to a slot, and then go straight up to obvious undercuts. Using these, traverse boldly right around the arête to a peg. Move up and left onto the arête proper. The arête gradually eases to finish in a little black groove.

Troy   27 metres   E1 5b   (6.79)

An interesting and exposed climb, which provides a good introduction to the crag. It follows the crack in the left wall of the large open groove of *Chreon*. From the foot of the groove on *Chreon*, step left into the snaking crack and climb it past a few tufts of heather.

Variation

Direct Start   E3 6a

Climb straight up to the crack from the start of *Tufty Club Rebellion*.

★Chreon   26 metres   E2 5b   (6.79)

This fine, sustained pitch takes the large open groove with a sapling at 6 metres. Climb a square-cut groove, which becomes a thin crack, to an exposed finish.

Soupa Mario   27 metres   E6 6a   (7.99)

A direct eliminate line based on *Romany Soup*, which is just about protectable by small wires. Start 3 metres left of *Romany Soup*. Climb the open, black groove to a bold exit leftwards to join *Romany Soup* at its crux, and climb that route for 5 metres. Continue direct up the headwall where *Romany Soup* goes right.

★Romany Soup   27 metres   E5 6a   (6.87)

A bold and intimidating line requiring a certain amount of cunning to protect it. Start 1½ metres left of *Killerkranky*. Climb straight up into a steep black groove. Exit left at its top to an area of undercut flakes. Pull out right and over onto a slab, and then move up and right onto some blocks. Finish directly up the arête.

★★Killerkranky   27 metres   E4 6a   (4.10.86)

The hair-line crack just right of the large open groove of *Chreon* is reasonably protected, giving good climbing. A technically difficult start leads up to where the cliff leans back a little. Continue in the same line to reach a groove, which leads to the top.

★★The Kicker Conspiracy   27 metres   E5 6a   (8.87)

An impressive route taking the big curving line right of *Killerkranky* by some very bold climbing at the start. Start at a large pinnacle, move up, and then traverse left along a slab. Go up into a scoop just right of *Killerkranky*. Follow this with interest (technical and strenuous but well protected), past two pegs, to finish.

Esgair Maen Gwyn (Scimitar Ridge)

1 The Roc-Nest Monster   E4
2 King Wad   E6
3 Tuffy Club Rebellion   E5
4 Troy   E1

5 Chreon   E2
6 Killerkranky   E4
7 The Kicker Conspiracy   E5
8 Agamemnon   E1
9 Hermes   VS
10 Kitten versus Pig   E5
11 Achilles   E3

★★The Trumpet Blowers   24 metres   E7 6c   (10.6.92)
An outrageous pitch, both testing and technical. Start as for *The Kicker Conspiracy*. Follow *The Kicker Conspiracy* until it moves left along the slab. Climb boldly straight up (past a hidden small wire placement) to arrive at a peg. Move right to a second peg, and then ascend direct to a niche below an obvious groove. Swing right around the arête to gain another groove. Follow this, moving rightwards to the top.

★★The 39 Slaps   21 metres   E7 6b   (17.8.87)
Strenuous, dynamic and dramatic. Start just right of the last route, below a line of 6 pegs (not one of which is bombproof: they are either sawn-off, tied-off, something equally unreliable, or missing). A series of radical slaps up the leaning wall, allied to a strong sense of motivation, enable you to reach a large wire placement (quite handy for protecting the top moves).

Agamemnon   21 metres   E1 5b   (6.79)
Slabby columns lie against the main face, forming a central groove, which rises from left to right. Starting from the perched pinnacle, ascend diagonally right to an easy finish. Rather disappointing.

Scabbard   28 metres   Very Severe   (20.6.53)
The original way up the crag. Start at the foot of a crack about 6 metres up from *Agamemnon*.
1 14m. 4c. Climb diagonally along the crack and groove to a spike stance on *Agamemnon*.
2 14m. 4a. Traverse right along a sloping ledge and across the rib. Continue diagonally left into the corner, which is taken with care to finish.

Hermes   23 metres   Very Severe 5a   (6.79)
Interesting enough. Start 12 metres up the gully from the pinnacle of *Agamemnon*. Follow the shallow ramp up left, past a small gorse bush at 6 metres, to join *Agamemnon* at the top.

★Kitten versus Pig   24 metres   E5 6b   (16.6.87)
This route has a slightly scary start, but protection is better in the upper reaches. The start is 3 metres right of the start of *Hermes*: a pinnacle of tottering flakes below a dead-straight crack/seam. Climb the stubborn crack direct to finish on the right in an easy but mossy groove.

Mutiny on the Mouse Organ   24 metres   E4 6a   (16.8.87)
A good route following the narrow ramps through the steep walls right of the dead-straight crack/seam, and left of a large bulge with an obvious downward-pointing spike at its top, below which *The Bells…* starts. Climb up to and onto a mottled black and white ramp with some difficulty. From the top of this ramp, move left onto the next ramp and continue up to a ledge at its top left-hand side. Climb up the easier mossy ramp above to finish in the final groove of *Kitten versus Pig*.

The Bells, The Bells, The Bells   27 metres   E5 6b   (16.6.87)
Yet another taxing pitch. Start 9 metres right of the tottering flake pinnacle
(*Kitten versus Pig*), just left of a prominent bulge with a downward-pointing
spike at its top. Trend up rightwards over the bulge on huge undercuts to
gain the spike, and pull over for a rest. Continue up a leftward-leaning
ramp until it is possible to finish up a vague, steeper groove, stepping left
to avoid loose rock at the top.

At the top right side of the crag is a corner with a sharp right arête, which is
taken by *Xerxes*.

Achilles   21 metres   E3 5c   (6.79)
Steep, strenuous and serious. About 9 metres left of *Xerxes* sits a huge
perched boulder, about 9 metres up the face; start below and just to its
right. Climb diagonally left and across to get established on a hanging
fang of rock. Go up to, and climb delicately over, the Damoclean block.
Continue slightly shaken to the top.

Sparta   21 metres   E3 5c   (6.79)
A technical and sustained pitch. About 5 metres left of *Thermopylae* is a
smooth red scoop, which is gained by a traverse from the right and is
finished direct.

Thermopylae   18 metres   Hard Very Severe 5a   (6.79)
The disjointed crack left of *Xerxes* is followed with interest.

Xerxes   18 metres   E1 5b   (6.79)
Climb the corner, which proves deceptively tricky.

Down and right of the gully leading up to Esgair Maen Gwyn is:

Are You Having It about the Mammoths   14 metres   E4 6b (1994)
Often wet and a bit loose. Follow the obvious line past a series of pegs.

Pen Craig   Rock Top   OS Ref 637 564
This is the prominent crag a few hundred metres above Esgair Maen Gwyn
and round to the right. It is easily recognizable by its central corner-line.
Approach from Pen y Pass: take the 'Red Dot' path up the ridge overlooking
the Pass, go left to the col where the path steepens, and then descend slightly
and round via a well worn sheep track. South-west facing, the crag provides
a pleasant situation with unusual views of the Pass.

Animal House Blues   30 metres   Severe   (11.6.94)
A good interesting route on solid rock but with poor protection. The route
takes the large prominent corner/groove-line. Exit right and then back left
to belay.

Sam Tân and the Pet Man   23 metres   E2 5c   (11.6.94)
A good route climbing the prominent groove left of *The Locum Agency*.
Start by the arête and make some awkward moves up and right to get

established in the groove. Climb this past a jammed block, and move up and left to finish up a rib.

The Locum Agency   23 metres   Hard Very Severe 5b   (11.6.94)
Start 5 metres left of the corner below an overhang. Climb the overhang and crack above to finish up a small pillar.

Craig Rhug Bach   OS Ref 638 563
This tiny crag is on the 500-metre contour line. Located at the foot of a gully-line, the crag consists of a narrow rectangular slab/wall. Above and left of this the crag breaks down, forming the east wall of the gully. There is an old sheep fold/shepherds' shelter below and west of the gully.

Approach from Pen y Pass and walk down the Pass until it is possible to cross the Afon Nant Peris. Head diagonally up and leftwards across the scree slope, aiming towards the skyline well above Clogwyn Blaen Coed. There is a vague sheep-path that will take you right to the base of the crag after about 20 to 30 minutes. Just after reaching the crag the path becomes more obvious just after a steep grassy step and leads to the next crag in this area, Pen Craig. The path then continues above Esgair Maen Gwyn and on towards Dinas Cromlech. Descent is straightforward from here to the Boulders.

Tosspot   20 metres   Severe   (3.7.03)
From the centre of the slab/wall climb up until it is possible to step right into the shallow groove system, which is followed to the top.

Franco/Russian/Anglo/Welsh Pact 20 metres Very Severe 4b (3.7.03)
Start as for *Tosspot*. Climb the slab/wall direct, rejoining *Tosspot* at the top.

Clogwyn Blaen Coed   Wood End Cliff   OS Ref 637 562
This area consists of three small buttresses, which lie further up the Pass from Esgair Maen Gwyn, low down, and below the level of the road.

The first has a south-west facing, short wall below a grass ledge and a slabby top. It has one route, descent from which is by means of heathery slopes on either side.

Thor   42 metres   Severe   (28.9.52)
Start at the left side of the crag on a large ledge beneath the right-hand end of a heathery bay, by a dirty chimney.
1 18m. Ascend the chimney, exit on heather, and then take the rock rib towards an oak tree. Huge flake belay.
2 12m. The steep wall on the left is climbed to the highest ledge. Step left into a crack (dubious holds). Go up and round the corner on the left, and then follow a glacis to belay.
3 12m. Take the continuation of the glacis and then a pleasant slab on the right; 30 metres of scrambling with an optional slab on the right remain.

One hundred metres further along to the right lies the most distinctive and best of the crags – a huge roof on its front face is an obvious feature. The bay on the left side of the crag has a deep chimney in the back and a steep wall sporting two hollies, the lower one being by far the larger of the two. *Bryn Rhedyn* is on the left wall.

Elegant Inevitability   18 metres   E5 6a   (25.5.97)
This tackles the obvious arête left of *Bryn Rhedyn*, with some good climbing in exposed position and just about enough protection from samll wires.

Bryn Rhedyn   18 metres   E4 5c   (4.9.93)
Start at the lowest point of the steep left wall of the chimney. Take a central line up the wall, past good horizontal wires, and then up a bolder central section. Finish leftwards up a good crack.

★The Berlin Wall   18 metres   E3 5c   (12.89)
A slight but serious route, which takes the wall immediately right of the deep chimney. Take a direct line up the wall, using the arête occasionally as required. The only runner is in the horizontal break at around 6 metres, but there is an easing from around 12 metres to the top.

Holly Cracks   27 metres   Very Difficult   (7.4.52)
Start at a crack below and right of the lower holly.
1 18m. Go up cracks on the right of the tree (or the wall on its left) to a crevasse on the edge to the right. Climb a 5-metre glacis and a short wall to a large ledge below an overhang.
2 9m. Climb awkwardly up the centre of the wall to the overhang. Pull up to the crack. Traverse left on a small handhold and then go up left by two hard moves.

Codswallop Flobalobalobalob
                    14 metres   Hard Very Severe 5a (10.12.89)
Over to the left of the central overhang and just right of a holly is a prominent, short, sharp arête. Climb it direct.

Watts the Crack?   18 metres   E1 5c   (13.10.86)
The thin crack in the wall left of the main overhang gives the substance of the route, succumbing only to a good jamming technique.

Berlin Philharmonic   18 metres   E1 5c   (10.12.89)
Start 5 metres left of the trees below the roof, at a block below a steep slab perched on top of a short wall. From the block, lasso the spike at the top of the short wall for protection. Go directly up, via the rib and slab above (avoiding the right arête) to a large ledge. Another steep 8 metres straight up the groove lead to the finish.

The Sheepwalk   41 metres   Very Difficult   (7.4.52)
Start on the main wall facing the road, 3 metres left of a large tree that protrudes horizontally from under the overhang, at an inverted corner below a thin vertical crack.

1 12m. (of climbing). Go up the corner pulling out left. Traverse left for 3 metres, and then go up the edge for 2½ metres. Move back right and ascend a cracked V-groove (concealed hold on the right around the corner).

2 9m. Go easily up a crevassed ledge to the base of two cracks.

3 9m. Climb the right crack (in the corner) leading to the glacis of *Holly Cracks*.

4 11m. Climb the steep awkward crack directly above the large block on the right-hand end of the grass ledge (Severe), or finish up *Holly Cracks*.

Libel, Smears, and Slander   21 metres   E3 5c   (26.5.87)
Much more accommodating than its sister. Start under the large roof, as for *Language, Truth, and Logic*. Follow that route to the base of the layback flake. Bridge over left and climb the diagonal left-slanting crack.

Language, Truth, and Logic   21 metres   E4 6b   (24.4.87)
Start below the left-hand tree, under the large roof. Climb up to the tree and take the right-hand crack to the base of a groove/layback flake. Climb this, exiting left at the top (peg), and move right to enter a shallow groove leading up to the break. Move right to a peapod-shaped crack, and then traverse left to finish on a perched block.

★★**Marlene on the Wall**   23 metres   E4 6b   (25.6.86)
This takes the right-hand side of the overhang above the prominent tree. Climb the roof with difficulty and continue up the groove for 5 metres. Traverse 6 metres left to a crack splitting the wall. Ascend this to its top and traverse left again, for 5 metres, to finish by a perched block.

Felix the Crack   12 metres   E1 6a   (29.9.86)
The diagonal crack in the short white wall just above and right of the large overhang gives a pleasant little problem.

P F Putrid   12 metres   Very Severe 4b   (13.10.86)
The slanting crack just right of *Felix the Crack* is short but pleasant.

A further 60 metres up the Pass sits a small outcrop of short walls and large blocks which, although climbed on in the past, has little to commend it. A prominent arête here is **The Grim Dower Tower** (Hard Very Severe).

Bryn Gwynt   Wind Hill   OS Ref 639 565
This crag lies on the skyline some 250 metres directly above the Clogwyn Blaen Coed. It has three faces, which form a sort of pillar. The lower section is a semi-detached plinth.

Ridge Route   40 metres   Very Difficult   (10.78)
A direct line up the centre of the cliff. Start at the toe of the buttress, at a crack. Climb the crack for 9 metres to where it eases. Now take a groove near the left-hand end of the wall. From the top of this, a pleasant scramble leads up to finish.

Bryn Du   Black Hill   OS Ref 639 569

This crag lies well above and to the right (east) of Dinas Cromlech, at about 700 metres, on the ridge Glyder Fawr sends down to Pen y Pass. It is the only large crag in the area, its white broken south face being clearly visible from below the Cromlech. The cliff's right-hand face is steeper and gives several interesting routes.

The crag is well worth a visit to do some quality routes in a high-mountain setting. The aspect is sunny, the rock is generally of very good quality, and the climbing is only partly spoiled by the terrace-line.

The best approach is from Pen y Pass, crossing the ridge that runs down from Glyder Fawr above Cwm Ffynnon (35 minutes walk). It can also be approached in about 45 minutes from the Pen y Gwryd hotel. The crag lies some 600 metres to the east of the cliff shown as Bryn Du on the Snowdon OS 1:25,000 Outdoor Leisure Map.

Ragged Wall   84 metres   Very Difficult   (11.10.52)
This lies on the slabby south-west face of the crag. A pleasant route, vegetated at first but steepening and becoming more exposed higher up. Start at a heather depression, 45 metres from the left-hand end of the south face.
1 30m. Go up the depression on heathery rock to a large heather ledge on the left.
2 30m. Traverse right up the rake to where it ends in a corner.
3 24m. Climb over the belay block and down a little groove on the left. Traverse left across the wall, and near its end head for a sharp notch on the ridge skyline. A fine open pitch.

The following routes all lie on the steeper, south-east face:

Geriatricks   67 metres   E2 5c   (15.9.02)
This generally follows the arête left of *Genesis* and then the fine headwall above. Start 6 metres left of *Genesis*.
1 30m. 5c. Follow a rightward line of incuts, and then go up to a quartzy ledge. Move up just left of the arête on awkward slopy flakes to a *Friend* placement in an undercut. Up and left is a rest on good footholds. A long hard move gains a precarious exit onto a sloping ledge on the arête. Climb the flaky wall to belay as for *Genesis*.
2 37m. 4c. As for *Genesis* to the top of the pedestal. The smooth headwall above is easier than it looks, so head up left boldly and then up and right to a prominent square niche. Easier climbing remains up the flaky wall to heathery ledges. *RPs* are needed on this pitch.

Genesis   70 metres   Very Severe   (18.5.73)
Not such a strong line as some of the other routes, as it cunningly avoids
the challenge of the upper wall. Start at the left-hand end of the face,
below an obvious steep nose of clean rock. A cairn marks the start, left of
the crackline.
1 27m. Climb the grooved rib left of the crack to a small ledge. Continue
up the corner with difficulty to another small ledge. Step left onto the
overhanging wall and make an awkward move up to better holds. These
lead to a good stance.
2 6m. Go easily rightwards up the rake to a stance with a flake belay
below a very steep smooth wall.
3 37m. Follow the line rightwards to a short corner, which is taken to a small
ledge below the smooth section of the wall. Climb the wall just left of another
corner, with several steep awkward moves. Finish up an obvious recess.

The combination of pitch 1 of *Genesis* and pitch 2 of *Geriatricks* gives the
best route on the cliff at a surprisingly amenable Hard Very Severe grade.

Josh   82 metres   Hard Very Severe   (26.8.02)
The steep wall and corner left of Jeremiah give a good route. Start on a
big block 6 metres left of *Jeremiah*.
1 37m. 4c. Pull up right and follow the rightward-trending flakes for 8
metres. A reach to a good pocket leads to the corner-line left of the prow.
Follow this to the left end of the shattered ledge, and then pull steeply over
the left side of the quartzy overhang. Belay as for *Jeremiah*.
2 8m. Walk left round the corner to flake belays.
3 37m. 5a. Climb the smooth corner with difficulty to a pedestal on the
right. Go over the bulge above, and follow flaky cracks to the top.

Jeremiah   74 metres   Very Severe   (16.6.73)
A steep route, but a lot easier than it looks. Start 3 metres left of the
prominent crackline (*Jonah*).
1 37m. 4c. Climb the steep wall to a small ledge. Step right and
continue on good but slightly mossy holds just left of the rib. Move left at
the top onto a shattered ledge. Traverse right on the ledge to avoid an
overhang; then go back left onto a good grass stance below a very small
overhang split by a crack.
2 37m. 4a. Easily climb the overhang and follow the slabby crack,
passing a prominent finger of rock on the left of a steeper, smoother
section. Climb this at the left-hand end to the top.

Jonah   74 metres   Very Severe   (19.5.73)
This is a prominent crackline approximately in the centre of the cliff, which
continues in the upper section. Start at the foot of the crack, in a small bay.
1 37m. 4c. Climb the crack (strenuous) to a niche. Move right onto the
arête and step back left into the crack above an overhang. Stance and
belays on the right.
2 37m. Gain the foot of the crack via easy slabs, and follow the line to
the top.

Joe   74 metres   Hard Very Severe   (26.8.02)
This follows the crackline on the right side of the prow between *Jonah* and *Joshua*.
1 37m. 4c. Gain the crack by some tricky, steep moves and follow it, with a hard move over the final bulge. Belay on flakes 6 metres higher
2 37m. 5a. Right of the crack of pitch 2 of *Jonah* is a buttress with a shallow groove above a grass ledge, just right of a patch of quartz. Bold moves up the groove (block runner on the right) lead to a slab. Follow the corner-line to finish left of the double-pointed quartz overhang. Not a well-protected pitch.

Joshua   74 metres   Very Severe   (19.5.73)
Six metres right of *Jonah* is another crackline.
1 37m. Climb the crack, moving left at the top onto a good ledge with twin cracks above. Take the right-hand crack steeply on good holds.
2 37m. Finish easily up broken slabs.

Claude   55 metres   Hard Severe   (26.8.02)
Something of a filler-in at this end of the crag, and not as satisfying as it appears. At the right-hand end of the crag is a prominent triangular overhang about 18 metres up, above a grass ledge. Start below this, at a big block (cairn).
1 18m. 4a. Climb the pillar to a wide crack, which is climbed to a belay below the continuation corner.
2 37m. 4b. The corner, left of the prominent overhang, is followed with interest to flake runners. Trend to the right and follow easier ground to the top.

The Teryn Bluffs

These fine little cliffs lie in the upper part of Cwm Dyli, just below and south of Llyn Teryn. The pipeline from Llyn Llydaw runs between two hummocks. The nearer, on the Pen y Pass side of the pipes, and easily visible from the Miners' Track, is Clogwyn Pen Llechen. On the far (south) side is Craig Aderyn. Both crags can be reached in less than 30 minutes from Pen y Pass and are useful for a short day or in bad weather.

Craig Aderyn (The Teryn Slab)   Bird Crag   OS Ref 639 543
The main feature of this crag is the fine south-east facing slab at about the 320-metre level, which catches the morning sun. Descent from the top of the arête, where most of the climbs finish, is by making a slightly descending traverse right for 12 metres to reach the top of a low-relief rib. Follow this carefully down and round to the left (facing out) and then back right below a short rock wall (with a rowan tree and a spiky stump) to a slippery, slabby step leading to a short grassy gully and the foot of the crag.

Ash Tree Rib   54 metres   Difficult   (20.8.48)
The broken buttress forming the left boundary of the slab. Start at the foot
of the rib.
1 18m. Keep on the right up broken rock to a ledge at 9 metres.
Continue up to a ledge. Traverse 6 metres left, and then go diagonally
back right to a spike belay at the foot of a rock section.
2 18m. A short overhanging chimney is climbed awkwardly to a
shattered ledge. Traverse 6 metres left, and then go diagonally back right
to a spike belay at the foot of a rock section.
3 18m. Ascend airily up the arête on good holds (steep) to the top.

Broad Marsh   Vegetably Severe   (20.8.48)
This interesting ramble across the left side of the cliff is possibly the most
vegetated climb in North Wales, and has an amazing variety of plants.
From the top of *Ash Tree Rib*, walk left across a broad grassy ledge with
fallen columns. After a narrowing, stroll across marsh grass below
overhangs to reach a narrow undercut ramp. Make a hard move up onto
it, and struggle along left through dense undergrowth to the clutching
embrace of some ancient stunted oaks, the Coppice. Ascend a mossy
3-metre wall on jugs, and then a quick move up a mossy slab leads to
grassy scrambling.

Treasury Climb   48 metres   Severe   (7.10.24)
Similar climbing to *Via Media*, but a bit mossy and often greasy. Start on
the left, immediately right of a mossy patch.
1 30m. Follow a sloping ledge up to the left; then go over a tiny overlap,
keeping just right of the mossy patch. At 18 metres, make a rightward
traverse to easier climbing just beyond a grassy rake and so to the *Via
Media* belay ledge.
2 18m. Finish as for *Via Media*, or go steeply up grass and break out left
after 6 metres to join *Ash Tree Rib*.

Via Media   48 metres   Very Severe   (24.8.25)
A very good route up the centre of the slab, though most of the difficulties
may be avoided at Severe standard. Start in the centre of the slab below
an easy gangway.
1 30m. 4b. Follow the gangway up right to its apex at 6 metres, and
then go straight up to reach a heathery break just left of a small gorse
bush at 15 metres. Continue direct for about 11 metres until shallow
cracks lead to a small ledge on the left in another 5 metres.
2 18m. Traverse right for a short way, and then move up to a
leftward-slanting crack. Follow this to good holds and ledges. Spike belay
at the top of the arête.

Jacob's Ladder   37 metres   Very Difficult   (7.10.24)
Artificial in line but good climbing. Start 5 metres left of the right arête.
Ascend direct to quartzy holes at 14 metres. Continue up parallel to the
arête via a weakness leading to two small scoops to join *The Arête Climb*;
finish up this.

★★Jacob's Media   50 metres   Hard Severe   4a
The best outing on the slab: a combination of the previous two routes. A 50-metre rope is necessary unless the team is prepared to climb together for a metre or two. Follow *Jacob's Ladder* for about 24 metres. Trend left and follow the left-slanting crack to the apex of the slab (pitch 2 of *Via Media*).

The Arête Climb   52 metres   Difficult   (1913)
A pleasant and popular route. Start at the extreme right-hand edge of the slab.
1 30m. Ascend the right-hand arête and go into a small groove at 3 metres. At 8 metres take the groove to the left under the overhang, and then follow the right arête of the slab, past possible stances, to a better stance on the arête at 30 metres.
2 22m. Continue easily up the arête to a good ledge at 14 metres (optional belay). Small stance and spike belay 8 metres higher at the top of the arête.

Subsidiary Slab   55 metres   Moderate
Start below the subsidiary slab to the right of the main slab.
1 26m. From the foot of the slab, straightforward moves lead up past a sapling to a good rowan tree.
2 29m. Climb up leftwards onto the arête. Follow this pleasantly to belay near the top on a large ledge, or better at a small stance with a good spike 8 metres higher, at the top of the arête.

Clogwyn Pen Llechen   Slabby Top Crag   OS Ref 641 545
This little cliff is the nearer of the Teryn Bluffs to the Miners' Track. It has two faces: one looking south, which overhangs; and the other looking east, which lies back. Unfortunately, both are rather scruffy by modern standards, with copious amounts of vegetation growing on many of the ledges and carpets of moss covering the slabby areas; these receive a lot of drainage and require at least a week of good weather to dry out. However, when dry, the rock offers good friction and sports mainly incut holds. In contrast, the South-East Corner provides a classic Very Difficult climb, which is quick drying, on good rock and with little vegetation. Well worth a visit on a short day or afternoon.

The South Face
Ledge Climb   39 metres   Very Difficult (Very Dirty)   (11.5.43)
An awkward and unpleasant climb, which accepts the vegetable challenge of the left side of the face. Start 12 metres left of the South-East Corner, in a vague corner 8 metres left of a rowan tree growing 3 metres up the face, and directly below an oak tree 12 metres higher.
1 27m. Gain a ledge at 2 metres, and then go left up a little grassy groove to a second ledge. Traverse awkwardly back right for 9 metres to a 3-metre leaning flaky corner. Climb this and gain the ledge on the right. Step back left and climb a heathery slab to a stance. A pitch with more than a smidgeon of loose rock.

2 12m. Ascend a short overhanging wall on the left, and then move left to a whitened tree stump. Continue in the same direction for a short way to a finish up over grass ledges.

Little Audrey   61 metres   Very Severe   (22.8.53)
This takes the diagonal gangway running up the left edge of the steep wall on the right-hand side of the south face. Start 50 metres left of *Winthrop Young's Climb*.
1 12m. Scramble easily up heather to a ledge level with the foot of the gangway, and belay on the right.
2 15m. Move awkwardly onto the gangway. Step right and ascend delicately, moving back left to an obvious recess.
3 34m. Climb the crack on the right of the gangway to gorse. Traverse left and go up diagonally left with difficulty to finish.

Persons Unknown   46 metres   E4 6a   (19.7.96)
The obvious line in the middle of the cliff has finally gone free. Start up ledges to gain two pegs (one old, the other newer). Follow the ramp diagonally rightwards to a niche, and then go back left along a crackline (passing numerous rusty pegs) to gain easy ground leading to the top.

The South-East Corner
Winthrop Young's Climb   69 metres   Very Difficult   (1913)
The best climb on the cliff. The hard section is very short. Start above a prominent quartz boulder at the south-east corner of the cliff, by a short grassy chimney on the left of the rib.
1 12m. Take the chimney for 5 metres, and then make an awkward step left onto a detached block. A pleasant traverse left along a diagonal crack leads to a stance.
2 21m. Cross easy slabs on the left to a large detached block on the skyline.
3 15m. Surmount the block and go easily up to a broad terrace.
4 12m. From the far end of the terrace, climb a short and strenuous flake crack (much harder than anything else on the route). Continue up ledges to a belay.
5 9m. Finish up the clean rib on the right.

The Grey Rib   60 metres   Difficult   (17.8.15)
This goes up the left side of the mossy slab. After the first 24 metres, which are taken on the rib, continue up to a grassy bay. Escape across to the left via some piled-up stones and scramble up to finish.

Two Tree Route   60 metres   Difficult   (20.8.48)
A mediocre route, with an airy finish and only one remaining tree. Follow *The Grey Rib* for 24 metres and continue up to the grassy bay. Climb a steep groove on the right, past a small tree, and continue in the same line to the summit.

The East Face

The routes on this face are approached from the right. The clean slab seen in profile from the Miners' Track divides this face, which has steep subsidiary cliffs below it. The crossing between the foot of the slab and the top of the lower rocks is awkward and hazardous, and it is probably easier to go right down to the bottom.

Plato's Cave   60 metres   Very Severe (1 pt aid)   (1987)
An intriguing line up steep rock about 30 metres left of the central slab. A hawthorn stands at the foot of the crag with a grassy slope above. Start at a slanting overlap marking the left edge of a mossy slab. The 'cave' is a niche in the blunt arête high up right. It holds a small sapling.
1 30m. Follow the crack, with a few moves out on the slab, until it is possible to traverse right and climb a short corner on wedged blocks. Move right to where the ledge ends at a short rib.
2 30m. Step around the rib and move up right, entering the niche with an awkward mantelshelf. Surmount the bulge (crux) using a peg for aid, and continue up the steep slab on good holds to reach a long ledge below broken rock. Traverse right along the ledge to a summit cleft.

Pastoral   54 metres   Hard Severe   (23.9.72)
After a heathery, and annoyingly indirect, start the route gets onto good rock and a fine finish. It uses the shallow gully-like feature just left of the central slab, reaching it and finishing by leftward excursions. At the foot of the crag, left of centre, is a hawthorn with a grassy slope above. Start from the ledges at the top right-hand corner of this slope, at a break below and right of the hanging gully.
1 30m. Climb up to a leftward traverse across a long narrow heather ledge (beneath the gully) to reach the rib on the left. Climb this via a steep mantelshelf and go up the slab on the left. Traverse back right into the gully and climb it on good holds to a stance 3 metres short of the steeper rocks; awkward belays.
2 24m. Step left into the corner and go up to a big block. Move round the rib on the left and step across onto a bottomless slab, with two small incuts before good holds are gained. Finish direct.

Tongue and Groove   65 metres   Hard Severe   (20.9.72)
A good route on sound rock taking the right-hand side of the large central slab. Three starts have been made, that described first being the easiest. Above and right of the large slab is a spreading oak tree. Start at a suspect flake directly below the tree. There is a large hanging flake 9 metres higher.
1 9m. Follow the rock ledge to the left until an awkward move gains a steep little corner. Ascend this and move left to awkward nut belays at the foot of the slab.
2 23m. Traverse right to a (belayless) ledge. Climb the left-slanting groove until it finishes; then cross the right wall on hollow flakes to ledges and a block below the oak tree.

3 18m. From the block stride left onto the slab and follow a line of big holds leftwards to the top. From here escape is possible along the terrace to the right, or via the grassy gully on the left. However, the slab above gives the best finish.
4 15m. Climb the slab directly or traverse onto the right arête at mid height.
Variations
1a Original Start 24m. Very Severe. From the suspect belay flake, climb directly into a short groove and mantelshelf onto a traverse-line. Move left to the belayless ledge of pitch 2.
1b Aboriginal Start Very Severe. The stance at the top of the first pitch can also be reached from the start of *Pastoral*.
3a Original Finish. Climb up through the tree, past a small rowan, to the foot of the upper slab.

After Eden   42 metres   Very Severe   (1.11.72)
Steep and strenuous. Towards the right-hand end of the crag is a big block overhang which caps a right-facing corner-crack, the substance of the middle pitch. Start from large blocks at the foot of a leftward-slanting grassy break.
1 18m. Scramble up the gully for 6 metres, and go along the upper ledge to the right to reach an undercut niche holding a perched block directly below the big overhang. Using the block, surmount the bulge. Vegetated climbing leftwards leads to the foot of the crack.
2 9m. Climb the crack to the overhang and a sitting belay by a perched block.
3 15m. Cross the ledge to the right and with a delicate step join the finish of *Ann Cornwall's Climb*.

Ann Cornwall's Climb   24 metres   Severe   (24.10.72)
This climb takes the centre of the recessed wall at the right-hand end of the face. The left side of this wall is bordered by a large corner-crack with a block overhang above. The right side is also bordered by a short corner-crack; start at the foot of this. Walk along the ledge to the left for 5 metres, climb a shallow groove and step onto the ledge on the left (possible belays). Go up to the right, moving right and then back left to pass over the bulge. Follow the left-slanting groove and finish up a little wall.

Lichen Arête   37 metres   Very Difficult
A somewhat artificial route on the extreme right of the East Face. Start left of and lower down than *East Ridge*. The line follows mossy slabs, heather, a short wall and a grooved arête.

East Ridge   24 metres   Easy
The right arête of the East Face shows signs of having been used from time immemorial.

Carreg Gwalch   Hawk Crag   OS Ref 643 554

These little crags lie just above the PyG Track, about 500 metres from Pen y Pass. They have yielded several routes over the years, the best of which are fully described. A few scruffy lines remain for the climber to rediscover.

On the slabby wall to the left of *Cul-de-Sac* lies a prominent crack, the old classic climb **The Gauge** (18 metres Difficult 20.8.25). Immediately to its right, the wall offers the somewhat lichenous **Micrometer** (18 metres Very Severe 4c 25.8.64).

Cul-de-Sac   30 metres   Hard Very Severe 5a   (c.1964)
Nearest the path is a sombre-looking crag with a steep front face. This good climb takes the prominent damp green flake overhang on its left side, and it is worth waiting for a dry spell. Start below and left of the overhang, in the corner. Climb awkwardly up to the right, normally damp and dirty. Turn the overhang and finish more easily up the fine corner-crack.

Pyg in the Middle   42 metres   Hard Very Severe   (26.8.64)
An interesting climb that wanders across the front of the buttress, with an airy finish. Start below the arête on the left side of the cliff, just right of *Cul-de-Sac*.
1 30m. 5a. Ascend the arête for 8 metres and traverse right into a V-scoop. Take the diagonal crack in the back of this rightwards and around the corner. Continue along the crack, below roofs, to a hanging belay at the top of the slab.
2 12m. 5b. Pull out over the roof and finish delightfully up the crack.

★Into the Groove   18 metres   E4 6c   (1988)
A technically precocious and strenuous little pitch. Start to the right of the previous routes. Enter the large, central V-groove, and then move left up the slab to gain its left arête and a good rest by a prominent block (thin tape runner and a peg in a recess). Move right along the obvious crack and, having clipped another peg, enter a hanging groove round to the right. Sustained climbing up the groove/crack leads to a distinguished finishing move.

Summer Groove   15 metres   E3 6a   (3.7.01)
The obvious groove-line about 6 metres right of the central V-groove. Follow cracks to a roof and step left into a hanging groove, which leads to the top.

About 100 metres further up the hillside, near the crest of the ridge, is a cliff with a very steep wall on its left and a gentle right-hand flank.

The Green Beam   27 metres   E2 5c   (31.7.92)
A reasonable route. Start just right of the large flake, below and left of the finishing crack of *Shadow of Youth*. Climb direct past a good runner to a

sloping ledge (runners). Climb a bold sloping section up and then rightwards for 6 metres to the top crack of *Shadow of Youth*. Finish up this.

Shadow of Youth   27 metres   E2 5c   (20.6.85)
A stiff proposition taking the diagonal crack in the centre of the wall. Start below this. Attain the ledge at 3 metres. Go steeply up via flakes, moving left to a layback-flake and small ramp (crux). Continue more easily to finish via a scoop. Excellent strenuous climbing.

Captain's Bluff Direct   34 metres   Very Difficult   (20.8.25)
The original route of the crags, once popular with Pen y Pass *habitués*. The line follows the arête of the buttress; start at its foot. Climb the arête (steep to start) and continue on improving holds in a delightful position. An alternative starts up a groove just round to the left.

Well round to the right of the *Cul-de-Sac* crag is a large but more broken cliff (OS Ref 641 553) sitting in its own little cwm. The ancients have scrambled here since at least the 1920s and probably before that. In fact it is possible to climb almost anywhere at Very Difficult. One route has been recorded:

Moch Up   45 metres   Very Difficult   (7.9.52)
Start well round to the right, at the top of the scree, level with some large boulders.
1 15m. Ascend the slab to a small heather ledge.
2 18m. Gain a ledge on the right. Continue right and enter a hollow (possible belay). Move up left, and traverse the sloping ledge leftwards. Climb a small groove to an awkward stance.
3 12m. Climb up to the overhang line. Move right along to a jutting ledge, where a steep move gains easy ground.

Nearer Pen y Pass, and adjacent to the PyG Track are many traditional problems such as The PyG Track Slab, which one of the old pioneers, Geoffrey Winthrop-Young (who had a wooden leg), could only surmount with a flying (hopping) start.

Clogwyn Gafr (Craig Fach)
Goat Crag (Little Crag) OS Ref 634 554

This impressive little cliff, until the 80s much neglected, lies on the 400-metre contour line, about one mile west of Pen y Pass Youth Hostel, just below the PyG Track. It can be approached from Pen y Pass or from a small lay-by directly below the crag (space permitting).

The crag stands about 30 metres high. Its steep walls of rough, sharp rock are cut at half height by a line of black square overhangs, which enhance its sombre appearance. Facing north-west, the crag only receives the sun in the

Clogwyn Gafr (Dinas Fach)

1 Satsuma Special   E3
2 Diapason   E1
3 Outspan   E5
4 Hanging Flake Route   VS
5 Satsumo Wrestler   E6
6 The Nectarine Run   E5

7	Sacred Idol	E3
8	Pulsar	E3
9	The Slash	HVS
10	Clingstone	E3
11	Buck and the Noise Boys	E1

afternoons and evenings, and is a good spot on a hot summer's day. The climbs all tend to follow features such as cracks or grooves. Some, which were originally done with aid, now go free to give reasonably well-protected technical problems; these lie in the steeper central area. On the left flank of the cliff are short amenable climbs, which are suitable for beginners. A descent can be made down the slopes on either side of the cliff.

Ruddy Groove   14 metres   Difficult   (11.8.55)
Well worth doing. Start at the left-hand side of the cliff, 9 metres left of the huge black overhang. Climb the delightful groove, which has runners in its cracked red right wall.

Alex in Wonderland   14 metres   Severe 4b   (8.8.88)
Pleasant climbing up the blunt rib and cracks to the right of *Ruddy Groove*.

Preliminary Groove   14 metres   Severe   (11.8.55)
A good introduction to the grade. Start 3 metres right of *Ruddy Groove*. Go up to the bulge at about 5 metres. Make an awkward pull round this, and then finish more easily up the slab.

Mur y Fester   18 metres   Severe   (11.8.55)
Good moves and positions. Start between *Preliminary Groove* and the groove to the right, below a smooth wall. Climb directly up the wall via twin cracks, which start 6 metres up.

Staircase Groove   18 metres   Very Difficult   (3.1.55)
A reasonable starter route. Start just to the left of the huge overhang, below a groove. Go pleasantly up the blocky groove on good holds to a steep finish.

The Gangway   24 metres   Very Difficult   (7.55)
Another fine introduction to climbing. Start 5 metres right of *Staircase Groove*, below the centre of the hanging flake. Step up, and then follow the diagonal ramp leftwards to finish up *Staircase Groove*.

★Satsuma Special   30 metres   E3 5c   (23.6.92)
A fine route at its standard. Follow *Diapason* up and through the roof, but move immediately back left on small positive pockets until a long stretch gains a large pocket on the left. Tricky moves up and a foot-change in the aforementioned pocket lead to yet another stretch left to a good spike. Finish up the rib. The route can be split at the *Diapason* stance to avoid rope drag.

★Diapason   30 metres   E1   (23.8.64)
A good little route with an intimidating first pitch and much more open climbing above. Start below the huge black overhang, 5 metres right of *Staircase Groove* (as for *The Gangway*).
1 15m. 5c. Climb up to the foot of the corner-crack, which is followed to the roof. Cross the 2-metre roof with difficulty (easier for the small) to gain

a sloping ledge on the wall above. Move up to the right end of the ledge. Nut and cam belays.

2 15m. 5b. Climb the steep crack past a peg at 3½ metres (awkward). Continue up to a small pocket. Climb diagonally right, delicately, to the steep arête. Move right around this 3 metres from the top to finish up a crack.

★Outspan   24 metres   E5 6b   (22.6.88)
A direct approach to the final crack of *Diapason*. Ascend leftwards to a large pocket/hole, then move up right to a hair-line crack and a peg. A difficult section up the crack leads to better holds and the finish of *Diapason*.

Hanging Flake Route   27 metres   Very Severe 4c   (24.12.55)
A pleasant climb which follows the right edge of the huge hanging flake. Unfortunately, the lower section is rather dirty. Start from the top of a flake, by a rock spike directly below the right end of the flake. Climb the steep dirty slab and pull round into the crack that bounds the right edge of the hanging flake. Follow this awkwardly to a heathery ledge. Continue up the crack to the top.
Variation
More pleasant. Start 3 metres further right, climb a cracked red wall to a heather ledge, and traverse left to reach the crack.

★Satsumo Wrestler   34 metres   E6 6b   (27.4.87)
A fearsome outing, which utilises the obvious gap between *Hanging Flake Route* and *The Nectarine Run*. A fitting companion to the latter. Start left of *The Nectarine Run*, below a crack and climb it to a grassy ledge. Bridge up the groove above and enter the crack, exiting right onto a ramp (rest). Exit up a crack by bold and tenuous moves (crux) to reach another rest and a poor wire. Move left and continue up, sustained and serious, to finish.

★★★The Nectarine Run   37 metres   E5 6b   (25.6.86)
Hard, technical climbing up the wall, groove and roof left of the left-facing corner in the centre of the crag. Start just left of the corner. Climb the lower wall to a *RURP* just below the short hanging groove. Layback into this from the right and ascend it with difficulty. Make committing moves back down and right to a foothold just above the lip of the roof. A scary high step and rockover up the wall above gains easier ground, a flake and a good cam placement just above. Finish direct.

★★Sacred Idol   30 metres   E3 6a   (9.5.84)
A brilliant, very sustained pitch, which gives thin technical climbing up the left-facing square-cut corner in the centre of the crag. Start below the corner. Climb precariously up the white right-angled corner.

★★Pulsar   30 metres   E3 6a   (26.5.74)
This excellent crack provides a superb test-piece of arm-barring and finger-jams. Start 2½ metres right of *Sacred Idol*, at a thin vertical crack. Ascend to the overhang, where the crack becomes difficult. Continue up,

the crack proving more stubborn than it looks, to a ledge at about 21 metres. Traverse right a short way and finish direct.

★Red Giant   24 metres   E4 6a   (30.6.88)
A stiff pitch, high in the grade, taking the wall right of *Pulsar* before crossing it to tackle the obvious direct finish. Start up the crack on the right and then move left on the obvious holds. Step up to gain the crack, which is followed on user-friendly holds to a junction with *Pulsar*. Finish fiercely up the headwall (past one ancient and two newish pegs).

The Slash   30 metres   Hard Very Severe 5a   (7.57)
A fine little climb on excellent rock. Start 5 metres right of *Pulsar* and climb the obvious chimney to a ledge. At the back of the ledge, on the left, is a thin corner-crack. Climb this to a small roof and move left (hard) to another ledge. Continue up the wall above, trending slightly left to finish.

Clingstone   30 metres   E3 6b   (8.8.88)
The difficulties are short but sharp. Climb the first thin overhanging crackline right of *The Slash*; difficult moves up the brown bulge lead to easier climbing.

Buck and the Noise Boys   30 metres   E1 5b   (8.8.88)
An amenable route starting under some large flakes, about 6 metres right of *The Slash*. Climb the flakes to reach a steep wall with a flat-bottomed crack. Follow this to a ramp, step left and finish up the pocketed wall and slabs above.

The Last Outpost   23 metres   Very Severe 4b   (5.75)
A slight and somewhat broken route. Start 20 metres right of *Pulsar*, at the foot of a steep slab. Easy climbing up the slab leads to a tree and a grassy ledge. From the left end of the ledge, step up onto a large block. Good jams up the steep crack on the right quickly lead to the top.

The Craig Fach Girdle   95 metres   E3/A3   (5.67)
A sustained expedition, which is described in its most free form to date. A completely clean ascent will prove very hard indeed. Start at the left-hand base of the cliff.
1 21m. 4b. Make an ascending rightward traverse to a stance on *Preliminary Groove*.
2 14m. A1/5c. Move right a short way and descend slightly. Continue right to join *Diapason* (A1). Climb the roof of *Diapason*, and continue to the stance at the end of its first pitch.
3 15m. 5b. Make a hard move right and hand-traverse the horizontal crack to the arête. Climb this and the crack of *Hanging Flake Route* to its top.
4 21m. 5a/A3. Stride right to a peg. Move right and downwards to a flake with a peg. Tension right and down for 5 metres to reach a thin traverse-line with difficulty. At head level there is a very thin crack formed by a rock overlap. Using thin blades in the crack for fingerholds and tension from the rope, traverse right to a hanging belay on *Sacred Idol*.

5 12m. 6a. Climb *Sacred Idol* to the top of its overhanging section and an awkward stance.
6 12m. 5a. Traverse right along the obvious line, and then go up to gain the arête. Finish up this.

Craig Cwm Beudy Mawr
Big Cowshed Cwm Crag OS Ref 628 556

This crag is situated on the north-east slope of Crib Goch, high up in the left-hand corner of the cwm. It is most easily approached from Pen y Pass along the PyG Track. After about one mile, just beyond a long flight of steps where the path turns left to cross Bwlch y Moch, contour across the hillside for about a quarter of a mile to a small cwm with a broken rib of quartz-marked rock, which is **Ysgar – The Quartz Rib**, a fine 60-metre Moderate. Either climb this, scramble up for a further 25 metres and traverse round to the upper left side of the crag, or move across at a lower level to a point below the crag. Alternatively, you can make an excellent day by visiting Dinas Bach first, then Craig Cwm Beudy Mawr, and finishing with a pleasant walk to Crib Goch – sadly this itinerary no longer seems very popular.

Bounded on the right by a deep wet gully, the cliff rises from right to left parallel to the scree slope, a long tapering mass of rock which loses itself in the hillside on the eastern side. It is about 75 metres high. In the central part the rock is quite clean and solid, but it becomes more broken on either side. The main features are a series of overhangs on the left and a smooth slab on their right. Lower down the hillside is the gently rising V-shaped *Dodo Gully,* which steepens higher up. There is a stream running down it. To its right lie two large broken buttresses, *Dodo Buttress* and *Minor Buttress*. Between these is a large expanse of heather and broken rock, which provides a descent.

The climbs are described from **right to left**, in the order by which they are approached as you go up the scree slope.

Minor Buttress 55 metres Moderate
On the extreme right of the cliff, a slabby buttress on the left of a watery gully gives a pleasant enough route. Start at the left edge of the buttress and follow the rib overlooking the gully as closely as possible.

Dodo Buttress 81 metres Difficult
A pleasant route up the broken buttress right of *Dodo Gully*, reminiscent of the climbs on the East Face of Tryfan. Start where the buttress meets the scree, just below the gully.
1 15m. A short wall leads to a grassy slab. Climb this to a large grassy stance below an overhanging wall.

2 18m. Climb the short slab on the left to a ledge at 6 metres. Ascend the rib steeply for a short way. A small wall at 15 metres leads to a stance below a prominent nose.
3 12m. Go round the right of the nose to a grassy ledge.
4 21m. Cross heather to the next rock rib. Climb this, keeping left.
5 15m. Go slightly left over perched blocks into a shallow groove. Good holds abound, and the angle soon eases.

Dodo Gully   76 metres   Difficult   (1909)
A traditional expedition with a good water supply. Keep to the bed of the gully and take the right-hand branch.

Slab Variant   55 metres   Very Difficult   (1910)
At the top of the initial scrambling section of *Dodo Gully*, move left to grassy ledges below the prominent overhanging corner. Follow the steep grassy crack up the left side of the steep slab on the right; then traverse right on grass into the left-hand branch of the gully. The gully is dirty at first but gives a fine airy finish.

Phoenix Buttress   79 metres   Very Severe   (27.8.25)
Higher up the scree slope from *Dodo Gully* is a large, prominent slab with a smooth overhung corner on its right. The route climbs the grassy breaks left of the slab, finishing up a steep arête on the upper buttress. Interesting climbing with a short desperate section when wet. Start about 35 metres up the scree from *Dodo Gully*, at a grassy break.
1 24m. Scramble easily up heather and rock to a small grassy platform and twin spike belay at the foot of the slab. Or, better, take the first pitch of *Mortuary Slab* to the same spot (4b).
2 14m. Move left across the foot of the slab to reach the grassy break on the left. Follow this to a small stance below a slabby groove.
3 18m. Climb the slabby groove. Awkward when dry, it is a little horror when wet. Belay on the large grass terrace above.
4 15m. Move left and climb the steep arête on good holds; care is needed in handling a couple of hollow spikes.
5 8m. 4b. A short, tricky, mottled wall provides the final obstacle.

Mortuary Slab   90 metres   Very Severe   (5.8.55)
An entertaining route along the slabs and through overhangs on the right of *Phoenix Buttress*. Start as for *Phoenix Buttress*, 35 metres up the scree from *Dodo Gully*.
1 24m. 4b. Climb the steep shallow groove and go diagonally right along a slabby ramp to a grassy platform and twin spike belay.
2 24m. 4b. Take the left edge of the prominent slab overlooking the grassy break of *Phoenix Buttress* to reach a diagonal grassy break. Follow this rightwards; then step down onto the slab again, and make a semi-hand-traverse across to the top of the corner. Belay on a vegetated ledge.
3 24m. 4b. Climb the next slab, trending back left to easy slabs.
4 18m. 4a. From a pinnacle, trend left up a gangway; then go back right to the arête and climb easily to the top.

Variation
2a Direct Finish 46m. 4c. Follow the left edge of the slab. Instead of traversing right, continue up the slabs in a direct line to the top.

The Ashes Route 66 metres Severe   (18.8.48)
A pleasant but slight route working its way up through the overhangs to the left of the two previous routes. Start 25 metres further up the scree from *Mortuary Slab*, at a little green gully, the first break on the left of some steep walls.
1 15m. Climb the gully for 9 metres. Traverse right along the top of a massive perched block to a deep recess on the other side.
2 9m. Climb the right-hand side of the recess and go up the steep crack on the right to the top of a block. Climb easily to join *Phoenix Buttress* on the large grassy terrace.
3 21m. Climb easily up the dirty groove on the right to a pinnacle.
4 21m. From the top of the pinnacle, take the short crack on the right to a slab. Move left under steep walls to join the last pitch of *Phoenix Buttress*.

Burnt Out Buttress 56 metres Very Difficult   (10.8.55)
A tricky exercise on poor rock and steep grass. Start at the lowest point of a broken-looking buttress left of an unpleasant gully, some way up the scree from *The Ashes Route*.
1 9m. Climb the short steep wall with curious white markings to heather and a steep chimney.
2 11m. Climb the chimney to heather and a spike belay; loose but interesting.
3 21m. Move right behind a large pinnacle and go up until it is possible to traverse out over the gully. Climb into the bed of the gully on very doubtful rock and pull up to grass over detached spikes, or traverse right over steep grass into the other branch of the gully (both are exposed). Climb easily up the gully to a grassy stance.
4 15m. Finish up pleasant slabs.

Clinker 49 metres Hard Severe   (10.8.55)
Much further up the scree from *Burnt Out Buttress* is a large rounded pinnacle (best seen from left of the crag). About 25 metres left of this is a light-coloured slab topped by a grass rake and a reddish subsidiary slab. Start in the middle of the slab.
1 11m. Climb the slab, bearing left, until a corner-chimney leads to a grassy ledge, or go directly up the slab.
2 14m. Traverse right over a little slab into a corner-crack forming a pinnacle. Climb this to a stance and belay on the pinnacle.
3 24m. Traverse right over easy slabs, round a corner, and go up a difficult crack.

Craig Beudy Bach   Little Cowshed Crag   OS Ref 631 558

This is the small clean easy-angled crag midway between Dinas Bach and Craig Cwm Beudy Mawr. It has one worthwhile route, which gives a pleasant way into the upper cwm.

Yellow Scoop   63 metres   Very Severe   (17.6.79)

After the initial scoop and a short wall, the climbing is about Difficult. Start in the centre of the crag, at the foot of a scoop.

1 27m. 4c. Friction up the unprotected scoop (which is often greasy) via two good pockets, and then scramble up for 12 metres to belay.

2 6m. A section of steep rocks leads more easily to the foot of the upper area.

3 30m. Climb up clean, pocketed rock past spikes and tiny ledges, keeping as near to the nose as possible. A delightful pitch.

North Face of Crib Goch   OS Ref 625 553

Below the summit of Crib Goch (Red Crest 923m), the tall clean Crib Goch Buttress rises for 75 metres from the scree slope of the upper cwm (Cwm Uchaf Cwm Glas). It is a pleasant little climbing-ground, well known for *Reade's Route*. The crag is well positioned, with spectacular views across the Glyders and the routes finishing on one of the finest summits in Wales. A visit here may be combined with a trip round the Snowdon Horseshoe to give an enjoyable mountain day, particularly if finishing in late afternoon sunlight. To the right of Crib Goch Buttress lies Crazy Pinnacle Gully with the broken buttress of Crazy Pinnacle next to it. **Western Gully** (1887) flanks this on the right, an Easy scramble either up or down – the short chimney near the top is best taken on the left.

Route III   88 metres   Very Difficult   (27.8.46)

A mediocre route on poor rock. Start at the foot of a rib left of *Reade's Route* and at a much lower level.

1 30m. Ascend the easy rib.

2 23m. Follow an easy diagonal line up left for 9 metres, and then keep left until a move leads onto a tricky slab. Go up right to belay.

3 12m. Climb the rib on the left above the ledge, and then cross into a grassy corner.

4 23m. Ascend a steep wall on the right for 5 metres, and then traverse out on the wall for a short way. Climb the slab above to a grassy recess. Surmount the large capstone and finish easily out to the right.

Route II   98 metres   Hard Severe   (26.8.46)

A parallel line to *Reade's Route*, which gives good climbing in its upper half.

1 30m. *Route III* pitch 1.

2 12m. Continue in the same line to an overhanging wall.

North Face of Crib Goch

1	Route II	HS	3	Reid's Route	HVS
2	Reade's Route	VD	4	Crazy Pinnacle Face	D

3 27m. Avoid the bulge by a move round to the right. Climb a crack and a short wall on the left, and step onto a slab above the overhang. Go steeply up the slab and then diagonally up right to a stance close to the pinnacle of *Reade's Route*.
4 14m. 4b. Climb the slab on the left to a good ledge.
5 15m. Step out to the right and then go straight up, almost parallel to the last pitch of *Reade's Route*. Move left near the top to finish.

★★**Reade's Route**   66 metres   Very Difficult   (8.08)
A classic outing: the stride across from the top of the pinnacle is quite memorable. Start immediately left of *Crazy Pinnacle Gully* and scramble up broken slabby ground until it steepens. Belay on a stance overlooking the gully.
1 30m. Climb easily up the rib, past numerous ledges, to a large platform below a steep wall. An easy rake leads into the left-hand branch of the gully.
2 6m. Ascend the wall with a difficult move up to the left, and go up to a stance at the foot of a large pinnacle.
3 15m. Climb the pinnacle and stride across to a crack in the wall (crux). Ascend the crack to the top of another pinnacle.
4 15m. Finish up the rib by a shallow groove.

Reid's Route   24 metres   Hard Very Severe 5a   (16.6.83)
A rather artificial climb up the blank wall right of *Reade's Route*. Start at the belay above pitch 2 of *Reade's Route*, by the pinnacle. Make an easy traverse right into the gully at the base of the wall. Climb the middle of the wall, with a hard move to gain a pocket on the left. Go up to a horizontal break, and continue diagonally left to reach good holds on the arête. Climb this to another break before trending up rightwards to the top.

Crazy Pinnacle Gully   55 metres   Moderate   (1887)
One of the earliest routes in the Pass. Scramble easily up the bed of the gully for 30 metres to where it divides. Take either branch, the left-hand one giving an interesting cave pitch. The rib up the centre of the gully may also be climbed.

Crazy Pinnacle Face   30 metres   Difficult   (1894)
Scramble up for 30 metres to a grassy nook and belays. Ascend to the summit of a minor pinnacle on the left, and continue straight up for 15 metres to finish.

Dinas Bach Area

Below the main crag and only a little way above the road is a small buttress with a drystone wall abutting its base (OS Ref 634 559). A large 'surfboard' block can be found on the right. The easiest approach is from one of the lay-bys between Pen y Pass and Pont y Gromlech

Cut Back Crack   15 metres   Severe   (28.8.93)
Start directly above the drystone wall. Once past a slimy start, the deep jamming crack provides some interest, with one precarious move near the top.

Going over the Falls   15 metres   Very Severe 4c   (28.8.93)
Takes the obvious flake crack on the right, which gives an entertaining pitch on perfect rock. Layback up to a break, and then keep powering up to the top, with difficulties easing all the time.

Totally Tubular   15 metres   Difficult   (28.8.93)
The surprisingly easy chimney on the right is partially obscured by a tree.

Dinas Bach   Little Fortress   OS Ref 632 560

Five hundred metres on the Pen y Pass side of Dinas Mot and 90 metres above the road, this little cliff with its generally excellent rock gives a few pleasant routes and four hard short pitches. The east wing is clean and steep, with a noticeable flake, *Flake Chimney*, rising from the lowest point. The west wing is separated from the east by a large grassy gully and is characterised by a smooth slab rising like a house roof above the line of overhangs.

North-east facing, the cliff receives very little sunshine: a few rays may be caught early in the morning. At an altitude of 330 metres, the cliff is 15 minutes walk from Pont y Gromlech. Descent is by means of the large grassy central gully.

About 100 metres up and left of the main area is a small isolated buttress.

The Silver Backed Gorilla   15 metres   E2 6a   (2000)
Climb the obvious diagonal crack.

The East Wing
The large flake on the east wing forms two chimneys: a short one on the left and a larger west-facing one on the right. The face of the large flake has been put under the microscope to produce three boulder-problem-type routes.

★Dinas Bach Crack   12 metres   E6 6b   (2002)
A bold climb taking left wall of the arête left of *Felony*. Climb the overhanging and unprotected left side of the arête to a peg and a *Rock 2*. Pull left into the crack proper and finish up this.

Body Rock   15 metres   E4 6c   (19.7.85)
The front face of the left arête of the flake. If you like a hard well-protected problem, then this is for you. Start at the foot of a small flake just left of *Felony*. Climb the flake to a junction with *Felony* (protection). Step left and make a desperate move up and left to a jug. Continue for 5 metres to a ledge on the pinnacle on the left.

★Felony   18 metres   E5 6b   (3.7.84)
The large peg that was originally in place has been replaced by a poorer
one, so as not to facilitate its use as a foothold, and the pitch is now
finished direct. Climb a crack in the centre of the flake and continue with
difficulty to a peg. Either make a desperate move right to better holds (E4),
or go straight up with even more difficulty.

The Boys of Summer   15 metres   E4 6b   (20.6.85)
Short but serious. Climb an incipient crack just left of the right arête of the
flake. Continue boldly up the wall to a sloping finish.

Flake Chimney   30 metres   Difficult   (27.8.25)
The route takes the long chimney on the right-hand side of the flake and
then the buttress above.
1 15m. Ascend the flake, which is similar to *Monolith Crack* in Ogwen.
2 15m. Step across onto the wall and move right to a good ledge. Finish
up the steep crack on the right.

Right of Flake Chimney *is a slabby wall known as Mortlock's Slab. It is split by
three large cracks.*

Route 1   30 metres   Very Severe 4c   (28.6.59)
The left-hand crack, which unfortunately takes some drainage. From just
right of *Flake Chimney*, climb up and move right at 6 metres. Follow the
flaky crack past a tedious, central, grassy section to a cleaner finish.

Route 2   30 metres   Very Severe 4c   (2.4.60)
The central crack. Start 3 metres right of *Route 1*. Climb the flake crack on
good holds to join a crack on the right at 18 metres. Finish up twin cracks,
a grim struggle with grass and heather.

Route 3   30 metres   Hard Very Severe 5a
Some good little moves. Start 3 metres left of the holly and climb a thin
crack to a ledge at 5 metres. Move 2½ metres left and go up the crack to
join *Route 2* at 18 metres. Finish as for *Route 2*.

Route 4   27 metres   Hard Very Severe 5a
The right-hand crack keeps coming at you. Start just left of the holly. Climb
the crack, awkward at first, and continue up with good protection. At 21
metres, step right to finish up the heathery crack.

Freefallin'   27 metres   E3 5c   (5.92)
A bold initial section leads to easier climbing above. Start at the holly, just
up and right from the start of *Route 4*. Boulder out the shallow groove
above the holly. Step right to get the first protection, a chockstone behind
the large layback flake. Continue either by laybacking the flake or by
climbing the face slightly to the left of it to a ledge. Climb up and around
the arête to finish via a crack.

Ash Tree Gully   18 metres   Difficult   (8.48)
Immediately right of Mortlock's Slab a wooded gully rises up from a holly
at its base. Climb up via two pleasant flakes, and then bushwhack and
scramble to finish.

The Play-away Flake   26 metres   E1 5c   (1.8.92)
Technical and tenuous. Start a few metres left of *Flake Traverse*. Climb the
right-hand side of the arête to a small horizontal slot. Swing round
leftwards to an undercut flake. Continue up the groove above and an
excellent layback flake. Delicate and insecure moves up this gain a
continuation groove, which gives a pleasant finish.

★**Flake Traverse**   26 metres   Difficult   (30.5.31)
A popular climb on very good holds. Right of *Ash Tree Gully*, this is an
obvious line of well-scratched flakes up the left wall of the wide central
gully. The difficulty can be varied and some care is needed with the rock.

The West Wing
Slanting Buttress   43 metres   Very Severe   (3.8.55)
This takes the vegetated buttress that slopes diagonally left of the slab of
Crack and Slab. Rather artificial, but it adds yet another avenue for
masochistic pioneers. Start from the foot of the buttress by scrambling over
loose blocks to a grassy platform.
1 12m. Ascend easily over rock and heather to a large block. Go left to a
light-coloured slab leading to trees.
2 11m. Climb the undercut chimney on the right with difficulty to a
bilberry ledge.
3 14m. Go left over blocks to a layback crack leading to a large ledge
and pinnacle belay.
4 6m. Climb the rib to the top.

Crack and Slab   41 metres   Severe   (27.8.25)
Start 5 metres left of the drystone wall.
1 18m. A series of reddish-coloured ledges lead to a deep crack that is
hard but short. It leads to the Annexe.
2 14m. Walk up left and climb a fault in the upper wall. Continue to a
higher ledge.
3 9m. Step round the corner onto the edge of the slab. The right edge
provides a difficult finish, but the centre is easier. Scramble up to finish.
Variation
Wall and Traverse Finish   53 metres   Severe
2a 18m. Walk to the left for 6 metres to an obvious traverse-line below
the overhangs. A balustrade of large blocks leads to a stance on the left.
3a 9m. Follow a grassy rake left to a leaning bollard.
4a 11m. Swing across into a groove on the right and go up this for a
short way until it is possible to break out onto the edge. This is the left edge
of the roof slab. Follow the edge to a good belay.
5a 15m. Traverse easily back right. Above and left of The Annexe is an
obvious stone spike. The roof 5 metres left of this gives a 5a problem.

Wall Direct   57 metres   Difficult
An interesting training climb: there are many variations but this is the best
line. Start on the right-hand side of the West Wing, above the drystone wall.
1 20m. Climb the steep wall on good holds to a perched block. Ascend a
mossy groove in the same line to the Annexe.
2 37m. From the back of the grassy area of the Annexe, climb direct via
a mantelshelf, a crack and an arête.

Dinas Mot Area

Between Dinas Bach and Dinas Mot, nearer to the latter, is a small crag (OS
Ref 630 563) comprised of jumbled boulders and grassy ledges with a
prominent twin-spiked overhang at its left edge. In the centre of the crag is a
large triangle of grass. Above its apex rises an obvious flake crack, the
substance of *Dracula Spectacula*. The crag is approached by starting up the
track to Dinas Mot from the Pont y Gromlech car-park and then breaking up
the hillside to the left.

Salem's Slab   18 metres   Hard Very Severe 5a   (28.8.93)
A filler-in. Start at the base of a slender slab with a perched block at its top
about 45 metres left of *Dracula* Spectacula, just right of a wide crack. Step
up and right to reach a thread, and climb directly up the slab via a couple
of juggy breaks to finish at the perched block.

The Bat Passage   15 metres   Very Severe 5a   (19.5.87)
A good companion to *Dracula Spectacula*. Start left of that route and
either chimney or bridge the crack using the pillar to the left of that route,
or boldly layback the crack and continue to the top (good protection).

Vlad the Arête   8 metres   E4 7a   (9.88)
The arête left of *Dracula Spectacula* sports two pegs and may be very
frustrating on first acquaintance.

Dracula Spectacula   15 metres   E1 5b   (17.11.83)
A worthwhile little pitch in the esoteric vein. Start by scrambling up to the
foot of the flake, the bottom metre or so of which is green and grassy.
Avoid the green section by climbing jammed blocks on the left for 5
metres. Use the left-hand corner to gain the crack (crux), and then rapidly
layback the batwing-shaped flake to the top.

Dinas Mot Outcrop   OS Ref 630 565

This outcrop lies just up and across the road from the Cromlech Boulders,
upstream of Pont y Gromlech. The slabs are popular with outdoor groups,
offering a selection of routes from Very Difficult to Very Severe; however,
belays take a little finding. There are many steep problems, yet of a slabby
nature, the hardest of which appears to be a short 'holdless' wall at the

Resurrection (E4, page 101)
Dinas Cromlech
Climber: James Ibbertson
Photo: David Simmonite

SOUTH SIDE OF THE PASS ~ EAST

Pen y Pass

DINAS MOT

CLOGWYN
GAFR

Dracula
Spectacula

CARREG
GWALCH

DINAS BACH

THE
NOSE

WEST WIN

DINAS MOT
OUTCROP

The Cromlech Boulders lay-by

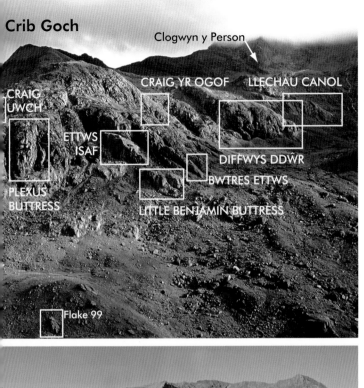

Crib Goch

Clogwyn y Person

CRAIG YR OGOF

LLECHAU CANOL

CRAIG UWCH

ETTWS ISAF

DIFFWYS DDŴR

PLEXUS BUTTRESS

BWTRES ETTWS

LITTLE BENJAMIN BUTTRESS

Flake 99

Cenotaph Corner (E1, page
102) Dinas Cromlech
Climber: Colin Scotchford
Photo: David Simmonite

right-hand end at about 5c. The prominent arête next to the bend in the road has been regularly ascended since the 50s at about 5b – no more claims please. There are a couple of routes in the modern idiom, however, which justify description. Left again past the prominent arête is a series of broken walls and corners, which are bounded by an obvious overhanging arête with a thin crack to its right. The arête is taken by:

Beginner's Mind   11 metres   E7 6c   (3.6.93)
Climb the obvious and vicious arête, past two poor pegs and an *RP2*.

Grin's Twins   9 metres   E6 6b   (30.6.94)
The twin cracks in the overhanging wall just right of *Beginner's Mind* are safe but strenuous.

My Favourite Route in the World, Ever   10 metres   E7 6c   (2001)
This is based on a short wall 20 metres down and right of *Beginner's Mind*. Climb a corner, and then follow thin edges out to the arête. Finish up this in a fine position.

Dinas Mot   Mot's Fortress   OS Ref 627 563
Dinas Mot forms the gable end of the north ridge of Crib Goch and it dominates the south side of the valley when seen from almost any direction. It is around 120 metres high and about a quarter of a mile wide. It is easily reached from the Pont y Gromlech car-park. The cliff has three main facets, the most dominant being the detached buttress of the Nose, the huge triangular slab at its centre. Above this broken rocks arbitrarily divide the main cliff into the Eastern and Western Wings. The Eastern Wing, although bristling with overhangs, has no modern desperates on it – as yet. Routes generally weave their way up through intimidating territory at a relatively modest standard with good protection when needed. This is in marked contrast to the smooth open slab routes on the Nose, which have the occasional long poorly-protected run-out. On the two-tiered Western Wing, routes tend to follow devious lines, which are difficult to identify on first acquaintance, and there is more vegetation. Further right, beyond the narrow Groper Buttress, sits Plexus Buttress with its superb climbing on rough compact rock.

The Eastern Wing
The Eastern Wing of the Mot is bounded on the left by the vegetated *Staircase Gully*, and its right edge is defined by Eastern Gully and the steep broken arête above the Nose. Beside the upper part of *Staircase Gully* is a tower-like buttress split by a groove in its upper half (taken by *The Toad*). This tower is well defined on its right by the sloping slab of *The Mole*. Right of *The Mole* the cliff becomes much longer, extending down to the level of Eastern Gully, and is divided by an obvious grassy rake which slants up right (*Troglodyte Wall*). Below the rake are steep mossy walls, and above it are large overhangs and grassy ledges. The structure of the cliff is such that route-finding can be very complicated. Most climbs have been drastically transformed from their original vegetated state, but grassy ledges and

Dinas Mot: The Eastern Wing

1	The Toad	E3	4	Molehill	E3	7	Gandalf	E1
2	The Mole	HVS	5	Molehill Direct Finish	E3	8	Beorn	E1
3	MPP	HVS	6	Gollum	HVS	9	Mordor	E3
							(pitch 1 not shown)	

lichenous rock are still encountered. A lack of traffic on a number of the routes has led to some of the gear placements having filled up with soil, and it is worth carrying a broddler on the lead. These features detract little from the quality of climbing and amplifies the cliff's impressive atmosphere.

South-east facing, this part of the Mot receives sunshine early in the morning. The base of the cliff is found at over 400 metres and is about 15 minutes from the main road at Pont y Gromlech. The best descent from the Eastern Wing is via a shallow gully and broken rocks, left (east) of Staircase Gully.

The first two routes are not on the Eastern Wing proper but lie on a small wall well up and round to the left. It is in fact the retaining wall of the descent gully.

Honky Tonk Corner   36 metres   Severe   (11.9.71)
Interesting but rather dirty. The first prominent feature when coming down the descent gully is a corner on the left (facing out). Start directly beneath the corner.
1 27m. Climb the corner to a ledge on the right (possible belay). Step left and continue in the same line as the corner, passing an overhang on the left, to belay below an overhanging chimney.
2 9m. Climb the overhanging chimney.

Tarotplane   42 metres   Very Severe (1 pt aid)   (11.9.71)
Start just down the gully from *Honky Tonk Corner*, at the base of a rib beneath a fine-looking flake crack that leads to the ledge on the right 18 metres up *Honky Tonk Corner*.
1 24m. 4c. Climb delicately up the rib to the foot of an overhanging groove. Climb the groove (sling for aid) until it is possible to layback into the flake crack above. Follow this to the ledge 18 metres up *Honky Tonk Corner*.
2 18m. 4c. Above the ledge is a white tree. Starting from the right, climb a leftward-slanting crack to the tree. Climb the groove behind the tree to a horizontal crack leading to the arête on the left. Layback up this and step left into the short groove above the overhang.

Staircase Gully   101 metres   Moderate
The normally damp gully climb that defines the eastern limit of the cliff proper. The fairly sound rock gives an interesting scramble for 46 metres. The gully now steepens, with a 6-metre crux wall 24 metres higher, and then eases off to finish.

Although a scramble rather than a climb but with some historic interest, details of **Terra Incognita** (6.6.49) are given in the First Ascents section.

The Toad   60 metres   E3   (10.63)
A serious and technical route on good rock and in a fine position. It goes up the tower-like buttress just right of *Staircase Gully*. The peg that used to protect the crux has long since gone, making this a bold lead as nut protection only exists way down to the right. Start from a small bay in the

gully (above the start of *The Mole*), below a short pocketed wall which leads to a large grassy ledge at the foot of the steep tower.

1 12m. 4a. Pleasantly climb the pocketed wall to the grassy ledge on the right.

2 24m. 6a. Follow the horizontal crack right to join the short rib of *The Mole*. Climb this and move left and then up to the left to surmount the overhang. Go easily up slabs to belay by a flake.

3 24m. 5b. Climb the shallow groove on the left, with difficulties soon easing. Finish up short easy walls on the left.

★M P P   60 metres   Hard Very Severe   (4.10.64)
A good climb, which starts up *The Toad* and then the crux rib of *The Mole*. Well worth seeking out. The crux traverse is delightfully exposed and quite bold for its grade.

1 12m. 4a. *The Toad* pitch 1.

2 27m. 5a. Climb the horizontal crack rightwards to the rib of *The Mole*. Follow *The Mole* to the thread runner in the corner. Hand-traverse sensationally out leftwards, around the arête, to where a startling move gains a tiny ledge and peg. Traverse left again to meet the easy part of *The Toad* above its overhangs (care should be taken to ease rope drag on this section). Scramble up to the flake belay as for *The Toad* pitch 2.

3 21m. 4c. Move right to the arête, and take the left-slanting crackline over some bulges to a small ledge. Finish up a short wall.

★★The Mole   84 metres   Hard Very Severe   (8.4.61)
A justifiably popular route on superb rock, although it is often wet and is then harder. The steep tower taken by *The Toad* has a prominent line of undercut slabs running up underneath it from left to right. These give the substance of the route. Start in the gully above the grassy rake of *Troglodyte Wall*.

1 27m. 4a. A small grassy rake leads to a short steep slab. Climb this to a grassy bay just right of a huge flake.

2 34m. 5a. Ascend the huge flake and walk left to a steep rib. Climb this (crux) and move right to the diagonal slab (thread runner up in the corner). Move right to the slab's edge and go up a corner. Traverse right below the overhang and go up a short groove to a ledge.

3 23m. 4c. Move into the groove on the left and follow it until an obvious traverse right to ledges leads to a finish up easier rock – a pitch which is often wet.

Troglodyte Wall   91 metres   Very Severe   (5.2.55)
Disappointing. The easiest line up the Eastern Wing provides good views of other routes but has little else to commend it. It follows the narrow, grassy rake winding out of *Staircase Gully* and crosses *Beorn* at the prominent L-shaped block seen on the skyline from the foot of the crag. Above this it breaks back left to finish near the top of *Beorn*.

Tales from the Riverbank   72 metres   E3   (1989)
Surprisingly good, sustained and technical climbing tackling an impressive part of the cliff. Start left of *Gollum/The Molehill*, at a thin crack leading to a groove, just left of groove of *The Molehill*.
1 24m. 6a. Climb the crack and step slightly right to gain a sharp downward-pointing spike below the roof. Layback up leftwards to enter the groove; then move up onto the right wall to climb a small groove and pillar above. Belay on the large ledge.
2 12m. 5b. Move left and layback up to gain a small niche. Exit awkwardly left to reach a belay above pitch 1 of *The Mole*.
3 18m. 5c. Pull directly up the rib on the left and continue to the right to the traverse on *The Mole*. Follow the rightwards-leaning groove above after a worrying start. Continue to a good handhold, and move up diagonally rightwards to the thread on *The Mole*.
4 18m. 5c. A very deceptive pitch. Follow the traverse of *M P P* to the arête, move right and climb the groove direct to a sensational pull-out rightwards. Trend back left over easy ground to belay on a large thread on the top pitch of *The Toad*.

The Molehill   95 metres   E3   (16.7.77)
An impressive route up some very steep rock, technical and bold. Start as for *Gollum*.
1 37m. 6a. From the belay, bold moves lead fiercely up into a short groove. Climb this and the small easy slab to a flaked wall that funnels into a groove leading to small trees. Trend left up easier rock to belay at the top of *The Mole* pitch 1.
2 24m. 5c. (*Mole Direct*). Go up the slab into the corner. Boldly negotiate two roofs by agonizing bridging (all very technical) and continue via a bulging crack to an awkward exit. Continue up to a stance about 5 metres below the top of *The Mole* pitch 2 (nut belays).
3 34m. 5a. Traverse left along the obvious line of slaty holds, and then move up left to blocks on the arête. Climb the arête and eventually finish up the final crack of *M P P*.
Variations
3a Molehill Direct Finish 21m. E3 5c. The poorly protected arête immediately left of *The Mole* proves to be a serious, soul-searching lead.
3b 34m. 4c. Instead of traversing left under the overhangs, continue up to the stance above pitch 2 of *The Mole*. Traverse left, around the arête (of the *Direct Finish*), to join *M P P* and the normal finish.

★★Gollum   91 metres   Hard Very Severe   (27.3.63)
A fine route with a spectacular overhang on its second pitch that more than compensates for the grassy terrace on its first. The climb takes a shallow groove up the lower walls and the slabby groove under the overhangs of *The Mole*. Start from a grassy pedestal right of the gully.
1 30m. 5a. Go diagonally right up to and over a bulge. Climb the slabs to a ledge below the flake crack. Follow the crack to a tree belay on the rake of *Troglodyte Wall*. Stroll 15 metres left to *The Mole* pitch 1 belay.

2 34m. 5b. Climb the slab diagonally right for 9 metres. Power up the overhang on good holds in a sensational position. Climb a shallow groove, move left and go up to the belay above pitch 2 of *The Mole*.
3 27m. 4b. Traverse right across a slab to an enjoyable finish up the exposed, juggy arête.

★★A New Austerlitz   100 metres   E3   (25.4.82)

An excellent route, with sustained and interesting moves in impressive surroundings. Start just left of, and below, the huge perched block of *Gandalf*, at a wide shallow groove in a slab.
1 21m. 5c. Climb the groove or the crack to its left into a dirty niche just left of the huge block. Bridge up its left-hand side via a huge protruding spike, to pull boldly over the bulge onto a short slab. Belay at the base of the flake.
2 18m. 5b. Step right round the corner onto a slab, then climb a thin crack to its end, and continue direct up the edge of the slab to easy ground. Walk 12 metres left to belay on the right-hand side of a flake.
3 34m. 5c. Starting 1½ metres right of the flake, pull over the initial roof at a slim groove to gain good holds. Pull up to the next roof and traverse right to a groove at its right-hand end. Climb this to below the overhang of *Gollum*. Step right and surmount the overhang on massive holds to a resting place on a big flat-topped block. Ascend directly up the slab on small hidden holds. Take the short groove above and exit to a grassy ledge; nut and *Friend* belays.
4 27m. 4b. *Gollum* pitch 3.

★Gandalf   104 metres   E1   (24.8.66)

An excellent climb, similar to *Beorn* but cleaner, with an intimidating first pitch. Scramble (or rope up) up grassy corners to a good flake belay just right of the cave formed by the large overhang.
1 37m. 5a. Move left into the recess below the overhang and climb up onto the large protruding block. Step right round a spike, and turn the roof on its right-hand side to good holds. Follow the flaky crack and move left to finish on a grassy ledge. Good holly tree belay 3 metres higher in a grassy bay.
2 40m. 5a. Climb the small rib on the right to a ledge. Go diagonally left and pull up into a small corner (good cam in a horizontal break). Climb diagonally rightwards for 3 metres to a peg and stride left to a ledge. Pull up, step right, and slant up rightwards, making for the left end of a diagonal band of overhangs. Pass these on the left, and then step right immediately onto the slab. Climb this for 2 metres, step left and go up into a corner below the uppermost of two large overhangs. Traverse left along the lip of the lower overhang and swing round the arête to belay in a corner as for *Gollum*.
3 27m. 4b. *Gollum* pitch 3.

The Wobbler   97 metres   Hard Very Severe   (3.66)

Not a very good route. Start as for *Beorn*.

1 34m. 5a. Descend a short way and surmount a line of overhangs to a small ledge. Go left along a ramp to more ledges, which are climbed until a step left can be made into a groove. Ascend the groove, moving left at the top to a large grassy ledge and tree belay.

2 21m. 5a. Climb the rib and grass on the right to poor belays. Climb over creaking blocks on the left to a small ledge (ancient peg). Move right, and go up a steep groove and the wall above to a small stance and peg belay.

3 18m. 5a. Traverse left under a line of overhangs to a groove. Go up this until a mantelshelf move out left leads to a grass ledge.

4 24m. 4b. Climb straight up the rib to finish.

★Beorn 71 metres E1 (3.4.64)

A very good route, with exciting positions, that takes a devious yet logical line up through the overhangs on the right-hand arête of the wall. At the time of writing, pitch 1 is very dirty. Start by scrambling up rightwards from below the *Gandalf* cave to belay in a small corner directly above the start of Eastern Gully, below and just left of a square black overhang with a small white tree above it.

1 34m. 5c. Climb a short wall and then a 6-metre groove to the roof. Make a hard traverse left from an ageing peg to gain the arête. Move left into the next groove, and then go back up right and climb the slab to cross the long diagonal overhang at its weakest point. Pull over to a small grassy stance and flake belays.

2 37m. 5b. Climb 3 metres to a higher grassy ledge. Ascend a 3-metre wall and pull leftwards over the roof at the top. Traverse left to the big groove and ascend it leftwards to the main overhang. Surmount this and go up airily to the top overhang, which is avoided by a mantelshelf on the left. A short groove leads to the top.

Mordor 66 metres E3 (24.6.68)

This fierce climb sees very few ascents and is almost always dirty. It is, however, in a good position and has some interesting climbing. Most of the dangerous loose blocks have been cleaned off, but care should still be exercised. Start as for *Beorn*, below the prominent groove that leads to a roof.

1 15m. 4c. Climb diagonally rightwards up a heavily vegetated ramp and groove until it is possible to move left at the top of the groove to a grassy ledge and prominent tree above the square, black overhang of *Beorn*. Belay in a cave (good thread).

2 24m. 6a. Move 2 metres left and climb the blocky wall to an old peg at the foot of a blank V-groove. Move right with difficulty (crux) below the level of the peg to gain a niche below a roof. Move back left under the roof on good holds until beneath a groove in the vague arête. Climb the groove between two huge, suspect pinnacles to a sloping stance. Belay to any number of rather hollow blocks.

3 27m. 5b. Move slightly left and climb an awkward, out-of-balance groove beneath the loose flaky-looking overhang. Good protection is difficult to arrange. Layback the roof boldly on the flakes (which turn out to be solid), move up and turn the large roof on the right to finish up the arête. Belay well back.

Variation

1a 18m. 5c. Follow *Beorn* until it is possible to break out right to the white tree and cave belay. Cleaner and more in keeping with the route's standard.

East Wing Girdle   108 metres   Hard Very Severe   (1966)

A disappointing climb. Start from the top of the Nose and scramble up to a belay below the steep wall.

1 24m. Climb diagonally left just above the lip of the overhangs to a stance beyond the skyline.

2 12m. Descend for 8 metres, and then move left to a stance and belay.

3 15m. Move down a short way to a slab on the left. Climb the groove on *Beorn*, moving left at the top to a small stance and peg belay on *The Wobbler*.

4 18m. *The Wobbler* pitch 3.

5 9m. Traverse left to belay on *The Mole*.

6 30m. Climb the corner for 3 metres, and then move round the arête to finish up the slanting crack and short wall (as for *M P P* pitch 3).

Flammarian   60 metres   Very Severe   (2.6.68)

From the top of the Nose, traverse left for 15 metres to a grass-topped pinnacle and then across more grass to a slabby wall.

1 9m. Cross the wall, and then go up to two trees below overhangs and a large ledge.

2 15m. Go left again, and climb straight up easily to the belay above pitch 1 of *Beorn*.

3 18m. Step right to take a rightward-slanting crack, finishing in jammed blocks. Climb over these and traverse round the overhangs into a wide easy corner.

4 18m. Go up left into a pleasant V-chimney and then up a slab to the top.

Eastern Gully   Difficult   (1901)

The short straight gully defining the Nose on its left side is a quick way up, or a tricky descent from its summit. A rock step near the gully foot may prove to be a 'stopper' in the wet.

The Nose

The smooth slabby face of the Nose, with its good sound rock, is a worthy counterpart to Dinas Cromlech opposite. Above its undercut base are some 15 metres of steep rock with fine holds, which merges into smooth slabs at a lesser angle with good, but widely-spaced, holds. The final steep section, rising from two large recesses separated by a central rib, provides cracks and corners. Just to the right of the very foot of the Nose is a large rock scar where part of the initial band of overhangs collapsed; all the climbs between *The Direct Route* and *Diagonal* now have a common starting-point, although the *Zeta* start has been re-climbed at a loose and dirty 5c.

North-east facing, the Nose only receives sunlight early in the morning and late on in the summer. At about 330 metres the base of the crag is about 10 minutes walk from Pont y Gromlech. Western Gully provides the easiest descent from the top of the Nose.

Warning: climbers should not gather at the base of *The Direct Route* and *The Cracks*, as the groove-system of the former naturally funnels any debris knocked off the top down onto this area. The potential for a serious accident is quite alarming. Climbers should gear up well to the right or the left of this point.

The first three routes are approached by scrambling up to the left of *The Cracks* to where a grassy ledge runs rightwards from the foot of *Eastern Gully*.

You're Not in Poland Now   9 metres   E1 5a   (20.5.87)
The delightful pocketed arête left of *Sombrero Fallout* pitch 1.

God Help the Sailors on a Night Like This! 9 metres E1 5b (20.5.87)
The thin seam with two pockets next to it just left of *Sombrero Fallout* pitch 1 is climbed using a useful crack for the right hand.

Sombrero Fallout   38 metres   E2   (23.6.84)
A powerful and painful little route. Start from the right-hand end of the ledge, below a steep wall.
1 21m. 5b. Climb the thin crack in the middle of the wall, past a resting-ledge, to a stance.
2 17m. 6a. There is a thin crack behind the belay (left of the crack on *G B H* pitch 3). Attack this (stubborn at the start) and continue without much respite to finish at the final belay of *The Cracks*.

★**Truncheon Meat**   15 metres   E6 6c   (20.5.87)
The overhanging groove between *Sombrero Fallout* pitch 2 and *G B H* pitch 3 used to be one of the most taxing pitches on the south side of the Pass, and it is still a stiff proposition. Crank up the desperately strenuous and technical groove to a rest. The boulder-problem cracklet in the even steeper headwall provides a stubborn, fitting finale. One poor peg and a rack of wires protect.

★★**The Cracks**   90 metres   Hard Severe   (4.30)
A classic climb, one of the finest at its standard in the Pass. The last pitch has a Very Severe mantelshelf, which can easily be avoided. Start just up and left from the lowest point of the buttress, by some blocks above polished slabs in the path.
1 12m. 3c. Make a steep move up onto a ledge (well worn), and then follow a small corner/groove slanting back left to a ledge. Belay on another ledge 2 metres higher.
2 18m. 4a. Step across left for 1½ metres, and then continue diagonally left up a slender left-facing corner, finishing up a short crack (hard if wet), to a stance below an overhang and chockstone belays.

Dinas Mot: The Nose

1	The Cracks	HS	5	Superdirect	E1	9	The Link	E1

1 The Cracks   HS   5 Superdirect   E1   9   The Link   E1
2 Lorraine   VS   6 Zeta   E3   10 West Rib   HVS
3 Lorraine Variation HVS   7 Diagonal   HVS   11 The Chain   E1
4 Direct Route   VS   8 Stairway to Heaven E3   12 Western Slabs   VS
                                                            13 Crosstie   HVS

3 14m. 4a. Traverse delicately right below the overhang (often wet) into a short chimney, which leads to a good ledge.

4 14m. 4b. Climb the thin crack splitting the slab on the left to a large ledge and possible belay. Step up and walk rightwards to belay on a large pinnacle.

5 18m. 4a. From the top of the pinnacle, make an awkward move right onto a ledge. Climb the crack in the slabby left wall of the corner to another ledge.

6 14m. 4c. Climb up to the right and make the infamous mantelshelf onto a smooth rounded ledge. Traverse left and climb the arête to the top of the Nose. The mantelshelf (which may be found to be 5a or more for those of less than average height!) may be easily bypassed.

Variations

Several inferior variations exist to the left of the main route.

G B H   83 metres   E2   (29.7.78)

A worthwhile route if only for the crack on pitch 3. Start as for *The Cracks*.

1 12m. 4b. Climb the rib on the right to belay as for *The Cracks*.

2 40m. 5b. Climb straight up between *Lorraine Variation* and *The Direct Route* to a good ledge. Slant left up a line of shallow grooves, pockets and cracks to move onto the good ledge at the top of *Lorraine Variation* after a few layaways up a crack. Pinnacle belay as for *The Cracks*.

3 17m. 5c. Climb the vicious crack just left of the arête, above the pinnacle.

4 14m. 4b. Finish up the arête on the left of the last pitch of *The Cracks*.

★★Lorraine   79 metres   Very Severe   (7.9.41)

A pleasant and enjoyable route just right of *The Cracks*. It is a parallel line to that route and the stances are shared.

1 12m. 3c. *The Cracks* pitch 1.

2 20m. 4c. Go steeply up and left over a bulge to reach a left-slanting groove formed by a scarp wall. Follow this past a hard section, and then step left into and climb the short chimney on *The Cracks*.

3 15m. 4c. Climb the thin corner-crack and a short corner to belay at the large pinnacle on the right, shared with *The Cracks*.

4 18m. 4c. Step right off the top of the pinnacle and move across a ledge to climb a corner-crack to good block belays. This pitch can be split at the foot of the corner.

5 14m. 4c. Climb a series of steps up right as for *The Cracks*, and finish via the difficult mantelshelf.

★Lorraine Variation   37 metres   Hard Very Severe 5a   (7.6.65)

A superb pitch that is delicate and sparsely protected; harder but better than the original. From its first stance, follow *Lorraine* for 8 metres until a steep move across the bulge leads to another slab on the right. Climb delicately up past a steepening (good runner), and continue on to a ledge at the centre of the shallow scoop above. Traverse down leftwards to the foot of a crack in the arête. Climb this to the large pinnacle on the ledge of *The Cracks*.

Trauma   15 metres   E9 7a   (6.99)
This route takes on the blank-looking wall to the right of pitch 5 of *The
Cracks*. Belay on the ledge after climbing the pinnacle and moving right.
From the ledge, leave poor *RPs* and make a rising traverse to an obvious
crackline. Climb with some complexity to move right to a groove,
which is followed to its top.

★★★**The Direct Route**   74 metres   Very Severe   (22.6.30)
A superb and popular route, which requires a wide variety of techniques,
especially on the last pitch. It follows the obvious light-coloured groove up the
centre of the Nose. Start at the lowest point of the buttress, left of the rock scar.
1 15m. 4a. Scramble up to the top of short twin pinnacles, continue up
for 9 metres, and then move round to the left and belay on the first stance
of *The Cracks*.
2 27m. 4b. Climb diagonally rightwards, crossing a blunt rib, to the base
of the prominent shallow groove. Ascend this, steepening at the top, to
good belays in an open bay.
3 15m. 4c. Go easily up to the right up steps to the start of a steep
diagonal crack. Hand-traverse this for a metre or so, make a long step
right and ascend easily to a long ledge with huge flake belays.
4 17m. 5b. Ascend the smooth, polished corner on the left: layback,
bridge, or use a shoulder. Continue pleasantly up the flake cracks to finish
up a shallow corner.

★**Famine**   78 metres   Hard Very Severe   (28.8.78)
A surprisingly good eliminate. Start as for *The Direct Route*.
1 15m. 4a. Climb up and over the twin pinnacles (as for *The Direct
Route*) to belay on a spike below and left of the huge perched flake, or
step left to belay as for *The Direct Route*.
2 46m. 5a. Climb across to the flake, and from its top go up into a
scoop exiting onto *The Direct Route*. Follow the crest of the rib right of *The
Direct Route* to a bulge. Pull rightwards onto this and follow a crack for 6
metres to join the end of the hand-traverse on *The Direct Route*. Go easily
up to flake belays.
3 17m. 5b. *The Direct Route* pitch 4.

★★★**Superdirect**   75 metres   E1   (28.6.74)
A leisurely slab precedes an overhanging corner that is climbed with a
sense of urgency. Justifiably popular. Start as for *The Direct Route*.
1 21m. 4b. Scramble up over the twin pinnacles, and then move up to a
spike. Move down right and traverse the obvious line just above the rock
scar. Move up to belay on a ledge about 6 metres below a small overhang.
2 40m. 5b. Climb up past the overhang to the nut-slot on *Diagonal* and
continue for 2½ metres, where a short traverse leads left to a thin crack.
Follow this up to the long ledge and flake belays on *The Direct Route*. A
fine pitch.
3 14m. 5b. Climb up to the spike on the wall above, and finish up a
short overhanging corner-crack, which turns out to be surprisingly
strenuous.

★★Zeta   75 metres   E3   (5.67)

A fine, sustained and serious climb up the centre of the Nose. Pitch 2 is quite thin and leaders often have epics on it, but pitch 4 is the stopper. The original start has disappeared in a mammoth rockfall, so start as for *Superdirect*.

1 21m. 4b. *Superdirect* pitch 1.

2 18m. 5c. Climb up past the small overhang to the nut-slot on *Diagonal*. Bold moves diagonally right lead to the second stance on that route.

3 21m. 5b. Ascend the thin crack above the pegs. An easy flake now leads to a ledge. Step down right to a good ledge and belays.

4 15m. 6a. Move left and climb up to the overhanging arête. Ascend this past the remnants of a peg (small wires offer some comfort for the crux moves). The scoop is entered from the right, or from the left by the cleft, to an easy finish.

★★★Diagonal   78 metres   Hard Very Severe   (10.8.38)

A magnificent route that wanders boldly across the centre of the Nose from left to right. The third pitch is very delicate and requires finesse for success. Start as for *The Direct Route*.

1 24m. 5a. Climb the groove just left of the rock scar, and continue up the left side of a huge perched flake. From the top of this, move up a short way, and make a difficult traverse right across the slab to a stance and nut belays under a small overhang. Or (easier) start up the first pitch of *Superdirect*, but the pitch as described is more in keeping with the rest of the route.

2 12m. 5a. Above and slightly right is a large overhang with a bottomless chimney on its right-hand side. The chimney can be reached in one of two ways. Either climb up to the left side of the overhang (good nut-slot), and make a hard traverse underneath it; or, easier, climb diagonally right to good holds and step up left into the chimney. The chimney leads to a small stance with peg belays.

3 30m. 5a. Traverse right into a shallow scoop. Climb this and move right to make the famous mantelshelf onto a small ledge. A long reach to a good pocket leads to an easy sloping crack (possible belays). Follow the crack up into a recess below the steep corner-crack.

4 12m. 4c. The strenuous corner-crack yields to a determined approach.

★Crosstie   71 metres   Hard Very Severe   (27.7.55)

A good route taking a counter-line to *Diagonal*, going from right to left and finishing up the left-slanting groove left of the final pitch of *The Direct Route*. Start below the overhanging chimney of *The Link*, 12 metres left of the stile at the top of some quartz steps, below a break in the initial overhangs.

1 18m. 4b. Go diagonally leftwards, heading for the stance below the small overhang above pitch 1 of *Diagonal*.

2 27m. 5a. Follow *Diagonal* to the nut-slot left of the overhang. Step up and traverse left, rising slightly into the groove of *The Direct Route*. Climb this to the open bay stance.

3 26m. 5b. Ascend the corner-groove directly above the scoop to the foot of the final corner of *The Direct Route*. Step back left into the groove and climb its left wall on good holds to a steepening. A few strenuous moves lead to a good ledge (hard) – junction with *The Cracks*.

★★Stairway to Heaven   69 metres   E3   (9.78)
This very fine climb, both bold and technical, gives a sustained outing. Start as for *Crosstie*.

1 21m. 4c. Climb directly up to a block stance below the left wall of *The Link* (and 3 metres left of the *Blink! – Don't!* flake stance). Thread belay on the left.

2 15m. 5c. Ascend for 3 metres to good runners; then traverse left across the wall and pull boldly around the arête on small holds. Go straight up into the *Diagonal* scoop. Reverse the *Diagonal* traverse to belay at the top of its second pitch.

3 18m. 5c. From the right-hand end of the belay ledge, a thin crack runs up the steep slab parallel to the thin crack on pitch 3 of *Zeta*. Climb the crack direct, trending right near the top to exit on a large grassy ledge. Belay in the corner.

4 15m. 5c. Climb the middle of the three grooves between the top pitches of *Zeta* and *Diagonal*, past a peg. A technically absorbing exercise. Variation

★Stairway Direct   30 metres   E3 5c
A bold but escapable pitch, hard for the grade. Start at the first stance of *Stairway to Heaven* and follow that route to the *Diagonal* scoop. Continue straight up to reach a crack up on the left. Avoiding an escape (and runners) to the right, climb the centre of the rounded rib above on small widely-spaced holds.

The Laughing Buddha   15 metres   E4 6a   (7.3.96)
A precocious little pitch in a fine position, taking the obvious and oft-eyed groove left of the final pitch of *Stairway to Heaven*.

The Link   24 metres   E1 5c   (22.8.54)
The conspicuous overhanging chimney joining *West Rib* to the upper part of *Diagonal*. High in the grade and often greasy. Start at the top of *West Rib* pitch 1. Move up to grapple with the stubborn overhanging chimney/crack. A good continuation pitch (**The Chain** 15 metres 5b) can be done up the finger-crack between the last pitches of *West Rib* and *Western Slabs*.

★★West Rib   68 metres   Hard Very Severe   (13.9.31)
The long shallow rib to the right of the overhanging chimney of the *The Link* gives a fine airy pitch similar to, but slightly easier than, *Diagonal*. Protection is spaced but good. Start below the chimney/crack of *The Link*.

1 18m. 4b. Climb up towards *The Link*, and then move right to a stance just left of the rib.

2 32m. 5a. Traverse horizontally right and up onto the crest of the rib. Climb this with a high step up after 9 metres (good nut), and then continue delicately, trending slightly left and then right, up to a flake belay on *Western Slabs*.

3 18m. 4c. Move round the arête on the left to climb a thin crack using some doubtful flakes. Mantelshelf onto the steep arête and move right delicately to finish as for *Western Slabs*. Or, better, finish up *The Chain*.

Blink! – Don't!   63 metres   E1   (26.8.78)
A rather contrived line with some good moves but little independent climbing.
1 24m. 4c. Climb *Western Slabs* for 6 metres. Break out left and ascend to a small stance on a large spike 6 metres left of *West Rib*.
2 27m. 5b. Make a few moves up the diagonal crack and pull up into the groove just on the left of *West Rib*. Climb this to a junction with *West Rib*, which is followed for 3 metres. Continue along a flake crack that runs up left to meet a crack above *The Link*. Climb the thin crack in the slab to a flake belay.
3 12m. 4c. Scramble up behind the belay and finish via the corner-crack of *Diagonal*.

★★Western Slabs   60 metres   Very Severe   (6.8.31)
A popular and enjoyable route up the right-hand side of the Nose. Start just left of the drystone wall.
1 15m. 4b. From the top of a quartzy block, pull up onto a ledge and climb to a rightward-slanting groove. From the top of this, go round the arête to a ledge with small belays.
2 27m. 4b. Gain the ledge above and ascend to the lower of two small overlaps. Pass this on the right to a small sharp spike (sling). Step right and climb across under the second overlap; then follow the groove up to a ledge. Continue up into a shallow groove that leads rightwards to a ledge overlooking *Western Gully*.
3 18m. 4c. Step down left and climb the easy groove to a higher ledge by a large flake. Climb the groove on the right to the top of a block. Make a hard move past a steepening and exit right onto a ledge. Finish easily.
Variation
1a 4b. Start 6 metres left of the drystone wall, on a sloping platform and climb diagonally right into the slanting groove.
2a 4c. From the small sharp spike above the first overlap where the original line moves right, step left and ascend directly to the ledge.

Speeding Fine   60 metres   E2   (29.7.78)
A bold but enjoyable route to the right of *Western Slabs*. The second pitch, although not technically hard, is sustained and has sparse protection. Start 11 metres right of the drystone wall and 2½ metres left of a seeping crack.
1 12m. 4c. Climb up trending left to the ledge above pitch 1 of *Western Slabs*. Belay on the extreme left of the ledge.
2 30m. 5b. Go up right into a broad scoop; bridge up this and exit right. The bold and precarious slab immediately left of the arête leads to the second stance of *Western Slabs*.
3 18m. 5b. Traverse left around the corner to finish up *The Chain*.

Spaghetti Western   56 metres   Hard Very Severe   (7.6.82)
This takes the left edge of *Western Gully* with some poorly protected
climbing – an easier version of *Speeding Fine*, with which it shares some of
the climbing. It is marred only by the close proximity of the gully. Start 1½
metres left of the leftmost crack of *Western Gully*.
1 11m. 4a. Ascend via flakes and ledges on the rib on the right to join
the gully.
2 24m. 5a. Go easily up the rib about 2½ metres left of the arête for 9
metres. Continue up the crest and over the bulge; then traverse 2½ metres
left and go up a thin crack to join *Western Slabs*. A delicate pitch.
3 21m. 5a. Traverse 1½ metres towards the gully-bed, and then climb a
crack and its continuation to meet *Western Slabs*.

The Girdle of the Nose   47 metres   Very Severe   (6.8.31)
A short high-level crossing of the Nose: mainly Severe in standard with the
exception of the hand-traverse on *The Direct Route*. It may be taken in
either direction but is normally climbed from left to right. Start as for pitch
5 of *The Cracks*, at the pinnacle belay.
1 12m. 4b. From the top of the pinnacle move across onto the ledge
(runner in the corner). Descend a short crack and an easy-angled slab to
the open bay above the long groove of *The Direct Route*.
2 17m. 4c. Follow *The Direct Route* along its hand-traverse (crux), and
then continue more easily to a large ledge and belay.
3 18m. 4b. Traverse on good flake holds to reach the groove of *Western
Slabs*; finish up this.

The New Girdle   68 metres   E2   (28.4.78)
A pleasant open route which crosses the Nose at half height. Start on
ledges on the left-hand side of the Nose, level with the traverse on pitch 3
of *The Cracks*.
1 9m. Step across the gap and traverse round and down to the stance on
The Cracks.
2 26m. 5c. Step down and cross easily to a rib. Go up to a flake, and then
move down across *The Direct Route* to some spikes on the arête. Reverse
Crosstie to *Zeta*, which is followed with interest to the *Diagonal* stance.
3 15m. 5a. Traverse the obvious line onto *West Rib*. Move round to a
pocket, and climb the wall rightwards to a large ledge overlooking
Western Gully.
4 18m. 4c. *Western Slabs* pitch 3.

Western Gully   60 metres   Moderate   (1901)
The easiest way to the top of the Nose. Start up either of two short cracks
or more pleasantly by a traverse across slabs from the right. Continue up
on excellent holds. This is also the normal descent, when it is trickiest at the
bottom (when wet a small smooth spike can be used to abseil the final
steep section – the rope runs easily).

North Ridge of Crib Goch   Difficult   (1901)
The upper rocks of Dinas Mot are weakest directly above the Nose and
provide a useful exit for parties wishing to continue the day by a walk
along Crib Goch or by a climb on one of the higher crags. On a wet day
this tricky line is not obvious and great care should be taken whilst
following it. From the top of the Nose, cross the quartz-veined rib above
Western Gully, and go up a mossy chimney and then a smooth corner.
Traverse left to a pile of large blocks about 18 metres above the rib.
Scramble leftwards over blocks into a small cave, and traverse left to a
large grassy avenue where the angle eases.

The Western Wing

This area, between *Western Gully* and *Jammed Boulder Gully*, gives long
rambling climbs with interchangeable finishes owing to the cliff being split
horizontally by a series of grassy ledges, the Great Terrace. Below the
terrace are steep open slabs of compact rhyolite similar to the Nose, while above
the terrace the rock is similar to that of the Eastern Wing, giving complex
route-finding.

When approaching from *Western Gully*, the first feature is an area of steep
black slabs, often wet, which are taken by the fine 'Black' routes. This is
bounded on the right by a dirty gully, *Dolerite Dump*. Below this gully is a tall
pear-shaped flake that marks the starts of both *Tremolite* and *Bluebell
Cracks*. Right of the flake, the compact slabby rock of the lower tier continues
to the top of the crag. The Great Terrace is the line of *The Western Wing
Girdle*. It also provides a way of escape either into *Jammed Boulder Gully* or
to the top of the Nose by Moderate scrambling.

The cliff is generally north-facing, but does receive sunshine from late
afternoon onwards if there is any. Descent is by means of *Jammed Boulder
Gully*, which is quite tricky in parts – particularly when wet.

★★**Slow Ledge Climb**   63 metres   Severe   (30.3.34)
A delightful route that cleverly finds a way through the many overhangs of
the upper tier. The climbing is continually interesting and the rock is sound.
A good continuation to *The Cracks* or a better finish to *Dolerite Dump*, but
it becomes much harder in the wet. Start from the top of the Nose. Slow
Ledge, a severely undercut sloping shelf, protrudes from the cliff face to
dominate the right skyline. Cross the quartz rib above *Western Gully* and
scramble 15 metres right to a flake belay.
1 23m. Climb easy ledges, moving right. A short wall with a tiny tree
leads to a good stance. Move right up the slab and semi hand-traverse
across to the Slow Ledge (a person sitting on this ledge would slowly slide
off!). Step right and go up a small groove to make another short traverse
to a grassy rake. Belay at the top of this.
2 40m. Go straight up to a mossy groove. Cross the rib on the left into a
cleaner groove. Climb this, moving left or right to avoid difficulties.
Scramble up slabs to finish.

Dinas Mot:
The Western Wing

1	West Rib	HVS
2	Western Slabs	VS
3	Black Shadow	E3
4	Black Spring	HVS
5	Coon's Yard	E2
6	Black Foot (lower pitches only)	E3
7	Dolerite Dump	VD
8	Tremolite	E1
9	Sych	E2
10	Bluebell Cracks	VD
11	Hiawatha	HVS
12	Jublilee Climb	HVS
13	Boulder Buttress	VD

At the base of the cliff right of *Western Gully* is:

★★Black Shadow 131 metres E3   (14.6.69)
A delicate and sustained climb up the edge of the black wall that overlooks *Western Gully*. It dries faster than its neighbours. The peg that used to protect the entry into the finishing groove on pitch 5 is no longer in place, making this the crux pitch. A rightward escape at the end of pitch 4 along *Slow Ledge Climb* for the sane and the faint-hearted reduces the grade to E2. Start 9 metres right of the foot of *Western Gully*.
1 15m. Climb the wet wall to a dirty terrace below the slabs.
2 21m. 5a. From the left-hand end of the ledge, move left across the slab and climb a thin crack near the arête until it peters out. Step left and go up the arête and onto a slab below a large overhang. Nut and peg belays.
3 37m. 5c. Move right up the slab and step left onto the lip of the roof. Climb 5 metres to the foot of a blank groove and move right to a rib. Climb the short blank wall past a peg (hard) and step left into a slabby groove, which leads to a grassy ledge. Ascend the groove above the right end of the ledge until a pull left onto the quartz rib leads to easier climbing and a belay on the Great Terrace. A pitch that has stopped many leaders.
4 24m. 4a. Scramble up across the Great Terrace, over broken rock to the left of two small trees, to reach a flake belay just left of the foot of the rightward-curving groove with a crack in it (junction with *Black Spring* and *Slow Ledge Climb*).
5 34m. 5c. Traverse left for 3 metres, move up to a good hold, and then go back right into a slabby groove directly above the stance. Follow this, heading for the wide shallow groove that breaks through the capping overhangs. Enter the groove boldly and continue on better holds to a large ledge (or scuttle off right along the obvious break). Nut belays 9 metres back on the left; scramble up to finish.

Black and White 73 metres E3   (26.8.78)
A worthwhile addition to the 'Black' wall. Start as for *Black Shadow*.
1 15m. *Black Shadow* pitch 1.
2 24m. 5c. Climb the wall left of *Black Spring*; then traverse left to a line of shallow pockets, which lead up into a shallow groove. Exit left at the top to belay on *Black Shadow*.
3 34m. 5c. Climb the overhang on its gully side by a long hard pull. Climb the groove on the left to an overhang below a grassy crack. Step round right below the square-cut roof, and then move out right and up to a grassy ledge (on *Black Shadow*). Finish more easily up the obvious quartz ramp/groove.

★★Black Spring 177 metres Hard Very Severe   (3.4.65)
An excellent route which gives delicate climbing up the steep black slabs right of *Western Gully*. The second pitch is unfortunately often wet.
1 15m. *Black Shadow* pitch 1.
2 27m. 5a. Climb a prominent crack for 9 metres, and then move left for 3 metres until pockets lead up the steepening slab to a bulge. Pull around

this and ascend delicately left and up to gain a cave stance right of *Black Shadow*. Peg and nut belays.

3 34m. 5a. Climb the overhang just right of the stance and swing round right onto a steep slab. Ascend the shallow groove for a short way, and then trend diagonally left to a quartz groove. Climb this to the Great Terrace.

4 27m. 4a. Scramble over broken rocks, past two little trees, to a steep wall and huge flake belay (on *Slow Ledge Climb*).

5 37m. 4c. Go up a crack on the left to below the big roof. A long easy traverse right leads to a belay (also on *Slow Ledge Climb*).

6 37m. Fine open slabs lead to the top.

Variation

3a 37m. 5b. Follow pitch 3 over the overhang to the shallow groove, and then take an obvious diagonal line up right with difficulty. Regain the main line up easy ledges to the left.

★Coon's Yard   143 metres   E2   (28.6.74)

A fine technical route with a superb third pitch under the diagonal band of quartz overhangs which break out rightwards from the *Black Spring* cave. Pitch 4 is always a bit dirty and lichen-covered, and has stopped a few parties.

1 15m. *Black Shadow* pitch 1.

2 27m. 5a. As for *Black Shadow* pitch 2 to its belay, and then traverse right to the cave belay of *Black Spring*.

3 43m. 5b. Climb diagonally right under the overhangs with increasing difficulty until a hard move leads round the arête on the right. Move up to grass and scramble up to a flake belay 5 metres below a small tree.

4 21m. 5a. Climb easy rocks and move up into a square niche. Swing left onto a prow. Climb the wall to the roof beneath the Slow Ledge. Move right and climb the groove to a good belay.

5 37m. 5b. Climb the roof above the short groove with difficulty, and step right to the foot of a groove. Climb this (with slightly less difficulty) to a small sloping ledge where the groove narrows. Step right to jammed blocks. Finish up easier rock.

Variation

3a 37m. 5b. It is possible to pull through the quartz overhangs and traverse along the lip – easier and a little bit cleaner.

Black Foot   156 metres   E2   (3.7.65)

A serious and technical route, which because of this is becoming increasingly dirty. Start right of *Black Shadow*, below a large grassy pillar.

1 24m. Climb easy rock, and then go up a grassy crack on the left side of the pillar. Move right and climb to a stance and good belay 5 metres below the apex of the pillar.

2 26m. 5a. Climb the groove formed by the pillar and the wall, then the wall above on pockets to the overhang. Traverse right to a grassy stance. Peg belays.

3 37m. 5b. Climb the arête behind the stance for a short way. Traverse left across the steep wall to a quartz ledge on the lip of the overhang. The steep crack above leads to easy ground.

4 23m. 5b. Scramble up left to a large detached block. Traverse right to a large flake, go up this and step right into the bottom of a groove (the large round overhang of *Slow Ledge Climb* is just on the right). Climb the groove with a very hard finish. Move right to belay. A serious and poorly protected pitch.

5 46m. Move right to below an overhang. Traverse under it to the foot of a long broken groove. Climb this to the top.

Variation

The Black Page E1

A direct alternative to pitch 2. Start on the other side of the pillar.

2a 21m. 5b. Climb the grey walls, a groove and the overhang above.

Dolerite Dump 163 metres Very Difficult (26.6.44)

Below the Great Terrace is a large corner facing left, which gives the line of this poor route. Above, the climb deteriorates into a grassy scramble. Best done as a start to *Slow Ledge Climb*. Start 18 metres right of *Western Gully*.

1 20m. Easy rock leads to a short overhanging crack. Avoid this by traversing left and then going up to another steep crack.

2 18m. Either climb the crack direct or more easily by excursions onto the slab on the right. From a grassy ledge, go up a path below steep walls and traverse left round the corner to a grassy bay.

3 14m. Ascend the long mossy groove.

4 18m. Go easily up the gully to the Great Terrace. It is possible to scramble up leftwards to join *Slow Ledge Climb* from here.

5 18m. Climb up on heather to the foot of a smooth slab, overhung on the left.

6 21m. Climb broken rocks on the right of the slab and then up a short steep corner.

7 24m. Scramble up a subsidiary groove on the left, until forced further to the left by an overhanging wall. Continue in the same line to the base of the final groove.

8 30m. Continue up the long wide groove straight ahead. Where the scrambling becomes awkward near the top, break out right and finish on clean rock.

Tremolite 121 metres E1 (29.8.63)

A varied and interesting climb. Start at the pear-shaped flake that marks the start of *Bluebell Cracks*.

1 18m. 5a. Climb the difficult bulge and go up on good holds to the top of the flake.

2 15m. 5b. Move right across wet sloping ledges to a tree. Climb the strenuous overhanging crack onto a slab. Good thread belay.

3 30m. 5a. Traverse right from the belay across a slab to a thin crack, which is climbed (hard to start but it soon relents) into a shallow groove. Climb this, exiting left at the top onto the Great Terrace.

4 40m. 5a. Climb the arête left of an open corner leading up to a huge overhang. Move right above the overhang, and then zigzag up the wall to avoid difficulties. Follow *Dolerite Dump* to a belay below a large overhang.

5 18m. 4b. Climb the arête left of the roof and go up a cracked groove to join *Boulder Buttress* just below the top.

Variation

Dole-ite Variation   E1
Scramble rightwards from the top of pitch 1 to belay below the second pitch of *Sych*, on hollies.

2a 37m. 5b. Climb up to the two large pockets and step left onto a small ledge as for *Sych*. Traverse left for a short way, and then follow a rising line to reach the base of the groove on pitch 3. Finish up the shallow groove as for that pitch.

Bluebell Cracks   56 metres   Very Difficult   (2.8.48)
Pleasant but hard for its grade. Thirty-five metres right of *Dolerite Dump* is the only other easy break below the Great Terrace, a cracked groove facing right. This is reached by a long traverse from the left. Start at the pear-shaped flake at the foot of the crag.

1 12m. Climb the corner right of the flake by a series of shallow caves to the passage between the flake and the cliff.

2 12m. The quartz-veined slab leads right into an overhung recess. Traverse right to a ledge below a holly tree.

3 20m. Traverse right along a narrow ledge, and go slightly up to a grassy niche at the foot of the cracked groove. Climb the steep groove to a ledge with a tall flake leaning against a corner.

4 12m. Climb the flake and then the crack or the slab on its left. Escape rightwards along the Great Terrace.

Sych   144 metres   E2   (19.8.76)
A steep line on the right of *Tremolite*. The name is Welsh for 'dry'.

1 21m. *Hiawatha* pitch 1.

2 46m. 5c. Climb up to the two large pockets and step left onto a small ledge. Make a series of difficult moves, first left and then straight up, to a good handhold. Swing right to the thin crack and climb this, via a very hard move, to reach the Great Terrace. The crack can be climbed direct, which is easier (5b).

3 40m. 5b. Above is a huge overhang. Climb onto the steep slab below the overhang and traverse right for 5 metres to the arête. Climb up (peg) to pass the roof on the right, and follow a groove until a step left over loose blocks leads onto *Tremolite*. Follow that climb to a flake belay in a large grassy bay.

4 37m. 5b. Climb up behind the belay, step right and climb over detached blocks to below a small roof. Make a hard move over the roof, and then take a crack and easier rock to the top.

★Sidewinder   165 metres   E2   (29.8.83)
Interesting and varied climbing up some impressive rock.

1 21m. *Hiawatha* pitch 1.

2 37m. 5b. Follow *Dole-ite Variation* to the base of the groove on *Tremolite*. Move 3½ metres left and go directly up the wall to a good small pocket. Continue steeply to reach a crack, which is followed to good belays on a terrace.

3 12m. Climb easily up heathery rock to a small tree and good belays below the upper part of *Tremolite*.

4 34m. 5b. Move left and climb various ribs and bulges, heading for a roof below a prominent triangular slab below a larger roof. At the level of the first roof traverse left (peg), passing a precarious-looking flake with difficulty. Step round the arête onto a steep wall and continue to a comfortable exposed ledge below Damoclean blocks. An exhilarating pitch.

5 21m. Climb over the blocks up to a short chimney. Follow this steeply until a move left to a stance on *Slow Ledge Climb*.

6 40m. Finish up *Slow Ledge Climb*.

Hiawatha   136 metres   Hard Very Severe   (2.7.61)
A good route building up to a great finish. The lower section is a series of variations on *Bluebell Cracks*. The upper section takes the left-hand side of the well-defined slabs, just left of the top part of *Jammed Boulder Gully*. Start below the cracked groove of *Bluebell Cracks*.

1 21m. Climb quartz and heather, moving right at the top to belay on hollies.

2 50m. 5a. Ascend the steep awkward crack, and move right near the top to the tall flake of *Bluebell Cracks*. Make a rising traverse right and go up a shallow groove (just in front of the skyline) to the heather terrace.

3 15m. 5b. Climb the stepped groove in the steep wall to the grassy rake of *Boulder Buttress*. Cross this and continue to a good spike belay.

4 50m. 5a. Layback into the heathery groove in the wall above, and climb the slab and heather grooves to the line of overhangs (*Flake Traverse Variant* crosses here). Traverse 3 metres right and go over the overhang to an obvious foothold. Either traverse left (thin) to the corner groove and go up to another overhang; or, pad up the slab 'Red Indian' style and traverse left to the same point (harder). Traverse left and continue up the left edge of the main slab proper to a large ledge. Scrambling remains.

The Watha Thin Variation   E2
4a 50m. 5b. Layback into the heathery groove as for *Hiawatha*, but step right at a small overhang capping the groove at 10 metres to gain a rib. Follow a thin seam up to the line of overhangs, joining *Hiawatha* at the prominent foothold. Move up to the next break, traverse left, and follow the very edge of the slab to the top.

Intruder   130 metres   Hard Very Severe   (14.6.65)
A vague route, in essence a harder variation on *Hiawatha*. Start 9 metres right of *Hiawatha*, just right of a grassy corner.

1 18m. 5a. Climb over a bulge to the right. Step left and go straight up to a grass ledge and peg belay.

2 37m. 5a. Climb up to the left and follow the prominent groove. Scramble up broken rock and belay below a deep groove above the terrace.

3 27m. 5a. Climb the groove and step left at the bulge. Climb this to a ledge and belay.

4 21m. 4c. Climb a short slab to the right and go up a crack to a roof. Belay on the right.
5 27m. 5a. Traverse left and over a small overlap to a peg. Continue up to the next small overlap and finish up *Jubilee Climb*.

The next two routes are in the area between *Hiawatha* and *Jubilee Climb*. Both routes end at the obvious grassy terrace dividing the upper and lower sections of the West Wing. You can traverse off rightwards, for which it is best to keep roped up, to gain the base of *Jammed Boulder Gully*; or finish off with the top sections of *Hiawatha* and its *Watha Thin* variation.

Pokeyhuntas   55 metres   E3 5c   (16.8.03)
Good climbing but with some poorly protected sections. Start where a large embedded flake props up the left end of an overhang, just right of the corner of *Intruder*. Obvious thread belay. Pull through the overhang on flakes and a long reach; then climb the slab direct to heathery ledges and a poor spike. An easier start can be made by moving in from the start of *Ghost Dance* on the right. Head up right to arrange protection around a flake somehow attached to the slabby wall. From here a committing move left onto an obvious foothold gains a crack. Go up until it is possible to swing left onto the arête; try to keep out of the damp groove and stay on the arête as much as possible to finish at the terrace.

Ghost Dance   50 metres   E3 5c   (16.8.03)
A pleasant enough filler-in with some good moves. Start at the large embedded flake 3 metres to the right of *Pokeyhuntas*, where the overhang disappears. Spike belay. Climb the slab boldly but easily to heathery ledges below an obvious crack system (possible belay). Step up right onto the slab right of the crack, and follow flakes and cracks curving over right to gain a steep vertical crack just left of the hollies on *Jubilee Climb*. Difficult moves up the crack gain easier ground and a huge flake belay just below the terrace. Finish off by climbing up easily to the terrace.

★★**Jubilee Climb**   84 metres   Hard Very Severe   (23.4.59)
This fine climb takes a parallel line up the slabs to the right of *Hiawatha*, giving a climb of contrasts. The lower section goes via an obvious square-cut niche. The crack above this is strenuous but safe, and the final pitch gives delicate climbing in a marvellous position. Start at the left-hand side of a large flake directly below the niche.
1 30m. 4b. Go up easy slabs for 18 metres and climb difficult twin heather grooves to a small holly tree in the niche.
2 9m. Traverse left to a good flake and go up easily to the heather terrace.
3 15m. 5b. Above is a steep little wall with a crack near its right-hand end. Move up right round the corner of the wall and ascend on spikes until a move back left leads onto the front wall. Climb the crack to a good spike belay. The coffin-shaped recess on the left of the lower wall also leads to the same point.
4 9m. 4a. Follow the crack up a mossy slab to a huge belay at the end of *Flake Traverse Variant*.

5 21m. 5a. Make a difficult rising traverse left up the slab to the central scoop. Regain the crackline above a small overlap and climb it. A fine exposed finish.

War Drum   45 metres   Hard Very Severe 5a   (17.7.03)
A fine pitch on perfect rock, just about reaching the grade. Start on the right-hand side of the large rectangular flake at the base of *Jubilee Climb*. Ascend the easy but bold slabs to a booming flake, and move up to an obvious flake hold at the base of a slab right of the twin cracks of *Jubilee Climb*. Climb the delectable slab to a ledge below a short corner just left of the holly, and go round and up right to make a high step past an obvious cam pocket. Easier climbing leads to the terrace; belay on the large flake. It is possible to scramble off right into the base of *Jammed Boulder Gully*.

Boulder Buttress   93 metres   Very Difficult   (30.3.34)
A scrappy route up the grassy break left of the final slab of *Hiawatha* and *Jubilee Climb*. Start by scrambling up *Jammed Boulder Gully* to grassy ledges at the foot of a few steep outcrops. The first section of the buttress lies on the left.
1 21m. Go pleasantly up rough slabs to the heather terrace.
2 18m. Move left under the steep walls. The break on the left is ill-defined at first. Climb a short corner to a grassy rake, which is followed left round the steep buttress into the groove.
3 9m. Scramble up, keeping close to the rocks on the right.
4 18m. Follow the groove until you can break away left to a heather ledge below a wide rock bay.
5 12m. Ascend to a holly tree, bear right and go up split blocks to a maze of belays.
6 15m. Traverse 6 metres left and finish up the arête on excellent rock.
Variations
4a 37m. Go straight up the groove. It is now better defined. At 30 metres is a short steep bit, above which the vegetation can be avoided on the right.
6a 12m. Instead of traversing left to the arête, cross the slab on the right and ascend a steep corner (about Severe).

Flake Traverse Variant   64 metres   Very Difficult
A dry alternative to the top of the boulder. Despite vegetation, the traverse is worth the diversion. Start at the foot of the gully and scramble up to the heather terrace on the left, which can also be reached by *Boulder Buttress* pitch 1.
1 37m. As for *Boulder Buttress*. Go into the large grassy groove up on the left via a short corner and grassy rake, and scramble up to the left end of a horizontal crack under a small overhang.
2 9m. Hand-traverse right, along the crack, finishing awkwardly on a heathery ledge with belays.
3 18m. Scramble across right into *Jammed Boulder Gully*.

One Inch Punch   42 metres   E7 6b   (8.01)
A bold undertaking in a fine position. The rounded arête forming the
right-hand edge of the Western Wing, right of the *Jubilee Climb* slab,
provides the meat of the route. Start on the right below an obvious
rectangular overhang in the arête.
1 24m. 5b. Climb up to the overhang (as for the first part of pitch 3 of
Jubilee Climb) and use cracks to pull round this on the left. Easy cracks then
lead up to some ledges below the arête, where you can view the problem.
2 18m. 6b. Climb the slab to the left of the arête until it is possible to
move right to the arête proper. Lonely moves up this prove to be the crux.

Western Wing Girdle   Difficult   (30.3.34)
A vegetated scramble needing very little technique, but giving some views
of the other routes. From the top of the Nose it follows the vegetated
terraces across to the foot of *Jammed Boulder Gully*. Scramble up *Eastern
Gully* to the top of the Nose. Cross the quartz rib above *Western Gully* and
continue for 30 metres or so, descending slightly, to an excellent belay.
Descend a grassy rake to the right for 15 metres; then continue along the
heather terrace to the foot of *Jammed Boulder Gully*.

Jammed Boulder Gully   60 metres   Moderate   (1900)
A typical gully with good rock and an interesting cave pitch. It is the
obvious wide recess in the centre of The Western Wing where a massive
rock has become wedged about 60 metres above the screes. A tricky
descent when wet.
1 30m. Scramble to the cave below the boulder, or climb the harder slabs
on the right, which are often wet and not so pleasant.
2 6m. Enter the cave and struggle through a narrow hole in the roof, the
cause of much amusement.
3 24m. Continue up the main gully-line, starting via a shallow groove on
the right and passing a second, much smaller jammed boulder.

Groper Buttress
This is the small buttress between *Jammed Boulder Gully* and *Black Cleft*.

The Lymph   70 metres   E2   (10.8.68)
A poor route taking a groove and then slabs, essentially a left-hand
variation of *Groper*. Start below the buttress by scrambling up to belay
below the obvious groove.
1 34m 5c. Climb up and step right into the foot of the groove. Start this
by hard moves (peg), and continue up to the big roof. Step right onto the
slab and go straight up to a heathery bay.
2 18m. 4b. Ascend easily rightwards to the belay above pitch 2 of
Groper.
3 18m. 5b. *Groper* pitch 3, or escape left along a ledge to reach
vegetation, up which it is possible to finish.

Groper   79 metres   E3   (1965)
A good varied route, quite high in the grade. Start as for *The Lymph*.

1 46m. 6a. Climb the groove as for *The Lymph* until it forks. Traverse right (peg high in the right-hand groove and another peg on the wall) to a slab and move up right to a shallow scoop. Climb the steep crack past a hidden spike to a ledge on the arête. Move left and go up to a stance.
2 15m. 4b. Follow the rib to a sloping ledge and peg belays.
3 18m. 5b. From the right-hand end of the ledge, climb a crack until level with an overhang on the right. Hand-traverse left to a layback crack. Ascend this to an overhang, move right and continue up to a good stance. Scrambling remains.
Variation
1a It is possible to climb the thin crack in the arête of pitch 1 at the same standard. Finish up *The Lymph*.

Zyklon 'B'   45 metres   E4   (23.6.84)
A bold and spectacular route taking the centre of the buttress after going over its initial roof. At the time of writing, it is very dirty. Start below the centre of the buttress.
1 26m. 6a. A crack on the right leads to a steep wall below the roof (peg on the left). Climb the wall and thug across the roof on large holds (peg).
2 19m. 5b. Finish up the centre of the wall.

Runnymede   75 metres   E2   (26.10.77)
An exposed and poorly protected route, whose main pitch takes the right arête of the buttress. Start below the right end of the big roof.
1 9m. Scramble up to a field just left of *Black Cleft*.
2 27m. 5b. Ascend a short groove in the right arête of the buttress and move left to join *Groper* just above the big roof. Climb the scoop of *Groper* to two obvious pockets. Move right round the arête and climb to a horizontal crack. Follow the arête, mainly on the right, to a spike belay. A fine pitch.
3 18m. 5a. Move down right and go up a steep ramp. Trend slightly left and go back up right to reach the belay above pitch 2 of *Groper*.
4 21m. 5a. Traverse left 3 metres, climb an open scoop for 6 metres and move right to the layback crack of *Groper*. Ascend this, and then surmount the overhang to finish up a short groove.

Runnymede Easy Variations   60 metres   Hard Very Severe   (18.6.78)
Slight but entertaining. Start at the grassy field above the start of *Runnymede*.
1 21m. 5a. Climb a line of flakes to join *Runnymede*.
2 18m. 5a. *Runnymede* pitch 3.
3 21m. 4c. Climb the smooth slab on the left of the upper wall.

Black Cleft   118 metres   Severe   (1897)
This classic gully, usually wet and repulsive, is the exclusive preserve of masochists and is generally deemed to be 'a fine climb in the traditional idiom'. It is the deep rift right of *Jammed Boulder Gully*, and has been known to turn grown men into quivering wrecks in all but the most perfect of conditions.
1 24m. Scramble up into a wide bay.
2 12m. Follow the narrowing gully, passing a chockstone on the left.

3 18m. The crux: climb the steep waterworn bed of the gully (good protection is very hard to find). In the usual wet conditions reserved for such routes this pitch may be found taxing in the extreme.
4 18m. Another interesting gully pitch, thankfully a little less steep than the previous one.
5 46m. Scramble to the top (and question your sanity).

Plexus Buttress

On the right of *Black Cleft* is a large area of slabby rock split at two-thirds height by a line of huge overhangs, the continuation of the Great Terrace faultline. This is the magnificent Plexus Buttress, which has a high concentration of top quality routes.

North-facing, it can receive some sunshine in the late afternoon and evening. An approach from the road can take between 20 and 25 minutes. Descent is by means of *Jammed Boulder Gully*, or down open slopes well to the west.

★Sexus   127 metres   E4   (27.3.65)
A difficult and sustained excursion up the left-hand side of Plexus Buttress; the roof on pitch 4 looks innocuous enough from below, but proves to be a ferocious obstacle. Start 6 metres right of the arête.
1 30m. 5a. Climb the leftward-slanting flakes to a shallow groove, which leads up to a grassy ledge. Move left to nut belays by a tree.
2 30m. 5c. Traverse 6 metres right and go up to a thin vertical crack in the arête. Climb this (very hard), trending left up a steep ramp. Move right at the top of the arête to the belay above pitch 2 of *Plexus*.
3 21m. 4a. Traverse left under the roof to a thread belay at its left end.
4 46m. 6b. Power over the roof (or more usually siege it) onto the slab. This transition from the strenuous to the delicate has bewildered many leaders. Traverse right on the slab to a prow (poor peg). Step down right and go up a hidden groove. Traverse left for a short way and climb a short groove to the slabs above; possible belay. Scrambling remains.
Variation
Direct Start   57 metres   Very Severe
The original start follows the left arête of the buttress.
1a 30m. 4c. Climb the left arête of the buttress overlooking *Black Cleft*, moving right up the face until a swing down can be made to a tree stance and nut belay on the arête.
2a 27m. 4a. Climb the crack, step left, and continue to the huge roof.

★★The Red Ring   93 metres   E5   (4.81)
A bold, intimidating and sensational route through some airy territory.
1 & 2 5c. As for *Sexus* to belay under the roof.
3 9m. 6b. Launch out across the massive roof, which sometimes succumbs to technical thuggery, and pull round the lip to climb an easy slab – not a pitch for the faint-hearted. Belay below the biggest roof above.

Dinas Mot:
Plexus & Groper Buttresses

1	The Lymph (with the independent finish)	E2
2	Groper	E3
3	Black Cleft	S
4	Sexus Direct Start	VS
5	Sexus	E4

6	Plexus	HVS
7	Ten Degrees North	E2
8	Nexus	E1
9	Nexus Direct	E5
10	The Windmill	E3
11	The Smodge	E4
12	Gardd	HVS
13	Hornets Attack	
	Victor Mature	E2

4 24m. 6a. Take the 2½-metre roof direct, an anticlimax after the previous pitch but still difficult. Step right into a groove, which leads to a hard exit onto easy slabs.

★★**Perplexus**   100 metres   E5   (13.7.89)
A tremendous eliminate based on *Plexus*, with some sensational climbing in its upper reaches. Start right of *Sexus*, directly below the first groove of *Plexus*.
1 18m. 5b. Climb up to an obvious vertical crack and use layaways on the left to gain height. Continue to slabs and a belay in the long scoop of *Plexus* at a peg.
2 34m. 6a. Follow *Plexus* pitch 2 to stand on a flake where *Plexus* moves right onto the slab. Make a move left into a groove and bridge up it to a sloping shelf on the edge of the arête, gained by a mantelshelf. Take the crack above to a ledge. Trend first right and then left, and continue directly up the arête. Belay just below the overlap.
3 15m. 5b. Move across a grass ledge on the right to reach the groove leading up to a belay below the crux groove of *Plexus*.
4 18m. 6b. Climb the overhang as for *Plexus*, and then traverse right along the lip of the overhang to where a high step-up gains a nick in the slab. Follow the faint depression above to stand on a rounded boss. Move right to a crack on the edge of the arête and belay at the end of the traverse of *Nexus* pitch 4.
5 15m. 6b. Layback the arête above to easy ground. A *Friend* ½ up and left and a hand-placed peg in a slot half-way up the arête give the only comfort.

★★★**Plexus**   138 metres   Hard Very Severe   (14.10.62)
The superb original route of the buttress provides delicate climbing in exciting positions on sound rock, bolder now that the peg protecting the crux has gone. Start at the right side of the buttress where the lower wall relents.
1 21m. Climb the easy groove to a large ledge. Traverse easily left above the lower wall to a stance and flake belay below the long scoop that runs up to the large overhang. Or start direct (5a).
2 46m. 5a. Climb to a bulge (peg), and go over it into a groove. Step right on to a slab (thread runner). Move left and climb a crack and the groove above until it steepens. Traverse left to the arête. Climb slabs to the big overhangs; peg belays.
3 37m. 5b. Traverse right to where the overhang is smallest. Climb up, and step left into a corner (crux). Ascend for a short way; then traverse right and up a delicate slab to a ledge beside a large detached block. Move left over the block to enter a scoop, and leave this on its right side by an awkward mantelshelf. Climb diagonally left to a stance and belay.
4 34m. 4b. Shallow grooves and slabs lead to the top.

★★**Ten Degrees North**   127 metres   E2   (27.6.74)
This excellent groove and slab between *Plexus* and *Nexus* gives sustained, delicate climbing with spaced but good protection.
1 21m. *Plexus* pitch 1.
2 15m. 5b. Climb a short wall and then move right to a peg. Go up to the groove, step left and ascend with difficulty to a nut belay on a slab.

Gollum (HVS, page 149) Dinas Mot
Climber: Mike Poppitt   Photo: Dave Ferguson

The Cracks (HS, page 153) Dinas Mot
Climbers unknown   Photo: David Simmonite

Black Shadow (E3, page 164) Dinas Mot
Climber: Tony Morley   Photo: Dave Ferguson

3 27m. 5c. Move right and balance up the open groove to a roof. Step right and go up to a peg. Step left and climb the slab to a small overhang. Continue up right to the huge roof and move right to belay on the flakes as for *Nexus*.

4 18m. 5b. Climb the crack on the left side of the flake above to join the *Nexus* traverse. Follow this to the left to belay as for Nexus.

5 46m. 4b. The last 12 metres of pitch 3, and pitch 4 of *Plexus*.

Dinas in the Dog 94 metres   E3   (21.8.95)
Though fighting for independence, this route has some good climbing and fine situations, as it makes a passing acquaintance with other lines. Start 8 metres left of *Nexus*, at a grass ledge.

1 18m. 6a. Climb a shallow corner with a move left at the top, and then go up past the peg on *Ten Degrees North* to gain a rest ledge. Climb direct, via a slim groove, for about 8 metres, and then traverse right to belay at the foot of the ramp of *Nexus*.

2 24m. 5c. Ascend the left-slanting corner above to a jug on a seemingly detached block. Swing left round a blunt arête to gain holds on the right wall of *Ten Degrees North*, which is climbed to a rest below a peg. Move right and follow a slab to the right-hand end of the overhang. Pull over the jutting but round end of the overhang to move up and right to belay on the flakes as for *Nexus*.

3 18m. 6a. Follow the flake crack above (*Ten Degrees North*) for 5 metres, and then traverse left steeply to gain a flat foothold near the left arête. Teeter round this and climb the slabby scoop above to gain some big flakes and the belay ledge of *Plexus*.

4 34m. 4b. *Plexus* pitch 4.

★★★**Nexus** 128 metres   E1   (21.5.63)
A companion route to *Plexus*, but slightly harder and better, making it one of the best routes of its grade on the crag. It takes the right-hand arête of the buttress, overlooking *Garden Groove*.

1 9m. As for *Plexus* to the first ledge.

2 46m. 5b. A magnificent pitch which climbs the slab on the right of the corner to the overhang. Hand-traverse left to a thread on the arête. Layback round the roof to gain the foot of a narrow gangway slanting up and right. Follow this in a superb position and where it steepens make a difficult move up to a sloping ledge on the right. Climb a short overhanging crack on good holds, and continue up a shallow groove to a stance and flake belays at the right-hand end of the big overhang.

3 12m. 4b. Climb the slab on the right until it steepens, and then go up to a ledge with a perched block on the right. Peg belay.

4 15m. 5b. Traverse left along a horizontal crack. Swing round the arête to join the upper part of *Plexus* pitch 3. Belay in the scoop.

5 46m. 4b. The last 12 metres of pitch 3, and pitch 4 of *Plexus*.

Variation
2a The Texas Start 46m E3 6a. A boulder-problem arête left of the usual start leads to a junction with the parent route at the thread runner.

★★**Nexus Direct**   24 metres   E5 6b   (26.8.66)
   Despite its benign appearance, this is a fierce and technical pitch with little
   in the way of protection, which still sees many failures. For the route to be
   in very dry condition is only *one* of the prerequisites for a successful ascent.
   Start from the belay above pitch 3 of *Nexus*. Climb up into the foot of the
   groove. A small wire provides the only protection. The blank groove above
   is climbed direct and yields only to sustained wide bridging.

★**The Windmill**   109 metres   E3   (7.5.74)
   An intricate but pleasurable first pitch up steep rock. Start as for *Nexus*
   pitch 2.
   1 46m. 5c. Climb the slab and the overhang above. Ascend the groove
   and move up to the roof. Go right on undercuts and then layback round
   and up to a small stance below a slab. Go delicately across the left wall
   and round the arête onto *Nexus*. Move up a short way to the overhangs
   and go right under these to a hidden flake in a groove. Move up to a
   ledge and then go right to easy ground. Belay as for *Nexus* pitch 2.
   2 12m. 4b. *Nexus* pitch 3.
   3 24m. 5b. Follow pitch 5 of *The Plexus Girdle* to easy ground. Go right
   and up to large blocks, and then move right across a slab to a peg belay
   in a niche.
   4 27m. 5a. The overhanging crack above leads to a ledge. Continue up
   the wide crack to finish.

★★**The Smodge**   64 metres   E4   (17.6.89)
   A surprisingly good line to the right of *The Windmill,* of which it is a
   mirror-image. Start by scrambling 9 metres up to a ledge below the
   groove immediately right of *The Windmill*.
   1 37m. 6a. Climb up into the groove, and exit left at its top to a junction
   with *The Windmill*. Trend precariously right across a slab below the obvious
   groove. More tenuous moves gain a solid handjam in a pod (*Friend* 1½).
   Move up the groove with interest, then cross some easier ground, and
   climb a slab to a peg belay below the arête by a block.
   2 27m. 5c. From the top of the block, climb directly up the arête to reach
   pitch 5 of *The Plexus Girdle*, which is followed to its belay.

★**The Plexus Girdle**   127 metres   E3   (1.5.65)
   A brilliant route, though never unduly difficult, which gives sustained and
   delicate climbing in an exposed position. Well worth the epic approach.
   Start up grassy terraces on the left of the buttress to below a small roof. A
   better start is up *Sexus*.
   1 24m. 4b. Traverse right under the roof to wet slabs. Cross these high
   up, passing a large spike to reach a grassy ledge. Climb onto a slab
   above large spikes and descend to these.
   2 18m. 5a. Traverse the slab to a prow and go up the groove as for
   Sexus (peg). Move out right below the roof until a descent can be made to
   a sentry-box stance.
   3 12m. 5b. Step down and traverse right on a steep slab to the arête.
   Ascend to a stance and belay in the scoop of *Plexus*.

4 15m. 5b. Descend the block of *Plexus* pitch 3, go round the arête and reverse the *Nexus* traverse. Belay in the corner.
5 43m. 5b. Climb the steep slab under the overhang (peg) to the arête on the right. Climb this, stepping round right and then back left (or direct at 5c) to easy ground.
6 15m. Ascend easily to the top.

Right of Plexus Buttress the rock degenerates considerably, but immediately to the right is the attractive slab of *Gardd*.

Garden Groove   92 metres   Difficult   (30.6.44)
This is the shallow groove that defines the right-hand side of Plexus Buttress. A thoroughly vegetative outing: not recommended, but it could be used as a winter playground.
1 15m. Avoid the first steep section by a detour on the left.
2 15m. Climb to the first overhang and pass it on the right. Continue up vegetation to a stance.
3 27m. Follow the groove until it widens into a heathery bay below an outcrop of quartz, and continue up to the slab below the second overhang.
4 11m. Climb the slab to a ledge on the right level with the overhang; thread belay.
5 24m. Climb the short slab, and then go left up a loose groove.
Variation
The left-hand exit makes the route independent of *Twin Groove*.
4a 14m. Go up the left side of the bay using a slab and some blocks to gain the edge of the buttress.
5a 15m. Finish up the easy arête.

★**Gardd**   49 metres   Hard Very Severe 5a   (2.12.62)
A worthwhile route on superb rock. It serves as a good introduction to the style of climbing to be found on the main buttress, and is surprisingly overlooked. High in the grade if climbed direct, but short variants off to the right or left of the main line bring the grade down to Very Severe. Start at the bottom left-hand corner of the slab. Step up, then traverse right for 10 feet, and go up over the bulge to gain the slab. Climb straight up the centre of the slab, with some long reaches and delicate moves. Ascend a short groove; then step right to the base of the crack system leading up to the wide crack, which gives an entertaining finish. It is possible to abseil off the big rounded pinnacle.

★**Hornets Attack Victor Mature**   36 metres   E2 5c   (30.4.83)
A very enjoyable pitch on good rock. Start by scrambling up to a point below a small square overhang 7 metres right of *Gardd* and 13 metres up. Climb a short groove to the overhang and surmount it using a good jam crack. Follow this to a small triangular overhang, which is skirted on the left by climbing easy ground to the slab above (much harder if taken direct). Make several precarious moves on small edges and sloping footholds to reach a last nut-slot. Layaway up left to make a long reach, or slap rounded slopers on the right. Finish up the arête to belay and abseil off as for *Gardd*.

Twin Groove   97 metres   Difficult   (22.6.35)
Much better than *Garden Groove*. Start at the foot of the groove right of
the *Gardd* slab.
1 24m. The slabby bed of the groove leads to the foot of the square-cut
chimney.
2 20m. Climb the chimney and the steep crack above it. A wider crack
leads to the grassy terrace above *Gardd*.
3 18m. Scramble across to the junction of two grooves.
4 11m. *Garden Groove* pitch 4.
5 24m. *Garden Groove* pitch 5.

Right of *Twin Groove* the cliff is very vegetated. Several very poor routes have
been recorded, all of them struggling to achieve mediocrity. Fifty metres right
of *Gardd* is a prominent pillar split by a wide crack on its left.

Calluna   55 metres   Very Severe   (3.11.68)
A vegetated outing that is cleaning up slowly. Start below the pillar about 15
metres up the heather slope, in a jungly gully with a large jammed block.
1 46m. 4b. Climb up to the left and go up to a rowan tree. Ascend
rightwards up the slab to a steep crack. Jam this to a crevasse. Traverse left
and grovel up the chimney to the top of the pillar.
2 9m. Escape rightwards through the jungle.

The Lectern   72 metres   Severe   (17.7.49)
A route of sorts, if you can find it. Start near *Calluna* below a
lectern-shaped rock above a wall.
1 12m. Climb the wall to the lectern.
2 15m. Traverse into a grassy groove and then out onto the face along
an obvious line.
3 15m. Move round the rib on the left. Hand-traverse onto the face, and
then go up to a large recess.
4 18m. Climb the right-hand of four grooves.
5 12m. Go easily up to finish.

The Blade   60 metres   Hard Very Severe   5a   (5.65)
At the right-hand end of the crag is a vegetated gully with a steep clean
tower high up on its right. The route finishes up a crack splitting the tower.

Ettws Isaf   Lower Ettws   OS Ref 624 564
This buttress lies some 200 metres right of Plexus Buttress, where the path from
Dinas Mot to Cwm Glas passes above Little Benjamin Buttress. It is in fact the
spur thrown down from *The Blade*, on the right-hand side of the wide vegetated
gully. The tip of the spur is dominated by a square-cut overhung corner.

Wimpey Pa   120 metres   Very Severe   (6.82)
A rather disjointed route, with some pleasant pitches, broken by large
grass ledges. Start about 9 metres left of the overhung corner, at the
second groove left of its arête, by a large polished spike. This can be
reached direct by a 6-metre rock pitch.

1 30m. 4c. Climb up left for 3 metres to gain the groove. Follow it for 9 metres, go across left and ascend past a loose sapling to a heathery ledge. Traverse this for 8 metres to its right end, and hand-traverse right and down to an obvious corner. Climb the crack/groove on the left to finish on a grassy terrace marking the top right-hand limit of the lower crag.

2 18m. Scramble up to a large terrace with a cave at its top right-hand end.

3 18m. 4b. Six metres right of the cave is a 5-metre leaning pillar on the arête. Climb this and the two steps above, and walk across the grassy ledge.

4 24m. 4a. The Delaminated Wall. This excellent pitch lies left of the smooth arête of the buttress and in between two heathery grooves.

5 30m. Pleasant scrambling leads to a surprise view. Walk off down to the right.

Although the following four routes are only single pitches, they are worth a visit, being of similar quality to those routes found on Plexus Buttress.

★Silent Thunder   37 metres   E4 5c   (30.6.83)
Superb bold climbing on excellent rock, although it may need some cleaning prior to an ascent. Start just left of the left arête of the overhung corner, below a square-cut overhang and just right of *Wimpey Pa*. Make a difficult move over the overhang and go up into the corner on the right, which is followed to a large block. Move right with difficulty to a sloping ledge on the arête proper (poor peg above). Pull up onto a small slab on the left and a good hold. Make a committing traverse right around the blunt rib and across the slab to a poor foothold on the arête. Follow the arête by long reaches to a hidden easy groove. This leads to good holds and easier climbing.

Gorty's Triangle   37 metres   E4 6b   (10.7.83)
A desperate roof problem with extreme bridging, unfortunately often wet. Start right of *Silent Thunder*. Climb the left edge of the triangular-shaped bay and slab below the overhanging left wall with increasing difficulty, passing two pegs near the top. Make a difficult move up the slab to the foot of the overhanging crack. Climb the crack (two wire runners were pre-placed on the first ascent) with a good finishing-hold out to the left.

★Stalling Out   40 metres   E2 6a   (10.7.83)
Extremely good, amply protected climbing, although escapable in two places. Start below a steep wall and rightward-trending flake crack. Climb the steep wall via the flake crack to a large ledge below a roof (the ledge can also be reached from the right by a difficult traverse). Move right from the ledge and climb the superb, very steep finger-crack to a good flake hold (wire runner). Move up right, around the arête, to the large roof and a peg. A delicate traverse right leads to a cracked block. Pull over the roof and go up the surprisingly exposed slab above to the top.

The Dark Side   40 metres   E8 6c   (6.99)
This shocking modern route tackles the wild overhanging prow dominating the upper section of the crag. Follow *Stalling Out* past the finger-crack and

up right around the arête to a peg. Back the peg up with a good wire and launch onto the prow. Dynamic and worrying moves lead through very steep territory to a final nervy snatch to easier ground (where brittle pockets provide protection). Pull over the lip slightly leftwards and move back rightwards to gain the top.

Huge Frog   30 metres   Hard Severe   (6.70)
Above the previous routes and further up the spur is a large grassy pasture below a short wall. This is reached via a gully on the right. Start just left of a 3-metre chimney that leads to a heather terrace on the right.
1 18m. Climb delicately up a short open groove until it is possible to mantelshelf up right. Traverse left to a cannon of rock. Follow short twin cracks behind the ledge to a small cave.
2 12m. Climb out of the cave to a small slab on the left. Take the wall above to an obvious traverse-line leading to an arête on the right.

Little Benjamin Buttress   OS Ref 623 564
This is a two-tiered buttress split by grassy bays, and with a chimney to the left of its upper half. It sits directly below Ettws Isaf, about level with the top of the Nose. The climbing is clean and steep.

Jacob   24 metres   Very Difficult   (9.9.79)
On the left flank of the buttress is a big central overhang. This route takes the break on the left and above the overhang, making for a bilberry ledge and a chimney. Start at an arête 3½ metres left of the line of the chimney. Follow a cracked scoop, and then go slightly right and up into a small V-groove. Traverse right to the bilberry ledge and finish up the chimney.

Big Ben   24 metres   E1 5c   (26.7.02)
Climb up to the large fangs on the right side of the overhanging area. Strenuous but well-protected moves (crux) lead into a steep corner. A hanging flake leads left to cracks in the arête. Continue up easy ground to the top.

Candice Marie   27 metres   Very Severe 4c   (26.7.02)
Pleasant enough climbing just to the right of the right arête of the overhangs, starting at a quartz vein. Steep moves up a flake crack lead into a broad slabby corner. Pull up onto the left wall using thin flake cracks, and continue via flakes and rounded ledges.

Master Blaster   20 metres   E1 5b   (1990)
Still a bit friable. Start just left of an obvious block, below a flake crack. Climb up and make a long reach to gain a further crack and a good flake at its top. Step right and follow easy slabs to the top.
Variation
The flake can be gained by taking the diagonal line leading up from the top of the block of *Skidmaster*. This reduces the overall grade to Hard Very Severe 5b.

Skidmaster   21metres   Very Severe 4b   (30.9.89)
Difficult and sustained. Start at an obvious block on the left end of a grassy
ledge. Step off the block and then climb the rib to reach the rightward-
trending groove/ramp-line, which is followed to the top of the pyramid.

Freudian Slits   18 metres   E3 6a   (1992)
A bit stiff but short-lived. Start at the base of the corner, to the right of
Skidmaster. Follow the thin crackline to the top of the arête. The upper
section of *Little Benjamin* then leads to the top.

The Amazing   18 metres   Very Severe 4c   (1992)
The wider diagonal crack on the right, joining *Little Benjamin* at the
pinnacle. Finish as for *Little Benjamin*.

Loves-a-Scent   40 metres   Very Severe 4c   (1.4.90)
A filler-in. Start 3 metres left of *Little Benjamin*, at the base of a steep slab.
Climb straight up the slab to reach the bay left of the arête and a ledge on
the left. Finish up *Skidmaster* or *The Amazing*.

★Little Benjamin   35 metres   Severe   (30.8.25)
An entertaining climb. Start on a boulder below the buttress.
1 20m. Climb a crack to a ledge, traverse left and go up the edge via a
crack to a bay.
2 15m. A crack on the left leads up a pinnacle. Ascend this and step off
the pinnacle to finish steeply over a nose.

Piggy's Arête   18 metres   E2 5c   (1990)
An unbalanced and bold route. Start at the base of the arête 12 metres up
Little Benjamin. The prominent arête left of pitch 2 of *Little Benjamin* is
unprotected to begin with. Fortunately, the difficulties are short-lived. Finish
easily up *Little Benjamin*, or (better) traverse right a short way to join and
finish up the top part of *Accept for Access*.

Accept for Access   15 metres   E2 5b   (10.6.88)
The wall right of *Little Benjamin* and left of the finishing crack of *Zimmer
Frame-up*. Start just right of the belay above pitch 1 of *Little Benjamin*. Go
up slightly leftwards via vague flakes to a small ledge. Finish direct up
shallow scoops, pleasant.

Zimmer Frame-up   30 metres   Hard Very Severe   (23.5.90)
A slight route, but pleasant enough. Start 2 metres right of *Little Benjamin*,
under a thin crack in the wall.
1 21m. 5a. Problematic starting moves lead up to the crack. Move up
and right to a shallow groove. Ascend this exiting right onto a slab. Head
back left to belay at a vertical crack near the centre of the wall.
2 9m. 4a. Climb the delightful crack.
Variation
1a 16m. 4a. Take the wide crack to the right of the original line to a
ledge. Move up to another crack, step left, and go up to reach slabs. Belay
below the crack.

On the right is a grassy gully. The next routes take various lines in the rather scruffy area of rock to the right of the gully.

B Series   24 metres   Very Severe 5a   (1990)
Rather disjointed, a technical slab leading to easy ground. Start at a slab 5 metres left of a holly tree. Follow a crack in the slab to a ledge. Head towards the prominent jammed block, but before reaching it trend left via cracks to finish up the left side of the final 'tower'.

Still Smiling   20 metres   Hard Very Severe 5b   (25.8.02)
Blinkers are required; but there are some good moves. Start below the holly. Mantelshelf onto a small sloping ledge, and go up to flakes on the right of the holly. Ignoring the easier ground above, make a long stride left to the obvious foothold on the edge of the slab above the overhang. Climb the centre of the slab boldly on small holds, passing a flake.

Pooper Scooper   23 metres   Hard Severe 4a   (1990)
Interest is short lived. Start down and right of the holly, below a crack in the slab. Follow the crack to the overlap directly below a protruding flake. Go past the flake and gain easy ground.

Drain Surgeon   25 metres   Very Severe 4b   (1990)
Pleasant enough climbing to start with. Start at the very toe of this buttress, below a rounded rib. Climb up the rib to below an overlap, and step up and left to continue up easier ground to the top.

Well below Little Benjamin Buttress and 100 metres above the Climbers' Club Hut Ynys Ettws is an obvious block with organ-pipe features.

99 Flake   7 metres   E1 6a   (1993)
Climb the prominent crack in the middle of the overhang. A fall would involve a lengthy examination of the slope below.

Bwtres Ettws   Ettws Buttress   OS Ref 623 564
Lying 150 metres right of and above Little Benjamin Buttress, this slabby buttress consists of a sheet of rough red dolerite, with a drystone wall abutting it. The climbing is of good quality if a little escapable, and the rock is immaculate.

Cinderella Penguin   40 metres   Very Severe 5a   (4.4.90)
An escapable route taking the slabby left arête of the buttress. Start just right of this, at a crack. Climb the awkward crack to a scooped area. Pad up to the upper scoop and step left onto a block pedestal. Ascend the parallel cracks above.

Willy Two Goes   6 metres   V8   (2000)
A searingly thin smearing problem. Climb the tenuous technical slab right of *Cinderella Penguin* to the thin crack, which eases as you climb it. Traverse off or down-climb *Cinderella Penguin*.

Bon Mot   210 metres   Very Difficult   (22.6.79)
A discontinuous mountaineering route, but with some pleasant sections. It
is a good way to gain height. Start up to the right of the drystone wall.
1 30m. Ascend grass on the right for 12 metres until a line of pockets,
scoops and cracks leads up and diagonally left for 15 metres to a large
heather ledge. (A direct variant starts from the top of the drystone wall at
Very Severe. It is quite delicate.)
2 60m. Go left and up to a rowan tree, and continue up slabs. Climb the
intermittent arête, which is like easy gritstone in places, to arrive at an
enormous field.
3 60m. Walk across the field, from where a slab leads to a scooped
arête, which starts with a smooth corner/groove.
4 60m. The rib soon peters out, so cross a grassy trough on the right and
continue up slabby humps and grooves.
Variation Start
Such a Pretty Nose   24 metres   Very Severe 5a
1a Start just down and left of the drystone wall. Initial difficult moves give
way to easy climbing.

The Glass Flipper   43 metres   Hard Very Severe 5a   (30.8.89)
An eliminate on *Bon Mot*, which saves its crux for the top section. Start 3
metres right of the drystone wall. Climb the steep slab to reach a vertical crack.
Easier climbing on *Bon Mot* leads to a tiny flake. Follow a groove up right to a
steep tower of slabs with a shallow crack, which leads up leftwards to finish.

Chilli Willie and the Red Hot Peppers
                40 metres   Hard Very Severe 5a (23.5.90)
Escapable, but it makes the most of the rock between *The Glass Flipper*
and the grassy gully on the right. Start as for *The Glass Flipper*, but move
right to pockets (*Bon Mot*) and the first shallow groove on the right. Climb
the groove and then go directly up the rib past a loose flake to cracks.
Finish direct (to the right of *The Glass Flipper*).

A little bit further round the corner from the *Bon Mot* area towards Craig y
Rhaeadr is a short section of steep rock, which is gained by clambering over
an old drystone wall.

Basil's Baby   21 metres   E4 6a   (1998)
Good moves with a precarious crux. Start at the right-hand side of the
craglet. Climb up a vague groove to gain the base of a leftward-trending
ramp-line; follow this insecurely until easier ground is reached. Further
difficult moves surmount the final bulge.

Craig Uwch   Upper Crag   OS Ref 626 562
A little above Dinas Mot, in the Jammed Boulder Gully area, is a small
hidden crag of perfect rock. It still retains the characteristic scoops and
grooves ground out by the passing ice during the last Ice Age. On the
left-hand side of the crag is a large flake directly below a shark's fin of rock
perched on top of the crag. The first route starts here.

Basking   30 metres   Severe   (17.7.94)
Ascend the centre of the flake to reach cracks and ribs, where one tricky move allows you to gain easier ground.

Tiny Is as Tiny Do   34 metres   Very Severe 4c   (17.7.94)
Climb past a coffin-shaped flake at the foot of the route to reach two cracks, and take the left-hand crack to a large bulge. Move up to and climb a rib and a short groove in the upper bulge. Belay well back.

Central Scrutinizer   34 metres   Hard Very Severe 5b   (17.7.94)
Climb a slab a little to the right of *Tiny Is as Tiny Do* to a ledge. The crack above allows you to pull through the bulge. Enter a short groove with a thin flake and then head for the top.

Nunatak   24 metres   Very Severe 4b   (17.7.94)
Just right of a series of wide cracks, follow the obvious line, past scoops and bulges, to the top.

Revision   18 metres   Hard Severe 4a   (17.7.94)
A couple of entertaining moves can be found on this route, starting just left of a steep area of rock. Cracks and bulges lead to easier ground.

Craig yr Ogof   Cave Crag   OS Ref 623 562

About 300 metres left of Diffwys Ddŵr is a buttress with a large cave on its right-hand side. It is well worth going up to, and it has good clean rock and fine views. When combined with a route on Ettws Buttress as an aperitif, it gives a fine day out away from the crowds.

The Wrath of Grapes   74 metres   E1   (27.4.90)
A damp start leads to good rock and a fine upper pitch. Start on the left side of the buttress, at some slabs 9 metres below a downward-pointing, slabby finger of rock.
1 34m. 5b. Climb the slabs to a roof, surmount this, and ascend the continuation slab and grooves to a belay.
2 40m. 4c. Follow the grooves up the left-hand side of the buttress with some hardish moves towards the top.

Cave Buttress   80 metres   Very Severe   (20.6.65)
Not an obvious line. Start at the lowest point of the rocks below and to the left of the cave.
1 40m. 4c. Climb a vegetated groove diagonally left for 9 metres, and cross a slab rightwards above the overhanging wall to the prominent central groove. Climb this (crux) and the rocks above to a ledge.
2 40m. 4b. Ascend steeply and follow the shattered crack.

★Anturiaethau Dic Preifat   80 metres   Hard Very Severe   (27.4.90)
Two very good pitches. Start to the right of *Cave Buttress*, at some slabs
under a diagonal crack slanting leftwards.
1 40m. 5a. Climb the slabby rib to the crack, and climb this (crux) to
reach a groove. Follow ribs on the left above the groove to belay down
and left of the *Cave Buttress* belay.
2 40m. 4b. Traverse left above an overhang to reach a series of grooves
in the centre of the buttress. Follow these to the top.

★Pocketful of Kryptonite   14 metres   E6 6b   (28.6.95)
A small compact arête in the gully left of Diffwys Ddŵr, on the right-hand
side of a stream. Climb the arête on its right-hand side, passing two pegs.

Diffwys Ddŵr (Craig y Rhaeadr)
Water Precipice (Waterfall Crag) OS Ref 622 562

Low down on the left side of Cwm Glas, this prominent, wet, reddish-black
crag rises steeply for some 100 metres. A waterfall cascades over a line of
black overhangs near the top onto the Pedestal, a massive sail-shaped block
at the foot of the cliff. Way over on the far left is a large pillar, Cwm Glas
Pinnacle. Right of the waterfall a steep nasty-looking gully runs the full height
of the crag. The buttress on its right is at a slightly easier angle and rather
more broken. A vertical furrow marks it on the right. The main cliff routes are
worth doing for their fine positions and unusual atmosphere; the rock is
compact and protection can be difficult to find and arrange.

North-facing and hidden in a cwm, the cliff receives very little sunshine. It is a
good spot in a hot spell. The base of the cliff lies at around 420 metres. The
approach should take about 30 minutes from the road. Descent is down a
grassy slope on the left of the cliff, or by heading up over the ridge and
coming back round the right-hand side of the cliff.

Verglas Slab   75 metres   Very Severe   (19.3.55)
Very grassy and not to be recommended. An artificial and indefinite line
starting just left of Cwm Glas Pinnacle.

Cwm Glas Pinnacle   Difficult   (9.3.35)
A short entertaining climb. Back-and-foot up behind the flake until the
chimney becomes too wide, swing across and climb the edge to the top.

There are other lines further left at Very Difficult/Severe in standard.

Down and right of Cwm Glas Pinnacle is a fine white wall, which is reached
by walking across left from the waterfall and a short scramble up to grassy
ledges.

★★Ghosts   73 metres   E3   (18.5.80)
A much sought-after route, giving good climbing up the open face to the left
of *The Wall*, with spaced protection but good rock. Low in the grade. The
second pitch is safer but steeper to start. Start at the left side of the white wall.
1 27m. 5b. Climb fairly directly to below a small overhang at 11 metres;
move left and then up to pass this. Continue direct for 6 metres until it is
possible to traverse right to the base of an obvious groove. Enter the
groove to gain a restricted stance but good belays.
2 46m. 5b. Step left and then go diagonally leftwards along a thin crack
to a bulge; then move left across a scoop to gain footholds above the
overhangs. Continue up and slightly left to easier ground. Finish up this.

★'T'ouse Wall   103 metres   E3   (7.69)
A fairly direct line up the area of steep rock between *Ghosts* and *The Wall*.
The climbing is good despite the implications of the name.
1 30m. 5b. Follow *The Wall* to the top of its crux groove. From here, climb
straight up the wall to enter the groove above, and belay as for *Ghosts*.
2 27m. 5c. Step left and then climb diagonally leftwards along a thin
crack (as for *Ghosts*). At the bulge, difficult and strenuous moves on small
but positive holds lead quickly straight up to reach easier ground.
3 46m. Ascend uninterestingly to a large grassy ledge.

★The Wall   107 metres   E1   (31.8.59)
A fine steep route, with just about adequate protection, up the obvious white
wall half-way between Cwm Glas Pinnacle and the red walls in the centre of
the crag. Route-finding will be found to be the crux. Start below the wall.
1 43m. 5a. Go up right on an obvious traverse-line until it is possible to
move back left along another traverse to the foot of a smooth groove.
Climb this for 6 metres (crux) and trend steeply rightwards to some grassy
ledges. Climb diagonally rightwards again to a small grassy ledge.
2 46m. 4c. Traverse left for 3 metres and climb up on good holds to a
shallow V-groove, which leads to grass and rock. Continue more easily to
a good grass ledge.
3 18m. 4c. Climb the awkward corner and ascend direct to the top.

Red Wall   79 metres   Hard Very Severe   (11.10.53)
A direct line up the red walls in the centre of the crag, passing a minor set
of overhangs on the right. It is easier but grassier than the other routes,
and it needs a long dry summer. Start from a large terrace midway
between Cwm Glas Pinnacle and the Pedestal.
1 34m. 5a. Climb a shallow groove for 6 metres, and traverse right to a
grassy ledge at the foot of a smooth groove. Climb on the right of the
groove until a step left leads into it. Follow the groove to a ledge on the
right. Go up to a stance and peg belays.
2 27m. 4c. Climb left up a series of awkward ledges. Go up a short crack
and step left onto a steep slab. Trend right up the slab, to gain a small ledge
below and at the extreme right edge of the overhangs. Step round the corner
on the right, and go straight up to a stance and belay on the edge of the overhang.
3 18m. Step right and climb direct to the top.

Chequered Wall   121 metres   Hard Very Severe   (6.9.59)
A wet, but mostly clean, route up the centre of the crag. Start below and
left of the Pedestal.
1 21m. Ascend the groove to a large grassy ledge.
2 9m. 4c. Climb the obvious crack on the left of the Pedestal to its top.
3 37m. 5a. Climb the wall for 6 metres and then go up the obvious
groove, trending left to an awkward corner. Go up this to a stance and
peg belay 6 metres higher on the left.
4 24m. 5a. Traverse 5 metres left along the ledge. Go up to enter and
climb a steep shallow groove with difficulty to a tiny ledge with a rickety
block. Climb delicately up to a tiny grass ledge at the right-hand end of an
overhang. Awkward thread belay.
5 30m. Go round the rib on the right, traverse 9 metres to a white slab,
and finish up this.
Variation
4a 18m. 5a. From the stance, stride across and go steeply up right to a
grassy ledge at the end of the enormous overhangs.
5a 30m. Go left and ascend directly up the white slabs.

★**Lung Fish**   99 metres   E4   (20.4.74)
A good route when dry. It takes a very direct line above the Pedestal. Start
near the right-hand side of the Pedestal, below some pockets.
1 12m. 5c. Climb up and left to a tiny spike on an arête. Move up with
difficulty and go right to the pockets. A difficult rising traverse leads to the
edge of the Pedestal.
2 30m. Scramble easily up to the very top of the Pedestal.
3 18m. 5b. Climb directly up the wall, making for a deep V-groove. Go
up this and exit left to a small stance and peg belay.
4 24m. 5c. Continue in the same line up to the overhangs. Climb
through these, past a peg, and go up to a grassy stance.
5 15m. Finish easily.

★★**Silent Spring**   107 metres   E4   (18.5.80)
An excellent route on perfect rock taking a central line up to and through
the overhangs. Start as for *Lung Fish*.
1 43m. 6a. Climb diagonally left for 9 metres to a good runner below a
shallow groove. Climb this to reach a horizontal line of handholds. Step
right and go straight up the face to easy ground. Climb to the crest of the
Pedestal, and ascend obvious grooves above as for *Waterfall Climb* to a
good spike.
2 34m. 5c. Above is a smooth black groove. Climb to the base of it, then
move left, and climb steeply to gain the slab. Go up left slightly to the apex
of the slab, and move back right across the top of the black groove. Climb
up for a short way and then go up left on improving holds until a slight
groove leads up to the right to some ledges below the main overhangs
(and just left of the obvious way through them). Good belays.
3 30m. 5c. Climb out to the right through the roofs and then go up a
clean white slab to an easy rib leading to the top.

Diffwys Ddŵr (Craig y Rhaeadr)

1	Ghosts	E3	4	Red Wall	HVS
2	'T'ouse Wall	E3	5	Chequered Wall	HVS
3	The Wall	E1	6	Lung Fish	E4

7 Waterfall Climb	S	11 Botany Climb	VS
8 The Sewer	E3	12 Grooved Slab	VS
9 Llwch	E2	C Cwm Glas Pinnacle	
10 Mushroom	VS	P The Pedestal	

Waterfall Climb   126 metres   Severe   (9.32)
A unique and serious expedition, which is seldom dry as the line traverses
along the obvious terrace under the waterfall. Although technically
straightforward, some care is needed in handling the loose rock. Start from
the foot of the easy chimney that leads up the right-hand side of the Pedestal.
1 15m. Climb the chimney to a rock rake leading to a good stance on
the crest of the Pedestal.
2 12m. Descend a short way and traverse right into a steep groove.
Climb this to a small ledge on the right and continue easily to the left-hand
end of the terrace. Consider retreat.
3 11m. Follow the terrace easily to the right, under the waterfall (which
provides a brisk cold shower), to a rock bay beside the gully.
4 12m. The wall on the right bulges but soon has good holds. Traverse
into the gully as soon as possible to a grassy stance on the right.
5 18m. Keep to the right over broken rocks and grass.
6 12m. Go straight up and then trend left to a prominent white rock.
7 46m. Climb indefinite broken rock to the top, with various possible stances.
Variation
The Direct Start   Hard Severe
The lower easy section of the gully is climbed direct. Difficult at 12 metres.

The Sewer   88 metres   E3   (17.6.67)
This extreme endurance test follows the drainage line up the wet wall just
right of the Pedestal. It never dries properly. Start 5 metres left of the Direct
Start to *Waterfall Climb*.
1 24m. 5a. Climb the steep wall just right of a wet flake. Traverse left
along an obvious ledge to belay at its end.
2 9m. 4c. Ascend the groove on the left to the terrace of *Waterfall Climb*.
3 18m. 5c. Climb the precarious and technical slimy groove directly
below the right-hand end of the overhang past a rotten peg (crux) to a
small stance. Peg belay about 9 metres below the roofs.
4 37m. 4c. Climb diagonally rightwards onto the rib and follow it,
keeping left, to the top.

Llwch   92 metres   E2   (14.5.99)
A direct route taking the arête right of the Direct Start to *Waterfall Climb*,
which covers some interesting ground. Start as for *Mushroom*.
1 37m. 5b. Climb the arête to the obvious overhang, and pull through
this to gain a vague ramp-line leading up left to some flakes. Drop down
left to belay in the corner.
2 37m. 5b. Climb back right to the flakes, and go straight up to a blunt
rib. A high step attains easier-angled ground. Trend up and right to a
shallow scoop and climb the rib on the right to belay on some flakes.
3 18m. Scrambling remains.

Mushroom   91 metres   Very Severe   (30.4.67)
A steep line with reasonable holds, which takes the buttress just right of the
chimney of the Direct Start to *Waterfall Climb*. A groove capped by an

overhang 30 metres up is an obvious feature. Start at the left corner of the buttress.
1 27m. 4c. Climb the arête or easy cracks to a grassy terrace. Layback up the prominent undercut flake, and go diagonally left over an overlap to a ledge. Continue to a belay on the left of the groove.
2 46m. 4c. Climb the groove, moving left at the overhang, and then ascend an easy arête and grassy slabs.
3 18m. Finish easily up vegetated rock.

★**Sphagnum** 100 metres E2 (1.6.81)
A good route with some intriguing climbing. Best completed with the variation. Start midway between *Mushroom* and *Botany Climb*.
1 12m. 4c. Pull over a slight bulge onto the wall and climb to a large mossy ledge. Belay on the left.
2 27m. 5c. Ascend the middle of the steep wall to an obvious undercut. Make hard moves to reach a block where the angle eases. Continue up the slab, keeping left of a shallow groove, to gain the left-hand end of a large grassy ledge. Climb short cracks above to a small stance and high spike belay near the foot of the groove on *Botany Climb*.
3 43m. 4b. Climb the right-hand edge above; then move out left onto the slabs and continue to a stance and spike belay.
4 18m. Easy rocks lead to the top.
Variation
3a 43m. 5b. Above and left of the belay is an undercut flake. Reach this and go left to easier ground. Climb the slab to join the original line. More in keeping with the grade of the parent route.

Botany Climb 113 metres Very Severe (19.3.55)
A rather grassy route ascending the long shallow groove right of *Sphagnum*. Start at the lowest point of the buttress.
1 15m. 4b. Climb a steep wall to a rowan tree. Easy slabs on the left lead to a grassy terrace.
2 23m. 4b. Layback a short crack; steep walls and grassy grooves lead to ledges below and to the right of the main groove.
3 41m. 4a. Take the obvious line left up pleasant slabs into the groove and climb this to grassy ledges.
4 34m. Walls and grassy scrambling lead to the top.

Grooved Slab 91 metres Severe (19.3.55)
Right of *Botany Climb* is a slabby light-coloured buttress flanked by grassy grooves. Shallow grooves are followed up the slabs, bearing left to a grass gangway and trending leftwards to the top.

Rubble and Strife 46 metres Hard Very Severe 5a (18.6.00)
A vegetated upper section mars a pleasing slab. Start just right of the shallow grooves of *Grooved Slab*. Weave up the centre of the slim slab, sometimes searching for protection: as difficulties ease, the heather begins to encroach. Either abseil off large flakes, or scramble a further 45 metres on heather to gain the top.

Rhaeadr Girdle   230 metres   Hard Very Severe   (26.4.56)
Hydroponics gone haywire. Start up a little grassy gully just right of *Botany Climb*. Follow *Botany Climb* pitch 2 and then traverse left into the Direct Start of *Waterfall Climb*. Go up this and traverse easily across the terrace swept by the waterfall. Continue in the same line until a line of weakness ascends diagonally left to an awkward corner (junction with *Chequered Wall*). Above the corner, traverse left to an area of grass on *Red Wall*, and then ascend diagonally across a wall to a poor stance. Traverse left to a spike on the skyline, and then climb diagonally to finish on an obvious terrace with a cave.

Sunshine Breakfast   46 metres   Very Severe   4c   (14.12.68)
A steep little route. Start at the foot of a pink wall in the descent gully at the right-hand side of the crag. Climb straight up to a flake crack and follow this until it is possible to stride right to a sloping ledge. Finish directly up the wall.

On the right-hand wing of Diffwys Ddŵr is an area of pink rock. To the right and below these is a slabby wall facing the path up to Diffwys Ddu. It has an obvious overlap at its right-hand end, the location of *Nos-mo-king*.

Esgairgeiliog   18 metres   Very Severe   4b   (5.8.02)
A filler-in. Start below a crack, where the upper of three quartz seams reaches the ground. Follow the quartz out left, and then go up to the crack and follow this to slabs. Easy climbing leads up to a belay well back.

The Famine Road   18 metres   E1   5b   (8.95)
Good rock and quite airy climbing. Start as for *Esgairgeiliog*. Climb the slab to a large flake right of the crack, then step up and move right past a big spike to finish up the groove above. Belay on the slab above.

★**Rock Oil**   15 metres   E4   6a   (8.95)
Fine moves on good rock. Start down and right of the obvious corner/groove on the front face leading up to the steep corner. A bold start leads to the base of the corner; move up and then step left to climb the rib. The angle now eases as you head for the top.

Eden   21 metres   E2   5b   (18.6.00)
Good moves, if rather bold in places. Start below a V-chimney. Climb up left to reach a horizontal crackline. Pull up into the V-chimney, via a block, and bridge up to a long flake. Step left and pad up a slab. Belay well back.

West End   37 metres   Very Difficult   (19.5.60)
A good little route on superb rock. Start near the centre of the buttress, at a gangway trending left.
1 20m. Ascend the gangway to an awkward mantelshelf, and then traverse right for 10 feet to a narrow ledge. Climb flakes to a large grassy ledge on the left.
2 17m. Climb the steep slab, trending right, and finish direct.

Little Jim   23 metres   Very Severe 4b   (19.5.60)
A worthwhile route. Start 5 metres right of *West End*, at an arrow on the
rock. Climb the bulging wall to a narrow ledge on the left. Climb a vague
crack on the right to a ledge under an overhang. Pleasant slabs lead up
leftwards to the top.

Easy Rhaeadr   21 metres   Hard Very Severe 5b   (6.95)
A pleasant enough route that starts a little further right, below a hanging
slab. Climb this to the break (arrange protection) and then go slightly right
to stand on a ledge. Pull over the bulge and finish pleasantly.

Nos-mo-king   21 metres   Hard Very Severe 5a   (6.95)
Another diverting climb. Start just left of the obvious pinnacle at the
right-hand end of the wall. Climb up vaguely rightwards (with poor gear)
towards the overlap; surmount this to reach an easy finish up slabs.

Llechau Canol Intermediate Slabs   OS Ref 618 559

On the eastern side of Cwm Glas, between the two streams to the left of
Diffwys Ddu, is an outcrop called Castell, with a clean stretch of slabs up to
75 metres high. The main slab lies between the right-hand edge and a
prominent black chimney on the left, *Intermediate Chimney*. Further up and
left is another area of slabs, and to the left again is a third area of slabs.

To the left of the left-hand, upper slab is a short sweep of good rock covered
in pockets.

Polling   18 metres   Very Severe 4c   (1.5.97)
Nice climbing. From the right-hand side of the slab, ascend a shallow
groove to the half-way break; then move up and right to finish up the
clean crack.

Up Your Hacienda Jimmy   49 metres   Very Severe 4b   (1.5.97)
Good rock but poor protection. Start some 12 metres left of *Spring
Chimney* on the upper slab, after about 12 metres of scrambling to belay
below a shallow groove. Ascend the groove for 6 metres and move right
to a steepening. Trend left via a high step and follow the line leftwards up
the slab to the top.

Spring Chimney   59 metres   Very Difficult   (6.3.49)
A good introduction to some old-fashioned moves. Start at the foot of a
continuous buttress well to the left of the black chimney. An overhanging
chimney starts half-way up.
1 15m. Scramble to a heathery ledge.
2 23m. From the right-hand end of the ledge, go diagonally up to the
right to the chimney, which leads to a small ledge below a groove. Climb
the groove to a recess below the overhangs.

3 21m. The steep chimney splitting the overhangs is hard to start. Above the chimney, finish up a wall.

Election Flight   61 metres   Hard Severe   (1.5.97)
Takes the buttress just right of *Spring Chimney*.
1 24m. 4a. Climb the shallow groove to an awkward move at 8 metres. Climb the bulge above via a crack and move up to a good nut belay.
2 37m. Follow the slab to the top.

Intermediate Chimney   39 metres   Very Difficult   (18.4.49)
Very little time is spent in the chimney. Start in the black chimney.
1 21m. Climb the groove right of the chimney. Bear left near the top to a stance in the chimney.
2 18m. Keep in the right-hand corner and go up steeply to a pull out right, or finish up the chimney direct.

Tradition   60 metres   Severe   (6.3.49)
Rather rambling. Start to the right of the black chimney, at the foot of a groove leading up to an overhang.
1 18m. Climb the groove for 9 metres until it becomes awkward. Swing out right, and go over a rib and across a short steep slab to a detached block. Climb up above the block to a grassy stance.
2 15m. Step out left onto a slab. Climb this to a broad ledge. A good pitch.
3 27m. Walk along the ledge to the first break on the right. Ascend a short way and then go diagonally left, underneath a poised block, to the top.

Conway Climb   54 metres   Difficult   (12.6.49)
A straightforward beginner's line. Start at the lowest point of the right-hand section of the slabs.
1 15m. Climb the shallow groove and then the slab.
2 12m. Go diagonally left with ease.
3 27m. Climb the steeper rocks ahead and continue up in the same line to finish.

Clogwyn y Person & Clogwyn y Ddysgl

From the ridge of Crib y Ddysgl, a rocky promontory juts out into upper Cwm Glas dividing it into two cwms, each having a tiny lake. The crest of the promontory is called Crib y Person or the *Clogwyn y Person Arête*. The western flank of the promontory is a steep rock face, Clogwyn y Ddysgl. At the extreme end of the promontory, a prominent nose of rock, some 45 metres high, is separated from the main cliff by a vertical break. The nose is Clogwyn y Person and the clefts defining it are *Eastern Gully* and *Western Gully*.

Clogwyn y Ddysgl is an extensive cliff varying in height from 60 to nearly 150 metres. On the left, towards Clogwyn y Person, the rock is clean and solid. As you move right, the quality deteriorates until the main cliff ends in a mass of broken ground, unstable 'organ pipes' and scree-filled gullies. Along the base of the cliff is a wide rake, the Parson's Progress. Most of the climbs start from this rake. About 150 metres from *Western Gully* is the huge Fallen Block with a prominent crack above it. On the left of this is a large recess with a broken chimney. To the right of the Fallen Block is a large area of partially explored rock; the main lines have all been climbed, but there may yet be some scope for the pioneer. The lower section of the cliff here is very steep for 45 metres but above it is broken and loose. To the right a V-shaped stone-shoot marks the line of *Waterslide Gully*. The cliff ends with the large triangular buttress taken by *The Infidel*. Beyond this is a jumble of broken rocks and scree.

Most of the cliff is above the 750-metre contour, and if not in the clouds some parts of the cliff can be in sunshine from mid-afternoon onwards. An approach time of about 50 minutes will be seen to be quite fast. The best descent from Clogwyn y Ddysgl is down the *Clogwyn y Person* Arête and then down *Western Gully*.

Clogwyn y Person   Cliff (of) the Parson   OS Ref 617 555
Square Gully   59 metres   Severe   (18.4.49)
'A very entertaining cave pitch'. Start at the foot of the first break left of *Eastern Gully*.
1 30m. A wet rake slanting up left leads into the gully. Continue up over grass to a stance below an overhang.
2 14m. Back-and-foot or bridge over the overhang to good holds. Step left and over the rib to a good stance.
3 15m. Scramble up some grass to a stance. Climb the angular chimney on the left, over a loose flake, and then climb the right-hand branch. Scramble up to finish.

The rocks on the left of *Square Gully* are more broken, but odd interesting routes up chimneys can be worked out.

Eastern Gully   49 metres   Moderate   (1879)
The left-hand boundary of the nose gives a loose scramble with two small cave pitches.

The Eastern Edge   67 metres   Severe   (19.3.49)
An interesting route on the left side of the nose, with poor rock. Start at the foot of a grassy slab slanting up leftwards below the front of the nose.
1 18m. Scramble up the slabs to a band of quartz.
2 17m. Climb the quartz to an awkward sloping shelf. Step across to a chimney, which leads to a stance.
3 14m. Ascend the corner, first left and then right, almost to the foot of another chimney. Follow a natural traverse-line right, and climb steeply to a grassy break.
4 18m. Finish easily up grass or more pleasantly up the rib.

★The Parson's Nose Direct   40 metres   Very Difficult   (c.1900)
A fine climb with airy situations but with poor protection; it is best done in
one run-out. Start 24 metres above the foot of the nose. Easy scrambling
over loose rock leads to a sloping triangular ledge. Step out to the left and
go up towards an arête on the skyline (possible stance on the arête below
a small overhang, shaky belay). Climb the steep gangway on the right of
the arête for about 11 metres and swing over onto the arête. Good holds
lead to a grassy corner near the top of the nose.

★★The Parson's Nose   75 metres   Difficult   (1884)
One of the earliest routes in the Pass, with pleasant open climbing on
good holds. Start at the lowest point of the rocks, at some slabs.
1 24m. Ascend the easy-angled slabs.
2 21m. The slab steepens but good holds still arrive. The route curves
over slightly towards *Western Gully*. Stance at the foot of a shallow groove.
3 15m. A rising traverse along a faint crackline leads to a large ledge
overlooking the gully.
4 15m. Easy scrambling leads to the final section of *The Right-Hand Edge*.

The Right-Hand Edge   46 metres   Moderate   (1892)
A short but pleasant route, which follows the western edge of the nose.
Start just left of *Western Gully*. Numerous stances etc.

Western Gully   46 metres   Easy   (1879)
Useful as a descent. The top pitch is about Moderate and can be taken on
the right wall or up through the cave.

From the summit of Clogwyn y Person, the **Clogwyn y Person Arête**
(1879) gives a fine ridge scramble. The route is well marked, and climbing
the various obstacles direct can vary the standard.

Clogwyn y Ddysgl   Cliff (of) the Dish   OS Ref 615 554
Gargoyle Route   81 metres   Very Difficult   (24.8.48)
A varied and engaging climb, quite high in its grade, which makes the
best use of the area to the right of the gully. Start at an obvious V-groove
about 30 metres right of *Western Gully*.
1 15m. Climb the V-groove and exit left onto the slabs above. An easier
start can be made up the slab on the right.
2 15m. Broken rock leads to the foot of an overhanging chimney.
3 12m. Traverse across the right wall, and then bear up and slightly left to
a small chimney.
4 18m. Ascend the chimney and climb the corner on the right over
immense piled blocks.
5 21m. Step off the small quartz-topped block on the left and climb the
crack above. Cross grass below the gargoyle to the foot of the left-hand
crack. Ascend this to join the arête.

Choristers' Cleft   65 metres   Very Difficult   (17.3.39)

A pleasant and worthwhile route, even if a little contrived. Start between the V-groove of *Gargoyle Route* and the start of *The Gambit Climb*, where slabby ground on the left becomes a wall.

1 15m. Climb the corner on good holds to an awkward exit onto the slabs above. Continue easily to a large bollard.

2 12m. Step off the bollard into a shallow scoop in the right wall and follow this up to a tiny groove, which leads to a slab. Belay in the left-hand corner of the slab.

3 15m. Take the overhanging crack above the belay to a grassy ledge. From a higher ledge, climb the right wall to a large grassy ledge (the Green Collar of *The Gambit Climb*).

4 23m. Climb the interesting flake crack on the left to a stance. Ascend the crack on the right to a grassy bay. Finish up the left wall.

Hooded Crow   119 metres   E3   (13.8.83)

A good route with much varied and interesting climbing. Start as for *Choristers' Cleft*.

1 30m 6a. A technical and strenuous sequence up a right-slanting groove gains an overhang. Pull round this into a groove. Climb the groove (crux), exiting right after a few moves, and then go up to ledges (on *The Gambit Climb*).

2 15m. 4b. Trend easily rightwards until a step right can be made round a corner to reach a crack. Climb this to grassy ledges.

3 26m. 5b. Ascend to a ledge at 5 metres and go up the middle of the slabby wall above, finishing by a short right-facing corner. Superb bold climbing.

4 18m. 5a. Climb cracks direct to a grassy ledge.

5 30m. 4b. Follow a crack, move right to a corner and climb this to easy rock.

★★**The Gambit Climb**   83 metres   Very Difficult   (9.10)

An excellent route at its grade, with sustained, interesting and airy climbing with the crux being saved for the last pitch: an absolute classic. The Pass's answer to *Grooved Arête*. Sixty metres to the right of *Western Gully*, and 5 metres left of a curious pocketed wall is a crack containing a hanging flake.

1 23m. Climb the crack with the flake for 3 metres, and then step left. Make a step down and across onto the left edge of a slabby ramp and climb this (exposed) to the foot of a corner-crack. Go up this to a small ledge, and then climb the short awkward crack above to belay on broad ledges.

2 17m. Take the easiest direct line above the belay to the obvious broad grassy ledge – the Green Collar.

3 14m. An exciting traverse rightwards on small holds leads to the foot of a short broken chimney. Climb this to gain a good ledge.

Clogwyn y Person and Clogwyn y Ddysgl

1	The Parson's Nose	D	4	Choristers' Cleft	VD	7	The Ring	VS
2	Western Gully	E	5	Gambit Climb	VD	8	Fallen Block Climb	M
3	Gargoyle Route	VD	6	Nunc Dimittis	VS	9	Fallen Block Crack	VS

10	Black Gates	VD	13 Three Cave Gully VD	W	Waterslide Gully
11	Rectory Chimneys	VD	14 Lecturn Grooves HS	V	The Vestry
12	Duet Chimneys	HS	15 Russet E3		

4 14m. Move left to the base of an impressive chimney. Climb this to the to the top of the pinnacle on the left. Step right and climb the short crack to arrive on scree-covered ledges. A cracking pitch.

5 15m. Climb the rightward-sloping ledge above to the bottom of a right-angled corner containing a thin crack. Climb this strenuously for a few moves (crux) and finish on broken ground. A sting-in-the-tail finale, which can be avoided on the left.

Variations

4a The 'He-man' Variation 15 metres Very Difficult
Climb the slab above pitch 3, starting on the right, to a ledge below a quartz-mottled corner.

5a Longland's Variation Very Difficult
At the top of the 'He-man' slab, and just to its left is a steep arête. Climb this to a small platform and large belay. Traverse up and across the wall to the left to finish level with a mottled recess,

Many other variations can be made above pitch 3. The arête of Longland's Variation direct is Severe.

Nunc Dimittis 107 metres Very Severe   (1.6.57)
A pleasant and sustained series of variations on The Ring. It is hard for its grade. Start 1½ metres right of The Gambit Climb, below a clean-cut groove higher up the crag.

1 12m. 4c. Climb the layback crack for 3 metres up to a grassy recess at the foot of the groove.

2 17m. 5a. Climb the deep V-groove, moving right at the top (crux).

3 23m. 4b. Ascend the crack for 3 metres and move left onto the narrow ledge. Trend rightwards across the wall until you gain a crackline, which is followed to a stance at a perched block (junction with The Ring).

4 18m. 4a. Above is a steep wall. Climb it on the right by cracks in a groove above an initial slab to a large bay.

5 37m. 4b. Climb the left arête and move right to join the last cracks of The Ring. Ascend easily to the ridge.

My Best Friend 108 metres Hard Very Severe   (4.7.91)
Essentially a direct start to The Ring. Start just right of Nunc Dimittis, at the crack in the steep slab.

1 21m. 5a. Jam the crack in the slab to a spike belay – a superb pitch reminiscent of gritstone.

2 6m. Move up to join Nunc Dimittis at its second stance.

3 23m. 4c. Ascend the crack for 3 metres, moving left onto a narrow ledge. Take the wall above, finishing steeply, to join Nunc Dimittis at the perched block.

4 21m. The Ring pitch 5.

5 37m. 4b. The Ring pitch 6.

The Ring 115 metres Very Severe   (23.8.48)
A steep, pleasantly exposed, but somewhat rambling route. Start to the right of My Best Friend, and 3 metres right of two ill-defined chimneys, at a steep groove that is slightly overhung at its base.

1 15m. 4a. Climb the groove (awkward for 3 metres) and then move left round the corner to a small grass ledge.
2 12m. Head up and slightly left over three large steps to a corner.
3 15m. 4b. Ascend the corner for 3 metres and step out left. Traverse left to a small stance and belay beside a tiny slab.
4 15m. 5a. An awkward traverse up right across the slab leads to a stance at a perched block.
5 21m. Traverse left and go up the cracked corner to a spiky stance. Climb a short wall to a corner slab, which leads to a ledge below a corner with twin cracks.
6 37m. 4b. Climb the left-hand crack for 5 metres to a ledge. Step right into the corner and jam steeply up the twin cracks. Broken rocks lead up to the ridge.

Ribbon Route   91 metres   Difficult   (9.08)
Loose and not recommended, a rather broken route and very ill defined in its upper reaches. Start about 8 metres left of *Fallen Block Crack*, by a pock-marked block. Climb up, zigzagging to avoid difficulties. At 30 metres a prominent quartz ribbon is crossed, after which the route deteriorates into scrambling.

Fallen Block Climb   87 metres   Moderate   (9.08)
The obvious but disappointing gully left of the Fallen Block.
1 27m. Scramble up into the bed of the gully and climb the broken crack in the left corner of the chimney on the right. Ascend the upper part of the chimney.
2 60m. Loose scrambling up the gully-line leads to the arête; numerous stances and belays.

Bad Moon Risin'   37 metres   E3 6a   (19.8.84)
A fierce route, which gives good climbing up the imposing crack in the wall left of *Simulid*. Start just left of *Simulid*. Climb directly up the wall to the detached flake/pillar on *Simulid*. Continue up the crack to finish.

Simulid   43 metres   Hard Very Severe 5b   (27.6.81)
A worthwhile climb. Start just left of *Fallen Block Crack*. Climb left up a series of flakes to the top of a detached flake/pillar. Traverse right and down along the obvious line to the foot of a steep groove. Climb this, past a ledge, making a difficult move out right just below the top. Step back above the groove to belay.

★★Fallen Block Crack   72 metres   Very Severe   (11.9.27)
Interesting and enjoyable. The wide crack may prove to be slightly easier in boots, the traditional footwear for this esoteric outing. Start from the Fallen Block.
1 9m. 4a. The strenuous crack leads to a chockstone belay.
2 26m. 4c. The crack is very steep up to a resting-place at 9 metres on some loose blocks. The middle section of the crack can be avoided by the

harder, thin crack on the right. The crack eventually eases and leads to a large ledge shared by *The Black Gates*.
3 37m. *The Black Gates* pitches 4 and 5.

★**Route of Knobs** 53 metres   Hard Very Severe   (26.8.52)
An exposed and technical route that takes the right wall of *Fallen Block Crack*. Good climbing in a fine position makes it well worth the walk.
1 9m. 4a. *Fallen Block Crack* pitch 1.
2 29m. 5a. Use a hold on the right wall to reach the outer edge. Climb the arête for 5 metres to a ledge. Traverse right past a thin vertical crack to a groove/crack on the right. Climb this for a short way, and then move back into the centre of the face. Ascend trending right until a crack leads to the arrival ledge of *Fallen Block Crack*.
3 15m. 4b. Traverse left across the crack and climb the left wall.
Variations
Direct Start   Hard Very Severe
1a 5b. Follow a steep crack on the right to join the main line.
1b 38m. 5a. From the base of *Fallen Block Crack*, climb the right arête to a junction with the parent route. Follow this and then continue up the obvious crack to a stance.
2b 15m. 4c Traverse 3 metres right to the base of a clean-cut 12-metre corner and climb this.

★**The Black Gates** 66 metres   Very Difficult   (12.15)
A hidden gem. Start 15 metres right of *Fallen Block Crack*, at a shallow depression or groove in a small steep wall and just down and right of the obvious pinnacles.
1 9m. Ascend the groove to a stance below large boulders.
2 15m. 'The Black Gates'. Go over the boulders to a niche below a leaning pinnacle. Leave the niche strenuously and climb the crack to the top of the pinnacle on the left. Belay 5 metres higher in a corner.
3 12m. Climb the corner for 3 metres, till an exposed step can be made round the corner on the left to a small ledge. Climb the wall to a larger ledge, and go on for 3 metres to a ledge with a belay.
4 10m. From the left end of the ledge, climb the chimney for 6 metres (the upper part of the line of *Fallen Block Crack*). Move right for a short way, and some 10 metres of scrambling leads to a chimney on the right.
5 20m. Climb the chimney past a chockstone at 3 metres, and then go up to a ledge on the right. Finish up the fine steep slab by using the left-hand corner-crack.

Genesis 120 metres   Hard Very Severe   (29.8.70)
A well-protected climb up entertaining cracks. The exact line is quite hard to find. Start as for *The Black Gates*.
1 40m. 5a. Follow *The Black Gates* for 9 metres, and then go right up a wall at a leaning block. Corner-cracks and then steep thin cracks lead to a good belay ledge.
2 30m. 5a. Traverse 6 metres right into a right-angled corner. Go up the strenuous corner-crack and the continuation chimney.

3 23m. 4b. Step right and climb a groove to a ledge. Step right to a short crack and ascend to a huge crevasse below thin water-worn cracks in a prominent steep wall.

4 27m. 5a. Ascend the steep left-hand crack on good jams.

★★**Rectory Chimneys** 130 metres Very Difficult (27.8.25)

An excellent route, one of the best of its standard in the Pass. It is harder but not unreasonable in the wet. Start 9 metres right of *The Black Gates*, at a narrow chimney, which has a small flake leaning across it at half height.

1 18m. Use the flake to climb the chimney, and then go up a groove in the steep wall. Easier than it looks.

2 21m. Ascend a short steep wall on the left, and then a short crack, with a mantelshelf to a niche below a pinnacle. The crack above is strenuous but can be avoided by a crafty deviation. Step round to the left and enter the crack from behind. Five metres of easy climbing above the crack leads to a good stance.

3 12m. Step up in the corner and then traverse a narrow ledge to a large chimney. Climb this to a ledge.

4 18m. From the ledge at the top of the chimney, climb over broken rocks in a grassy gully.

5 37m. A grassy rake leads up to the right above a huge crevasse. Follow this to an immense cairn of bollards, the Vestry, (numerous stances).

6 24m. Traverse 6 metres right into a broken chimney, which leads easily up to the final arête.

Quintet Route 107 metres Severe (9.6.35)

A vague route right of *Rectory Chimneys*. Start 6 metres right of the line leading to a conspicuous recess near the foot of the crag. A 9-metre crack leads to a stance. Traverse left and go up a vertical corner with a rib in it to a broad platform. Above this is the Grey Chimney, which is difficult to start and is climbed for 14 metres to a belay. Move left onto an arête and climb this to a stance after 12 metres. Traverse right onto a steep exposed slab, which is followed pleasantly to a perch on its left edge. Continue up in the same line to finish.

Duet Chimneys 97 metres Hard Severe (8.9.35)

A worthwhile route despite some dubious rock. Immediately right of *Rectory Chimneys* is a steep buttress, whose right-hand side defines the route. Start by scrambling up to a quartz-topped bollard below a smooth V-chimney.

1 23m. Go easily up to the smooth chimney, which is climbed (quite difficult) to a stance. Work up into the roof of the chimney and swing round to a higher ledge using good holds well up on the left.

2 14m. Climb up behind the perched block and continue diagonally up to a stance beside a chimney. A good pitch.

3 9m. The narrow dirty chimney leads to a cave in the wider cleft above (loose). Belays in the cave floor.

4 18m. The chimney is strenuous and the flakes forming the roof are difficult to get round. Continue more easily and leave the chimney to reach a stance at a long finger of rock.
5 18m. Continue in the same line to the foot of a steep wall. The piled bollards of The Vestry are above and to the right. Climb the wall to a stance.
6 15m. Descend slightly left and go up a break in the wall until it is possible to move round onto the face. Follow the right edge and finish in a niche just below the ridge.

Hexagonal Phase   93 metres   E1   (19.8.84)
A direct line, which gives interesting but rather disjointed climbing. Start 3 metres left of *Three Cave Gully*, at the base of the buttress.
1 21m. 5b. Climb thin cracks in the front of the buttress to a grassy ledge.
2 40m. 5a. Climb a wide flake crack above the belay and go across broken rock to avoid the overhang on the right. Continue directly up the wall to a stance.
3 32m. 5a. Scramble up for 6 metres, and then follow a crack in the thin slabby buttress left of the gully.

The Quartet Wall   79 metres   Very Difficult   (21.9.35)
This pleasant and exposed route leads directly to the Vestry, via the loose wall left of *Three Cave Gully*. Start as for that route.
1 11m. Climb to the floor of the cave, and climb up a pinnacle on the left wall to a ledge.
2 14m. Traverse to the end of the grassy ledge and climb the wall on a diagonal line of holds to a good stance.
3 15m. Climb diagonally up right below the overhang into a shallow groove. Climb the right edge of the groove and cross to the roof of the overhang. Pinnacle belays.
4 15m. Take a direct line up the wall to the Vestry.
5 24m. *Rectory Chimneys* pitch 6.

Three Cave Gully   92 metres   Very Difficult   (16.5.37)
A poor route on bad rock. Right of *Duet Chimneys* is a steep broken buttress with an obvious overhang about half-way up. The route follows the prominent chimneys on the right. Start by scrambling up to the foot of the gully.
1 20m. Climb the gully to a cave. Ascend the right wall and traverse to a stance on the edge. Climb a small corner near the edge to a slab on the right, and then traverse back across a smooth slab into the second cave.
2 27m. Ascend the deeply-cut chimney to the third cave.
3 21m. Climb out of the cave and follow the gully continuation to join *Rectory Chimneys* at the crevasse and so to the Vestry.
4 24m. *Rectory Chimneys* pitch 6.

Lectern Grooves   51 metres   Hard Severe   (6.10.62)
The walls to the right of *Three Cave Gully* are smaller, but are very steep and split by some impressive cracks. About half-way between the gully and

the large triangular buttress on the right is an inverted V-chimney. The route follows twin grooves up the wall on the left. The escape above the route is exceptionally loose. Start by scrambling up to ledges at the foot of the steep upper walls.

1 30m. Step left onto a rib and go up to the foot of the first groove. Move left immediately onto the wall on the left. Climb this on small positive holds to the second groove and ascend this steeply to a good ledge.

2 21m. Climb the easier continuation of the groove for a short way, and then move right to a grassy ledge. Scramble up with caution to finish.

★Russet 52 metres   E3   (19.9.71)
An excellent crack pitch, well worth the walk. Towards the right-hand end of the cliff is a well-defined and steep red groove. Start below this.

1 43m. 5c. Climb the overhanging groove (very fierce at the start). Continue more easily up the groove and past the overhang.

2 9m. Scramble easily to the top.

The Curate's Egg 66 metres   Very Severe   (9.7.67)
A poor route that starts left of *Waterslide Gully*, at the lowest point of the buttress.

1 24m. Climb easily to grassy ledges and belays below a large detached pinnacle.

2 12m. 4b. Ascend the pinnacle and groove above on dubious flakes. Move right to a stance.

3 30m. 4b. Climb the flake cracks behind the belays, then traverse left across a slab for 5 metres and finish up the wall above.

The Organ Route Easy   (9.08)
From below the waterslide of the next route, break out left over loose rock to a subsidiary gully on the left. Follow this to the upper sills of felstone, which seem like stacks of organ pipes when viewed from the cwm. Care should be taken as the rock is very loose here.

Waterslide Gully 122 metres   Moderate   (9.08)
The left side of *The Infidel* buttress is defined by a scree-filled gully running the full height of the cliff. In the lower half it gives typical gully-climbing for about 30 metres to the steep waterslide, a tricky pitch that leads out of the main gully to the right. The rock then deteriorates. Not recommended.

Sedilia 63 metres   E2   (14.9.68)
The first pitch is steep and on rotten rock. Start below and left of *The Infidel*, some 3 metres right of the short chimney that defines the edge of the buttress.

1 30m. 5b. Climb up to a sloping ledge and continue with difficulty into a shallow scoop below a diagonal overhang. Move left and climb a hidden flake crack. A short loose groove on the left leads to a good ledge and peg belays. Serious.

2 21m. 5a. Climb a shallow green groove behind the stance and traverse left below an overhang. Step across a groove and ascend to easier ground.
3 12m. 4b. Traverse right across a slab and go up a short rib to a grassy terrace.

★★The Rosy Crucifixion   60 metres   E3   (20.9.63)
A fine open route that accepts the challenge of the wall left of *The Infidel*; perhaps a tad easier for the tall. Start at grassy ledges down and right of a huge block with a chimney behind it, reached by scrambling as for *The Infidel*.
1 30m. 6a. Climb diagonally up left to a tiny ledge level with the foot of the flake crack of *The Infidel*. Move up in the same line and layback a blind flake crack (hard) to a small loose spike. Traverse right to a ledge in the middle of the wall. Move up 3 metres and follow a thin diagonal flake crack (peg), which leads to the foot of a bottomless groove on the right. Climb this via a very hard move to a small roof and move up into a long narrow ledge. Belay well to the left or take a hanging belay in the crackline above.
2 30m. 5a. Move back right and ascend the steep crack-line on good holds moving left near the top. Continue up easily to ledges and belays near the top section of *The Infidel*. About 45 metres of scrambling leads to the top.
Variation
Direct Start   27 metres   E4 6a
1a 27m. 6a. Climb straight up on creaking holds, and then make some difficult and delicate moves diagonally left to gain the diagonal flake crack.

The Infidel   118 metres   Very Severe   (20.4.63)
An interesting climb with some enjoyable moves. At the right-hand end of the cliff is a large triangular slabby buttress. The route follows a flaky crack up the right side of the buttress. Start by scrambling up the easy slabs for 30 metres to a ledge 12 metres below the flake.
1 43m. 4c. Climb a thin crack and then the flake or the wall on the right. Move right at the overhangs (crux) to a ledge on the arête. A short steep groove round the corner leads to a ledge.
2 30m. 4a. Climb the short diagonal flake crack in the wall above, and then trend left up rough slabs to a huge flake belay in a grassy bay.
3 15m. 4a. Climb either crack in the steep back wall.
4 30m. 4b. Move up left to a huge spike at the foot of the prominent arête. Step left off the spike and climb the arête to a ledge near the top. Move left again to finish up a steep and very loose groove.

Right of *The Infidel* the rocks are very broken and give no scope for continuous routes. Well up in the cwm, **Grey Gully** (Easy 4.06) gives a good scramble to the crest of the ridge.

Clogwyn y Ddysgl Girdle   Difficult   (1913)
An arbitrary outing that can follow a variety of lines in either direction.

The Gambit Climb (VD, page 199) Clogwyn y Ddysgl
Climber: Simon Cardy   Photo: Mary Niklas

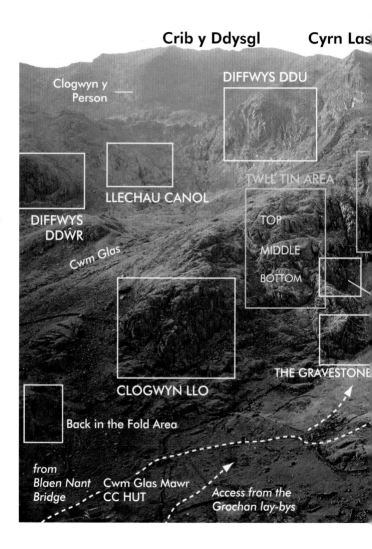

Crib y Ddysgl   Cyrn Las

DIFFWYS DDU

Clogwyn y
Person

LLECHAU CANOL

DIFFWYS
DDŴR

Cwm Glas

TWLL TIN AREA

TOP

MIDDLE

BOTTOM

THE GRAVESTONE

CLOGWYN LLO

Back in the Fold Area

from
Blaen Nant   Cwm Glas Mawr
Bridge   CC HUT   Access from the
Grochan lay-bys

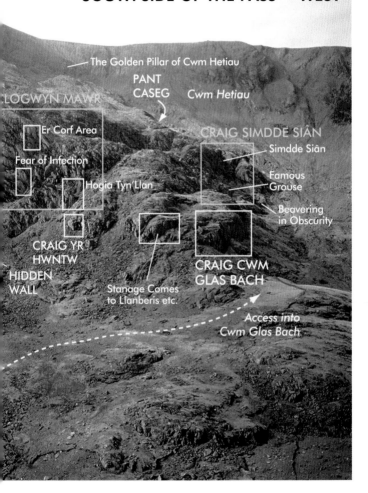

The Golden Pillar of Cwm Hetiau

PANT CASEG

Cwm Hetiau

CLOGWYN MAWR

Er Corf Area

Fear of Infection

Hogia Tyn'Llan

CRAIG SIMDDE SIÂN

Simdde Siân

Famous Grouse

Beavering in Obscurity

CRAIG YR HWNTW

HIDDEN WALL

Stanage Comes to Llanberis etc.

CRAIG CWM GLAS BACH

Access into Cwm Glas Bach

Main Wall (HS, page 214) Diffwys Ddu
Climber: Grace Hurford   Photo: Wil Hurford

Diffwys Ddu (Cyrn Las) Black Precipice (Grey Horn)
OS Ref 614 561

At the head of Cwm Glas, Diffwys Ddu rises challengingly some 180 metres above the scree. It is a lower offshoot of Cyrn Las proper, the prominent great step in the ridge between Cwm Glas Mawr and Cwm Glas Bach. The earliest climbers for no very good reason bestowed the name Cyrn Las upon the cliff.

Seen from low down the cwm, the cliff appears as a huge dome, with large and impressive overhangs forming the final nose. The most obvious feature is the huge vertical gash of *Great Gully*, which is deeply cut and divides near the top. Left of *Great Gully* the rock is more broken and on the lower sections the structure is similar to that of Lliwedd. The Upper and Lower Chasms are two obvious vertical rifts separated by a broad terrace of scree and heather. Left again the cliff breaks away into the stream which runs down from Llyn Bach below Clogwyn y Ddysgl. Right of *Great Gully* is Great Buttress, which sweeps up from the screes to end in a large overhang. The first vertical feature right of the gully is the curving crackline of *Subsidiary Groove* and part of *Main Wall*. Right again is a short black cleft in the shape of a curved L. This is part of *The Great Buttress* and the girdle connections. Right of this are the prominent leftward-slanting cracks of *The Grooves*, which lead up to the grassy area right of the final nose.

The deep vertical chimney of *Schoolmasters' Gully* defines the right-hand section. The rest is broken. Two gullies, the first ill-defined and the second of yellow rock, run up to the right of *Schoolmasters' Gully*. Then Gwter Fawr, an easy gully which gives a descent on that side, marks the end of the cliff.

The rock is not always perfect and a good deal of competence is needed even on the easy routes. The major routes are long, exposed and as good as any climbs in Wales. The crag faces north-east, and you have to be up early, in the summer, to catch much sunlight on it. The crag can often be very windy and cold, even in good weather. With the base of the cliff lying at about 530 metres the approach from the road can be made in about 35 minutes.

The best descent is by traversing over to the main path from Upper Cwm Glas well over to the left of the cliff.

The Chasms   213 metres   Moderate   (1903)
A pleasant scramble, which can be used as a way of descent. The Lower Chasm is left of *Great Gully* and just above the stream. It is an obvious inverted L-shaped cleft. Scramble 30 metres from the scree into the bed of the chasm. A 12-metre pitch up the cave is taken as a through route or on the outside. From the cave, ascend the left wall and go up to the slab on the left; this can be avoided on the right. A short 6-metre chimney leads to a broad ledge of red scree. The Upper Chasm starts with a scramble of 18 metres into the gully and goes up a short chimney, finishing on the right.

Continue for 18 metres up to the cave. From here, make a delicate traverse across the wall on the right and go up over doubtful blocks (14 metres). It is possible to traverse the left wall instead, but this is more difficult. Ninety metres of easy scrambling up the scree-filled gully leads to the top.

Bogus Mountain Journey   75 metres   E1   (16.9.02)
Not the best route on the crag: pitch 2 is serious, with poor protection and some loose rock. Start right of *The Chasms*, at a pillar running up to the left of the prominent overhanging nose.
1 21m. 4c. Follow the crest of the pillar to a spike belay on the crest below an overhang.
2 24m. 5a. Go over the overhang to a ledge. Steep moves above poor wires gain good holds below a small cave (behind the grass). Easier slabs lead to a terrace.
3 30m. Pleasant rightward-trending ramps lead to the main terrace.

Lonely Corner   42 metres   Very Severe   (16.9.02)
The main terrace dividing the lower and upper Chasms peters out on the right below an obvious corner. Start down to the left of the corner.
1 12m. 4c. Trend right along the grassy ledge, over the top of a gully, to the bottom of the corner. Climb the corner to a good stance about 6 metres up.
2 30m. 4b. Climb the corner to the top, with good, steep, juggy moves high up.

Central Route   136 metres   Hard Severe   (1903)
A long and intricate mountaineering route with its share of both good and bad rock. The lower pitches are the hardest part of the climb. After the first pitch it is possible to ascend the cliff more or less direct, at about Very Severe. Start on the heather band below *Great Gully*.
1 18m. Climb the rib on the left, and then move left below a large flake to an awkward groove, which leads to a good ledge on the left.
2 20m. Climb the large block above and step left. More grass and a short traverse right lead to a short steep wall. Ascend this and the groove above to a stance below an overhang.
3 15m. Move left at the overhang and climb easily to a belay below orange-coloured slabs.
4 24m. Ascend the clean slab on small holds to an open chimney on the right. Good holds on the left of the chimney are the key to the problem. Exit on jugs to reach a large terrace.
5 23m. Follow an easy gangway up right to a good stance below a chimney.
6 15m. Climb the chimney and move out right to a sloping ledge.
7 21m. Move back left and ascend a steep exposed wall. A crack on the left of a big flake leads steeply up to finishing cracks.

Great Gully   133 metres   Very Difficult   (1904)
One of the best gully climbs in the valley. Much harder when wet. Stances should be arranged beneath overhangs to protect the second from loose

scree. Start by scrambling up the bed of the gully until it steepens about 100 metres above the scree. Keep to the right, on a heathery rib, to a heathery band that runs across the gully at the same level as a triangular cave and about 12 metres to its left.

1 24m. Descend slightly and follow the heathery gangway to the centre of the gully. Go steeply up the bed to a stance.

2 15m. Start up the slightly overhanging wall on the right. It leads strenuously to a short chimney.

3 27m. Ignore an easy leftward-rising traverse. Keep in the main gully-line up the right-hand chimney to a large chockstone forming a cave. Good belays.

4 12m. Turn the cave on the left and scramble up to where the gully divides.

5 37m. Follow the central line up a chimney to grass at 18 metres (stance possible). Continue easily to a cave below a capstone.

6 18m. Ascend the chimney until a step can be made onto the right wall. Climb to a good belay above the capstone. A short pitch of scree leads to the top.

Variations

3a 30m. The rising traverse above pitch 2 can be taken and the gully regained by a rising traverse to the cave.

5a 46m. The left-hand branch of the gully after pitch 4 gives less interesting climbing.

Trauma Grooves 105 metres E1   (26.5.62)
A disjointed line of grooves on the left of *Main Wall* with loose rock and some dangerous blocks, which need trundling. Start as for *Main Wall*.

1 30m. 4a. As for *Main Wall* for 9 metres; then continue left to belay at the foot of the first groove.

2 18m. 5a. Climb the grassy groove on the left, and then make a difficult traverse right to reach a small ledge. Pass the large loose flake jammed in a crack to the short chimney beyond. Go up this to a grassy ledge and belays.

3 30m. 4c. Climb the groove on the left to a long narrow ledge overlooking the gully. Move left and go up the shallow vertical groove to a ledge on the left. Move up a little and traverse right to a grassy ledge. Flake belays below overhangs.

4 12m. 4c. Climb diagonally back left and go up the groove over the overhangs to a ledge below the final slab of *Main Wall*.

5 15m. 4a. Finish up the rest of *Main Wall* pitch 6.

Druid's Dilemma 122 metres Severe   (6.8.56)
A rising traverse which meanders up the left-hand part of the cliff starting at the top of pitch 1 of *Main Wall*, crossing *Great Gully* 12 metres above the overhanging wall and continuing to the left up ledges and grass with some rock towards the top. Not really recommended

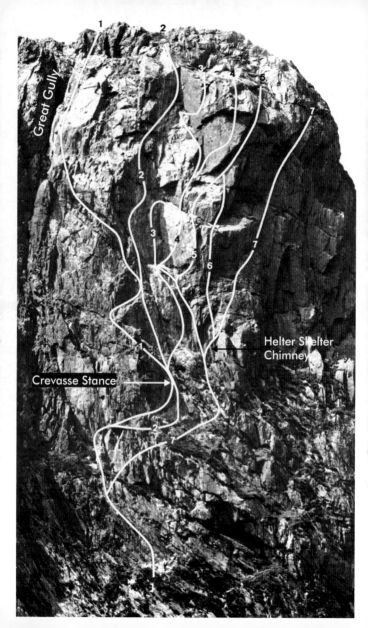

Great Gully

Helter Skelter
Chimney

Crevasse Stance

Diffwys Ddu (Cyrn Las)

1 Main Wall	HS	5 The Skull	E4
2 Subsidiary Grooves	E1	6 Hindenburg	E5
3 Lubyanka	E3	7 The Great Buttress	E2
4 Long Kesh	E5	8 Sunday School Outing	E4

9 The Grooves	E1
10 The Edge of Time	E4
11 Pedants Buttress	VS

★★★**Main Wall**   140 metres   Hard Severe   (27.7.35)
One of the most enjoyable expeditions in Eryri, a tremendous Welsh
classic. Exposed and serious for its grade, the route zigzags up the steep
wall between *Great Gully* and *Subsidiary Groove*. Start about 100 metres
above the scree, near a conspicuous triangular overhang with a grassy
field above. From the scree fan on the left, scramble to a slab left of the
overhang and at a lower level.
1 21m. 4a. Climb diagonally left up the well worn slab to a vegetated
ledge at 9 metres. Ascend a short corner for 3 metres. Move right across a
slab and round a rib, and then go up to a pulpit stance.
2 24m. 4b. Make some difficult moves up the rightward-sloping
gangway on the right of the pulpit to the chimney of *Subsidiary Groove*.
Climb this for a short way and then traverse back left along a ledge to a
corner overlooking the gully. Peg belay.
3 14m. 4a. Ascend the arête above, and then go diagonally right to a
large triangular platform in the corner.
4 27m. 4b. Descend slightly and climb a flaky pinnacle on the left. From
its tip, step left onto the steep wall and pull up into a niche. Go round the
corner on the left and up a steep arête until a step leads across a chimney
to a short slab. A fine pitch.
5 24m. 4a. Go up to an overhang and move left across a broken
chimney to the foot of a large slab overlooking *Great Gully*. Climb the left
edge of the slab on excellent holds to a good stance at its top – delightfully
exposed.
6 30m. Climb up left to a ledge and ascend a slab to the right. Finish by
scrambling to the summit.

Main Wall Eliminate   85 metres   Hard Very Severe   (27.5.73)
The left-hand arête of *Subsidiary Groove*. Start at a stance just before the
crevassed stance of *Subsidiary Groove*, which is gained by climbing *Main
Wall* pitches 1 and 2.
1 18m. 5a. Climb the crevasse until a difficult step leads out left onto the
nose, which is climbed to reach good ledges. Move right onto the wall and
climb direct to a stance and belay on *Main Wall*.
2 37m. 5a. Traverse left for a short way and climb the steep wall on
fragile holds to a shallow depression leading to a short wide crack. Climb
this to reach the top of the pinnacle on *Main Wall* pitch 4, and step right
from it onto the wall. Follow a shallow groove and then a crack to a loose
finish onto easy slabs. Belay as for *Main Wall*.
3 30m. 4b. Follow the right-hand edge of the slabs and then the
grooved arête. Move left near the top onto easy-angled slabs.

★**Subsidiary Groove**   112 metres   E1   (22.3.53)
A very fine route. Sustained climbing and an exacting final corner-crack
make for an invigorating outing. It is the obvious line of curving chimneys
defining the left side of the Great Buttress.
1 27m. 4a. As for *Main Wall* to the stance above pitch 1. Move across to
the foot of the chimney/groove.

2 15m. 4b. Ascend the chimney/groove, joining *Main Wall* part way up. Step out right at the top to a crevasse stance.

3 41m. 5a. Climb the crack in the same line on dubious rock (hard if wet) to a junction with *Main Wall*. Make a rising traverse across a steep wall for 6 metres, and then go back right up a small gangway to a resting place higher up the corner. Climb the steep wall above, moving left at the top. Last possible escape.

4 14m. 4c. Ascend the groove to the overhang. Step round the corner on the right on poor rock, and then climb easily up the slab on the right to a stance and belay.

5 15m. 5b. Ascend the crack on the left of the slab to the bottom of the steep corner. Climb this (sustained) to a stance and belay. Scramble up to finish.

★★**Lubyanka**   117 metres   E3   (21.8.76)

An excellent and varied route that is very popular. Bolder than *The Skull*. The climbing is sustained, technical and in a dramatic situation, particularly on the crucial top pitch. The climb follows a series of grooves and corners between *Subsidiary Groove* and *The Skull* before breaking out onto the headwall above the top pitch of the latter.

1 & 2 42m. 4a. *Subsidiary Groove* pitches 1 and 2.

3 18m. 5c. Above the stance is an obvious groove. Enter this with difficulty from the left and climb it without much respite to a large bay.

4 15m. 5b. Climb the corner behind the belay; then exit right and descend the slab for a short way to a spike belay.

5 21m. 5c. Climb directly up the slab, over an overlap, and enter a short open corner. Climb this and exit left at the top (hard), and then continue up the short slab to a small ledge.

6 21m. 5c. An exposed pitch. Hand-traverse to the right along the quartz band above the roof for 3 metres until a finger-hold enables a standing position to be attained. Climb the groove (good holds round to the left) until it curves round to form a roof. Layback boldly through the roof and continue easily up the slab to nut and spike belays.

Variation

The Left-Hand Finish   E4

6a 21m. 6a. A bold pitch, harder than, though not as exposed as, the original way. Hand-traverse the quartz band for 2 metres to an awkward step up. Pull out leftwards onto the wall. Sustained climbing up and leftwards on small holds leads to a slab 2 metres above the roof.

★★**Long Kesh**   130 metres   E5   (1.7.85)

A very good climb with tremendous exposure.

1 & 2 57m. 4c. *The Great Buttress* pitches 1 & 2.

3 18m. 5c. Follow *The Skull* pitch 3 to its belay, and then go up 3 metres to a larger ledge. Belay as for *Lubyanka* pitch 3.

4 12m. 5c. From the right end of the ledge, step up right onto the wall. Climb a thin crack for 2 metres and then move right to the arête. Follow this to a spike belay as for *Lubyanka* pitch 4.

5 43m. 6b. Climb directly up the slab and over an overlap to enter a short open corner (as for *Lubyanka*). Step right, then go up to a peg, traverse right to an *RP* placement, and climb up onto a slab on the right (crux). Ascend to the roof (two poor pegs), move rightwards underneath the roof to the arête overlooking *The Skull*, and pull boldly over the roof onto the slab above. Continue to the top, and belay on a flake at the top left corner of the easy-angled slabs.

★★★**The Skull**   127 metres   E4   (1.5.66)
A thrilling and spectacular climb with a memorable top pitch. It is the arête right of *Subsidiary Groove* and the prominent slanting groove left of the final overhanging nose.
1 & 2 57m. 4c. *The Great Buttress* pitches 1 and 2.
3 15m. 5c. Step down left, and then climb awkwardly left using a dubious flake to reach a thin crack. Climb this strenuously to a stance.
4 15m. 6a. Move right to a shallow groove in the overhanging arête. Ascend this with difficulty and continue up a slab to a peg belay.
5 40m. 5c. Climb the slab above, trending right to the foot of the obvious slanting groove (peg). Make a hard step right and climb the right wall of the groove to a small ledge. The groove above is very technical, but has good protection, and is best climbed by painful wide bridging (which somewhat amplifies the exposure). The groove now eases, and an easy slab and block belay are soon reached. A superb pitch in a magnificent position. Scramble up to finish.

★**Hindenburg**   121 metres   E5   (30.8.79)
A hard direct line between *The Skull* and *The Great Buttress*.
1 & 2 57m. 4c. *The Great Buttress* pitches 1 and 2.
3 15m. 6a. From the top of the pinnacle, step left onto the wall and climb up to enter an open groove. Ascend this and continue a further metre or so to a sloping ledge. A very serious lead. Nut belays over on the right at a poor stance.
4 12m. 5c. Climb up and slightly left to obvious undercuts and, using a crack on the left, go up to a sloping ledge. Nut and peg belay under the bulge.
5 37m. 6a. Climb the problematic groove above, which is hard to enter, and continue to a junction with *The Skull* part way up its last pitch. Finish as for *The Skull*.

★**The Great Buttress**   139 metres   E2   (4.5.63)
A good and varied route on good rock; the start of pitch 3 is, however, quite bold for the grade. It takes a line up the centre of the buttress, finishing up a series of overhanging grooves right of the final nose. Start as for *Main Wall*.
1 27m. 4c. Climb a steep slab and a short strenuous chimney to the field at the foot of pitch 2 of *Subsidiary Groove*.
2 30m. 4c. Climb a steep flake crack on the left of the arête. Descend slightly and move right round the arête to a wall. Trend left to the foot of

the L-shaped Helter Skelter Chimney. Go up this to a stance level with the crevasse of *Subsidiary Groove*.

3 24m. 5b. Climb to the top of the flake of Helter Skelter Chimney and make a bold and committing move onto the wall above, where the climbing soon eases. Step right to a shallow vertical groove/crack. Climb this and move left along a narrow ledge for 3 metres. Go steeply up to a diagonal flake and follow it to the right to a niche.

4 12m. 5c. The strenuous overhanging crack leads to a niche and an exit right. Fierce jamming/laybacking leads to a stance on the left and a well-earned rest.

5 46m. 5b. Trend right and climb a steep cracked wall, a rightward-slanting groove and the final groove of *The Grooves*. A fine, exposed pitch.

The Green Caterpillar   120 metres   Very Severe   (22.4.49)
A grassy route, connecting the lower part of *Subsidiary Groove* with *The Grooves* and finishing up to the right of the latter. Some interesting ground is covered and the grade of the route is open to debate depending on your attitude to grass-climbing. Start as for *The Great Buttress*.

1 18m. Scramble up rightwards and climb the short strenuous chimney to the grassy field. Move right and ascend a grassy crack in the same line to a stance with a thread belay on the right.

2 18m. Above and on the left, another grassy crack leads to a gangway, which is followed to the left. Pull out on grass, and climb a short way to a small corner and a belay.

3 18m. Ascend diagonally rightwards into a grassy chimney, which leads up to a wall. Traverse 3 metres to a large flake below a corner.

4 12m. Climb the overhanging corner on good holds to a stance at the top of the blocks. Descend the crack on the other side and traverse to a good grassy ledge and belay. Junction with *The Grooves*.

5 27m. Ascend the rib above the stance for a short way, and then step across the corner to a ledge with an overhang above. Make a difficult traverse to a mossy slab on the right, and traverse the slab with even more difficulty to a grassy ledge. Go straight up over a mossy bulge and continue to the grassy slab, keeping near to the corner when difficulties appear. A small rock stance is thankfully reached above a short corner. Twin flake belays.

6 27m. Easier climbing up to the right gains the top of *Schoolmaster's Gully*.

The Prune   129 metres   E2   (1.5.66)
Essentially a direct start to *The Great Buttress* but harder and not so enjoyable. Start at a 3-metre block 9 metres left of *The Grooves*.

1 24m. 5a. Traverse left a short way to a steep groove with a loose block forming part of its right wall. Move right at the top of the groove. Climb a steep wall to a peg, where an awkward move leads to a wide crack. Follow this to a pinnacle belay.

2 24m. 4c. Traverse awkwardly right to good holds, and climb the wall, trending slightly left at first, to a junction with *The Grooves* at a grassy ledge. Scramble up grass to a block belay.

3 23m. 5c. Descend the far side of the block to a ledge. Step left and climb a thin crack to the foot of a corner. Ascend this with difficulty past the bulge to a ledge below the crack on *The Great Buttress*.

4 & 5 58m. 5c & 5b. *The Great Buttress* pitches 4 & 5.

Sunday School Outing   117 metres   E4   (1.7.94)
A good route, which follows an independent line between *The Prune* and *The Grooves*. It is worth taking two sets of *Friends 0*, ½ & 1. Start 6 metres left of *The Grooves*, on a ledge with a spike belay. This is just left of a prominent 3-metre-high pinnacle.
1 46m. 5b. Climb directly above the belay to the overlap and pull over it onto the wall above. Traverse up and rightwards for 6 metres to gain a horizontal break below the grassy rake descending from the right of the huge perched block. Move up the left arête of the wall on large holds and cross rightwards onto the face just above a prominent undercut hold. Climb the wall on small holds until a wet groove can be gained on the left. Move delicately past a perched block, stand on it, and climb the right arête to join *The Grooves* at its first big ledge. Move left and ascend the crack in the wall to the first belay of *The Grooves*. Move left and up to belay on the pinnacle below the large inverted V-groove.
2 37m. 6a. Climb the groove with interest to the roof. Layback and bridging moves gain the sloping quartz ledge above (the rotting pegs are not necessary as other good protection exists). Climb the awkward crack/groove above to a good grassy belay ledge. *Friends 1 & 3* useful for the belay.
3 11m. 6a. Climb up and rightwards onto the arête. Make a difficult move right onto a ledge and pull up left over the bulge above to reach the base of the groove on *The Grooves* pitch 3. Move right to belay just below the overhanging arête.
4 23m. 6a. Climb the right-hand overhanging groove above the stance past a dubious peg to good jugs on the lip of the overhang. A hard pull gains easy ground above and the belay of *The Grooves*. A sensational pitch in a position of tremendous exposure.

★★★**The Grooves**   114 metres   E1   (13.9.53)
One of the best mountaineering routes at this standard in Britain. It follows a series of impressive grooves, which slant up leftwards, just right of the centre of the cliff. The climbing is strenuous and the difficulties sustained though at no point excessive. Start at the foot of the prominent groove-line with an overhang at its base.
1 43m. 5b. Go up easily to the overhang. Pull round this (hard if greasy, and it generally is) and enter the groove above. Follow the groove (frequent runners) to a small bay. Climb a short wall on the left to a large platform.
2 37m. 5b. Climb a rib on the right to a little groove. A hard move up this and awkward jamming lead to an impending wall. Make a tricky step left to the foot of the main groove. This is sustained but well-protected and

soon leads to a ledge. Continue more easily up a short corner to a larger ledge.

3 34m. 5b. Above the stance is the overhanging groove in the arête taken by *Sunday School Outing*. Gain the leftwards-slanting ledge below this and keep traversing left until a second groove is reached just around the arête. Climb this quite awkwardly until easier ground leads to the top.

Variations

★★The Overhanging Arête   E2

A sensational pitch to the right of pitch 4 of *Sunday School Outing*. Start at the base of the huge open corner 6 metres right of the last stance of *The Grooves*.

3a 37m. 5b. Climb the corner direct to a good runner at about 9 metres. Traverse left to the arête and grasp a huge jug. The rock above now overhangs alarmingly, the view below is impressive, and the weight is on your arms, so quickly pull up to a second huge jug. Continue to a point where a delicate step right gains good holds and easier-angled rock. Finish via the easier top part of *The Grooves* pitch 3.

The Right-Hand Finish   42 metres   E2

A good sustained pitch, which provides a fitting alternative to the final pitch of *The Grooves*. Start at the foot the corner of *The Overhanging Arête*.

3b 24m. 5b. A thin awkward crack in the right wall leads to a slab below the overhanging corner. Climb the slab and corner with a difficult finish on flat holds right of the bed of the corner. Climb more easily to a stance and belay.

4b 18m. 4a. Make a rising traverse left below the overhangs.

★★The Edge of Time   114 metres   E4   (18.6.89)

A classic expedition with breathtaking situations, which tackles the prominent right-hand skyline arête of the crag, starting as for *Times Past* and continuing up where that route moves right. Start just right of *The Grooves*. Spike belays.

1 27m. 5c. Climb up to the large overhang as for *Times Past*. Undercut leftwards to enter the groove. Continue up this until just below the overhang, where a move up and right brings a good spike to hand. Stand on the spike and move left, to pull round the overhang on huge holds. Thread and nut belays below the overhanging arête.

2 27m. 5b. Climb directly up the right-hand side of the arête to good runners in a horizontal break. Pull up on the edge of the arête and continue in the same line until a small left-slanting groove leads onto the slab above. Go left to belay below the hanging prow – or descend further to a more comfortable belay on *The Grooves*.

3 30m. 6a. Climb up to the overhang (*Times Past* takes the right-hand twin cracks). Pull around left to gain and follow a thin crack just right of *The Grooves*. Layback into the groove above, and then bridge up to a good spike where it finishes. Stand on the spike and pull up to a pancake-flake and small spike just to the left (line runner). Move left and down to a foothold on the arête and, using pinch grips, move down again

to reach a rest in the groove near a curious hole. Go left again and move up to stand on the huge fin. Climb the crack above to good belays on the terrace. Be careful to avoid rope drag.
4 30m. 5c. Climb directly up the true line of *The Overhanging Arête*, entering from the left. Gain the spike of *The Overhanging Arête* and finish as for that route.

Times Past   117 metres   E3 (31.5.77)
A challenging line, now somewhat superseded by *The Edge of Time*, with which it shares all its stances. Start just right of *The Grooves*, below two bottomless grooves.
1 24m. 5c. Climb to beneath the large overhang. Move left to the groove, climb up into it past an old peg, and make a bold move into the right-hand groove. Ascend this and go left to a good spike. Continue up to the overhang and surmount it to gain a belay.
2 24m. 4c. Climb the overhanging groove and move left to an arête. Go up this and move left to a slab.
3 27m. 6a. Traverse 3 metres left to a bottomless groove. Start this with difficulty, and then continue up to belay as for *The Right-Hand Finish* to *The Grooves*.
4 & **5** 42m. 5b & 4a. As for *The Right-Hand Finish*.

Caterwaul   96 metres   Very Severe (24.8.69)
Very steep and vegetated.
1 21m. *Schoolmasters' Gully* pitch 1.
2 24m. 4b. Descend 5 metres and follow ledges out left above the overhang. Climb diagonally left to the arête. Go up to a ledge, step right round a rib and climb a groove to a stance.
3 18m. 4a. Move easily out to the arête on the left and go up a slab to join *The Green Caterpillar*.
4 15m. 4a. Climb *The Green Caterpillar* to a wide corner.
5 18m. 4c. The tricky crack in the right wall of the corner leads to a ramp. Follow this to the top.

Schoolmasters' Gully   84 metres   Severe (12.8.06)
A good route of its type, fairly serious and with some loose rock. The upper chimney, known as Plaster Chimney, of this well-defined gully can be seen from low down in the cwm. Start on the heathery band below the gully an scramble up to the foot of the gully.
1 21m. Ascend the left-hand branch to the top of the broken rib in mid-gully.
2 9m. Easy grass leads to a platform, the Croquet Ground.
3 12m. Climb the wall left of the corner-crack and go up for about 3 metres. Traverse left to a stance on the edge.
4 12m. Go diagonally back right and traverse to the foot of the deeply-cut Plaster Chimney. Stance on the opposite side.
5 15m. Face right to climb the dirty chimney to an awkward grassy landing. Belay high up on the left wall.
6 15m. Scramble up to a short chimney, and then ascend to the top.

Variation

1a The Original Start 24m. Climb to a tiny cave and then up the wall on the right. After a short way, move back into the gully to a larger cave with a dubious flake. Climb out of the cave to a grassy ledge on the right (the Bowling Green). Step left and ascend a short groove on good holds to the top of the mid-gully rib.

Pedants Buttress 75 metres   Very Severe   (7.7.68)
A scrappy route up the narrow buttress right of *Schoolmasters' Gully*. Start at the toe of the buttress.
1 21m. 4b. Climb an easy groove to a big spike and step left to a slab. Climb this and traverse right along a ledge. Swing round the arête and go up to a grassy ledge.
2 21m. 4a. Climb the obvious crack on the left. Step right at the top to a ledge below a corner.
3 21m. 4c. Go up the corner, past a bulge, and step right onto the arête. Climb this easily to a ledge and a big block belay.
4 12m. 4a. Step off the block, climb the wall above, avoiding the overhanging chimney, and go into *Schoolmasters' Gully*. Scrambling remains.

Double Cave Gully   Difficult   (9.8.06)
Right of *Schoolmasters' Gully* is a shallow and ill-defined vegetated break. The main feature is a two-storeyed cave 45 metres up. A mediocre scramble.

Yellowstone Gully   Difficult   (6.8.06)
The poor gully on the right of the main cliff is easily identified by its yellowish rock. The first section, up the yellow chimney by its left wall, is steep and intimidatingly loose. After two pitches the gully deteriorates into a stone-shoot.

The Green Necklace 183 metres   Very Severe   (22.4.49)
A rambling expedition which girdles the cliff, pleasantly sustained. It traverses into *Great Gully* at about one-third of its height, and then across and down the hardest part of *Main Wall* before joining *The Green Caterpillar*. Start above the main pitch of *The Upper Chasm*, where a heather band runs along the cliff. Follow this to a stance overlooking *Great Gully*.
1 37m. Traverse down into the gully, via a large detached block. Climb above the cave and cross the gully to a large stance on the right wall.
2 30m. Follow the obvious quartz-marked traverse to the far edge. Descend for a short way, and then step right round the corner and down into a scoop. Continue the line of descent to a flaky pinnacle, and then down again to a large triangular platform in the corner (most of this is pitch 4 of *Main Wall* in reverse).
3 14m. Abseil down to the crevasse on *Subsidiary Groove*, or reverse *Main Wall* to the same spot.
4 6m. Move down and across to a flake at the top of Helter-Skelter Chimney on *The Great Buttress*.

5 12m. Descend the smooth curving chimney and traverse across to a grassy corner.
6, **7**, **8** & **9** 84m. Finish as for *The Green Caterpillar* pitches 3, 4, 5 and 6.

The High Level Girdle   95 metres   Very Severe   (15.6.58)
A route with some interesting positions, though rather pointless; it is probably best used as an approach to *The Overhanging Arête* or *The Right-Hand Finish*. Start from the top of pitch 3 of *Main Wall*.
1 14m. Climb the steep wall on the left, and then go back right up a small gangway (as for the top half of *Subsidiary Groove* pitch 3) to a chockstone belay and stance 2 metres from the corner.
2 18m. Step right across the groove onto an easy-angled ramp, which leads to a stance.
3 15m. Cross to the far end of the grassy ledge on the right. Step down and make a short traverse to a small ledge in the corner (junction with *The Grooves*). Climb the crack on the right to another large ledge.
4 12m. Walk across the ledge.
5 9m. Make a 5-metre abseil. A short ascent now leads to a good ledge on *The Green Caterpillar*.
6 27m. *The Green Caterpillar* pitch 6.

Crossbones   224 metres   E3   (17.9.77)
A lengthy and sustained expedition on good clean rock, which meanders diagonally up the cliff from left to right. Start as for *Great Gully*.
1 46m. Climb easy rock as for *Great Gully* to a grassy ledge. Move right to belay as for *Trauma Grooves* pitch 1.
2 40m. 5a. Go up the groove on the left for 5 metres as for *Trauma Grooves* pitch 2; then traverse right across the steep wall round the lip of the ledge to a crack. Climb this to a ledge. Go up a groove on the left and traverse horizontally right at the obvious fault to the peg belay at the top of pitch 2 of *Main Wall*.
3 21m. 4a. Climb diagonally right as for *Main Wall* pitch 3, and then go right to belay as for *The Skull* on the lowest ledge.
4 24m. 5a. Descend 3 metres down pitch 3 of *The Skull*. Traverse right to a rib. Cross this, and hand-traverse across a quartz break to *The Great Buttress*. Continue in the same line to a foothold-stance on the arête.
5 30m. 5a. Three metres up on the right is a small spike. Abseil from this 6 metres down *The Prune*. Traverse right along an obvious overlap into pitch 2 of *The Grooves*. Climb this for 6 metres. Belay in slings at a flake.
6 21m. 6a. Descend the groove (or abseil) and exit right to an overhanging groove. Climb the right arête past two pegs. Climb out into the left-hand of two grooves above. Go up this to a ledge and climb the crack above (as for *The Edge of Time*) to a block belay. Walk right to belay below *The Right-Hand Finish* of *The Grooves*.
7 & **8** 42m. 5b & 4a. *The Right-Hand Finish*.

The West Buttress   42 metres   Very Difficult   (1903)
A pleasant little climb with an interesting finish. West of the main cliff a broken buttress on Cyrn Las proper bounds the right side of Gwter Fawr,

the easy gully. A curiously-streaked slab with a broken chimney on the
right is the most obvious feature. Start by scrambling up 60 metres, first
right and then left, to the foot of the chimney.

1 12m. The chimney is entered by a mild layback. Climb up past a large
block to a good stance.

2 12m. The chimney is very broken, so climb the rib on the right
pleasantly to a stance above a pile of boulders.

3 18m. After a traverse right, which bulges awkwardly, ascend to a large
pinnacle. Climb this and then step into the corner on the left. The finish is
just below the Cyrn Las ridge.

Equator Walls

The Equator Walls lie to the right of Diffwys Ddu, and right of *The West Buttress*.
They are the much-eyed, golden-brown, slabby walls about 45 metres high
and divided into two sections by an easy grassy gully running down their centre.
The left-hand wall is split at half height on the right-hand side by an obvious
overhang with pockets forming a line out below it, and back across to the right
above. On the left side are two water-streaks (one of which rarely dries) down a
superb-looking crackline. Across the easy grassy gully lies the right-hand wall,
which from below appears to be the more unbroken and larger part of the cliff.
In its centre sits a prominent grass ledge that marks the belay of *Preamble*.

The rock is quick-drying and extremely compact, particularly on the left-hand
wall, and is similar in texture to a pocketed Clogwyn y Grochan. South-east
facing, this particular facet can retain sunlight until about midday. There is a
good terrace at the base of the walls for dumping gear, which is reached
from the right. The descent is down a gully on the right.

Extra big cams are useful for the various big pockets on these routes.
Although there is reason to believe that some of the pegs mentioned have
been replaced, they should all be treated with suspicion.

★★Steel Appeal   49 metres   E6 6b   (8.8.83)
A poorly-protected line with exceptionally good face-climbing, much steeper
than it looks but often wet. Start at the foot of the left-hand wall, just left of
New Era, below and right of a pillar and a flaky groove. Climb to the top of
the flaky groove and move up leftwards (small wire) to a foothold below a
crack sporting the remains of a peg (wire runners in pockets down on the
left). Ascend the crack with difficulty to a thin ledge on the right. Traverse
right to a poor peg on *New Era*. Climb up as for *New Era* to the remnants of
the top peg and a poor foothold. Using a small hold, make a very hard
move left, and climb quickly to a larger hold and the easier-angled slab.
Ascend first leftwards and then back right, and go up to the grassy terrace.
Easy ground on the left or the right leads to the top.

★★Alchemy   49 metres   E6 6c   (9.6.88)
The stunning rightward-trending hairline crack running the full height of
the left-hand wall is a modern masterpiece. Stamina, technical ability and
a cool head, *Friends 2 & 3* and a good rack of small wires (plus a week's
dry weather) should constitute the necessary criteria for a successful ascent.
Start by *Steel Appeal*. Climb up to a poor peg at about 6 metres and pass
it by difficult moves, and then trend slightly right and go up to the pocket of
New Era. Move left and clip what remains of the first peg of that route.
Layback into the obvious niche, and bridge up this to clip an ancient peg.
Stand on the good incut hold next to the peg and step right to a
reasonable rest. Make desperate moves up and slightly leftwards to grab
the huge pocket near the end of *New Era*. Continue, still quivering, to
finish as for *New Era*.

★New Era   49 metres   E6 6b   (8.8.83)
Another superb but serious wall pitch: like *Steel Appeal*. Start on the right
side of the left-hand wall, at the foot of a grassy gully. Climb easily up the
grass-filled gully on the right to a large block at 5 metres. Traverse out
leftwards on amazing pockets across the very smooth wall. At the end of
the pockets move up to a small flat-topped flake; then make a series of
difficult moves left past another pocket and go up to a poor peg. With
increasing difficulty climb up to reach a poor resting-foothold and another
poor peg. Make a huge reach up right to a poor small pocket. Swing right
in a crucifix position across a very smooth wall to a large pocket. Gain the
right-hand pocket and go up to a broken groove and easy ground. Climb
up leftwards to a grass terrace; belay on the right. Climb the corner on the
right or the smooth slabby wall above.

Mild Steel (49 metres E6 6b), a combination of the *New Era* start and the
Steel Appeal finish is also a noteworthy route.

Across the grassy central gully lies:

★Preamble   61 metres   E1   (19.6.65)
An excellent route. Start below an obvious flake crack on the left-hand side
of the right-hand wall.
1 46m. 5a. Climb the flake to a small grassy ledge. Step up right to
large holds. These lead right to a spiky block. Step right onto a long ledge
below a short slab. Traverse right and balance around a rib to reach
broken ledges. Ascend the small right-facing corner to a thin crack, which
leads up the slabby wall to a groove. Climb the groove to a grassy terrace
that crosses the buttress.
2 15m. Climb the loose rock to an overhang. Traverse left and ascend to
the top.

Flicker of Hope   40 metres   E5 6c   (12.5.88)
In the centre of the buttress, right of *Preamble*, a smooth leftward-slanting
groove, sporting an old peg at 6 metres, gives relatively safe yet technically
desperate face climbing. Lasso the peg. Using this as protection, climb

directly up the water stains left of the groove to gain flakes on the left and a good incut left of the peg. Continue up and left to a groove leading to a ledge on the right. Move about 3 metres right, and then climb straight up the face, following various cracks to finish.

Cyrn Las Fach   Little Grey Horn   OS Ref 615 563

This fairly broken cliff lies on the western side of Cwm Glas Mawr, at the same level as the foot of Diffwys Ddu. Several routes have been done here involving scrambling, grass and some loose rock, before petering out near the ridge of Chwarrennog (Lumpy – as with swollen glands), which leads to a pleasant scramble up the ridge of Cyrn Las proper.

Tiercel   84 metres   Very Difficult   (30.5.54)
Helps to make the walk over to Cwm Du'r Arddu more interesting. Start near the left-hand end of the crag, some 9 metres right of the foot of a grassy gully that slants gently leftwards.
1 37m. Climb the steepish open groove to a small ledge. Follow the groove and finish up the heathery gully; belay on the rib on the left.
2 18m. Scramble in the same general line over broken ground to the foot of a corner/chimney. Thread belay.
3 11m. Climb the corner/chimney.
4 18m. Follow the slabs, trending left to the top of the cliff.

Impromptu Buttress   82 metres   Difficult   (8.9.54)
The steepest buttress on the Chwarennog ridge, about half-way along, to the right of a clearly marked col and immediately left of a deep gully, is split from right to left by a diagonal groove. Start just right of the groove and almost at the lowest point of the buttress.
1 12m. Climb the wall to the right of the groove for 5 metres, traverse left and climb the groove on its left edge.
2 23m. Take the steep crack in the wall above and continue up it to quartz ledges. Scramble up a grassy ledge for 9 metres to the left and climb blocks to the top of the rake to land on a prominent nose.
3 11m. Swing right into a chimney and climb it to a ledge. This is followed by a mantelshelf to reach a large spike belay.
4 21m. Traverse left along a quartz ledge into a chimney. Climb this, escaping onto its flaky right edge. Ascend diagonally right to a grove of bollards. The steep wall above leads to a grassy rake, which can serve as an inferior finish.
5 15m. The slab above gives pleasant climbing for 6 metres. Scramble to the crest of the ridge.

Cwm Glas Bach Area

This is the area of broken mountainside opposite Clogwyn y Grochan and behind (the rather confusingly-named) Cwm Glas Mawr, the Climbers' Club hut. The hut, partially hidden by trees, is best reached by walking along a grassy track from the two wooden bridges near Blaen y Nant. Another, although damper, approach can be made from the upper of the two lay-bys below Clogwyn y Grochan; crossing the river and following a faint path up to the cottage. The area consists of a number of disparate crags. Commonly called 'Bumhole Buttress', Cwm Glas Bach offers a selection of almost gritstone-style climbing with good landings.

Ponc   Knoll   OS Ref 621 568
Above the CC hut is a sheepfold; the next two routes lie on the steep slab up and left of the fold and facing the bridge over to Blaen Nant.

Maia   17 metres   Very Severe   4b   (17.7.02)
An innocuous line, which gives a couple of tricky moves. Start left of the slab and follow the groove to an overhang. Layback round this to another groove and overhang, which provides an easier finish.

Heilyn   20 metres   Hard Very Severe   5a   (17.7.02)
Good moves and superb rock. Start at the very toe of the slab, below the obvious diagonal crack. Climb up to the crack and follow this almost into *Maia*; step back right and finish up the continuation crack.

Close to the right-hand wall of the fold is a slim coffin-shaped slab, with a holly tree at about half height on its right.

Back in the Fold   15 metres   Hard Very Severe   5a   (7.91)
A smart little pitch. Start below a stained crack. Ascend the crack system, with some difficult moves to start, to a heathery ledge. Continue up a final crack to a large ledge.

Raging Thesaurus   15 metres   E2 5b   (1991)
A nice way to finish off a day in this area of the Pass. Start at some pockets to the right of the crack system. Climb up to a horizontal crack, move up right to a vertical crack, and continue directly to gain a second horizontal break and the final slab. Precarious moves gain a scoop and a ledge. The belay is above the ledge.

Clogwyn Llo (Cwm Glas Facet)   Calf Crag   OS Ref 619 568
This is the first proper expanse of rock to be encountered when going up the hillside above the CC hut. Approach along a track from behind the CC hut until it passes round a ruined building and then becomes walled. At an old wire fence, bear up and left to reach a drystone wall below a broken area of

clifflets. Above is Clogwyn Llo, which is split in two by a grassy gully. High up on the right-hand buttress is a Y-shaped tree and the prominent pinnacle of *The Dolemen*.

North-west facing, the cliff can receive sunshine from late afternoon onwards. The cliff lies at 250 metres and is quite close to the road; an approach can be made in about 10 minutes. Descent from the longer routes reaching the very top of the cliff can be made down grassy slopes well back and away to the left, or by going up and then down to the right. Descent from the Left Buttress routes can be made down a hidden gully on the left.

Left Buttress

This is bounded on its left by a short gully slanting up leftwards from a damp and grassy bay. The gully is 12 metres to the right of three drystone walls perched on ledges on the left-hand side of the bay. Two heather ledges run across the buttress, the lower one being about 9 metres up, and below this lies a seeping red wall.

Aratnerphobia 42 metres E2   (1991)
Quite enjoyable but escapable climbing. Start in the gully on the left of the buttress, at a boulder about 3 metres below a grotty grotto.
1 30m. 5c. A difficult start to gain a flake leads to a slabby rib; follow this to the perched block. Step off the block, and climb the wall via thin cracks to reach a large ledge. Walk off, or:
2 12m. 4c. Ascend the flake and crack above the ledge to reach a heathery terrace.
Variation
Substance 30 metres E4 5c
A bold little extension, high in the grade. From the quartz band 18 metres up pitch 1, step left and climb the arête direct.

Catflea Massacre 24 metres E3 5c   (6.6.93)
A bit airy at the top. Start on a vegetated ledge below a slim groove, reached by climbing the first section of *Aratnerphobia*. Ascend the groove and an easy wall to a break, and move up again to an overlap. Climb the wall above to a sloping ledge, then swing up left to a further ledge and teeter up the final arête.

Foxglove 41 metres Severe   (10.7.49)
A poor, vegetated route, although the final corner gives it some reason for existence. Start down and to the right of the gully, where a heathery strip reaches the base of the cliff, a little to the left of the seeping wall.
1 21m. Scramble diagonally right up heather and up into a little hollow. Take the wall behind, starting up a flake. Continue for a short way to the foot of a heathery corner containing a holly.
2 8m. Climb the corner past the holly to gain a heather ledge with a gnarled yew tree.
3 12m. Ascend the short steep wall via the tree to another ledge. Finish up the clean steep corner-crack.

Of Mice and Men   54 metres   E3   (1991)
The route ascends good clean rock and the final pitch is quite tough. The
normal start is as for *Inoculation Wall*, although the wall just to the right of
the reddish wet streaks has been ascended at about 5a to give an
independent start.
1 15m. Move left as for *Inoculation Wall*, but continue leftwards to belay
behind a holly tree below two cracks, one straight, the other ragged and
heathery.
2 18m. 4a. Ignore the heathery crack and follow the left-hand crack to a
heathery stance below the upper wall.
3 21m. 5c. Ascend to a ledge, then gain the shallow groove in the centre
of the arête and climb this to its top. Step right and climb the wall just left
of the corner to easy ground. Belay in the corner above.

Tafod y Gors   49 metres   Very Severe   (28.5.89)
A good varied route in a fine position. Start on top of the rock steps to the
right of the wet streaks, below a leftward-slanting slab, the start of
Inoculation Wall.
1 34m. 4b. Climb up to the slab to reach cracks 5 metres to the right of
the holly, which lead up to a shallow left-facing corner. Go up cracks and
layback into the corner, then swing out right, and ascend the wall (crux) to
some jugs and a heathery ledge. Move left to belay as for *Of Mice and
Men*, at a crack.
2 15m. 4a. Gain the ledge above. Strenuous cracks then lead up and
right to the base of a leftward-facing corner with a spike at its base. Swing
up and right to finish at a ledge. Belay in the corner above.

Thema   45 metres   E1   (28.5.89)
Pleasant climbing leads to an excellent final pitch. Start just right of the
steep, seeping wall, directly below a small holly.
1 12m. 4b. Ascend the bulging wall to a slabby area just right of the holly.
2 12m. 5b. Attack the vertical crack about 2 metres right of the shallow
corner. The crack peters out but good holds through a bulge bring you to
a large ledge below some flakes and the final wall.
3 21m. 5b. Climb past the flakes to reach a thin crack, which leads up
with one entertaining move to a small ledge. Strenuous laybacking up the
continuation crack brings you thankfully to a jug and easier climbing above.

Inoculation Wall   90 metres   Hard Severe   (25.6.49)
A captivating route though not in the modern idiom. Start to the right of
the seeping wall, above a rock step.
1 27m. 3c. Climb the slabby wall trending slightly left, and then move up
right onto a heather ledge at 15 metres. Take the short steep corner
above, past perched blocks near the top, to reach a large ledge with a
holly. Belay behind this, at the foot of the obvious chimney.
2 18m. 4b. Ascend the chimney to belay on the short wall at the top.
3 30m. 4a. Climb the wall and then walk to the right across the grassy
terrace to reach the right-hand of two chimneys.
4 15m. 3c. Finish up the chimney.

Profound Lichen 52 metres E1   (19.7.94)
A bold initial pitch leads to a technical little crack. Start as for *Inoculation Wall*.
1 34m. 5b. Do not trend left as for *Inoculation Wall* but go straight up to
reach a slab and a vertical crack in a short wall, and take this direct. A
series of ribs and slabs then leads up right to the belay of *Inoculation Wall*
just below its crux chimney.
2 18m. 5b. Tackle the crack in the wall right of the chimney to reach a
ledge and follow the arête above.

Leurve Shack 46 metres Very Severe 4c   (19.5.94)
On good rock with generally steady climbing. Start just right of *Inoculation
Wall*. Climb up and onto some easy slabs. Follow these to a steepening,
gain the top of a spike, and then climb the wall and slabs above. Step
right through a bulge and follow the arête to the top.

The Wrath of Grapes II 30 metres Hard Very Severe 5b   (1991)
A steep start leads to easier climbing. Start to the right of *Inoculation Wall*
at the base of a slim groove in a steep arête. Ascend the groove until
forced out left onto a ledge at 8 metres. Continue up the slabby arête to
surmount a blocky overhang, and follow easy rock to a belay on a ledge
overlooking the gully that splits the crag.

Right Buttress
This section of the crag is to the right of the obvious gully slanting leftwards,
which can be used as a means of descent.

Lore and Hors d'œuvre 48 metres Very Severe   (6.92)
An entertainig trio of pitches. Start at the foot of the slanting gully, at a
small perched pillar leading up to the left end of the ledge system of *The
Band of Hope*.
1 18m. 4b. Gain the end of the ledge, and step back left past a block to
gain a steep juggy wall. This leads to slabs right of a holly-choked groove
and a grassy belay ledge left of a sharp arête at the left end of a
rectangular wall.
2 12m. 4c. Climb the flaky rib behind the stance to a small square roof,
just right of a prominent crack. Layback the crack and step left to gain the
broad terrace. Belay below the wide right-hand chimney of *Inoculation Wall*.
3 18m. 4c. From just below the chimney, step up and right onto a wide
ramp running up rightwards to the foot of a corner. Take the corner past a
hollow-sounding flake, and layback up to slabs. Belay well back.

The Band of Hope 75 metres Difficult   (10.11.51)
Unfortunately, a rather vegetated and rambling route that traverses from
left to right across the face to reach the pinnacle (taken by *The Dolemen*).
Start about 8 metres left of the prominent corner with a holly, just left of a
narrow slanting groove.
1 27m. Climb diagonally up the wall left of the groove, via a hard
mantelshelf at 3 metres, making for the left-hand end of a heather terrace.
Belay at its right end.

Clogwyn Llo

1	Aratnerphobia	E2	5	Thema	E1
2	Catflea Massacre	E3	6	Inoculation Wall	HS
3	Of Mice and Men	E3	7	The Wrath of Grapes II	HVS
4	Talfod y Gors	VS	8	Lore and Hors d'oeuvre	VS

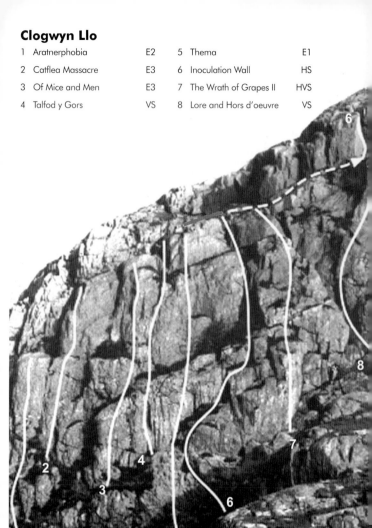

9	Beta	VS
10	Far from the Madding Throng	E2
11	The Triptych	E1
12	Whiplash Smile	E3
13	The Bed of Nails	E2
14	Melancholony	E7
15	Doleful	E4
16	The Dolemen	E3

2 27m. Mainly parkland walking towards the pinnacle, which is reached on the right by a mantelshelf half-way up a 3-metre wall. Climb the chimney behind the pinnacle.
3 21m. Cross into and climb the groove on the right of the grass shelf. Avoid the exit, and go right and climb the groove to finish.

★Beta   51 metres   Very Severe   (28.5.89)
Fine and varied climbing. Start to the right of the slanting gully, just below a vertical crack that curves over to the left and below an area of slabs.
1 18m. 4c. Pull up and layback the crack (large gear) until it disappears at a flake. The slab above is easier. Belay at the base of a steep crack slanting up to the left.
2 15m. 4c. Ascend the slanting crack to a large spike; further flakes and spikes lead up to a move right just below the broad heather terrace. Belay well back.
3 18m. 4c. *Lore and Hors d'œuvre* pitch 3.

Melons Rip My Flesh   12 metres   E5 6a   (23.8.95)
A bold offering, which takes the wall right of pitch 2 of *Beta* via the left-hand line. Climb the wall to a quartz ledge, rock up onto it, and continue directly up the wall above.

Kermit   12 metres   E6 6b   (23.8.95)
A technical pitch taking the wall right of pitch 2 of *Beta* via the right-hand line. Climb the wall, moving to the right, and make some hard moves to gain a flat hold. Go back left and finish up a small arête, passing a peg. A *Wallnut* 2 or 3 sideways in a pocket protects the crux – hard to place.

★★Far from the Madding Throng   57 metres   E2   (27.5.89)
A good clutch of pitches to give a fine route which deserves popularity. Start immediately right of *Beta*, under a vertical crack system on the left-hand side of a brownish rippled slab.
1 24m. 5a. Go up the crack, steep at first, (or take the faint rib on the right for 5 metres). The line leads to grassy ledges and a belay below the prominent left-facing corner.
2 18m. 5b. The steep corner is climbed with well-maintained interest to a wide ledge.
3 15m. 5c. To the right of the largest crack (*The Triptych* pitch 3) is an arête and then a steep wall with two shallow scoops at half height. Step off a block below the left-hand scoop and gain a small overhang. Traverse right until it is possible to layback into the right-hand scoop. Trend up left to a grassy stance. Scramble to finish.
Variation   E2
3a 15m. 5c. The left edge of the steep scooped wall.

The Triptych   42 metres   E1   (27.4.73)
An obvious line comprising three cracks. Sadly it is rather overgrown. Start 5 metres left of the corner with a holly tree 3 metres up, and 3 metres right of the previous route.

1 14m. 5a. Take the vegetated groove to a grassy stance.
2 14m. 5c. Continue up the difficult, overhanging and somewhat heathery crack to gain a broad ledge.
3 14m. 4b. Walk along the terrace and climb the slanting, continuation crackline, the crack now being wider and easier.

The only route that starts at the top tier, which can be used as an alternative finishing pitch for such routes as *The Triptych*, is:

The Bed of Nails   18 metres   E2 5c   (6.92)
A fine little pitch. Start at the foot of the arête to the right of the largest crack on the tier (*The Triptych* pitch 3). Climb the arête, using cracks on either side, for 5 metres. Swing round rightwards to reach a crack. The ledge above is gained by a hard move. The arête above becomes progressively slabbier and easier.

Whiplash Smile   21 metres   E3 6a   (24.6.88)
To the right of *The Triptych* is a corner with a holly tree 3 metres up. Start just left of the corner, beneath a damp crack. Climb moistly past a peg to reach a horizontal break, move left and continue up the upper crack to finish at the ledge of *The Band of Hope*.

The Fun before the Storm   12 metres   Hard Very Severe 5c   (1987)
Rather disjointed. Start right of *Whiplash Smile*, at the base of a small V-groove. A hard start leads to a holly tree, easier climbing and the safety of a heather ledge.

The only other route to start from the base of the cliff is to be found down and to the right of the pinnacle of *The Dolemen*. Near a damp area of rock, a clean white groove rises up just left of a swathe of moss. This is:

Llysiau'r Gwlith   79 metres   Hard Severe   (1991)
The difficulties are short and hard, and all in the first pitch, but the route is safe if somewhat escapable. The top two pitches can be done for their own sake at about Difficult. Start directly below the white groove, at some grassy ledges.
1 18m. 4b. Gain the base of the slabby groove. The climbing now becomes progressively harder until a monster jug above the right wall of the groove can be grasped.
2 15m. The obvious wide chimney above is easy – alternatively the jam crack on the right is a little harder.
3 46m. Climb up a little to the right of two large and hollow flakes, then go diagonally rightwards, and gain and finish via a delightful rib.

The following routes all start from the horizontal ledge that traverses into the right-hand side of the face at about half height to the pinnacle of *The Dolemen*. The easiest approach is to follow *The Band of Hope*, which traverses this ledge, to the base of the route required.

★Spanking for Beginners   15 metres   E5 6b   (11.9.86)
A good pitch, and quite high in its grade now that a protection peg used
on the first ascent has disappeared. It takes the square wall above the
point where *The Band of Hope* arrives on the heather terrace, just right of
the slanting grassy gully that splits the crag. Climb the thin crack in the
centre of the wall until it peters out at a sloping ledge. Move up and slightly
left to a shallow groove (crux) and finish up this via good holds on the left
at the top.

★Eager Submission   15 metres   E3 5c   (18.7.88)
A fine little pitch. Start on the wall round and to the right of *Spanking for
Beginners*, at a short corner. Climb the short corner to reach a thin crack,
move left to a ledge near the arête, and mantelshelf onto this to gain
better holds and then the top.

★★Melancholony   24 metres   E7 6b   (10.9.86)
A desperate test-piece taking the obvious rounded arête behind the rowan
trees, passing a flake to reach the hanging groove. Start below the arête,
about 25 metres along from the left end of the terrace. Move up and right
via a crack to reach a downward-pointing and hollow flake on the arête
proper. Climb straight up past the 'Cyclops Eye' to a hanging groove, and
continue past a gnarled and rusty *in-situ* wire to reach a ledge. Go up
leftwards to finish.

Doleful   23 metres   E4 6b   (18.7.88)
Decidedly tricky. Start at the base of the groove behind the tree to the right
of *Melancholony*. Ascend the groove and then the corner on the left with a
hard move at half height.

The Dolemen   12 metres   E3 6a   (11.9.86)
About 6 metres right of *Melancholony* is a prominent free-standing
pinnacle. The route climbs the left side of the pinnacle. Climb the left arête
for 5 metres and pass a peg to gain a spike. Move right to the centre of
the narrow face and 'span' this to the top; abseil off.

Grazer   15 metres   E6 6a   (11.7.97)
A fine climb ascending the arête to the right of *The Dolemen*.

Down and right of *The Dolemen* pinnacle is a large block above a prominent
yew tree, where you should find:

That's Life   12 metres   E4 6a   (7.97)
Takes the obvious front arête, starting at a short wall leading to a little
overhang.

Two Dogs   12 metres   E5 6a   (9.7.97)
The slab to the right has a difficult start.

Somewhere on the right-hand side of this buttress is:

Doldrums   85 metres   Very Difficult   (26.6.55)
A broken rambling climb with some interesting pitches which are difficult to
locate. The route lies above an area of broken ground on the right-hand
section of Clogwyn Llo, and close to where the crag disappears into the
hillside. Start by a boulder next to a rowan.
1 6m. Go up on the left corner. Traverse right behind the tree and finish
up a wide crack. Scramble for 6 metres to a belay.
2 12m. Go left from under the overhang, and then follow the ridge after
a step back right to a large thread belay.
3 9m. The left edge of the ridge – better than it looks.
4 15m. Go down to the left to find and climb a chimney (crux). Scramble
6 metres to large grassy ledges.
5 9m. The slabs just left of the heather groove lead to a ledge and belay
on the wall above.
6 34m. Climb straight up the slab, which soon eases to a scramble.

Above and left of the top of *Aratnerphobia* is a short cliff. On the left of this is
a rib with an obvious groove. A number of lines have been climbed and are
worth an ascent if you have done everything else.

Henri the Fiat   27 metres   Severe   (18.7.94)
Ascend the rib and the left-hand groove with one difficult move – not much
protection.

Hambon   27 metres   Very Difficult   (18.7.94)
Ascend the slabbier area of rock right of the rib.

Elmer   24 metres   E1 5b   (18.7.94)
The blunt arête is quite steep at one point and the crux requires a long
reach.

Huw Pobdim   21 metres   Hard Severe   (18.7.94)
Climb a groove to a ledge and then go past a flake to finish up a
delightful jamming crack.

Hell Hull   21 metres   Very Severe   (18.7.94)
Takes the steep slab to the right of the groove. After a ledge, go right past
a loose flake and trend diagonally up right.

The Gravestones   OS Ref 618 568
A good place on a hot day, particularly when you can watch the frazzled
hordes on Clogwyn y Grochan on the opposite side of the valley. To reach
this area, continue along the walled track above and behind the CC hut to
the second small ruin where the track peters out into open hillside. On the
left is a small rectangular crag with a drystone wall abutting its left-hand
side; it has an excellent landing-pad/picnic area. To its right, the drystone
wall continues, leading up to the base of the short Tapered Wall. Behind this
is the Headstone, a cracked tower with a slanting chimney to its right. *Pretty
Girls Make Graves* takes the obvious crack in this tower.

The Gravestones

7	Grave Diggers	E8	10	Ring My Bell	E6
8	Ugly Girls Make Slaves	HVS	11	Melondrama	E2
9	A Sweet Encounter	E8	12	Espasmos	VS

The area can be approached from the road in about 15 minutes. Generally north-facing, the cliffs only receive evening sunlight. There is a maze of grassy ramps and gullies, so unless mentioned the descents from the multitude of short cliffs and facets are left to the climber. The next crag, Hidden Wall, is approached via the broad and grassy scree fan to the right.

Tapered Wall
The first route is 5 metres left of the drystone wall below a damp scoop.

Prince of Deifio Muff   14 metres   E2 5c   (19.2.03)
Climb the pocketed scoop (past a double-clip thread) to reach some large pockets. Make some precarious moves to reach easier ground. Belay way back.

A rather unbalanced route would be possible up the cracks just to the right. The next route lies above the drystone wall.

King of Rumpy   11 metres   E6 6a   (5.9.88)
A short route, which is both delicate and very bold; landing on either the wall or the emasculating fin is not to be recommended. Start at the drystone wall. Step up to a short groove, follow this to a shallow scoop and make a series of precarious moves, which lead to the top.

The Moose's Toothpaste   8 metres   V5   (6.87)
A tough little number, reminiscent of gritstone. Start below a line of flakes to the right of the drystone wall. A hard start leads up past some layaways to an easing in the rock angle and the difficulty.

Nick's Sexual Problem   6 metres   V8   (8.87)
An even harder problem! Start 3 metres right of *The Moose's Toothpaste*. Move past a small pocket in the rounded rib to a slab – if you can.

The Headstone
This little crag has become a prime spot, where a number of technically fierce routes vie for attention.

Down on My Knee   14 metres   E7 6b   (16.6.97)
A technically precocious little pitch. Start left of *Pretty Girls Make Graves*, on the broad ramp. Climb the crack, and then head out leftwards on a diagonal line past a peg, making some 'groovy manoeuvres on undercut pockets'.

★★**Pretty Girls Make Graves**   18 metres   E6 6b   (5.6.86)
Powerful climbing up the innocuous-looking crack splitting the left-hand side of the buttress with a sloping top. A much sought-after route. Start on the broad ramp, below some overlaps, down and to the left of the obvious vertical crack. Span up the dank cracks to the overlap. Difficult moves might allow you to establish a position at the base of the vertical crack. A sustained sequence of finger-locks and jams now needs to be completed.

Grave Diggers 21 metres E8 6c   (15.6.97)
Another robust route, this tackles the crack and headwall to the right of
Pretty Girls Make Graves and left of the green groove. The crux is right at the
top, so it can give you some spectacular flight time. The wobbly spike was
not used as a runner, and the climbing is independent of the previous route.

To the right is a holly-choked chimney slanting to the right; this is where:

Ugly Girls Make Slaves 24 metres Hard Very Severe 5a (25.7.94)
Very well protected by a selection of big camming devices, the bigger the
better. Move up to a ledge, and then bridge up the groove, using the odd
hold on the right. Awkward moves up the mossy crack allow you to pull
into the upper chimney; squirm up this and flop out at the top.

To the right of the chimney-line of *Ugly Girls Make Slaves* is a painfully
obvious tower:

A Sweet Encounter 18 metres E8 6c   (22.6.98)
A powerful route that ascends the wall immediately right of the central
green groove via 'big moves on rounded holds' to reach a hands-off rest.
Traverse right; then go up to a break and attack the top arête in the front
face with difficulty. The use of a side-runner at the hands-off rest eases the
grade.

Down and right again is a steep little wall with a sloping ledge at half height.

Ring My Bell 15 metres E6 6b   (27.7.93)
A bold route, which starts down and to the right of the chimney. Ascend the
seam in the wall past a 'buried' peg to reach a pod (*Friend 2*). Pass this
with difficulty to gain the half-way ledge. Continue straight up, then slightly
right, to the top.

★Melondrama 15 metres E7 6c   (5.8.92)
Powerful and fingery. The tricky little wall past two pegs is *only* 6c every
move for the first 5 metres.

On a rib on the arête to the right you find:

Espasmos 24 metres Very Severe 4b   (4.87)
A slight but steep route, and good fun. Start on the right-hand side of the
rib. Climb up to a quartz-topped ledge, and move up the front face of the
rib to a heather break. Easier ground above leads to slabs and a belay.
Variation
Crook's Direct 6a. Boulder out the left side of the rib to finish up (or
even down) the original.

Directly above *Pretty Girls Make Graves* is a small grassy hollow with a pile
of boulders at its base. Above is a small rib leading up to a rowan tree.

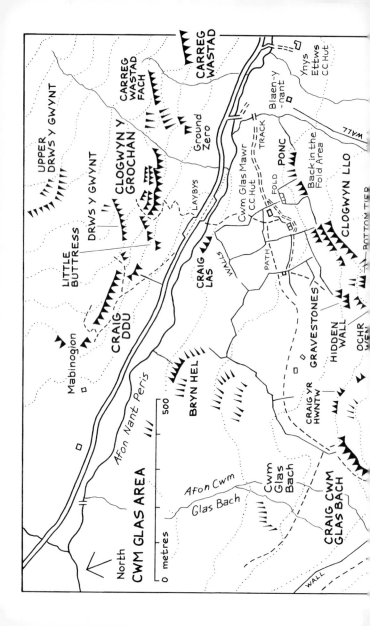

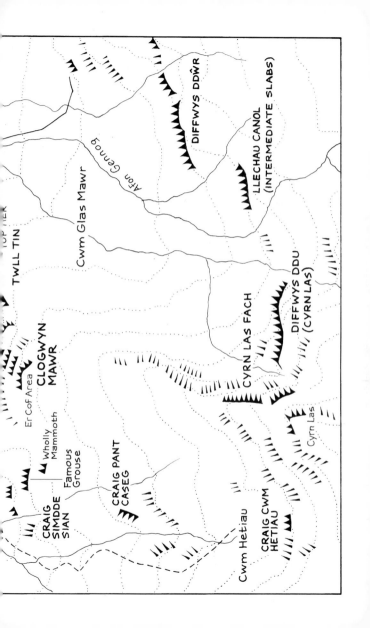

Buhlermaniac   24 metres   Very Difficult   (7.91)
The short jamming crack proves to be the crux, but is well protected. Start
at the base of the rib leading to the tree. Follow the rib to the rowan, jam
up the crack behind the tree, and step right to a further rib, which leads to
a large grassy ledge and spike belay.

Peter Panic   37 metres   Hard Severe   (7.91)
There are some bold and intricate moves, particularly above the scoop,
but the climb only just merits the grade. Start about 9 metres to the right of
Buhlermaniac, at the base of a slabby area of rock with a prominent scoop
up and to the left. Ascend the lower slab, step left into the scooped area,
and climb this directly via some bold moves to gain cracks. A series of
mantels up ledges leads to the belay blocks.

Round and up to the right of *Pretty Girls Make Graves* and roughly half-way
up to Hidden Wall is a slender rib with a holly tree near its base.

Xmas Dinner   55 metres   Very Difficult   (5.1.78)
A pleasant route requiring a blinkered approach, as it is easy to escape at
many points along the way. The original third pitch was quite a long way
off and on a different cliff! This is now described as a separate route, *Xmas
Dinner II*, on Twll Tin. Start at the base of the rib, below the holly.
1 37m. Climb up past the holly, step right and ascend the slabby rib,
keeping to the left, to reach ledges.
2 18m. A steep cracked wall is at first rough and juggy. An easy-angled
slab then leads to a broad grassy crest.

Level with the Gravestones but a little over 150 metres to the right, in the
middle of the bouldery scree bay is a tiny little crag, which gives:

The Cushion   6 metres   E6 6a   (16.6.97)
The small scooped and rounded buttress is climbed by its central line.
Watch out for the bad landing.

Hidden Wall   OS Ref 617 567

A gem of a crag, which should become popular with those of a technical bent.
Although this area of rock is directly above the Gravestones, it is very difficult to
pinpoint the crag until you are almost upon it. From the Gravestones, simply
ascend the open and fairly grassy scree cone to the right and up the left side of
a large bay of boulders. After about 100 metres you reach flatter ground with
a steep lozenge-shaped Hidden Wall to the left and the white slabs of Yr Ochr
Wen to the right. Descent is via the gully to the left of the wall, which has a
huge chockstone at its top.

★What a Difference a Day Makes   21 metres   E4 6a   (6.7.87)
A cracking route, much steeper than it looks and with a bit of a sting in its
tail. Start up the left-hand side of the crag, below a dark groove. A crack
leads up to a narrow, sloping ramp. Climb the crack to the ramp, move up
leftwards to a short wall, and surmount the wall to reach a small slab

Hidden Wall

below the groove. The groove is followed on surprising holds to a wide crack (large cam). Layback up leftwards to the top.

Lasagne Verdi   26 metres   E5 6b   (16.7.87)
An obvious rising line going from left to right, with some very technical climbing. Climb *What a Difference a Day Makes* for 5 metres, and move rightwards to reach the flake on *Melon Transplant* (crux). Step down and right to reach a crack slanting up diagonally right. Follow this to a slab and so the top.

★Melon Transplant   27 metres   E5 6b   (16.7.87)
A desperate, but well-protected, start leads to slightly easier but bolder climbing. Start 5 metres down and right of *What a Difference a Day Makes*, at a white scoop. Climb the scoop past two pegs to reach the obvious traverse-line. Move left to arrange protection; then climb the wall to reach a crack, and follow this to the top.

★★Rimsky-Korsakov   24 metres   E4 6a   (5.87)
A fine sustained climb, with only just adequate protection. Start in the centre of the wall, 5 metres right of *Melon Transplant* and below a slanting crackline. Move up to the crack and follow this leftwards to a shallow open groove and leaning flake/cracklines. Continue up the flakes and then go boldly up the wall above to a wide crack (large cam useful). Follow the crack into the large groove and finish easily.

★El Guide Direct   30 metres   E3 5c   (1989)
A good pitch that starts just right of *Rimsky-Korsakov*, by a rock step at the base of the cliff. Climb up to the diagonal crack, go up to a small spike, and move left and then up to the undulating weakness of the girdle. Shimmy rightwards to the arête (good *Friend* 1½ slot) and then climb the wall above boldly to a difficult step up onto a wide white slab. Climb directly up the cracked tower above. Scramble up easily to the descent gully.

El Guide   37 metres   E3 5c   (26.5.87)
This has the benefit of following the line of the arête throughout. Follow *Rambo* up to the flakes, swing out onto the wall, to the *Friend* 1½ slot. Continue as for *El Guide Direct* to the wide slab and cracked tower.

Rambo   74 metres   Hard Very Severe   (26.4.73)
A good route with just one hard move. Start at the lower right-hand end of the wall, where a flake crack leads up to a ledge at the base of a recessed rectangular slab. It is usually damp underfoot, so hop along stones to the base of the crack.
1 37m. 5b. Ascend the crack to the slab and then keep to its left edge. The step left round the rib to reach some good holds proves to be the crux. Gain the obvious line of flakes leading back right to a short corner. Move up the corner past a hollow flake to the slab above, and belay beneath a wide vertical crack.
2 37m. 4a. Follow the crack to reach easy vegetated slabs. Belay well back, almost in the descent gully.

Variation
Buck Warren Meets the Headmonsters   37 metres   E2 5c
Bolder and more sustained. Instead of going left round the rib to reach the
flake traverse, continue directly up the white slab to the right of the rib to
gain the flakes.

Wagner's Ring   55 metres   E3   (5.87)
A delightful girdle, that 'scamanders' its way along the undulating
weakness from right to left. Start as for *Rambo*.
1 18m. 5b. Climb *Rambo* to where it begins its flake traverse right.
2 37m. 6a. Swing left onto the wall and follow the snaking ripple or
weakness across the wall to quartz seams and the end.

Also, **Hidden Treasure** (55 metres E4 6a 15.7.02), an eliminate line which
offers little independent climbing, takes the rising crack left of *Rambo* to join
El Guide Direct and then *Wagner's Ring*. It then goes left to finish up *What a
Difference a Day Makes*.

Yr Ochr Wen   The White Side   OS Ref 617 567
This is is the slabby continuation of Hidden Wall to its right. The right-hand
side of the crag is white.

Y Lon Wen   74 metres   E2   (7.89)
Reasonable climbing on clean rock. However, the crux is difficult to protect.
Start at the lowest point of the buttress, beneath a flake crack, 6 metres
right of *Rambo*.
1 37m. 5b. Climb the crack and flakes to reach the base of a slender
rectangular slab. At the top left-hand end of the slab, at a short wall, make
a bold swing out to gain a flake crack and pull up to a larger slab. Belay
at its top (junction with *Rambo*).
2 37m. 4b. Move up diagonally rightwards through a bulge and finish
easily up slabs.

Pererindod   74 metres   Very Severe   (4.88)
The route weaves a clean path through some heathery slabs. Start at the
base of a stepped rib to the right of *Y Lon Wen*.
1 37m. 4b. Ascend the rib to a heathery ledge and follow a series of
small slabs, aiming for a vertical crack below a large ledge with a small
dead sapling directly above.
2 37m. Follow a groove direct, and then move up leftwards over slabs to
reach belays.

'Sgwd'   77 metres   Hard Very Severe   (1988)
A rather wandering route. Start 3 metres right of *Pererindod*, at some cracks.
1 37m. 5a. Climb the cracks to the rightward-leaning groove just to the
left of the wall taken by *Rembrandt Pussy Horse*. Follow the groove to a
vertical crack, climb the crack and then a rib to its top.
2 40m. Easier climbing leads diagonally leftwards to belays.

★Rembrandt Pussy Horse   21 metres   E2 5c   (16.5.88)
A sparkling pitch. Start to the right of *'Sgwd'*, at some cracks just down
and left of a clean tower split by a prominent leaning crack. Climb the
cracks to a ledge, foot-traverse right to a peg and step up delicately to a
downward-pointing flake. A further move gains the base of the crack.
Romp up the crack to where the last sequence of moves awaits. Spike
belay backed up by poor gear in a crack high up to the right.
Variation
The Pinocchio Start
The direct start is 6c, even for the tall. A damp landing-pad awaits all.

Twll Tin   OS Ref 617 566
To the left of Hidden Wall is a gully with a huge chockstone near its top. The
following routes are to the left of this gully on a series of short walls. The
Bottom Tier is best reached by descending a little way down the gully, going
through a sheep hole in a small wall and turning right (facing out). The
Middle Tier is roughly level with the top left-hand end of Hidden Wall. The
routes are described as they are approached. That is to say that on the
Bottom Tier they are described from **right to left**.

Bottom Tier
A grassy rake slants up leftwards. The routes on the first wall are described
from right to left.

Return to Melancholony   15 metres   E6 6b   (4.87)
Only feasible for those with very strong fingers. Start down and left of a
peg, at a very thin seam. Move up and then right to the peg with difficulty.
Continue boldly past the peg to finish more easily up a groove slightly on
the right.

★6B Melonoma   9 metres   E5 6b   (28.7.93)
Good sustained climbing, which starts as for *Return to Melancholony* but
goes straight up. Climb a thin seam past two pegs, the first being very
poor. From a good break near the top, go right and up to finish at a
notch. (The peg on *Return to Melancholony* is not clipped).

The Damp Squib   12 metres   E1 5a   (24.6.88)
A poor, wet and vegetated pitch higher up the grassy rake. Start up to the
left of *Return to Melancholony*. Squirm up the odious drainage line/crack.

To the left of the base of the grass rake, and level with *Return to Melancholony*
is a large easy-angled slab of perfect rock, easily seen on the descent from
the top of Hidden Wall. The slab is seamed with horizontal veins of quartz. A
small rock step lies below the left edge of the slab. The slab can be climbed
anywhere; however, the following routes are available:

Twll Tin: Middle Tier

1 Ribble Wobble	HVS	4 Celynen	VD
2 Rim with a View	E3	5 Vampire Butterfly	HS
3 Crack and Slab	HVS	6 Xmas Dinner II	VD

Strap Me to a Nubile   30 metres   Difficult   (7.91)
Only just merits the grade if the easier alternatives are not taken. Start 3
metres left of the rock step. Climb directly to some shallow scoops, move
left to some quartz veins, and follow the left edge of the slab. Belay to
blocks well back on the rounded top above.

The Gas Man Cometh   30 metres   Difficult   (7.91)
Quite pleasant. Start at the rock step. Go straight up to a crack, and then
gain a small gangway leading rightwards to a vertical crack. Follow the
crack to belay as for *Strap Me to a Nubile*.

Zirhalee   30 metres   Very Difficult   (7.91)
Probably the best of this quartet. Start at the lowest point of the slab.
Ascend the slab past grassy ledges to a short crack, where a hard move
gains a ledge at the top of the slab. The angle now eases, as does the
climbing. Belay on the blocks.

New Model Arm   30 metres   Difficult   (7.91)
Little protection but on sound rock. Start a little up and to the right of
Zirhalee. Climb the slab to a tiny overlap and then a grassy ledge. An
easier slab gains the blocks.

The top of the grassy rake reaches an area of rock with numerous quartz
ledges; this is the location of the following routes:

Rim with a View   12 metres   E3   5c   (4.87)
An interesting pitch, best gained from the bottom tier. Start 40 metres up
and left of *The Damp Squib*, at some quartz ledges. Ascend a crack to an
obvious flake and a tiny groove. Step left round the flake and finish
directly.

Ribble Wobble   11 metres   Hard Very Severe   5a   (4.87)
Short but succulent. Start below a crack to the left of *Rim with a View*.
Climb the airy crack in the rib on the left edge of the wall.

Middle Tier

Crack and Slab   14 metres   Hard Very Severe   5b   (24.6.88)
A rather unimaginative and incorrect name for a good little route. Start at
the left end of a heathery ledge, gained from the gully capped by the
chockstone left of Hidden Wall, below an overhang split by an obvious
wide crack. Move up to the overhang, pull through this, and climb the
crack above on jugs. Good protection.

Celynen   24 metres   Very Difficult   (5.9.91)
A rather unusual little route. Start on the right-hand end of the Middle Tier,
where a ragged crack leads up to reach an obvious traverse-line leading
off leftwards to a corner. Ascend the quartzy cracks and reach the
right-hand end of the undulating traverse. Follow this to the holly tree. A
fairly interesting little corner leads to a flake belay above.

Vampire Butterfly   18 metres   Hard Severe   (12.9.91)
A nice pitch on good rock but with sparse protection. Start as for the
previous route. From the quartz cracks, move boldly up and rightwards to
gain a small scoop in the arête. Continue up the arête to ledges and a
flake belay. Walk up the easy slab above.

Allegrophobia   18 metres   Severe   (12.9.91)
The route only just merits this grade due to a hard starting move and the
paucity of good protection above. Start just right of a short corner below
the arête of *Vampire Butterfly*. Difficult starting moves lead to a delightful
slab. Climb this direct to gain the easy-angled slab. A flake belay is found
down and to the left, or walk a long way up the slab to the ledge above.

Xmas Dinner II   37 metres   Very Difficult   (28.4.78)
The upper section or the sequel of the original route on the Gravestones
(perhaps it should be called Cold Turkey). Start in the gully directly below
the small rowan, at a wide crack under the chockstone. Follow the wide
crack to a vegetated ledge and the rowan sapling. Continue up the crack
and move right on ledges. Follow a second crack to the easy-angled slab.
Belay at the grassy ledge up and to the right.

Bjorn Again   27 metres   Very Difficult   (13.9.91)
A little filler-in. Start to the right of the wide crack. Move up and then right to
a horizontal break and continue up the slab just left of the massive
chockstone, or bridge up the groove formed by the slab and the chockstone.

Top Tier
Above the chockstone is a broad flat terrace with another short tier above.
On the far left is a small bottom-shaped craglet. The left cheek is taken by:

Mini Ha Ha   8 metres   E5 6c   (5.87)
A micro-route packing a macro-punch. The smooth buttock is ascended by
means of a thin seam.
The right cheek contains a thin crack; further to the right is a scooped area
of rock below a slab.

The Real Scoop   12 metres   Severe   (1987)
Gain the scoops easily and follow these with a high step to reach slabs
(unprotected).

To the right is a distinct right-angled corner with a flat grassy platform
beneath. On the left edge of the platform is:

Cyfrifiadurwyr   20 metres   E1 5b   (21.5.89)
After a hard start it soon eases. Start at a quartz ledge at the left-hand end
of the corner's left wall. Follow the vertical crack to where it curves over
leftwards, move up to slabs, and follow these to the top.

★Rim at the Top   18 metres   E2 6a   (5.87)
A cracking little pitch. Start beneath a vertical crack leading up to a quartz
seam in the wall just left of the corner. Boulder out the first crack to reach
the horizontal quartz seam. Now step left and continue up the second
vertical crack, which soon eases to slabs. Follow the slabs to the top.

Y Gornel   15 metres   Hard Very Severe 5b   (1988)
A pleasant route, which is occasionally damp. Start at the foot of the
obvious corner. Climb the corner by a series of jams, layaways and
bridging moves.

Ring Ouzel 2   15 metres   E5 6c   (7.92)
A complex and strenuous little number. Start at the obvious crack right of
the corner of *Y Gornel*. A series of difficult contortions up the initial crack
may sometimes lead to an apparently juggy ledge. Move right to the arête
for a rest. Move back left to finish direct.

Craig yr Hwntw   Southerner Crag   OS Ref 615 567
To the right of Hidden Wall is the large bay of scree and boulders, above
which is a huge area of broken slabs, ledges and walls; this is Clogwyn
Mawr. However, on the far side of the screes, to the right of Clogwyn Mawr, is
a broken escarpment of shorter crags. This is Craig yr Hwntw, and is best
approached by contouring round from Hidden Wall.

On the left is a short, steep, and undercut craglet cleft by two cracks.

The Mild Very Hard Hand Jam Crack   11 metres   E2 6a (25.4.87)
A well-protected route that feels much bigger than it looks. Start beneath
the left-hand crack. An awkward start leads to a difficult crack and a
desperate finish.

Yr Hwntw Bach   12 metres   E2 5c   (25.4.87)
Low in the grade, but with some good climbing. Start beneath the
right-hand crack. A hard start leads to a rest at the point where the crack
becomes horizontal. Finish up the wider section above.

The Stain   14 metres   E3 5c   (6.87)
A low crux with crumbly rock. Start beneath the right arête of the block.
Climb up to the arête and follow it until a swing rightwards can be made
to gain an easy slab.

Rumblecock   15 metres   E3 6a   (5.87)
Rather friable. Start 30 metres right of *The Stain*, at an arête. Ascend the
left side of the arête until it is possible to make a difficult move round onto
the right-hand face by a flake. Follow the wall above to easy ground.

A route has been climbed up the broken and rounded arête down to the
right, at about Hard Severe.

Clogwyn Mawr   Big Cliff   OS Ref 616 566

Apart from its most obvious feature, the straight wide crack high up on the right-hand side of the crag, the main cliff is the most disappointing cliff in the whole area. The wide crack is the line of a unique route for the Pass, *The Fear of Infection*. To approach this area of rock, scramble up the central slanting gully or climb *Hogia Tyn'Llan* to a traverse-line back left.

The first route lies at the very base of this large mass of crag and vegetation.

Wind in the Hollows   12 metres   E2 5b   (3.2.97)
An amusing if short arête.

The following route is gained by following a broad gully to the left of Craig yr Hwntw. This leads to a rounded slab with a dog-leg crack on its top right-hand side and a rib above.

Hogia Tyn'Llan   74 metres   Hard Very Severe   (5.87)
Two contrasting but interesting pitches. Start at the very toe of the slab.
1 37m. 5a. Climb directly up the centre of the slab, past a loose flake, to reach belays at the base of the rib.
2 37m. The rib above is fairly straightforward.

School's Out   30 metres   Hard Very Severe 5a   (27.4.94)
A neat little filler in. Start at the base of a crack just to the right of *Hogia Tyn'Llan*. Follow the crack to a groove and a further crack above to gain the obvious wide crack. Finish up the rib as for *Hogia Tyn'Llan*.

A Pointy Reckoning   8 metres   E5 6c   (1998)
The tiny flying arête down and right of *Fear of Infection* is climbed direct by a series of à *cheval* moves.

★★Fear of Infection   15 metres   E4 6a   (22.5.87)
A fierce and painful feature, this route has defeated a number of strong teams. *Friend 4s* and 5 or 6 are required for protection. Start at the base of the obvious off-width, about half-way up the face. Starting the crack is torturous, and difficulty then increases in proportion to height gained, until at half height the climbing becomes slightly easier.

Jargon Speaker Creature   14 metres   E5 6a   (26.4.87)
Another fine little route. Start 12 metres up and right of *Fear of Infection*, at a groove with an undercut flake. Follow the groove to a jug and move right to a rest. Go back into the groove and then climb up on undercuts to the top.

In the area above *Fear of Infection*, ending up at the very top of Clogwyn Mawr, are the following:

Er Cof   37 metres   Very Severe 5a   (5.87)
Only the initial moves are difficult. Start at a steep crack in a rib, which itself forms the left-hand edge of an area of easy-angled slabs. Go up to

gain the easy-angled but bold rib above (a crack to the right is easier).
Delectable climbing leads to the top.

Iachad   37 metres   E3 5c   (5.87)
A bold route. Start 30 metres left of *Er Cof*, at the foot of a steep, smooth
slab. Climb the slab to reach a wide flake crack beneath a short wall. Step
up to the next slab and trend up rightwards to gain a crack leading up to
the top of the crag.

Craig Cwm Glas Bach

Lesser Grey Cwm Crag   OS Ref 613 568

A really good crag, worth several visits. The rock, in general, is very good,
being very rough and in some places peppered with pockets. Heavy winter
drainage is conducive to moss growth, but this detraction is steadily
disappearing. Much of the cliff dries out faster than was initially thought,
and some of the best routes are also the first to dry out after rainfall. The
best approach is as for the Gravestones, and then to contour round to the
right into Cwm Glas Bach. On reaching a col just before a large drystone
wall, the crag comes into view.

The cliff is split into two sections by a grassy rake coming down to the top of a
triangular rock rib forming a step. The left part of the cliff has a fine blunt
arête, the location of *Weasels Rip My Flesh*; then to the right, starting at half
height, is the prominent bow-shaped chimney of *Skid Alley*. The crack
splitting the fine tower to the right again is *Spitting Image*. After the grassy
rake, the first feature of the right-hand section is a recessed and reddish wall,
which contains some of the hardest routes. Further right is a large wall of
rough rock and then a series of gradually descending overhangs.

North-west facing, the crag receives sunlight from the late afternoon onwards.
At about 300 metres and fairly close to the road, an approach can be made
in about 20 minutes. Descent from the main cliff is down a curious cleft
'tin-can alley' to the left of the cliff, reached by a grassy walk down and
along, but well back from, the cliff-top.

The first routes are on a short wall about 100 metres left of and slightly
above the *Weasels Rip My Flesh* area. The wall is easily seen on the descent
route from the main cliff.

Someone's Pinched My Winkles 18 metres Hard Very Severe 5a (5.94)
Good sustained climbing up the groove and overhang above a holly tree
and a sapling on the left-hand side of the crag. Start at two spikes to the
right of the sapling. Stand on the spikes and pull up and left into the
groove. Follow the groove to the overhang and pull through on hollow
blocks to finish up a slab. Belay well back.

Mr Kipling's Groove   18 metres   E4 5c   (1994)
A tad easier for the tall. Start below a groove on the left-hand side of the
facet. A serious start up the groove leads to a niche and a thin crack
through a slight bulge.

Rupert's Rib   15 metres   E5 6b   (10.7.97)
A typically trying, modern addition. Start at the rib in the centre of the crag,
pull over the overlap as for *Stanage Comes to Llanberis*, and climb
leftwards to blade peg (good if tied off). Some hard moves lead up slightly
right and then back left to the top.

Stanage Comes to Llanberis   15 metres   E2 5c   (23.8.95)
Start at a vague groove just right of centre. Climb the groove on rounded
holds to a break and finish up the crack above.

On the far left of the main crag is an obvious cleaned corner with a holly at
its base; down and to the right is a slab cleft by a wide crack. The first route
takes the wall above and left of the holly.

Microtrauma   18 metres   E6 6c   (20.8.95)
The searingly technical wall left of the obvious corner. Climb straight up to
a slot and good protection, and then continue up the wall past a peg via a
series of pockets and pinches.

Cornel Celyn   39 metres   Hard Very Severe   (c.1987)
A scrappy start leads to a good finish. Start as for *Stuff the Stoat*, below the
wide crack in the slab.
1 21m. 4a. Follow the crack until it is possible to belay directly below the
corner (rather prickly).
2 18m. 5b. Climb up the corner past an ancient nut. The difficulties soon
relent once the angle eases.

Stuff the Stoat   37 metres   E1 5c   (26.4.88)
Reasonable climbing in general, but the crux is problematic. Start at the
foot of a slab with a wide broken crack leading up to flakes below a
steeper wall. Gain and follow the crack to where it kinks left, and go left
and then back a little rightwards. To the left is a corner with a spike just to
its right. Move up to gain some thin cracks above the spike. Bolder but
easier climbing leads to the top.

Sheik Yerbooties   37 metres   Very Severe 4c   (14.5.88)
Pleasant enough. Large protection is required at some points. Follow *Stuff
the Stoat* to where the crack steepens, move right to a large flake at the
bottom of a corner/groove, and layback the corner to gain slabs and
easier rock.

★★**Weasels Rip My Flesh**   35 metres   E3 5c   (6.87)
A very entertaining pitch and quite popular. It is now done with a slightly
different start from the original. Start at some cracks below an obvious jug,
in a shallow groove. Gain the jug and a peg, and then climb up and

Craig Cwm Glas Bach: Left-Hand Section

1	Cornel Celyn	HVS	4a	Original Start	E
2	Stuff the Stoat	E1	5	Skid Pan	E
3	Sheik Yerbooties	VS	6	Skid Alley	HV
4	Weasels Rip My Flesh	E3	7	Spitting Image	HV

leftwards to reach a thread. Sustained and bold climbing leads up to easier ground and a crack. Swing right into a slim groove and follow this to the top.

Original Start   E3 6a
Start a metre or two down to the left, at the base of the arête. Go straight up to a peg, from where difficult moves up and to the right gain the obvious jug.

Skid Pan   34 metres   E1 5b   (1990)
A good route, though often damp. Start down and left of the obvious *Skid Alley* chimney. Steep starting moves and a step right enable one to reach the base of a zigzag crack. This is followed as directly as possible to the top of the crag.

Skid Alley   34 metres   Hard Very Severe 5b   (27.4.73)
A route for the connoisseur (or the perverted); it is always wet. Start at the left-hand side of the crag, below the clearly defined chimney, the bottom of which is half-way up the crag. Climb the steep wall, trending leftwards onto the damp section. Traverse right to gain the base of the chimney. Continue directly up the strenuous and greasy chimney to finish (a mammoth thrutch, the difficulties escalating as the height increases).

Ethel the Aardvark Goes Quantity Surveying
                                        24 metres   E4 5c (20.8.95)
A bold route. Start just left of *Spitting Image* and climb up to join the prominent upper crack of that route. From the base of the crack, climb out left and ascend the wall and groove to the top.

Where Angels Play   27 metres   E6 6b
A bold route taking the arête left of *Spitting Image* in its entirety.

★**Spitting Image**   27 metres   Hard Very Severe 5b   (17.6.84)
A fine pitch. Start just right of the *Skid Alley* chimney, below the prominent crack. Climb straight up to the foot of the crack (usually wet), or take a diagonal line up from the right. The crack above gives a razzling finish.

Vital Balance   24 metres   E3 6a   (5.8.96)
Ascend *Spitting Image* to the upper crack, and then follow a thin crack into the middle of the clean wall on the right. Move up and right to reach good protection at a flake on the arête, and then step back into the centre of wall. Make a move up to a line of holds leading diagonally up to a ledge. A short wall now leads to the top.

★**Beasts of the Field**   27 metres   E3 6a   (10.4.88)
On curious rock, this route is low in the grade and perhaps easier for the tall. Start to the right of the grassy rake and the rock step just down and left of the recessed wall, beneath a sapling. Climb up to the sapling (thread runner above), and then move right and up to another thread runner. Continue directly to a slab and then climb the overhang to reach easier climbing above.

Rimsky-Korsakov
(E4, page 244)
Hidden Wall
Climber: Chris Calow
Photo: Bill McKee

LLECHOG

NORTHERN SLABS

Bad Altitude

SOUTH EAST
FACE

NORTH EAST
SPUR

CRAIG UCHEL

Gully Slab

CRAIG Y
CRIBFLAEN

DISGYNFA

CAM CYNTAF

WALIAU ISAF

Access from
Cwm Glas Mawr and
the Grochan lay-bys

Poket-Lips Now   15 metres   E3 5c   (22.5.98)
Cunning is needed with some gear placements. Start 3 metres right of
Beasts of the Field, at a groove formed by a hanging flake. Climb the
groove (large cam needed) and then the pocketed wall above, heading for
a horizontal break. Continue straight up on better holds to the top.

Runner Up   36 metres   Very Severe   (18.6.89)
Takes the left-hand corner of the recessed wall above the ledge at
one-third height. Start under the wall, a little to the right of centre.
1 12m. Climb clean rock, and move left on the ledge to belay at the foot
of the corner.
2 24m. 4c. Ascend the corner-crack, wide at first, and continue up the
groove above.

The next two routes start from the ledge at one-third height below the
recessed wall, which is gained by climbing the first pitch of either *Runner Up*
or *Rufus*.

★★**Noah's Ark**   21 metres   E6 6b   (14.4.88)
A bold but excellent route tackling the reddish wall. Start at the left-hand
side of the ledge, below a crack in the recessed wall. Climb the crack past
two threads to reach a good hold. Difficult moves then lead up to and past
a peg to a further good hold; stand on this and move up leftwards to finish
(good nut out to the right near the top).

★★**Over the Beach**   23 metres   E6 6b   (18.4.88)
The harder of these two routes, and bolder now that the pegs are quite
poor. Start in the corner to the right of *Noah's Ark*, as for pitch 2 of *Pan
Alley*. Climb up, swing left, and then move up past two pegs to reach a
good hold and a tape runner. Move up to a flake and then a good pocket,
and layaway up a groove to reach another flake. Easier ground and
scrambling remains.

Pan Alley   36 metres   Hard Very Severe   (18.6.89)
A very good top pitch. This is the right-hand corner of the recessed wall.
1 12m. As for *Runner Up*, but then walk right along the ledge to the foot
of the corner.
2 24m. 5b. The steep corner is varied and interesting.

Rufus   46 metres   Very Severe   (26.4.73)
A good route. Start slightly down and right of the large heather ledge at
one-third height.
1 14m. Take the steep wall, trending left to a good stance at the
right-hand end of the ledge, below the corner of *Pan Alley*.
2 32m. Move out right onto the steep wall. Climb this delicately via a
faint, rightward-slanting weakness to the top.

★★**The Stebbing**   40 metres   E2 5b   (6.89)
A very good route on clean rock, which is one of the first to dry in this
area. Start a little to the right of *Rufus*, at the base of a slim groove with a

Craig Cwm Glas Bach: Right-Hand Section

1	Runner Up	VS	5	Rufus	VS
2	Noah's Ark	E6	6	The Stebbing	E2
3	Over the Beach	E6	7	Ecover	E1
4	Pan Alley	HVS	8	Rocky	VS

9	Belv-Eddie-Ere?	HVS	13 Outside Right	HVS
10	Slab and Groove	HVS		
11	The Booze Brothers	E2		
12	Outside Left	HVS		

small overlap at 12 metres. Climb the groove to the overlap; surmount this to reach a series of ledges leading up to a line of weakness trending diagonally up rightwards (the line of *Rufus*). Gain a steep crackline below a small tower. Step left and climb the crack, moving left, and then the tower to easier slabs. Going direct, all the way up the crack, is harder.

Mr Stiff   40 metres   E4 5c   (6.89)
A harder though slightly indirect version of *The Stebbing*. Start at the narrow groove to the right. Follow the slim groove to reach the line of *Rufus* and follow *The Stebbing* to finish.

★Ecover   40 metres   E1 5b   (6.89)
A pleasant pitch that wends its way up the wall. Quite low in the grade. Start 6 metres to the right of *The Stebbing*, at yet another groove (wider this time), just to the left of *Rocky*. Ascend the groove, difficult at its top, to trend leftwards up the slabby wall and then back right up a faint groove. Once at the slabs near the top, trend back left once again to finish near *The Stebbing*.

Rocky   37 metres   Very Severe   (26.4.73)
This follows a series of insidious cracks up the rough, pocketed wall to finish as for *Rufus*. Start 9 metres right of *Rufus*. Climb a steep rib, and then follow a line of thin cracks leading up to an open corner left of a large brown recess – delicate. Finish as for *Rufus*.

Belv-Eddie-Ere?   37 metres   Hard Very Severe   5b   (5.88)
A good route on fine rough rock with its crux at the top. Start to the right of *Rocky*, directly below the large V-shaped recess. Climb the wall boldly, but on good holds, to reach the base of the V-shaped recess. Climb the recess, moving out left at the top.

Rogue Trooper   37 metres   E2 5b   (7.02)
The main feature of this route is a slim groove in the arête right of *Belv-Eddie-Ere*. Start as for *Belv-Eddie-Ere*. Climb up and then right, up a crack and over a small overlap, to gain and climb the slim groove.

Slab and Groove   30 metres   Hard Very Severe   (18.6.89)
Not the most original of names, but a good first pitch. Start to the left of a large flake directly beneath a holly-choked groove.
1 18m. 5a. Go up the left-hand side of the flake. Traverse right to reach the base of a slim groove. Ascend this for a short way to a steepening. Trend diagonally leftward to gain slabs and a ledge sporting some hollies.
2 12m. Continue up the groove behind the hollies, moving left to finish.

The Booze Brothers   37 metres   E2 5c   (6.89)
A fine pitch with a surprising roof section. Start at a large flake directly under the holly-choked groove with a large triangular overhang to its right (taken by pitch 2 of *Slab and Groove*). Climb up to gain a clean groove and then up slabs above to reach the roof. Pull through this from left to right – much easier than it looks. Go directly up the slabby arête, ignoring the easier but dirty crackline on the right.

Outside Left   30 metres   Hard Very Severe   5b   (5.5.92)
Takes one of the few weaknesses in this part of the cliff. Start at a clean corner directly below a downward-pointing flake at a breach in the overhangs. Climb the corner to a ledge and step left to the Damoclean flake at the base of the groove (it is allegedly quite sound) left of the large triangular overhang. Climb the flake and continue steeply up, exiting right at the top of the groove.

Outside Right   30 metres   Hard Very Severe   5b   (26.6.92)
This route should improve with traffic. Start directly beneath the large triangular overhang. Climb the obvious flake crack and continue up the slab above to a possible stance left of a group of hollies. Traverse right into a short corner, which leads up to the short triangular roof. Pull out right to a good rest. Traverse awkwardly right to a thin crack, which proves stubborn. Continue to a stance and greasy slabs above.

Hairway to Steven   48 metres   E1   (13.5.88)
Fifty metres to the right of *The Booze Brothers* are some vegetated slabs. Start at the foot of a clean curving flake leading up to a roof.
1 30m. 5b. Climb the flake and stand on its top to pull through the overhang to reach parallel cracks. Climb these to gain slabs and a belay.
2 18m. Easy slabs lead up leftwards. Belay a long way back.

Chunder's Revenge   24 metres   Very Severe   4b   (14.5.88)
On the far right of the crag, a series of pocketed slabs lead up to a short wall. Start below the slabs. Climb the slabs to reach parallel cracks and use these to surmount the wall. Finish by scrambling leftwards.

A little to the right of Craig Cwm Glas Bach is a stone wall going from one side of the cwm to the other. Just above the stone wall is a short pyramid of superb rock. The central depression is obvious, and left of it lie two shallow ribs. The first route ascends the left-hand rib.

Roam if You Want to   10 metres   Very Severe   4c   (7.7.02)
After the obvious spike a long reach gains a horizontal crack; a further long reach leads to jugs and easy ground.

Roam around the World   12 metres   Hard Very Severe   5a   (7.7.02)
Climb the rib on the right via a crack and some quartzy seams. Fingery moves allow easier climbing to be reached.

Without Wings   15 metres   Very Severe   4b   (7.7.02)
After a hard start, the central depression is climbed on fine flake jugs to the top.

Field of Molten Flowers   18 metres   E1   5b   (16.8.02)
The slight scoop left of the arête goes with one difficult sequence.

Without Wheels   20 metres   Severe   (7.7.02)
A good little route, starting at the very toe of the buttress. Climb the groove
in the arête to a ledge, and continue up the quartzy slab.

Above the scarp lies the next wall, the slightly bigger Craig Simdde Siân (the
location of *Famous Grouse*).

Craig Simdde Siân   Siân's Chimney Crag   OS Ref 613 567
The following routes lie round and up to the right beyond Craig Cwm Glas
Bach and a broad grassy gully in lower Cwm Hetiau. (The name derives from
the fact that hats, which were blown from the heads of trippers riding the
original open carriages of the Snowdon Mountain Railway, tended to land in
the cwm.) The first landmark is the dome-shaped crag down and left of the
prominent cleft of Simdde Siân; this is where the majority of routes are to be
found. A second area is provided by the slabs a few metres to the left (the
location of *Wholly Mammoth*), while the rib taken by *Beavering in Obscurity* is
much lower down and to the right, directly beneath the chimney itself.

Sugar and Spice   18 metres   E4 6a   (1997)
Start to the left of *Famous* Grouse. Fairly high in the grade but on some
superb rock. Climb up diagonally right to reach a vague ramp-line sloping
up to the left. Follow this to a large flake on the edge of the face. Traverse
right and go up to a small stepped overlap at a steep wall. Climb past this
and move left to finish up slabs.

★Famous Grouse   17 metres   E4 6b   (1988)
A good route taking the central crackline in the face, which needs a
prolonged dry spell. Start below the obvious crack. Climb the crack, which
increases in difficulty to where the wall steepens. A finger-crack then
provides a frustrating but well-protected crux.
Variation   18 metres   E3 5c   (1997)
Instead of the steep finger-crack, make a move up right to gain a short
groove. An airy move right again allows you to finish easily. Well worth
doing as a route on its own.

Bunghole Buster   18 metres   Hard Very Severe 5a   (1988)
An enjoyable little offering, technically straightforward but quite bold,
rather reminiscent of some of the climbing on Diffwys Ddŵr. Start below
the central rib and right of the crack of *Famous Grouse*. Move up and right
to the rib, where good holds lead up to an obvious crack in a slab. Gain
the obvious flake-line leading up left to slabs. Finish easily.

Just to the right are a couple of lines based on the blunt arête.

Ari Lichenas   23 metres   Very Severe 4c   (1997)
The left-hand line is a good little pitch on fine rock, although a little mossy
at the top. Climb up to flakes and go straight up to a groove. A high step
up leads to easier climbing and slabs above.

A Break from the Norm   23 metres   Hard Severe 4b   (1997)
Pleasant enough climbing based on the right-hand ramp line. Start as for
Ari Lichenas and go up to the flakes, move right and follow a series of
stepped scoops up and left to the top.

A touch further round to the right is a steep little face, which gives:

La Hain   15 metres   E6 6b   (1997)
Concentrated climbing with no time to ease into it. Start just right of a
knee-height pocket opposite a protruding boulder. Climb up to another
pocket at 6 to 8 metres, step left and head straight up.

Get a Grip   14 metres   E6 6b   (1997)
The short overhanging groove to the right is protected by small wires and
gives another intense excursion.

Up and left of the main crag, a secondary area of rock, with an obvious
heathery crackline, is the location of:

Wholly Mammoth   26 metres   Very Severe 4c   (7.01)
Pleasant climbing on superb pocketed rock. Start near the toe of the
buttress down and left of the arêtes. Climb up to an overlap and move left
to step up and gain the base of a rib, which is climbed direct to get the
grade given.

Spice of Life   23 metres   Hard Very Severe 4c   (1997)
This route takes the obvious rounded arêtes; once again good climbing on
perfect rock but with not much gear. Climb the first arête to a ledge and
take the second arête direct.

The Grassy Knoll   20 metres   Severe   (1997)
A fairly pleasant pitch, following the obvious crack in the centre of the slab.

Whooah!   20 metres   E3 5b   (1997)
A bold route. Start just to the right of *The Grassy Knoll*. Climb straight up to
join that route at a heather bush in the centre of the crack, move out right
on crimps and head for the flake at the top of the slab.

The next routes lie on the little buttress with a very steep main wall and an
obvious rib on its right; to the right of the short escarpment below Craig
Simdde Siân. The escarpment lies behind the pyramid taken by *Roam if You
Want To* etc. The rib is the location of *Beavering in Obscurity*.

The short steep wall left of *Beavering in Obscurity* (and below *Famous
Grouse*) is in two sections with a couple of obvious corners in the middle. The
left-hand section has a short ruined drystone wall at its base. The first four
routes are on this part of the craglet, with the climbing being concentrated in
the first 10 to 12 metres.

Under Pressure   20 metres   Hard Severe 4b   (14.7.03)
Climb the crack-system 3 metres left of the remains of the drystone wall.
Easy slabs and grass lead to the top.

Weed It and Reap   21 metres   Hard Very Severe 5a   (14.7.03)
Easy climbing up amazing rock directly above the drystone wall leads to a
diagonal crack; pull up straight above this. Grassy slabs lead to the top.

Uchelgeilliol   22 metres   Hard Very Severe 5a   (14.7.03)
Start at a short groove to the right of the drystone wall. Ascend the obvious
red streak past two horizontal breaks. Finish easily.

Too Much Pressure   22 metres   Very Severe 4c   (14.7.03)
The crack-system 3 metres right of the ruined drystone wall, starting at
some flakes, gives one short hard section. Finish easily.

Beavering in Obscurity   21 metres   E1 5a   (4.10.87)
A bold little route, with only just enough gear. Start at the base of a narrow
rib leading up to a slabby area to the right of a steep little wall. Climb the
rib to the rounded slabs. Ascend these with some delicacy. Belay well back.

Craig Pant Caseg   Mares Hollow Crag   OS Ref 611 567
A little above the upper stone wall crossing Cwm Glas Bach, the stream forks.
Follow the left fork through an obvious miniature canyon. About 100 metres
above the top end of the canyon is an amazing slab of rock on the left.

Caseg Fraith   30 metres   Very Difficult   (7.7.02)
Follow the crack-system on the left-hand side of the slab, past a bulge, to
the large sloping grassy ledge. Continue up the easy slabs above.

Byd Bach   30 metres   Very Difficult   (7.7.02)
Climb diagonally up to the right on pock-marked rock until it is possible to
follow a diagonal line back left to reach the sloping ledge and the easy
slabs above.

Craig Cwm Hetiau   Hats Cwm Crag   OS Ref 610 561
Cwm Hetiau lies at the very top of Cwm Glas Bach. It is where hats, blown off
the heads of unsuspecting walkers on the Snowdon Path, can still be found
littering this secluded cwm. At the back of the cwm lies a rectangular cliff, the
left arête of which is the location of the following route, gained by scrambling
up grassy slopes on the right.

The Golden Pillar of Cwm Hetiau   23 metres   E2 5c   (1.9.02)
A climb with fine situations and some good moves. From the base of the
arête, step left into the corner; and then pull up onto good holds on the
steep slab. Move up and right delicately to gain the arête; difficult moves
then allow the ledge to be reached. A long reach for a good hold brings
you to easier ground. Belay well back.

Craig Las   Grey Rock   OS Ref 620 570
The steep walls and corners on the small outcrop just the other side of the
river from Clogwyn y Grochan have provided a little playground for a
number of years. Many of the routes have some nasty landings if you are
trying to solo them. The grades require a very blinkered approach.

1 8m. 4a. Climb the corner at the left-hand end of the crag to a ledge and
cracks above.

2 8m. 6b. The groove just right of the corner leads to slabby walls.

3 9m. 6a. Climb the hanging groove after laybacking the hanging arête.

The central arête has two groove-lines:

4 12m. 5b. The left-hand line.

5 12m. 5b. The right-hand line.

6 8m. 5b. The arête to the right of the grooves.

7 8m. 5b. The cracked wall right of the arête.

8 10m. 5c. The obvious jamming crack.

9 10m. 5c. The wall to the right of the jamming crack, coming in from left
to right.

10 10m. 5c. The overhanging prow above the drystone wall.

11 10m. 5b. The arête and reddish scoop at the right-hand end of the
crag above direct.

Bryn Hel   Gathering Hill   OS Ref 616 573
Opposite Craig Ddu, and just overlooking the river is a short steep scarp, the
location of a number of fierce little offerings (including an E2 5c crack).

Perhaps the most significant line on Bryn Hel is:

Heinous Hone   8 metres   E5 6c   (7.94)
The obvious thin, central crack.

Up and right, on the tier above *Heinous Hone* is:

Some Routes Are Smaller than Others   7 metres   E2 6a   (1994)
This takes a slabby wall above an awkward landing.

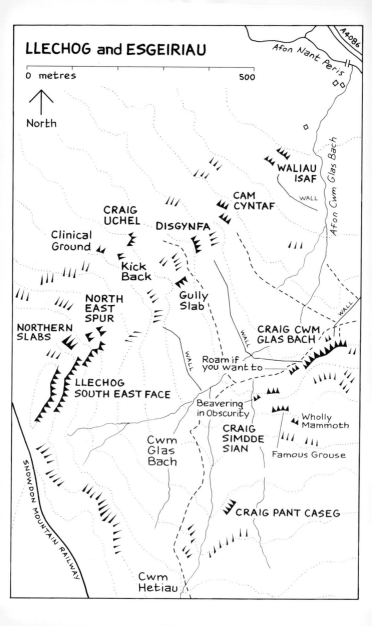

Llechog Area

Not to be confused with the crag of the same name in Cwm Clogwyn. Llechog itself is the impressive squat wedge-shaped crag high up on the west-bounding ridge of Cwm Glas Bach.

The climbing lies both on Llechog itself and on Esgeiriau, the ridge leading down to the valley floor from Llechog. The buttresses are described as they are encountered when walking/scrambling up the ridge. This is the best approach for Esgeiriau. Llechog itself is most easily approached up the Snowdon Mountain Railway although purists will prefer to scramble up the ridge.

Esgeiriau   Spurs   OS Ref 610 570

This is the long arm leading down from the main cliff in a jumble of craglets, slabs and boulders. It has a number of facets with differing aspects at various heights; with no clearly defined features and rock everywhere. It is difficult to describe exact locations, and careful use of the map in this book is recommended.

Waliau Isaf

These are the first walls or facets of the Llechog Spur to be of interest; they lie just above the cottage of Cwm Glas Bach, and stand out as satellites below the main spur. The upper crag has a huge perched boulder above. The climbs here were done many years ago but not recorded.

The first route lies on the lower wall just where an old drystone wall abuts the rock.

Cwm Glas   10 metres   Hard Severe 3c   (10.8.02)
Follow the weakness above the drystone wall to the top.

Esgeiriau   12 metres   Hard Very Severe 5a   (10.8.02)
Quite varied. Start just right of the drystone wall. Weave a way up the slab, passing a crescent-shaped feature to start, and finishing on large holds.

Bryn Fforch   13 metres   E1 5b   (2.9.02)
A fairly bold number. Start left of a vegetated cleft. Go up to a short vertical crack, and finish direct above the crack.

The next area of good rock on the lower wall lies down and to the right, at an obvious clean slab.

Mur Mawr   14 metres   Hard Very Severe 5a   (10.8.02)
Boldly gain the prominent crack in the slab, and follow this to make some delicate moves just before topping out.

Cadlas   14 metres   Hard Very Severe 5b   (10.8.02)
Very slippery when wet. Start about a metre to the right of *Mur Mawr*.
Climb up to a flake of sorts , and then trend right along cracks, past a
mossy section, to gain the final clean slab.

On the upper craglet, the first routes start from some quartz veins on the left.

Coed Gwydir   10 metres   Severe 3a   (10.8.02)
From the quartz, head up left and then go back right to gain a crack.
Follow this to the top.

Chwarae Poced   14 metres   Hard Very Severe 4c   (10.8.02)
Sparse protection. Start as for *Coed Gwydir*, but go straight up to the
pocketed slab, and then go up to the right, keeping away from the crack.
Move up to the right along this and swing right to finish boldly.

Yr Hollt   13 metres   Hard Very Severe 5b   (10.8.02)
Well worth doing. The painfully obvious diagonal crack provides a
powerful little line.

The next routes could be to the right of *Esgeiriau*, somewhere! The first two
may perhaps be to the right of *Waliau Isaf*, near a wire fence. All we have to
go on is the description, which was written up as follows: 'About 400 metres
up the hillside, across the road from Gwastadnant, is a collection of walls.'
Hat Shoe (8 metres E2 6b 24.5.87) takes the right-hand line up a small
wall facing Llanberis. **Boot Coat** (8 metres E2 6a 24.5.87) is the line left of
Hat Shoe. **Aesthete's Foot** (18 metres E1 5b 24.5.87) lies across the
hillside (up the Pass) and faces up the Pass. Left again is a slimmer wall
facing the main road, on which the line of **Surprisingly Goute** (9 metres
E1 5c 24.5.87) is marked by quartz. **Quantum Dump** (27 metres E1 5b
24.5.87) takes a curving wall up and left, behind the previous route.

Cam Cyntaf

Above and to the right of the lowest facet of the spur, which is rather broken
and messy, you arrive at a steep area of rock on the right-hand side. There is
an obvious triangular recess leading to a chimney and a diagonal crack on
the right. The first route tackles the recess and chimney.

Niche   20 metres   E2 5c   (13.7.02)
A good fight. Start down and left of the triangular nook. Hand-jam
diagonally up right to make a hard move into the base of the niche. Climb
the chimney above and emerge thankfully onto slabs, which ease off all
the time; walk way back to belay.

The next route lies up a slab above.

Triple A   53 metres   Difficult   (3.8.02)
Worth doing just to gain height. Start above a small rowan tree to the right
of the steeper face.

1 18m. Climb the heathery slab and belay at a crack on the left of the grassy ledge.
2 35m. A long thin slab above is followed, via some cracks.

Disgynfa
A bit of a walk up from Cam Cyntaf brings you to a scooped area of rock below the next steep facet.

Scoopy Doo   15 metres   Very Difficult   (13.7.02)
Enter the scoop on the right just above some quartz and follow a kind of crack or weakness up left, via some entertaining moves.

Triple Treat   15 metres   Very Severe   4a-4c   (3.8.02)
Different. Start just left of *Scoopy Doo*, at a short steep wall. Ascend the wall to enter the scooped area (the diagonal line of *Scoopy Doo* cuts across). Above are three grooves. The left one is 4a the others are harder – also, the lack of gear might make them seem a touch harder than they actually are.

On the upper left section of this particular scarplet is an obvious thin crack snaking up a short tower. The next route tackles this.

Over the Edge   12 metres   E2 5c   (13.07.02)
Delicate and devious. Start at the base of the obvious diagonal crack. Follow this until it is possible to reach a continuation crack leading straight up. Belay well back.

Craig Cribflaen
Diagonally up and right of the lower Llechog spur is a subsidiary spur, a prominent jutting prow of rock with many obvious lines. High on the left is a prominent, steep bulging wall, and to its right is a curved groove in the arête. The first route tackles this.

The Good Book   20 metres   E1 5a   (13.7.02)
A fine open route, but sparsely protected. Start just right of the wall, step up and move diagonally left on flakes to reach the groove. Climb this almost to the top, when weird moves into a short pod allow you to finish easily. Step down into the col to belay.

Craig Uchel
A little above this buttress is a wire fence, the next routes lie on the cliff above; the obvious jamming crack and the short corner on the left help define it.

Kick Back   15 metres   E3 6b   (28.7.02)
A technical little offering taking the short corner. Move right at the top.

Lazy Ray's   18 metres   E2 5c   (28.7.02)
The obvious jamming crack to the right is much harder than it looks.

Clinical Ground   20 metres   E3 5b   (28.7.02)
Round to the right is a bald bold slab.

Over on the other side of the spur, facing and overlooking Craig Cwm Glas
Bach, is an obvious square slab. This lies to the left of an obvious grassy gully,
half-way between two drystone walls. The lower wall is much better defined.

Gully Slab   25 metres   E1 5b   (17.8.02)
A good little route; if only there could be more! Start about 15 metres left
of the gully, below the slab. Ascend a rib to a bulge and pull over this to
gain the base of the slab proper. A thin crack on the right-hand side of the
crag then defines the line. Move left at the top.

Llechog   Slabby   OS Ref 606 567
North East Spur
As you approach up the spur of Esgeiriau from Gwastadnant, the lowest
rocks of Llechog proper form a number of ribs and slabs. Just above these is
the first continuous area of rock. The fine diamond headwall with a
prominent crack and groove on its left is an obvious feature, which is taken
by *Gochell*.

Gochell   52 metres   E2   (27.7.02)
A fine climb on good rock, the wide ledges hardly impinging on the
airiness of the situation. Start at a grassy terrace below an arête left of a
deep groove (some perched blocks share the terrace).
1 15m. 5b. Climb the arête until it is possible to move right onto the slab.
Bold moves now lead to easier climbing. A poorly protected pitch.
2 15m. 5a. Climb the diagonal crack above the ledge, then move left to
follow the thinner crack and go straight up to a short groove.
3 22m. 5b. From the large flake leaning against the headwall, move up
to gain a diagonal crack leading past a block to the arête. Follow this to
the top.

A scramble can be made by taking a groove-system just left of pitch 1 of
Gochell and crossing it at the ledge below pitch 3. Easy grooves well to the
right of pitch 3 lead to easy ground.

Northern Slabs
On the right, and higher up than the North East Spur, the rock forms a series
of overlapping slabs and ribs. The slabs are generally quite easy-angled,
and the rock is reminiscent of Lliwedd in structure. Descent for both routes is
fairly easy by going up or down the ridge.

Warlock   20 metres   E3 5c   (27.7.02)
A fierce little route, which should clean up. Climb the crack, which gets
steeper all the time, until a swing round to the left is needed to gain the
continuation crack. Jam gingerly past an apparently detached flake to
some even steeper ground. Good holds allows you to pull up onto the

gangway of *Cae Perthi*. (The Connoisseur's Finish, a continuation of the same line leftwards for 5 metres, has not been done yet.)

Cae Perthi   32 metres   Very Severe   4b   (27.7.02)
A bit bold to start, but it does ease off, particularly towards the top. In general it follows the arête overlooking the previous route. Start at the very base of the arête. Step up into a groove, follow this up the arête until it is possible to move right, and step back left to get on a gangway. This leads to easy ground.

The obvious off-width on the right has not been done.

South East Face
This is the main cliff of Llechog, the one seen clearly from the Grochan and Wastad areas. From a distance the crag seems to be broken, but the few routes that have been done there are surprisingly continuous and reminiscent of the East Face of Tryfan (though with superior situations). Once the first continuous rocks of Llechog are gained, follow a sort of bilberry terrace slanting up left along the base of the crags to get to the routes.

The routes are described from **right to left**.

Bad Altitude   162 metres   Very Severe   (17.8.02)
A neo-classic alpine training route, destined to become popular with those with big leg muscles. The occasional grassy breaks detract little; think of them as snow patches. Start about 100 metres along the terrace where it narrows, down and left of some mossy slabs. A small V-niche lies below a steep crack.
1 15m. 4c. Tackle the steep crack, awkward to start; then pull up onto slabs. Ribs lead left to a belay at a large flake.
2 20m. 5a. Pull up onto a slab via a flake-stuffed crack; move left and then back right to gain some left-slanting cracks. Ascend these to slabs and a belay on the left.
3 24m. 4b. Move left to a slabby area, and follow a crack back right to reach a large ledge. Swing left to a short groove and head up, past a block, to belay well back.
4 45m. 4a. Walk 5 metres left to the base of a steep rib. A difficult step up allows you to gain and scale the slab, which eases off all the time. An area of quartz leads up to a blocky rib; follow this, past flakes and blocks, to a belay below an overhang and a huge detached flake.
5 30m. 4a. Follow the arête just right of the detached flake to slabs. A grassy break then leads to a wide crack. Climb this to belay below another wide crack.
6 28m. 3c. The wide crack leads to an awkward position. Step left and follow further cracks to arrive at the summit. Belay to a fence.

Jug Handle   122 metres   Very Difficult   (1954)
The route is approximately centrally placed along the terrace about 50 metres left of *Bad Altitude*. Start from a large pointed block. It can be hard

to follow at times as it zigzags around a bit, but it gives several worthwhile pitches.

Slab and Tower   88 metres   Severe   (1954)
Start by a pinnacle at the foot of a large steep quartzy slab bounded on the left by a dirty groove. The climb heads for the prominent tower outlined against the sky from the ledge at the foot of the crag

Nice Chimney   84 metres   Very Difficult   (19.4.80)
Wends its way through impressive rock scenery. Start below the steep mossy slab on the left side of the main area, about 50 metres left of *Jug Handle*.
1 15m. Go up the slab to a grassy platform and spike belays.
2 24m. Continue up a slab on small holds, making for a crack on the right. Traverse right just below this and go up round the corner.
3 24m. Make for the obvious chimney (more pleasant than it looks). Above this is an easy step where two ledges converge.
4 21m. Go up left of a pinnacle by small cracks and then left under the overhang above to tackle the final steep wall.

Crags Overlooking Llyn Peris

Clogwyn Mawr   Big Cliff   OS Ref 596 586
This area is made up of ridges and ribs of rocks running up the hill from the end of Llyn Peris above the old copper mine building perched on a spur. Park at a lay-by and go up the hillside past small crags to obvious roofs. The bigger, right-hand roof is:

Little Foos   9 metres   E3 6a   (5.95)
Grab the mossy clump in the groove and gain the undercling. Pull out over the lip and scramble up above. Cams useful.

Also here is **Pinocchio Crack** (3 metres 6b), the obvious off-width just left of *Little Foos*.

About 200 metres back up the Pass, along a track heading towards Nant Peris, a small outcrop sits at the foot of the hillside offering a few problems, the best of which is an 11-metre *Left Wall* type crack (5b); the arête to the left is 6c. *All* the other obvious lines have been climbed.

Creigiau Conwy   Conway Crags   OS Ref 593 588
Well down the Pass towards Llanberis are several more rocky spurs running down on the north flank of the Snowdon ridge. The largest of these is in a small cwm overlooking Llyn Peris and opposite the slate quarries. The crag consists of rocky ribs protruding from a heathery hillside. Several 90-metre

routes have been put up here. Descriptions seem to have been lost, along with the old Wendy's Cafe new-route book. However, the main rib gave a fairly good outing at about Very Severe/Hard Very Severe.

Creigiau'r Cadeirydd   Chairman's Rocks   OS Ref 584 591

These pleasant little outcrops lie on the north-west face of Derlwyn, overlooking the Coed Victoria. They consist of a series of three grey ribs running down the hillside, parallel to each other and offering problems of between 14 and 25 metres in height. The area is rich in plant, bird and animal life, and climbers are requested to disturb this environment as little as possible. The rocks are best approached from a point on the Snowdon footpath, about 100 metres beyond the top of its initial hill. Contour around to the left, well below a small quarried face (which also has the odd problem) and across boggy ground to reach the top end of the nearest rib. This is the prominent group of high slabby rocks split by two wide cracks.

Cracked Spur   9 metres   Very Difficult   (20.2.71)
This is the short shattered buttress a short way to the left split by the second wide crack. A hard pull up right leads to jugs.

Mini Botterill   8 metres   Very Difficult   (9.6.73)
The small heathery slab immediately left, neat.

Original Route   11 metres   Difficult   (20.2.71)
Take the wall to finish up the right-hand crack.

One other route is perhaps worthy of recording. Go down onto the open grass below the trees, and continue left for perhaps 50 metres, beyond the second rib, below broken rock and a heavily vegetated gully. There is a large nose of rock left of the gully. Twenty metres left of this is another nose split by:

The Big Groove   12 metres   Very Difficult   (26.3.71)
Scramble up broken ground to the cluster of small trees at its foot and climb directly up the groove – a short excursion to the right may be necessary half-way up.

Bouldering   by Simon Panton

The Llanberis area has a long tradition of bouldering, providing many opportunities for easily accessible, quality problems. Recent years have seen a marked resurgence in the popularity of this age-old game, so much so that there is now an independent bouldering guide for the whole of North Wales that provides definitive details of all the latest test-pieces[1]. The casual

1 More detailed information and topos of the bouldering areas covered here can be found in the new *Bowldro Gogledd Cymru* (*North Wales Bouldering* guide) produced by Simon Panton (published in 2003, and available from climbing shops and Cordee).

visitor may wish to consider the following recommended venues, either as a starting point for further explorations, or simply as a pleasant diversion from roped climbing.

Fachwen

A historically interesting series of minor venues, which admittedly haven't captured the imagination of the modern generation. Nonetheless a circuit of the major lines on a sunny afternoon should prove sufficiently charming to please even the most cynical of visitors.

From the Caernarfon end of Llyn Padarn take the minor road to Fachwen; Electrocution Wall (OS Ref 563 622) lies immediately adjacent to the road, just before the lay-by after which the road narrows and starts to climb up the hillside. *Electrocution Wall* (V2) itself takes the central flake, and the crack further right is V1. Beware the padded telegraph wire across the top of the wall, the tarmac landing and the heedless cars. If you walk up, trending left through the trees from the back of the adjacent lay-by, you will arrive in about 100 yards at Split Rock (OS Ref 563 624). The roof-rack facing you on arrival is the hideous *Fachwen Overhang* (V2 – useful for a wet day!), and the arête to its right the hospitalising *Perrin's Arête* (V2 but bold). The classic *Shorter's Overhang* (V3) on a subsidiary boulder to the right is now slightly blocked by a tree but is still possible; other problems exist on the rest of the main formation. By following paths rightwards you will arrive at the most prominent feature in the Fachwen area. Lion Rock (OS Ref 566 624) is the obvious dome of white quartzy rock with black streaks running down its short overhanging west face. The two most important lines hereabouts are located on the scrubby hillside beneath the television mast and directly behind the village of Fachwen. The elusive *Harris's Arête* (V3 OS Ref 574 621), reputedly first done in the 60s, lies hidden, close to the lower wall that delineates the back of the village properties. *Accomazzo's Wall* (V3 OS Ref 576 622) can be found about 50 yards below the mast and recognized by a diamond-shaped pod to the right of a small clean wall. The groove to its left is about the same grade. (NB there is no formal access agreement to this last area. Visitors are advised to keep a low profile and to be careful not to damage any fences.) Finally, an hour or so's entertainment can be found on Yellow Wall (OS Ref 561 622), situated by the old Llanberis road on the other side of Llyn Padarn.

Wavelength

The extensive boulder-strewn hillside leading up from Ynys Ettws to below Diffwys Ddŵr offers the best quality bouldering in the area. There are numerous classic problems of all grades and styles. First-time visitors should make a beeline for the Utopia block (OS Ref 623 567), a large house-sized boulder reached by bearing rightwards up the hillside from the back of the CC hut. The front face contains numerous classic problems. The central flake line is a fine Very Severe route, and the prominent groove to its left is V2, exiting left at the top break. *The Pebble* (V6) is the thin high wall right of the central flake. The wide crack leading into and from the alcove to the right is V1, whilst the steep line to the right, exiting rightwards, is a superb V5. From Utopia, walk up past the obvious low roof (*The Pieshop*) and over to the Wavelength Boulder (OS Ref 622 565), a beautiful and immaculately formed piece of stone bearing the trademark 'wavelength' feature. The left arête is V1, whilst the right-hand exit from the shelf gives a bizarre V4. *King of Drunks* (V6) is the sitting-start problem to the left of the adjacent low block, swinging wildly leftwards at the top. *Wavelength* (V8+) goes rightwards into a desperate sequence above the low block. Across to the left (about 100 yards) lies the large Grooves Boulder (OS Ref 623 565), home to the classic *Boysen's Groove* (V3, the obvious feature on the Llanberis side of the boulder), first climbed by Paul Pritchard in 1997. Further left again, the Satellites offer endless opportunities for steep problems on clean rock, although most visitors are drawn up to the Meadow and the Dome beneath Diffwys Ddŵr, where yet more superb problems await their arrival.

The grounds of Ynys Ettws also offer the classic *Boysen's Roof* (V3), first done by Martin Boysen in the 60s: a thin crack splitting the overhanging roadward face of a boulder just across the stream 50 metres to the left of the track from the road.

The Cromlech Boulders   OS Ref 628 567

Easy access has guaranteed the popularity of this cluster of roadside boulders (the main area being the two enormous erratics by the road next to the lay-by beneath the Cromlech, but there are many outlying problems). The sheer density of problems throughout the full grade range V0 to V13 has made this a magnet venue for all climbers. Whilst the rock lacks the subtle frictional qualities of the Wavelength boulders, there is no denying the endless opportunities for perverse stamina links and arm-destroying traverses. There is something for everybody here, whether you have designs on the classic *Roadside Ramp* (V1), the apprenticeship test-piece *Edge Problem* (V5, situated at the right-hand side of the roadside face), *Jerry's Roof* (V9, a left-to-right rising line situated on a boulder on the Cromlech side of the road, about 100 metres towards Pen y Pass from the Ynys Ettws entrance), or the impossibly hard line past the high porthole, *Pools of Bethesda* (V12, first ascended by Paul Higginson). The last-mentioned now has an even harder (V13) low start on the left, the work of Malcolm Smith.

The Barrel   OS Ref 627 564

This is the obvious horizontal, cigar-shaped boulder, situated right of the path leading up to Dinas Mot. There are several up lines, including some very scary ones on the left, but most visitors come to try the right-to-left traverse on the steep right side of the face. This goes at V8+, exiting upwards onto the left side of the high slopy ledge after 6 metres of powerful and sustained climbing.

Graded List

The following list of a fairly comprehensive selection of the best and most popular climbs the Pass is in descending order of difficulty. The list has been prepared by the Plas y Brenin instructors and is based on their on-sight ascents of all the routes up to the mid to high E6s.

E9
Trauma

E8
Nightmayer
Agua Caliente
'Totally Wired 9'
Grave Diggers

E7
The Trumpet Blowers
Rumblefish
Overlord
The Bastard Practice
The 39 Slaps
Surgical Lust
Melondrama
Melancholony

E6
Alchemy
Truncheon Meat
Pretty Girls Make Graves
Lord of the Flies
Over the Beach
New Era
Steel Appeal
Tess of the d'Urbevilles
Satsumo Wrestler
Noah's Ark
King Wad

E5
Atomic Hot Rod
Ryley Bosvil
The Red Ring
Perplexus
Grand
Long Kesh
Dried Voices

Tufty Club Rebellion
The Bog of the Eternal Stench
The Kicker Conspiracy
Cockblock
Melon Transplant
The Nectarine Run
Quantum Jump
Venturi Effect
Ivory Madonna
Precious
Spanking for Beginners
J R
Hall of Warriors
Hindenburg
Right Wall
Buoux in a Tin (Without a
Tin-opener)

E4
Into the Groove
Marlene on the Wall
Killerkranky
Pus
Perygl
The Pump
Awesome
The Roc-Nest Monster
Silent Thunder
Sexus
The Heretic
Resurrection
Crucifix Direct
Zangorilla
The Edge of Time
Rimsky-Korsakov
The Skull
What a Difference a Day Makes
Tombstone Wall

E3
The Black Pig
Zeta
Stroll On
Leftover
Quasar
Blackhead
Corruption
Sacred Idol
Weasels Rip My Flesh
The Molehill
Brute 33
Stairway to Heaven
Memory Lane
Foil
Black Shadow
Lubyanka
The Windmill
Pulsar
The Plexus Girdle
Epitaph
Twisted Sister
Jupiter

E2
Surplomb
Left Wall
Spectrum
Divertimento
Sombrero Fallout
The Grim Jim
Jericho Wall
The Great Buttress
Ten Degrees North
Coon's Yard
Rembrandt Pussy Horse
The Cromlech Girdle
Shadow of Youth
Hornets Attack Victor Mature
Grond
Erosion Groove Direct
First Amendment
G B H
S S Special
Slape Direct
Yellow Wall
The Thing
The Monster

E1
Black Wall
Hangover
The Link/The Chain
Cenotaph Corner
Nexus
Elidor
Subsidiary Groove
Curfew
Ochre Groove
Beorn
Dracula Spectacula
Superdirect
Canol
Ivy Sepulchre
The Grooves
Overlapping Wall
The Vendetta
Scrog
The Nubian
The Wall
Rolling Stone
Rameses Wall
Cemetery Gates
Old Holborn

Hard Very Severe
Jubilee Climb
Hiawatha
M P P
Wind
Diagonal
Unicorn Direct
Gollum
Unicorn
Strapiombo
Gryphon
Sickle
Plexus
Black Spring
Sunset Boulevard
Red Wall
Karwendel Wall
Kaisergebirge Wall
Crosstie
Spectre
West Rib
Erosion Groove

Route of Knobs
The Mole
Brant Direct
Lorraine Variation

Very Severe
Slape
Lion
Noah's Warning
Phantom Rib
Slime Wall
Cobweb Crack
The Crevice
Fallen Block Crack
Ribstone Crack
Nunc Dimittis
Rift Wall
Lorraine
Mushroom
The Infidel
The Direct Route
Cave Buttress
Long Tree Gate
Brant
Rackstone Crib
Broad Walk
Shadow Wall
Trilon
Castor
Pedants Buttress
Pharaoh's Wall
Gardd (by the easiest variations)
Pharaoh's Passage
Ampyx
Holly Buttress
Mortuary Slab
Botany Climb
Western Slabs
Yellow Groove
Sabre Cut
The Ring
Zig-Zag
Little Sepulchre
Nea

Hard Severe
Main Wall
The Black Belt
Skylon
Central Route
Halan
Petite Fleur
Dives/Better Things
The Cracks
Hazel Groove
Main Scoop Route
Central Gully
Horseman's Route

Severe
Waterfall Climb
Slow Ledge Climb
Scrambler's Gate
Garlic Groove
Crown of Thorns
Crackstone Rib
Black Cleft
Schoolmasters' Gully

Very Difficult
Reade's Route
Great Gully
Bluebell Cracks
Cracked Wall
The Gambit Climb
The Black Gates
Flying Buttress
Wrinkle
Rectory Chimneys
Flake Traverse Variant
Parchment Passage
Spiral Stairs
Rib and Slab
The Parson's Nose Direct
Pedestal Route

Difficult
The Parson's Nose

Erosion Groove (HVS, page 81) Carreg Wastad
Climber: Ron Moseley (c.1955)   Photo: Don Roscoe col.

First Ascents

AL and VL mean alternate and varied leads respectively.

The dates given in the route descriptions are there to provide a cross-reference to the dates given below. All details of variations, free ascents etc. are listed under the date quoted in the text and the climb name used in the main text. In the route descriptions, dates for routes climbed in the last 100 years are given in full where available, whereas for routes climbed prior to 1904 only the year is given. Thus 1903 is used for *The West Buttress* (climbed on 3.4.1903) and 30.3.03 is used for *Feeding Station* (climbed on 30.3.2003).

Where the first ascent records have specifically mentioned that a route has been climbed on sight this is indicated below. Similarly, where details have been recorded of some form of preparation of a route, or in a few cases where there is known to have been some form of preparation, this is indicated. The absence of such information should not, of course, be taken to mean either than a route was not climbed on sight, or in the case of the harder routes that the first ascent was made without any pre-knowledge.

1879	**Western Gully, The Arête, Eastern Gully** (Clogwyn y Person) R Pendlebury
	'…behind them is a V-shaped nook, 15 feet high, peculiar attitudes are often seen here.' (H R C Carr, A Climber's Guide to Snowdon and the Beddgelert District, 1926)
1884	**The Parson's Nose** A H Stocker
	'This is one of the oldest climbing grounds in the district. It is named after the clergyman who frequented the mountains of Snowdonia in the 50s and 60s of the last century, and who was the first to hold the true religion of the hills.' (H R C Carr, 1926)
1887 July 30	**Crazy Pinnacle Gully** E R Kidson
	'The front of the Pinnacle can also be climbed from Cwm Glas, but the rock is 'crazy', to say the least of it…' (George D Abraham, British Mountain Climbs, 1909)
	'First Pitch. 20 feet. Select the most stable holds on a slope of debris.' (H R C Carr, 1926)
1887 July 31	**Western Gully** (North Face of Crib Goch) E R Kidson
1892 April 2	**The Right-Hand Edge** H B Dixon, Mrs Dixon, Mrs Commelons, F W Gamble, A M Marshall
1892	**Castle Gully** Only the date is known!
1893 March	**South West Arête** G W H Tunzelman
	On Craig Nant Peris. No details are known.
1894 Dec 9	**Crazy Pinnacle Face** J M A Thomson, H W Hughes, H Edwards
1897 March 16	**Black Cleft** J M A Thomson
	Considered for some time to be the hardest route in Wales.
	'Rotten rock, which may be compared to sugar toffee in structure, needs every care…' (George D Abraham. British Mountain Climbs, 1909)
	'After two brief pitches almost entirely concealed by the lush

herbage, a move to the left takes the party into the jaws of this savage chasm.' (H R C Carr, 1926)

1899   **Bryant's Gully**   G B Bryant and party

'A brief lunch was disposed of in a small hollow. We shared it with a well-nourished and contented-looking toad, living there in apparent freedom from all family cares. The general verdict was that, whilst containing nothing to attract the seekers after glory, yet it was an excellent gully.'

'Those who on occasion can be content to admire remarkable examples of rock structure, without having to scale anything very remarkable in the way of rock, may use the route described below as an unusual introduction to a day on the Glyders.' (H R C Carr, 1926)

1900   **Jammed Boulder Gully**   J M A Thomson, R Williams

'The exit is narrow, and the arrival of corpulent or clumsy followers will be watched with amusement by those who have gone before. A commodious theatre is provided for the spectacle'. (H R C Carr, 1926)

1901 April   **North Ridge of Crib Goch**   C G Brown, P A Thompson

1901   **Eastern Gully, Western Gully** (Dinas Mot)   W H Price, C G Brown, P A Thompson, P S Thompson

A cairn above the Nose showed that at least one of these had been climbed before.

1902 Sept 6   **Thomson's Routes**   J M A Thomson, T Williams, D Hunter

On Clogwyn y Person, in the region of Square Gully.

1903 April 3   **The West Buttress**   J M A Thomson, M K Smith, R F Blackwell

1903 Sept 13   **Central Route**   J M A Thomson, T Williams, R Williams

'...and the removal of earth with a penknife disclosed a succession of excellent niches; with the aid of these the ascent was accomplished with an unexpected ease. Strange sounds caught at intervals, and previously accredited to sheep, were now recognised as human voices. Our flanking column under Blackwell's guidance had reached their goal and were raising the paean.'

This was an attempt on Great Gully, the difficult pitch being avoided by a detour out to the left. The route described was probably first done on 22.4.49 by G Dyke, P R J Harding. A more direct version of the route was climbed by A Taylor 31.7.60; this is left for those with a hankering for adventure to rediscover.

1903 Sept 13   **The Chasms**   R F Blackwell, S Tetley, E R Turner

'An easy 20-foot chimney is climbed to the crux – the "leaning monster." This curiously poised splinter has, so far, defied the prophets and remained in place.' (H R C Carr, 1926)

1904   **Crib Goch Buttress**   G D Abraham, A P Abraham

Long since lost, but was near Route III.

1904   **Great Gully**   J M A Thomson

'At a point above a yard higher, a half turn was necessitated, and I found myself looking straight outward, with my back to the rock. The distribution of the holds lent themselves to this attitude...

1906 April   **Grey Gully**   J M A Thomson

'An amphitheatre of rocks of the Parsonic order is then reached.' (J M A Thomson, written in a notebook)

1906 Aug 6   **Yellowstone Gully**   A E Barker, G T Atchison, W J Drew, H Mitchell

1906 Aug 9	**Double Cave Gully** H Mitchell, G T Atchison, A E Barker, W J Drew
1906 Aug 12	**Schoolmasters' Gully** H Mitchell, A E Barker, W J Drew, G T Atchison

A remarkable climb for the period. 'Each of us insisted that the man before him made a ridiculous fuss and spent an absurdly long time over it. Criticism and advice flowed freely, but each of us modified his opinion when his own turn came.'
J M Edwards, J N Mahler repeated it on 2.4.34 and added the left-hand start, which they rather confusingly called Plaster Chimney, a name that the first ascencionists had already given to pitch 4!

1908 Aug	**Reade's Route** W R Reade, G L Bartrum

'A few feet higher is a conspicuous pinnacle 12 feet high. The leader stands upon it, and, bestriding the gulf like a Colossus, makes contact with the vertical wall above'. (H R C Carr, 1926) The climb was initially known as Route No. 1.

1908 Sept	**Ribbon Route, Fallen Block Climb** J M A Thomson

'I narrowly escaped being trepanned by a rock chisel'. Ribbon Route derives its name from 'a string of quartz visible at 100 feet.' (H R C Carr, 1926)

1908 Sept	**Waterslide Gully, The Organ Route** J M A Thomson, H O Jones, K J P Orton
1909	**Dodo Gully** G Winthrop Young

'The pitch looks difficult, and in no way belies its appearance. The upper part is scaled to the left of the waterline... A young river usually enhances the difficulty of this line.' (H R C Carr, 1926)

1910 Sept	**The Gambit Climb** J M A Thomson, H O Jones, K J P Orton

'The discovery, by means of this intricate and difficult route that these crags so formidable in aspect, were not wholly unassailable, encouraged the hope that a second breach could be made.'
Longland's Variation was climbed by J L Longland on 2.4.31.

1910	**Slab Variant** J M A Thomson
1913	**Clogwyn y Ddysgl Girdle** G Winthrop Young, C O'Brien

An Irish sailor, Conor O'Brien was renowned for climbing in bare feet. 'Often in climbing one has to support the entire weight of ones body on a couple of toes – but toes in stiff boots. Conor claimed he could force his naked toes farther into crevices than a boot would go.' (Robert Graves, Goodbye to All That, 1929)

1913	**The Arête Climb** (Craig Aderyn) S W Herford
1913	**Winthrop Young's Climb** G Winthrop Young, H E L Porter
1915 Aug 17	**The Grey Rib** J I Laycock, C T Lehmann, T B Burnet, Sir J B Farmer, Miss R Farmer
1915 Dec	**The Black Gates** G H L Mallory

After a Christmas spent with his parents, Mallory spent a few days climbing with H Reade and C O'Brien; it is likely that one or both of these men accompanied Mallory on his ascent.

1924 Oct 7	**Treasury Climb, Jacob's Ladder** F Graham

'Treasury Climb concentrates its principal difficulties in the initial 20 feet, from which a lapsus corporis would not be attended with serious consequences. It may, therefore, be considered the least serious of the three.' (H R C Carr, 1926)

1925 Aug 20	**Captain's Bluff Direct, The Gauge** C F Stoehr, W K McMillan, H R C Carr

1925 Aug 24	**Via Media** F Graham, M W Guinness

A little-known gem.

'This period between the war and the middle 20s was the real beginning of what may be termed modern rock-climbing. The traditional footgear of the mountains had been discarded and 'rubber' climbing was making its debut. The older generation no doubt stood aghast, as it always does at the doings of its children, but rubbers had come to stay.' (P R J Harding, Llanberis Pass, 1950)

1925 Aug 27	**Crack and Slab** (Dinas Bach), **Flake Chimney** (originally called **Tower Chimney**) H R C Carr, M W Guinness

'…climbing is of an exposed nature and of more than moderate difficulty for 30 feet'.

The Wall and Traverse Finish had been climbed by H R C Carr, M W Guinness, W K McMillan on 23.8.23. 'The party is still under the impending wall of the nose, and it is necessary to scramble a few yards along the ledge, upwards and to the left, before a weakness in this formidable bastion is discerned.'

1925 Aug 27	**Phoenix Buttress** M W Guinness, H R C Carr

'The groove proved to be a vexatious little problem…

1925 Aug 27	**Rectory Chimneys** M W Guinness, W McNaught, H R C Carr

The finish as described (The Vestry Variant) was first done by M W Guinness, H R C Carr on 30.8.25.

1925 Aug 30	**Little Benjamin** M W Guinness, H R C Carr

'On the final section, the leader runs out 50 feet of rope.'
(H R C Carr, 1926)

1926	**A Climber's Guide to Snowdon and the Beddgelert District** by H R C Carr

The first guidebook to cover the Llanberis Pass. It described some 40 climbs on the south side of the valley and one, Bryant's Gully, on the north side. 'Its (Esgair Felen's) cliffs crown the precipitous slopes which plunge into the Pass of Llanberis, and appear from the road as from the opposite side of the valley, to offer many opportunities to the climber. Some of the lower crags in this neighbourhood are also arresting in form, and have doubtless fired the imagination of many explorers, but no discovery of merit has yet been found on them.'

1927 Sept 11	**Fallen Block Crack** I M Waller

A fine lead taken straight out in one pitch.

1930 April	**The Cracks** (4 pts aid) B L Bathurst, H C H Bathurst

'First explored in 1926. The party traversed in from the foot of Eastern Gully and climbed the heather-filled crack direct to the twin cracks by means of two pitons, a bolt and top-rope. C F Kirkus led the first free ascent later in 1930.' (P R J Harding, Llanberis Pass. 1950)

'The Nose of Dinas Mot consists of 200 feet of depressingly steep rock.' (H R C Carr, 1926)

The top pitch was done by the arête on the left on 23.6.38 by A D M Cox, J L Longland.

1930 June 22	**The Direct Route** C F Kirkus, J B Dodd

A Kirkus classic. Much of the route had been done earlier in the year by C F Kirkus, C J A Cooper, G G Macphee. 'Time taken 4 to 5 hours – should long remain a record. A ladder would make the *final crack suitable for others than a few rock gymnasts.' A shoulder was used on the final pitch, but Kirkus later climbed it without.*

'No true mountaineer ever sets out with the object of making history, but the Nose of Dinas Mot was obviously the place on which to do it...' (P R J Harding, 1950)

1931 May 30	**Flake Traverse** P L Roberts, R D Crofton	
1931 Aug 6	**The Girdle of the Nose** J M Edwards A M D'Aeth	
1931 Aug 6	**Western Slabs** J M Edwards, A R Edge, A M D'Aeth	

The direct start was climbed on 8.6.46 by P R J Harding, R E Meyer.

1931 Sept 13   **West Rib**   C F Kirkus, I M Waller

Another brilliant lead by Kirkus.

1931 Oct 13   **Holly Buttress**   J M Edwards, S C R Walmsley

The first real attack on the north side of the Pass. An easy variation to the last pitch was done on 18.12.31 and the modern start on 9.6.31, both by J M Edwards. The route (now VS) was given a standard of II (corresponding to Difficult) in the 1944 guide.

1931 Dec 6   **Spiral Stairs, Valley Crossings**   J M Edwards, S B Darbishire

The former route was initially very vegetated. In describing Dinas Cromlech in the 1944 guide, Barford stated 'the possibilities of more difficult routes are obvious to even the cyclist's eye. It is a good cliff and it is surprising that it has been neglected so long considering that there is a large amount of quite straightforward climbing on it...

1931 Dec 18   **Flying Buttress**   J M Edwards

A fine classic discovery which has become exceptionally popular. Originally named Sodom. This shocked the CC Guidebook Editor who persuaded Edwards to change the name.

By the fifties the route had become a classic and the recipient of some curious attention, but no doubt provided good solid alpine training. 'One of the most interesting circuits is the ascent of Dinas Cromlech by the Very Difficult Spiral Stairs and the descent of the Difficult but superb Flying Buttress.' (J E B Wright, Rock Climbing in Britain, 1958)

Kamikaze Finish: D Roberts, P Williams, 15.7.78.

1932 Sept   **Waterfall Climb**   J M Edwards, A B Hargreaves

The Direct Start was taken on 12.7.45 by J Campbell, who took a slightly different upper line from the original and the whole climb was thought to be new. It was called Heather Climb.

1933 Feb 2   **Neb's Crawl**   J M Edwards, C F Kirkus

Originally named Nebuchadnezzar's Crawl.

...derives its name from the seven years that Nebuchadnezzar spent on his belly with the beasts in the field and his head buried in the long grass, as one may well do on this climb.' (J E Q Barford, 1944)

'Vegetation, overhangs, rotten rock, trees. Menlove is a connoisseur.'
(P R J Harding, 1950)

Crockett Crack start: 21.4.56 by M H J Baylis, J F Pagella.

1933 March 27   **Parchment Passage, Pharoah's Passage**   J M Edwards, O S Bell

'The overhang at the foot of another climb looks rather like the sort of hat which the Egyptians used to wear, hence the name...'

(J E Q Barford, Three Cliffs in Llanberis, 1944)
Variation Finish to Pharaoh's Passage: 2.9.51 J Brown,
M T Sorrell.

1933 April 17   **Pharaoh's Wall**   J M Edwards, A B Hargreaves
'A small but superlative class of climber already exists which
specialises in unsound or uncertain holds. By a technique
combining balance and a serpentine body-cling, the climber
crawls adhesively up the face of vertical mud-verdure or of
deciduous splinters unified by moss, not disdaining to use his teeth
to maintain his balance, and his faith in the tenacity of Celtic turf
to its native rock. This vegetarian technique has opened up for
climbing, of a super-select order, a number of cliffs formerly
shunned, or climbed only by their rotten gullies.'
(Geoffrey Winthrop Young, Mountain Craft Fourth Ed., 1945)
'Standard: V. Strong fingers required.' (J E Q Barford, 1944)
Direct Finish: 26.3.46 by M G Hughes.

1933 May 13   **Dives**   J M Edwards, T E Davies
Pitch 1 was climbed on 18.12.31 by J M Edwards as a variation
on Spiral Stairs. The original finish was as for Spiral Stairs. The
Better Things finish was climbed by T D Bourdillon,
J W T Tomlinson, M J Bell on l8.4.49.

1933 June 17   **Sexton's Route**   J M Edwards, G G Macphee, R W Stallybrass
'Sexton's Route was so named because of the sombre coat tails of
the third man who wore a black tailcoat to protect him from the
incontinent elements.' (J E Q Barford, 1944)
The hard variation to the last pitch had been led on 13.5.33 by
J M Edwards.

1934 March 30   **Boulder Buttress**   J M Edwards, J Gask
H A Carsten added the modern finishes on 28.5.48.

1934 March 30   **Slow Ledge Climb**   J M Edwards, J Gask
The long groove, now part of Dolerite Dump, was taken as a
finish. The final section was added by G W S Pigott, H A Carsten
on 29.5.48.

1934 March 30   **Western Wing Girdle**   J M Edwards, J Gask
1935 Jan 20   **Ledge Way**   J M Edwards, B McKenna
1935 Feb 17   **Hazel Groove**   J M Edwards, B McKenna
The left-hand crack in pitch 2 was led by P R J Harding in Aug
1948 and the Direct Start was added by P R J Harding,
P R Hodgkinson on 12.4.49.

1935 March 9   **Cwm Glas Pinnacle**   R V M Barry, J R Jenkins
1935 April 20   **Dead Entrance**   J M Edwards, C W F Noyce
'The three cliffs disappointed me. They seemed very low, there was
a lot of messing about in yew trees and holly trees and rowan
trees that climbed the cliff with us, and things that looked easy
were not.' (Wilfrid Noyce, Samson, 1961)
The easy way of reaching Green Park was discovered by R Hind
on Good Friday 1940.

1935 April 20   **Scrambler's Gate, Long Tree Gate**   J M Edwards,
C W F Noyce
Initially, Long Tree Gate was graded a V (Severe). 'A very steep
route. Extremely strenuous on the first pitch. A pleasant exercise in
technique… it is necessary to climb the first 20 feet almost
completely on the arms, the holds being much too far apart.'
(J E Q Barford, 1944).

'The tree could be seen on its large ledge less than fifty feet away. The opening pitch did not look difficult, and I lay on the grass at the bottom and shouted encouragement, wondering why he took so long. He worked upward very slowly, clumsily almost, and I can see now that it was strength of arm alone that kept him to the rock.' (Wilfrid Noyce, 1961)

1935 May 5   **Bluebell Traverse**   J M Edwards, Miss M Glynn, Miss I Corrie
'The route now lies through the waterfall and the next section is done as quickly as possible into the cave at the back. A short walk along the edge of a flake finishes on the large sloping ledge known as Lords. Crossing the pitch to the pavilion end (rain having stopped play), an easy downward scramble lands one on a small triangular grassy ledge, down which one slithers to a block belay at the foot. Fortunately, while poised over the abyss at this point, I could not see what was in store for me and had leisure to work out the posture in which my flesh had the fewest possible points of contact with my soused clothing. Transferring to rock, the way goes up to the left for a few steps until a foot and a hand can be wedged in a crack on the right. After a warming tussle, a small ledge is reached and the climber notes with retrospective alarm the exiguous belay provided by niggardly nature.' (F H Keenlyside, CC Journal, 1944)

1935 May 7   **Main Scoop Route**   J M Edwards, B McKenna
Koala Finish: 27.7.69 by M J Bell, J D Griffiths.

1935 June 9   **Quintet Route**   J K Cooke, E Holliday, W S Webb, E Pentir Williams, A Burns

1935 June 22   **Twin Groove**   C H S R Palmer

1935 July 14   **Shadow Wall, Crackstone Rib**   J M Edwards, J B Joyce
At the time Crackstone Rib was thought to be more technical than Shadow Wall. In the 1944 guide Crackstone Rib was described as 'Technically harder than Shadow Wall but better rock', and graded IV; whilst Shadow Wall was 'A very steep route up the cliff. Exposed on the most difficult move, loose, probably dangerous', and graded V. 'A stern test of anyone's vocabulary. Amid festoons of cowardice, the leader called upon ethereal beings for strength, and assuming sundry copulative postures eventually clawed over the mantelpieces.' (a 1954 ascent of Shadow Wall)
The five holly trees on Crackstone Rib are now no more.
The Rottish Monk start to Crackstone Rib was climbed by M Crook, P Clark ('Patric the Rottish Monk').

1935 July 25   **West Buttress Arête, Tweedledum, Tweedledee, The Rattle, Central Buttress Arête**   C H S R Palmer, H E W R...

1935 July 27   **Main Wall**   P L Roberts, J K Cooke
A bold route on a buttress previously dismissed as impossible. 'The steep edge of the slab gives a fine pitch. The holds arrive well, the rock is beautifully rough and sound.' (P R J Harding, 1950)
Pitch 1 was added by the same party plus E Holliday on 16.3.37, the original start having been made from Great Gully.

1935 Sept 8   **Duet Chimneys**   J K Cooke, P L Roberts

1935 Sept 21   **The Quartet Wall**   P L Roberts, G A Duckett, J K Cooke, L Milner

1935   **Sabre Cut**   E Pentir Williams, R G Williams
The first of the big Cromlech corners to fall.

1937 May 16   **Three Cave Gully**   P L Roberts, J K Cooke

1938 Aug 10   **Diagonal**   A Birtwistle, G F Parkinson
Named Diagonal Route up until the 1987 guide. An amazing route, well ahead of its time. It was not repeated for ten years. 'In parts it is very thin indeed and the problem is usually more of balance than brawn.' (P R J Harding, Llanberis Pass, 1950).
'Diagonal was one of the most important pre-war climbs in Britain. The puritanical, piton free climbing standards of Kirkus, Edwards and Birtwistle worked out in the Pass were at least the equal of free climbing standards on the Continent at that time. As important as the achievement though was the ethical line that they marked out for the post-war explosion of climbing in Britain.' (C T Jones, Rocksport, 1972)
The final crack was climbed by P R J Harding, A J J Moulam in May 1946. The original route took the final pitch of West Rib.

1939 March 17   **Choristers' Cleft**   G K Hodgkin, R C Evans

1939 Oct 21   **Cenotaph Corner Finish**   R Hind, J E Q Barford

1939 Oct 21   **Tributary Crack**   R Hind
It was believed to have been done before.

1940 Aug 5   **Brant**   J M Edwards, J E Q Barford
'Standard: VB. The hardest climb in this group of cliffs.'
(J E Q Barford, 1944). J M E after farming at Harlech for some days was in extremely good form and produced a climb considerably harder than any of the others which have so far been done on these cliffs, with the possible exception of Long Tree Gate. 'The Brant – Very Severe, strong arms required and a just appreciation of the value of loose holds'.

1940 Aug 8   **Slape**   J M Edwards, G F Peaker, R G Donaldson
A superb addition, though thought to be slightly easier than Brant at the time. 'A fine steep climb, good rock, very exposed, strenuous. Standard: VB.' (J E Q Barford, 1944)

1940 Oct 20   **Horseman's Route**   J M Edwards, J E Q Barford (AL)
'Edwards failed on the middle pitch, which Barford led without effort'.

1941 Sept 7   **Lorraine**   J E Q Barford, Mme N E Morin (AL)
All but the slab pitch had been done previously by J M Edwards on 9.9.31.

1941 Sept 10   **Nea**   Mme N E Morin, J M Edwards
Shoulder Connection (joining the main little square gully from the right where Nea joins it from the left) was climbed by J M Edwards, G Dyke on 8.8.49. Once graded Severe, a rockfall in the early spring of 1984 obliterated its third pitch making Spectre pitch 5 the only viable finish.

1943 May 11   **The Ledge Climb**   A W Bridge, J Kenny, J Lynn
The seconds were 'two commando stalwarts' of No. 4 Commando.

1944 June 26   **Dolerite Dump**   J E Q Barford, D Pepper
The corner and final groove had been climbed previously by J M Edwards in conjunction with Slow Ledge Climb. The continuation above the terrace was worked out by H A Carsten on 28.5.48.

1944 June 30   **Garden Groove**   J E Q Barford, R M P Hartog, M P Ward
The left-hand exit was led by H A Carsten, P R Hodgkinson on 1.4.48.

1944	**Three Cliffs in Llanberis** by **J E Q Barford**

A 24-page pamphlet reprinted from the Climbers' Club Journal. The grading went from I to V, with A and B subdivisions. A grade of II corresponded to Difficult; III was a V Diff, IV a V Diff to Severe and a route given V was classified as a Severe. The hardest routes were given VB.

1946 Aug 26   **Route II**   B L Bathurst, E D Carr, H R C Carr
1946 Aug 27   **Route III**   B L Bathurst, E D Carr, H R C Carr, W Fahie
1947 May 4   **Spectre**   P R J Harding, E H Phillips
'Not feeling like The Slape, a new climb was done: The Spectre (The Grochan Spectre)'. Harding had made the second ascent of Brant the previous day. The route originally finished up Nea. The present finish (and now the top pitch of Nea) was added on 12.3.49 by P R J Harding, K A W Herbert.
First solo ascent by P R J Harding in 1948.
A variation start, The Goat Start, starting up Goat's Gully, was climbed by C M G Smith, B L Blake, J H Swallow, 21.7.49.

1947 May   **The Crevice, Wrinkle**   M P Ward, J E Q Barford, B Pierre
The Crevice was originally named The Clevis. Pitch 1 of Wrinkle was climbed direct, taking a similar line to what is now First Test.

1947 Aug 29/30   **Ivy Sepulchre**   P R J Harding, E H Phillips (2 pts aid)
The second of the three big Cromlech corners to fall. 'Operation Garden was commenced on Ivy Sepulchre, P R J H abseiling down complete with trowel etc: the top 60 feet was found to be climbable, involving an all-in wrestling match with a rotten holly tree, which despite its age, still knows how to deal with would be climbers. ...reinforced by E H P, the party again visited this cliff – this time meaning business. The first ascent of Ivy Sepulchre was made; 200 feet. 120 feet of rope required. Exceptionally Severe – Rubbers or Kletterschue are advisable for nail fans... The crux involves some loose rock, vegetation, overhangs, a fight with a holly tree and delicate wall climbing.' (P R J Harding, 1950)

1948 April 24   **Trilon**   P R J Harding, N L Horsefield (1pt aid)
1948 June 12/13   **The Old Girdle**   P R J Harding, P R Hodgkinson
A two day expedition, split at the yew trees.
1948 June 19   **Pedestal Route**   P R J Harding, K A W Herbert
The first route on Craig Ddu.
1948 July   **Overlapping Wall**   M G Hughes
A bold and outstanding lead.
Pitch 1 was climbed on 18.6.49 by P R J Harding, F A Smith.
Pitch 3 was climbed in 11.51 by J Brown, R Moseley.
Soloed by P R J Harding in 1949.
1948 Aug 2   **Bluebell Cracks**   H A Carsten, P R Hodgkinson
1948 Aug 18   **The Ashes Route**   P R J Harding, A J J Moulam
1948 Aug 20   **Ash Tree Rib, Broad Marsh, Two Tree Route**
P R J Harding, A J J Moulam
1948 Aug 23   **The Ring**   P R J Harding, J I Disley
An attempt for an earlier route, The Clasp.
1948 Aug 24   **Gargoyle Route**   A J J Moulam, D Thomas
1948 Aug 28   **Kaisergebirge Wall**   P R J Harding, J I Disley, A J J Moulam
(7pts aid)
'Nothing was barred; pegs, knotted bootlaces... the leader went up again as last man to remove the attachments.' 'Much harder

Ribstone Crack (VS, page 81) Carreg Wastad
Climber: Ron James (in boots, c.1960)
Photo: Ken Wilson

The Mole (HVS, page 148) Dinas Mot
Climber unknown
Climbers on top pitch of *Gollum*:
Pete Allison and Jancis Baldock (c. 1966)
Photo: Ken Wilson

now. All the tiny flakes in the groove on which it was possible to hook a nail, have disappeared – it's as smooth as a baby's bum!'
(J Brown, 1985)

1948 Aug 30	**Cracked Wall, Little Sepulchre, Holly Gate** J I Disley, P R J Harding, A J J Moulam (AL)
1948 Aug	**Ash Tree Gully** A J J Moulam
1948 Oct 14	**René** R Thomas, A J J Moulam
1948 Oct 29	**Rib and Slab** V J Wiggin, D R Meldrum

An incredibly popular route, and rightly so.

1949 Jan 30	**Crown of Thorns** P R J Harding, C W F Noyce (AL)
1949 March 6	**Tradition, Spring Chimney** J I Disley, P R J Hodgkinson

John Disley was to go on to make his name in athletics.

1949 March 19	**The Eastern Edge** P R J Harding, J B Nicholson
1949 April 9	**Phantom Rib** G W S Pigott, Miss M Kennedy-Frazer, W H Stock
1949 April 11	**Short Tree Chimney** P R J Harding
1949 April 13	**Delphos** P R Hodgkinson, P R J Harding (AL)

'That crack is desperate.' (D Ferguson, 2002)

1949 April 17	**Unicorn** P R J Harding, P R Hodgkinson, M G Hughes (1pt aid)

Pitch 1 had been led two weeks earlier by J B Lawton.

1949 April 18	**Intermediate Chimney, Square Gully** P R J Harding, P R Hodgkinson
1949 April 22	**The Green Caterpillar** P R J Harding, G Dyke

'...boots in preference to rubbers.'

1949 April 22	**The Green Necklace** P R J Harding, G Dyke
1949 April 23	**Little Buttress Climb** J B Lawton, F A Smith, D P Davies, P Dellow, J S Stafford
1949 April 24	**Brant Direct** P R J Harding, J I Disley, P R Hodgkinson, G Dyke

'This pitch is definitely harder than anything else on The Brant. It is 75 feet long with no respite, strenuous and technically hard all the way – fine pitch.' 'The Direct Start was led clean by P R J Harding... after prolonged but unsuccessful mechanical attempts by another party.' (P R J Harding, 1950)

1949 April 24	**Fa** J B Lawton, F A Smith, D P Davies
1949 April 25	**Garlic Groove** P R Hodgkinson, J I Disley (AL)
1949 April 26	**Halan** P R J Harding, G Dyke
1949 June 6	**Terra Incognita** H A Carsten

'A scramble to the right of Staircase Gully – soloed in filthy weather. This is loose, full of overhangs and plants. The woods in the middle can be reached by way of either of two traverses from the bend of Staircase Gully. These lines are about 30 feet apart and obvious, with massive jug-handles – Flowers! Beyond Staircase Gully there is no coherent rock.'

1949 June 12	**Conway Climb** P R Hodgkinson, R W Beard, M Bosworth, B Meveen

Routes were climbed on the right-hand side of Llechau Canol by M W Guinness, H R C Carr on 30.8.25. 'An ascent can, therefore, be performed as a pleasant diversion during a walk up the cwm.' (H R C Carr, 1926)

1949 June 25	**Inoculation Wall** F A Smith, P R Hodgkinson

This was once quite a popular route; it 'disappeared' for many years.

1949 June 26	**Lion** P R J Harding, A J J Moulam

Most of it had been soloed before by P R J Harding.

1949 July 8	**Fatha** A J J Moulam, D Thomas

1949 July 10	**Foxglove** G W S Pigott, A J J Moulan, J Walmesley
1949 July 14	**The Black Belt** A J J Moulan, B L Blake, C M G Smith

A route called The Black Braces was climbed by D McKilvey, R Hughes on 30.7.52, which started along The Black Belt and finished up Zig-Zag.

1949 July 15	**Goat's Gully** C M G Smith, B L Blake
1949 July 17	**The Lectern** P R Hodgkinson, R W Beard
1949 July 23	**Central Gully** J M Edwards, R W Beard

Long thought to be impossible. 'Menlove led...turning the cave pitch on the right wall though we thought a strong and confident climber might take it direct.'

Left Hand Variation: 14.10.51 J M Edwards, M R Loewy – a shoulder was used to start.

The 'strong and confident climber' appeared in the shape of W Hurford, who, with M Parker, led the Superdirect Variation on 8.6.75.

1949 July 27	**Babel** C M G Smith, J H Swallow

Pitch 3 Variation: 8.3.69 by M T Taylor, A Booth.

1949 July 27	**Rift Wall** J M Edwards, K N Davies, F J Monkhouse

'...up the steep crack at the back, over a perched block (traveller, treat this jug with care, for other travellers travelling here)...' 'We climbed in rubbers, used slings for safety on the perched block and on the top traverse. Standard. Perhaps just into the Severes!'
Re-discovered by J Brown in 1952 who called it Anthropology, the name that was used in the 1961 guide.

1950	**Llanberis Pass** by **P R J Harding**

Affectionately known as the Bumper Fun Book, it also covered Clogwyn Du'r Arddu.

1951 March 22	**Ribstone Crack** J I Disley, A J J Moulan (AL, 2 pts aid)
1951 May 12	**Bole Way** A J J Moulan, G W S Pigott, A Hyde

Direct finish added in 1958.
Left-hand finish by J Brown, C E Davies, 6.84.

1951 May 18	**Hangover** J Brown, R Greenall, M T Sorrell, F Ashton

'With the production of Harding's guidebook the stage was set for the third phase of this short but eventful history. The doings in "the pass" were the subject for awed discussion by the majority of climbers, and a challenge to the small but expanding nucleus of "tigers" continually on the lookout for "virgin rock". It is not surprising therefore that, almost before the guide had been published, a small, wiry young climber appeared with the apparent intention of rendering it obsolete, a man with the ability to make first ascents of extreme difficulty, more often than not in appalling weather conditions, who, at the time of writing, still remains a living legend, Joe Brown.' (D Roscoe, Llanberis North, 1961)

'Since the removal of the large flake in the final groove on pitch 3 the character of the route has altered considerably. The final 10 feet is now the crux of the climb.' (CC hut book, 21.10.55)

1951 May 26	**Unicorn Direct** J Brown, M T Sorrell, P Hampson, R Greenall
1951 Sept 2	**Cobweb Crack** J Brown, M T Sorrell

So-called, because a spider had spun its web across the crack, ensuring that there were 'no flies on Joe that day'.

1951 Sept 3   **Noah's Warning**   J Brown, M T Sorrell
*A classic find. The finish as described was climbed by
C J S Bonington, G Francis on 20.7.54.*

1951 Sept 29   **Cromlech Grooves**   G W S Pigott, R M Viney, G P Hample

1951 Sept 30   **Cemetery Gates**   J Brown, D D Whillans (AL)
*A major discovery up fierce rock. 'I led the first pitch and took a
stance just above the holly tree and hung on to slings attached to
poor spikes sticking out of the rock. This was the first stance in
slings that we had taken. The position on the face was very
sensational and frightening. I brought up Don and he was
flabbergasted. "Christ this is a gripping place", he muttered
hoarsely. Neither of us seemed able to move. Then it started to
rain…all the way up it, little flakes of rock broke off when we
pulled or stood on them.' 'Definitely E5 1b.' (John Allen, Gritstone
guru, 1985)*

1951 Nov 10   **The Band of Hope**   A J J Moulam, A Francis

1951 Dec 16   **Leesled**   J R Lees, A J J Moulam, D Fisher
*'…Leesle across the mossy slab…' To Leesle – a leaning gliding
mantelshelf.*

1952 April 7   **The Sheepwalk, Holly Cracks**   P Carr, R A Brown
*Holly Cracks was later ascended as President's Climb by
A B Black, R Mann on 25.5.53.*

1952 April 13   **Skylon**   R Handley, E H Phillips
*Named after the rocket-shaped edifice built for the Festival of
Britain in 1951.*

1952 June 16   **Canol**   J Brown, D Belshaw
*The same team added the Direct Start on the same day. Variation
to pitch 3: T I M Lewis, 1965.*

1952 June 17   **Zig-Zag**   D Belshaw, J Brown

1952 Aug 24   **Cenotaph Corner**   J Brown, D Belshaw (2 pts aid)
*One of the great milestones in Welsh climbing. 'I was climbing in
socks and vainly tried to hook my feet onto rugosities below a
large patch of moss, oozing with water. Until then I had forgotten
that the conditions on the cliff were bad and the corner was very
damp.' By 1961 Cenotaph Corner was being described as a
'trade route.' 'The Corner, being one of the most terrifying climbs
to look at in Snowdonia, is particularly likely to cause long delays.
I have seen more than one party decide, after several hours of
watching other people climbing, not to bother after all.' (T Smythe,
Rock Climbers in Action in Snowdonia, 1966). 'There's no doubt
about it; it's a polished horror.' (Mark Pretty, 1986)*

1952 Aug 26   **Route of Knobs**   J M Edwards, H C Bryson
*For many years a greatly under-rated route, originally graded Mild
Severe.
Direct Start: 8.75 by R Newcombe
The variation was climbed by J Fotheringham, N Kekus,
D Hatwood on 14.7.02.*

1952 Sept 7   **Moch Up**   A J J Moulam, S Fry

1952 Sept 7   **Notanda**   E Marshall, M Ridges, D Penlington

1952 Sept 28   **Jericho Wall**   J Brown, D Cowan
*Pitch 1 was added as a direct start in summer 1958 by J Smith,
D Gray.*

1952 Sept 28   **Thor**   A J J Moulam, W R Caister

1952 Oct 11   **Ragged Wall**   P Hampson, Miss J Coates (AL)

| 1953 March 1 | **Surplomb**   J Brown, D D Whillans (AL, 1pt aid) |

Rumoured for many years to have been done wearing big boots during a snowstorm. That attempt failed. First free ascent P Gordon 1959.

1953 March 22   **Subsidiary Groove**   J Brown, D D Whillans (AL)

'You can pick out a Brown route in the same way that you can pick out a photograph by Cartier-Bresson or a speech by Churchill. It usually follows a great but forbidding weakness; it tackles overhangs in a very direct, unnerving, but logical way; it uses corners and grooves which look quite holdless from below but are not quite bare when you get on to them (although this must not be taken for granted); it is not afraid of mud and vegetation (but thank goodness, is not a glutton for them); and finally, it is almost always steep – very steep.' (T Smythe, 1966)

1953 April 26   **Erosion Groove**   D D Whillans, J R Allen, D Cowan, P White (1pt aid)

'An early Whillans route of considerable severity on a forbidding part of the cliff, where the rock should not be treated too harshly.' (T Smythe, 1966)

1953 May   **Millwood's Wall**   G J Millwood, A Taylor

1953 June 1   **Yew Link**   P Hampson, A Kopczinski (2 pts aid)

1953 June 20   **Scabbard**   A Kopczinski, Fraulein R Ohrtman

1953 July 3   **The New Girdle** (Carreg Wastad)   H I Banner, D J Abbot, B G N Page

1953 July 6   **Cornix**   H I Banner, D J Abbot

1953 Aug 22   **Little Audrey**   M H Westmacott, A Alvarez

The leader called for a top-rope on the last pitch to negotiate an unstable block.

1953 Aug 30   **Sickle**   J Brown, D Cowan

'A route of some technical difficulty with an exposure which is not appreciated until one is actually at grips with the climb.' (D T Roscoe, 1961)

1953 Sept 13   **The Grooves**   J Brown, D Cowan, E Price (1 pt aid)

'…the rock was decorated with rosettes of a thick, brown, blubbery fungus growth that one imagined only flourished in a primaeval jungle. Both Don and Eric fell off the second pitch and neither of them wanted to continue.' For a long time the hardest route on the south side of the Pass.

Right-Hand Finish: *J A Austin, D G Farley on 4.10.59 – the team got lost.*

Overhanging Arête: *H I Banner, J O'Neill (1pt aid) on 15.6.58 who approached along the first ascent of The High Level Girdle. Soloed on sight by R A McHardy c.1970.*

1953 Oct 11   **Red Wall**   D D Whillans, T Waghorn

The first hard route on this formidable cliff.

1954 May 7   **Ochre Buttress, Asphodel**   G W S Pigott, K K Hartley, M Hartley

On Cryn Las Fach but the descriptions have been long since lost.

1954 May 16   **Ochre Groove**   H I Banner, G W C Wilson (1pt aid)

Pitch 1 by P H Hill, M W Harvey, P C Henry on the same day. First free ascent C E Davies, 1964.

1954 May 30   **Tiercel**   G W S Pigott, J M Barr

1954 July 22   **Sunset Boulevard**   C J S Bonington, A C Cain, G G Francies (1pt aid)

1954 Aug 5   **Gryphon**   A C Cain, C J S Bonington (VL) S Lane
'Warning: The large rectangular block at the top of the layback flake on the crux has suffered during the winter. Since last Sept it has moved about a quarter of an inch away from the parent rock – it will now take a line, or maybe a quarter weight sling in lieu of the piton, which was removed. One hopes it will continue to function as a hold, or the climb may become very hard indeed.' (P H Biven, 9 May 1955). It didn't, and it is.

1954 Aug 22   **The Link**   J Brown, E Price, D Roscoe (several pts aid)

1954 Aug   **Black Wall**   D D Whillans, J Brown (1pt aid)
Variation to pitch 4: 1986 by F Hall and I A Jones.

1954 Sept 8   **Impromptu Buttress**   C Fishwick, D J Hewitt

1954 Sept 19   **Jug Handle, Slab and Tower**   F A Smith, R Summers (AL)

1954 Sept 23   **Slape Direct**   M W Harvey, D J Abbott (1pt aid)
A superb effort, with just one point of aid.

1954 Nov 7   **Broad Walk**   D D Whillans, J Brown (AL)

1955 Jan 3   **Staircase Groove**   A W Killingback, B Summers
The crag had been climbed on before but no records were kept.

1955 Feb 5   **Troglodyte Wall**   R Moseley, D T Roscoe

1955 March 19   **Botany Climb**   R Moseley, D E Shortall

1955 March 19   **Verglas Slab, Grooved Slab**   D T Roscoe, T Waghorn

1955 May 28   **Question Mark**   P H Biven, H T H Peck

1955 June 26   **Doldrums**   A J J Moulam, Miss P D Chapman

1955 July 17   **Scrog, Yellow Groove**   J Brown, D D Whillans
A similar line to Scrog was climbed on 21.8.59 by H Smith, C E Davies, M Tweed and called The Mantis.

1955 July 22   **N'Gombo**   J Brown, D D Whillans

1955 July 27   **Crosstie**   H I Banner, G W C Wilson, P H Hill
Pitch 3 had been climbed as the Grooves Variation to Direct Route by P Hampson, A Cowburn, B Usher on 26.7.52.

1955 July   **The Gangway**   A W Killingback

1955 Aug 3   **Slanting Buttress**   A D Baker, A W Killingback

1955 Aug 5   **Mortuary Slab**   A W Killingback, A D Baker
Direct Finish: W F Hurford, C B Fitzhugh on 10.7.71.

1955 Aug 10   **Burnt Out Buttress, Clinker**   A W Killingback, A D Baker

1955 Aug 11   **Preliminary Groove, Ruddy Groove, Mur-y-Ffester**
A D Baker, A W Killingback (AL)

1955 Aug 17   **Erosion Groove Direct**   D D Whillans, J Brown
For some years considered by many to be the ultimate in seriousness and difficulty, and as such it was given a wide berth until modern protection techniques improved. It is still no pushover.

1955 Dec 24   **Hanging Flake Route**   A W Killingback, A D Baker (some aid)

1955   **Llanberis Pass** by **P R J Harding** – reprinted, with a **Supplement of New Climbs** by **R Moseley**
The 10-page supplement was the first time that many climbers had access to even the briefest details of the Rock and Ice routes in the Pass.

1956 Feb 11   **The Thing**   J Brown, D D Whillans
'Extremely strenuous. A short vicious climb of great technical difficulty. Possibly the hardest problem in the valley. Difficulty is sustained, protection poor, retreat beyond the crux uninviting and the ground below nasty to land on.' (D T Roscoe, Llanberis North, 1961). One of two routes to be given the Exceptionally Severe

grade in the 1961 guide, the other route being The Cromlech Girdle.

1956 April 1/2   **The Cromlech Girdle**   D D Whillans, J Brown (3 pts aid)
A technical masterpiece, done in two stages. 'Had we relied too heavily on modern techniques, such as rope tension moves, and moral support from ropes arranged above and behind us, for crossing the Corner? One of the old guard thought so. "By Jove," he spluttered, "you should have seen it. Any of the old-timers could have done it with the gear that those young fellows were using."' The initial section across to the Forest had nearly all been climbed in reverse as Twisters Traverse by R Hope, P Walsh (AL) of the Creag Dhu on 11.7.53.

1956 April 15   **Little Whizzer**   P H Biven, H T H Peck
1956 April 26   **Rhaeadr Girdle**   R Moseley, J R Sutherland
1956 May 6   **Left Wall**   R Moseley, J Smith, J Sutherland (several pts aid)
'Chockstoning brought to a fine art.' (D T Roscoe, 1961) The present start was added later by D D Whillans. The route was climbed free by A Garlick on 21.9.70. 'Watch your language, there are MEN down here!' (Unknown climber below the route, upon hearing a string of four-letter expletives from a woman who had just fallen off the crux)

1956 Aug 6   **Druid's Dilemma**   R C Evans, C J Simpson, E J Clegg
1957 April 25   **Grey Wall**   P H Biven, H T H Peck (AL), C Fishwick
Originally climbed as part of two separate routes, Black Magic (VS) and The Dark Horse (HVS). These were revised and amended at a later date by the first ascent team.

1957 June 1   **Nunc Dimittis**   G J Fraser, M J O'Hara (AL)
1957 June   **Strapiombo**   J Smith, J Brown (2 pts aid)
1957 July   **The Slash**   T Panther, R Stephens (S & A2)
Direct Finish: T Panther, C Langley 4.71(VS & A1), in very poor conditions. Direct Start: S Mathewson (solo) 26.5.74. Both are now incorporated in the line described. First free ascent (including the Direct Finish): D Pycroft, D Lancely, 14.7.83. 'Yet another aid route that has gone free at a surprisingly amenable grade.' (P Williams, Llanberis Pass, 1994)

1957 Oct 6   **Rameses Wall**   C T Jones, A Beanland, J R Sims
1958 April 2   **Rackstone Crib**   H I Banner, K Judy, L Brown
1958 May 18   *Dinas: the wall left of overhanging prow was pegged at A2 by N Williamson. Others had pegged here before and climbed some easy lines. The overhanging prow and hand-traverse were both soloed by D Ellison, who developed the crag c.1963-64.*

1958 June 14   **Boston Spa Climb**   Miss J M Scarr, N C Peacock, H B Carslake
1958 June 15   **The High Level Girdle** (Cyrn Las)   H I Banner, J O'Neill
The last two pitches had been previously climbed by H I Banner, B Barlow, J Sutherland, so they finished up Overhanging Arête.

1958 Aug 1/2   **Karwendel Wall**   H I Banner, J O'Neill, R Beesly
1958 Sept 14   **Reluctant**   P Bell, G Stumock
1958 Sept   **Grond**   D D Whillans, J Smith, D Gray, J Brown
All four led the route.

1958   **Yellow Crack**   H I Banner, C T Jones
Possibly climbed previously.

1959 Jan 18   **The Thumb**   C E Davies, C T Jones, W A Trench
1959 April 23   **Jubilee Climb**   C J Mortlock, P M Hutchinson
The finish has been swapped with that of Hiawatha. The upper

slabs were climbed by J Brown, D D Whillans.
The route was thought to be new when climbed by J A Maguire
and E C Townsend on 14.6.64. They called it The Mekon.

1959 June 28	**Route 1** (Dinas Bach) C J Mortlock, A Taylor, L Noble

Also known as Mortlock's Slab and written up as Left Central. Led after a top-rope inspection, with a 27-metre run-out to the first piece of protection.

1959 Aug 31 **The Wall** J Brown, A C Cain, C T Jones (1pt aid)
1959 Sept 6 **Chequered Wall** A C Cain, C T Jones (AL)
1960 April 2 **Route 2** (Dinas Bach) A Taylor, M Hillman

'I placed a runner behind a little flake at 40 feet and I had slung a loop down by the heathery crack as a runner in case I couldn't do it. I gardened the crack standing in the loop and then led it clean.'

1960 May 19 **West End, Little Jim** I Clough, J A Bennet, D Cooknell, R Pottage

1961 March 6 **Petite Fleur** C E Davies, G D Verity
1961 April 8 **The Mole** J Brown, E D G Langmuir

A route which revealed the potential of the wings of Dinas Mot, which 'breached the grass ramparts.'

1961 July 2 **Hiawatha** D Turner, D Kerr

The Watha Thin Variation was climbed by A Leary, M Eade on 13.7.03.

1961 Nov 18 **Slime Wall** P Crew, C T Jones

The first new route from a very powerful climber. It was originally called Mank Wall.

1961 **Llanberis North** by Don Roscoe

'Don Roscoe's 1961 guide was a superb piece of work and at the time contained more hard climbs than any previously published guide, a fact which speaks for his ability.' (P Hatton, The Three Cliffs, 1974)

1962 May 20 **The Tickle** M J Cummington, J S Hobhouse
1962 May 26 **Trauma Grooves** B Ingle, P Crew (AL, 1pt aid)

'They came to look at the blank areas left by the little hard men from Lancashire. They were different from the little men though. Instead of a monosyllable a month there were torrents of words, arguments, beat music and open verbal competition. The North side of the Pass had been thoroughly exploited so the young Alpha climbers turned their attention to the cliffs on the South side.' (C T Jones, 1972)

1962 June **Grooved Rib** J Robson, D Cook

Also climbed as Mellow Yellow on 17.4.68 by P Donnelly, S Ashley.

1962 July 16 **Yellow Wall** D Yates, D Potts (AL)

A direct finish was added by J Harwood, R High on 3.7.65.

1962 Oct 6 **Lectern Grooves** B Ingle, P Crew (AL)
1962 Oct 8 **Epitaph** R James, M Petrovsky (several pts aid)

'Only one great problem comes to my mind as being yet unled, the arête of the left wall of Cenotaph Corner, and even this has been ascended on a top-rope.' (D T Roscoe, Llanberis North, 1961)

Although top-roped first, it was still a bold and serious lead. Climbed free by J Ewbank, T Murphy on 9.8.65.

1962 Oct 14   **Plexus**   B Ingle, P Crew (AL, 2 pts aid)
                *Major gardening altered this route considerably. 'If you are a
                short-arse you can't get gear in till after the crux.' (D Ferguson,
                2002)*

1962 Dec 2   **Gardd**   P Crew, V N Stevenson, B Ingle
                Barford and Moulam had led routes on this slab.

1963 Feb 23   **Ensis**   R G Wilson, W H Smith
1963 Feb 24   **The Bearded Crack**   R G Wilson, J H Russell (AL)
1963 March 23   **Pholidomya**   R G Wilson, J H Russell
1963 March 23   **Solen**   R G Wilson, B Hendrickson, J H Russell (AL)
1963 March 24   **Ampyx**   R G Wilson, J H Russell
1963 March 27   **Gollum**   B C Webb, A Harris, V Cowley (2 pts aid)
                First free ascent: J Perrin, 1966.

1963 April 20   **The Infidel**   P Crew, B Ingle (AL)
1963 April 28   **The Castle**   R G Wilson, J H Russell, B Hendrickson (AL)
1963 May 4   **The Great Buttress**   B Ingle, P Crew (AL, 1pt aid)
                A bold impressive line.
                First free ascent R Barley, A Barley c.1964.

1963 May 21   **Nexus**   M Boysen, P Nunn (1pt aid)
                *A brilliant discovery. 'A pattern seemed to be established here:
                Crew and Ingle invented the good, solidly hard climbs and then
                Boysen would pop in with a route of the greatest difficulty.'
                (C T Jones, Rocksport, 1972)*
                The Texas Start: P Pritchard, S Howe, 6.5.87.

1963 May   **Old Holborn**   P Crew, B Ingle, D Potts (1pt aid)
1963 Aug 29   **Tremolite**   P Crew, B Ingle (AL, 1pt aid)
                *Pitch 3 was gardened and then climbed on 14 9.63.
                Dole-ite Variation: M E Crook, B Schmidt, S Glowacz in 6.83.
                Proof if it were needed that all great climbers get involved with
                new-routing in the pass at some stage of their career.*

1963 Sept 20   **The Rosy Crucifixion**   P Crew, B Ingle
                *B Ingle, D Potts had previously done the top pitch.
                The Direct Start: M Pointon, I A Jones on 25.1.95. The first ascent
                was made more through Mick's refusal to believe the guidebook
                description of the start, rather than a conscious decision.*

1963 Oct   **The Toad**   M Boysen, A Harris (2 pts aid)
                *A sling was used to place the peg as high as possible.
                First free ascent: J Moran 19.7.77.*

1964 April 3   **Beorn**   B C Webb, B C Ruby (1 pt aid)
                First free ascent: A Harris 1965.

1964 June 21   **Elidor**   J Harwood, R High
                *Unrecorded at the time but climbed and named in 1977 by
                M E Crook.*

1964 Aug 23   **Diapason**   T Panther, P Sorrell, J Fisher (3 pts aid)
                Climbed free by D Pycroft, D Lancely on 14.7.83.

1964 Aug 25   **Micrometer**   W Hurford, D Moore
1964 Aug 26/27 **Pyg in the Middle**   W Hurford, D Moore
1964 Oct 4   **M P P**   P Crew, C Boulton
                *The 'micro precision product', which gave the route its name was
                Ken Wilson's camera and the resultant photo was used on the
                back cover of the 1966 Llanberis South guide.*

1964   **Quasimodo**   R James, A Earnshaw
                A much overlooked climb.

c.1964   **Cul-de-Sac**   First ascensionists unknown
'In 1964 I washed up at the (then) Pen y Pass Hotel every evening for 3 hours in exchange for free board and lodging! I did try Cul-de-Sac but it was wet and never finished it. However, there was evidence of others passing (cleaned holds).' (W Herford, 2003)

1965 March 27   **Sexus**   M Boysen, A Williams (3 pts aid)
Pitches 1 and 2 first climbed (2 pts aid) as part of what is now The Red Ring. Pitch 2 free by J Moran, G Milburn 28.5.77.
Climbed free by D Hollows on 29.5.77. A leading local activist made an early attempt at a free ascent of this route. After a number of failures, he handed the lead over to another member of the team, never thinking that success was to be his. The initial leader was so incensed that his thunder had been stolen that he locked off the ropes and told the other to reverse the crux by jumping off. Not enamoured with this, the climber was forced to untie his ropes and make some 5b moves above the lip to gain easy ground.

1965 April 3   **Black Spring**   M Boysen, A Williams
Variation: J Moran, G Milburn 24.4.76. A similar variation was done in 7.69 by D Cowans and B Goodwin.

1965 May 1   **The Plexus Girdle**   M Boysen, D Little (1 pt aid)
'Boysen again produced the pearl in his own languid fashion. The Girdle of Plexus Buttress is a sustained climb building up to a truly nasty last pitch. On this pitch, finding himself pressed (for a change), Boysen called for advice from a spectator on another route. This unwitting fool told him that good holds were almost within reach. The "good holds" turned out to be shallow hollows full of moss and a struggle ensued to finish the very thin pitch.' (C T Jones, 1972)

1965 May   **The Blade**   M Boysen, A Williams
A similar line, Wild Grass, was climbed by D Keeling, G Young on 13.6.71.

1965 June 7   **Lorraine Variation**   D E Alcock, C E Davies
1965 June 14   **Intruder**   D E Alcock, B A Fuller, A Williams (AL)
1965 June 19   **Preamble**   D E Alcock, B A Fuller, J Fuller
Re-discovered by S Cathcart on 8.8.83. He named it Black Eyes.

1965 June 20   **Cave Buttress**   D E Alcock, B A Fuller, J E Todd
1965 June   **Goldcrest**   J Harwood, B Burns (2 pts aid)
They did not record the route.
Climbed free by A Sharp, J Harwood on 6.9.83.

1965 July 3   **Black Foot**   B A Fuller, D E Alcock (AL, 1 pt aid)
Pitch 3 by D E Alcock, P Crew in 9.65.
The Black Page variation to pitch 2: G Griffiths, P Waters in 1970. In 1970 Cliff Phillips had a narrow escape when he fell from pitch 3 while soloing. He fell at least 60 metres on to the screes below and sustained numerous injuries, including two cracks to his pelvis, but he managed to get back to his car and to drive to Nant Peris, where he collapsed at the wheel. He was found around midnight.

1965 Aug 9   **The Mystery**   J Ewbank, T Murphy
A whodunnit? – solved at last.

1965 Oct 4   **Spectrum**   R Edwards, D Mellor, M Boysen (4 pts aid)
First free ascent: G Regan, 1975.
The variation start was climbed by P Littlejohn on 19.4.02.

1965 Oct 7	**Perygl** R Edwards, D Mellor (3 pts aid)

During the first ascent a huge trundled block created havoc by blocking the road for some time. Brede Arkless came out of her house nearby thinking that the Pass had fallen down. Brilliantly freed by S Haston, M E Crook in 1982. 'Technical and very worrying, it is also very good.' (S Haston, Pete's Eats New Routes book)

1965 Oct 23	**Joshua's Traverse** S Wroe, A Howard (AL)
1965	**Groper** R Evans, T Hurley (AL) (2 pts aid)

First free ascent with a variation: P Whillance, D Armstrong, 26.8.78.

1966 March	**The Wobbler** R Evans, T Hurley (AL)
1966 April 29	**Corruption** J Costello, D J Southall (3 pts aid)

Freed by L Brown c.1969

1966 May 1	**The Prune** J Brown, C E Davies
1966 May 1	**The Skull** M Boysen, A Williams, J Jordan (6 pts aid)

A tremendously impressive line. '…going through all possible overhangs – and being one of the few climbs to warrant a Hard Extremely Severe grade.' (C T Jones, Rocksport, 1972) Climbed completely free by R Evans, H Pasquill (AL) c.1974.

1966 May 17	**The Crucifix** L T Brown, E Jones

At the time it was thought to be the last great problem. The quote, 'Lew should be given a special pat on the back for his clean lead of this outstanding problem.' (P Hatton, The Three Cliffs, 1974) is perhaps the most embarrassing compliment ever foisted on a climber in the history of guidebooks.

1966 July 17	**Fever** D Yates, K McLoughlin, P Donnelly (1 pt aid)
1966 Aug 24	**Gandalf** R Evans, J Esplin
1966 Aug 26	**Nexus Direct** P Crew, D E Alcock (4 pts aid)

'Climb the groove until the angle eases, 4 pegs (1st native, 2nd and 3rd American – difficult to position).'
First free ascent D Roberts, 20.6.77 on sight. 'It didn't look too bad from below, so I gave it a blast. Suddenly, I found myself committed above a dodgy wire. I was too gripped to fall off. There was no chance but to go for it. I reached a tiny hold on the left and pulled like mad. The gods smiled – I made it.'

1966	**East Wing Girdle** R Evans, A Kellas

1966	**Llanberis South** by **P Crew**

The much belated companion to the 1961 Llanberis North guide, eventually taken on by Crew, who completed his first draft in a matter of months.

1967 April 30	**Mushroom** M R Sinker, R J Isherwood (AL)
1967 May	**The Craig Fach Girdle** T Panther, R Harpley, – plus B O'Connor, T Bartlett, J Malcolmson, R Stephens, P Sorrell (HVS & A3)

The route is still graded E3 & A3.

1967 May	**Zeta** A Willmot, J Tooke (AL, 3 pts aid)

One writer finding the moves on the slab pitch quite worrying, timidly asked for a pull on a dangling rope of a team on the Diagonal ledge. Just as he was going to grab the rope, the sonorous voice of his second shouted up, 'Don't do that, you'll regret it if you do.' He was right.

1967 June 8	**Castor** C J Phillips, R I C Kirkwood.
1967 June 13	**Orpheus** C J Phillips, R I C Kirkwood, J Arthy
1967 June 17	**The Sewer** M Boysen, R J Isherwood (2 pts aid)

Free climbed on 10.7.83 by S Haston, C Brear, P Norton – a gruelling effort.

The grade is given for an ascent when the waterfall stops running, but this will only occur when 'Llyn Padarn dries up', according to the first free ascensionists. In its normal state, slime, seaweed, dirt and streaming rock will be encountered making this a strong contender for 'The Most Unpleasant Route on the South Side of the Pass Award.' (P Williams, Llanberis, 1987)

1967 July 9	**The Curate's Egg** C H Taylor, R J Isherwood
1968 June 2	**Flammarian** C T Jones, T I M Lewis
1968 June 24	**Mordor** P Johnson, G R Birkinshaw (1 pt aid)

On the traverse, a block came off; the team now thought two pegs would be needed.

The climb repulsed many would-be free ascensionists. M Campbell, I Fox finally free climbed it in 1985. During the ascent, a huge tottering block peeled off 'I thought I was going for a monster.' (M Campbell)

1968 July 7	**Pedants Buttress** F A Wedgewood, C H Taylor, J J Wedgewood (AL)
1968 Aug 10	**The Lymph** G J Gilbert, B R Whybrow (AL, 1 pt aid)
1968 Aug 18	**Jawbone** M Kosterlitz, D Cook (2 pts aid)

Freed by J Moran, 21.7.77.

1968 Sept 14	**Sedilia** L E Holliwell, L R Holliwell
1968 Nov 3	**Calluna** K Cartwright, Miss.P L Serby

The line described is not the original route.

1968 Dec 14	**Sunshine Breakfast** S Johnson, R Perry
1969 June 14	**Black Shadow** D E Alcock, M Boysen (AL, 1 pt aid)
1969 July 27	**Fester** M J Bell, J D Griffiths (AL)
1969 July	**'T'ouse Wall** J Brown, P Crew

The Baron was finally prevailed upon to name this route late one night in the Padarn. The two apostrophes do seem to be necessary to record the route name in print. For 33 years, the route description described the line as going up right of The Wall. 'It does in fact go up to the left. The guidebooks have put it in the wrong place and it's about time the record was straightened.' (J Brown, 1992)

1969 Aug 10	**Carlos** R Perry, S Johnson (1 pt aid)
1969 Aug 24	**Caterwaul** M J Guillard, J L Carley
1969 Sept	**Last of the Summer, Whine** T Rolfe, N Phillipe

Re-discovered and named by J R Peart, J L Hardy 19.9.79.

1970 June	**Huge Frog** D Keeling, M Carter
1970 Aug 29	**Genesis** (Clogwyn y Ddysgl) B Cooper, E Lawther
1970	**Cwm Glas** by **P Crew** and **I Roper**

An updated version of the 1966 Llanberis South.

1971 Feb 20	**Original Route, Cracked Spur** P C Shone, M Knowles, P Knowles

The first of several probings on Chairman's Rocks by the Chester Climbing Club.

1971 March 26	**The Big Groove** E D Summers, P C Shone

1971 Sept 11	**Honky Tonk Corner, Tarotplane**	D Keeling, P Clein (AL, 1 pt aid on *Tarotplane*)
1971 Sept 14	**Roll On** R Evans, C Rogers	
1971 Sept 19	**Russet** J Brown, D Alcock (2 pts aid)	

Climbed free by A Sharp, P Lewis, 6.83.

1972 July   **Speedfreak**   B Molyneaux, R Schneider
A bold lead for its time.

1972 Sept 20   **Tongue and Groove**   H Drasdo, Ms A Cornwall
Aboriginal Start by A J J Moulam, H Drasdo c.1968.

1972 Sept 23   **Pastoral**   H Drasdo
Led on a long rope; the second did not follow owing to darkness.

1972 Oct 24   **Ann Cornwall's Climb**   Ms A Cornwall, H Drasdo

1972 Nov 1   **After Eden**   H Drasdo, Ms A Cornwall

1972   **The Monster**   M Boysen, E Volar
Not recorded at the time. M E Crook climbed it in 1977, with D Roberts, who named it.

c.1972   *Several routes on Clogwyn Mawr were climbed by various local climbers. Exact details as to what was done were recorded in the old Wendy's Café New Route Book, and have disappeared, along with the book.*

1973 April 26   **Rufus, Rocky, Rambo**   J Brown, C E Davies
Three fine additions to a hitherto neglected part of the Pass. The variation Buck Warren Meets the Headmonsters: I A Jones, E Jones, 6.5.87

1973 April 27   **The Tryptych, Skid Alley**   J Brown, C E Davies (1pt aid on the former)
The Tryptych now goes without the aid, first free ascent unknown.

1973 May 18   **Genesis** (Bryn Du)   J Brown, C E Davies

1973 May 19   **Joshua, Jonah**   J Brown, C E Davies

1973 May 27   **Main Wall Eliminate**   B Wyvill, R Evans

1973 June 9   **Mini Botterill**   A Mitchell, N Owen

1973 June 16   **Jeremiah**   J Brown, C E Davies

1974 April 20   **Lung Fish**   D Pearce, N Estcourt (AL, 2 pts aid)
Freed by G Tinnings, D Greenald in 5.80, after a very dry Spring.

1974 May 7   **The Windmill**   A Sharp, B Hall, S Humphries
The first of Sharp's fine trio of climbs on the West Wing of Dinas Mot.

1974 May 26   **Pulsar**   T Panther, P Warner, J Jiggins, S Mathewson (VL, Hard Very Severe & A3)
An excellent pitch free climbed by P Davidson, D Pycroft on 20.7.83.

1974 June 15   **Right Wall**   P Livesey
A new concept and a major step forward in Welsh climbing. Livesey abseiled down the route twice before his first attempt (which ended at the Girdle ledge, when he tied off his ropes and soloed up Cemetery Gates) and again prior to his successful ascent.
Possibly sharing a place with Cenotaph, as the 'most celebrated Welsh rock climb', it had become a trade route by 1980. '6b – terminal.' (Mountain Magazine 54, March/April 1977). 'I got half-way up your Right Wall and just ran out of gas.' (American Rick Accamozzo, 1977). 'It's only 5c —— eee.' (Chris Gore, taking a 60-footer from just below the Girdle ledge in 1979). One local activist fell repeatedly from the same point, just missing the

ground on the swing. On his next attempt, this time a couple of feet higher, he fell off again. His second managed to take in some slack and the leader got away with some scrapes to his back. Soloed twice by P Davidson in 1982 and 1983 (the second time for photographs). 'An easy and outdated crag.' (Jerry Moffatt after soloing Right Wall, Left Wall, Foil, Memory Lane, Cenotaph Corner and down Ivy Sepulchre, one afternoon in 1983).

1974 June 27	**Ten Degrees North** A Sharp, J J Zangwill

The route was supposedly named after Henry Miller's Tropic of Cancer (he also wrote Plexus, Nexus and Sexus). A slight error then, as the Tropic of Cancer is actually 23° north.

1974 June 28	**Coon's Yard** A Sharp, J J Zangwill
1974 June 28	**Superdirect** R Evans, H Pasquill

A variation start, since lost in the rockfall, was climbed by A Dilger, N McKenzie in 1976.

1974   **The Three Cliffs** by **P Hatton**
A return to an old title, but a misnomer in that, like the 1961 Llanberis North, it described all the climbing on the north side of the Pass. The first Welsh guide to have pitch gradings in the route descriptions.

1975 May	**Jayway** C J Phillips, M Barnicott
1975 May	**The Last Outpost** T Panther, S Mathewson, N Bradburn
1975 July 5	**Blackguard, Flying Trapeze** K Bentham, D W Shaw (AL)
1975 July 6	**Sheep in Situ** K Bentham, D W Shaw (1 pt aid)

Free climbed by P Williams, D Pycroft, 1981. '...a holly tree belay. – painful for the shorts and T-shirt brigade.' (P Williams, Llanberis, 1987)

1975	**Resurrection** R Edwards, N Metcalfe (4 pts aid)

A magnificent discovery.
First free ascent, including the Right-Hand Finish, (climbed by mistake), P Livesey, Ms J Lawrence in 9.75.
Left-Hand Finish, described as original way, free climbed by R Fawcett.
Redhead's Finish by J M Redhead in the 1980s.
'... it is hard to imagine any great new climbs being done. This has always been said by aged pundits like myself and it would be nice to be proved wrong and have a new teenage meteor to stagger the swaying crowds in the Padarn Lake.' (C T Jones, 1972)

1976 May 5	**Stroll On** R Fawcett, P Livesey

The first of many additions to the Pass by a very talented climber. 'Comparable to one of the harder moves on the Bradford Wall.' (The first ascent team, commenting on the crux)

1976 May	**Crucifix Direct** P Livesey, R Fawcett

Still a bold and serious lead, not to be underestimated.

1976 July 1	**Foil** P Livesey

A gem of a pitch, steep, sustained and well protected. 'When the going gets tough, it is possible to throw oneself into Sabre Cut.'

1976 July	**Memory Lane** P Livesey, Ms J Lawrence, Ms G Price
1976 Aug 19/20	**Sych** J Wincott, R Robson (1 pt aid)

Free climbed by D Howard-Jones, J Brown in 1979.

1976 Aug 21	**Lubyanka** E Cleasby, J Eastham, R Matheson (AL)

A superb route which was put up on sight.

Soloed by G Tinnings 1980.
Left-Hand Finish: A Smith, A Millsom in 7.87.

1977 May 8   **Mural**   R Newcombe, D Blythe (VL, 1 pt aid)
Previously known as Stone Child after an ascent by J Moran, M E Crook on 30.5.77. The start up to the Kaiserbirge Wall ledge was climbed by J Moran on 21.7.77.
The Scavanger's Daughter Finish was climbed by M Crook, D Cuthbertson on 17.9.82.

1977 May 26   **Wind**   M E Crook, J Moran
1977 May 31   **Times Past**   J Moran, D Hollows (AL)
Originally climbed as Black Mamba by C Foord, M J Guillard, 27.9.69 (XS & A1).
The renaming was controversial and it stimulated much ethical debate at the time.

1977 June 12   **Quasar**   J Moran, A Evans, E Marshall
1977 July 2   **Zangorilla**   A Sharp, C Dale
A route put up 'to sort the men out from the boys' just before Sharp left for America – suicidally undergraded at E1. The 'rattling block' on the top wall has long since gone.

1977 July 16   **The Molehill**   J Moran, G Milburn
Pitch 2 was climbed in 8.68 as Mole Direct (2 pts aid) by A Willmot, D Johnson. Freed by D Roberts, P Williams, 5.77. The Direct Finish was added by C Gore, D Greenald in 1980.

1977 July 19   **Curfew**   J Moran, G Milburn
Pitch 1 was climbed on 4.5.57 as a Direct Start to Sabre Cut by D T Roscoe, A C Cain, P Shotton, H McInnes.

1977 July 20   **S S Special**   D Roberts, P Williams, B Dunne
'Going round the top roof is like stepping out of an aeroplane.' (Anthoine Le Menestrel)
A line up the Sickle wall, which appears to be that now taken by S S Special, was climbed using artificial aids to an abseil point by R Hughes, P Hampson on 25.4.53. They named it Aimless Wall because it went nowhere.

1977 Aug 6   **First Test**   A Green, G Shanks (AL)
1977 Aug 17   **'C' Minor**   C Brooks, P Harrop
1977 Sept 9   **Leftover**   J Moran, S Horrox
Pitch 1 was climbed on 13.9.65 as Hangover Direct (4 pts aid) by G Homer, J M P Jones. First free ascent by G Regan 1975.

1977 Sept 9   **Sun Valley**   J H S Ashton, J G Jackson
1977 Sept 17   **Crossbones**   R E Millward, A Dilger (AL, 3 pts aid)
First free ascent by J Moran, A Evans, 21.5.78.

1977 Oct 14   **Vanishing Point**   M E Crook, P Sowter
1977 Oct 26   **Runnymede**   J Moran, G Milburn
1977 Oct 28   **Peeping Tom**   J Moran, R D Sykes, G Milburn

1978   **Llanberis Pass by G Milburn**
The two sides of the Pass were brought together again in the one book thanks to stricter editing and layout. E grades were tucked away in the back of the book.

1978 Jan 5   **Xmas Dinner, Xmas Dinner II**   P Martin, K Martin
Originally described as one route.
1978 April 28   **The New Girdle** (Dinas Mot)   P Burke, I Canton (AL) W Parker, D Hilling

1978 May 10	**First Amendment** D Roberts, P Williams (AL)	

So called because it put the newly published Pass guide out of date. The top pitch had previously been climbed by C Gore in summer 1975 in mistake for Slape pitch 2.
Also climbed as Walk On By by T Mitchell, M Dennis, 1981.
The Horizontal Departure variation was climbed by P Thomas, summer 1983.

1978 May 17   **Strapiombo Direct**   W Hurford, D Pycroft (AL), P Williams.
1978 June 5   **The Pump**   R Fawcett, C Gibb
Direct Start: J Silvester, 4.8.84.
1978 June 18   **Runneymede Easy Variations**   M G Mortimer, M G Allen
1978 July 15   **Gross Encounters**   D Roberts, P Williams
So called, because it lies next to The Monster.

1978 July 15   **Pegasus**   P Williams, D Roberts
N Shepherd and party made a serious start, Flying Fish, up the lethal wall below, in autumn 1978.

1978 July 29   **G B H**   G Gibson, D Beetlestone, M Hewitt
'Named after the initials of their surnames. Derek wanted to go third on the second pitch but I refused to let him. It would have ruined the pattern of the name!' (G Gibson)

1978 July 29   **Speeding Fine**   G Gibson, M Hewitt
The leader also recorded a new route, Tank, at Tremadog on the same day. A keen effort.

1978 July 31   **Advert**   A Sharp, S Lewis
1978 July   **Too Hard for Jim Perrin**   P de Mengel, P Thomas
De Mengel and Perrin were both instructing at Plas y Brenin. De Mengel wrote the route up in the log book at the centre, and jokingly wrote 'Too hard for Jim Perrin' against it as part of an ongoing banter the two were engaged in. The route description was then sent in (not by de Mengel) to the CC Journal as Too Hard for Mongols with the grade increased from HVS to E4!

1978 Aug 18   **The Heretic**   J Moran, P Williams
1978 Aug 26   **Black and White, Blink! Don't!**   G Gibson, J Perry
1978 Aug 28   **Famine**   G Gibson, J Perry
1978 Sept   **Stairway to Heaven**   S Cathcart, T Curtis
Stairway Direct was climbed by A Jones, T Carson on 2.6.85

1978 Oct 7   **The Puerile Ticker**   W Hurford, P Williams
The Scoop in Strone Ulladale was supposedly put in Hard Rock by Ken Wilson to stop 'puerile ticking'. The leader had done all the routes – bar one.

1978 Oct 13   **The Quaker**   P Williams, W Hurford
1978 Oct 22   **Corky**   P Williams, W Hurford
Named in honour of the leader's pet parrot!

1978 Oct 22   **Gruel**   P Williams, T Walkington
'The finishing holds were sloping and slimy, and with my gear a bit below, I was too gripped to fall off.'

1978 Oct 22   **The Nubian**   P Williams, T Walkington
1978 Oct   **Ridge Route**   P Martin, Ms F Martin
1979 April 24   **Zimbabwe**   P Williams, D Pycroft
1979 May 12   **Brute 33**   D Roberts, P Williams (AL)
After watching Williams 'thug' round the roof, Roberts pronounced him to be a 33-year old brute, amongst other things. '7a youth! Overhangs the road.' (J M Redhead, after finding the roof a struggle to second in 1981)

1979 May 15	**Misty Wall** L K McGinley, P Williams, M Brett, D Roberts
	For the third man, this was his first time out.
1979 June 17	**Yellow Scoop** K Martin, P G Martin
1979 June 22	**Bon Mot** K Martin, P G Martin, Ms F Martin
	The variation start, Such a Pretty Nose: I A Jones (solo) in 5.95.
1979 June 25	**Golgotha** L K McGinley, P Williams
	During cleaning operations, a huge flake 'soundly' attached to the rock became airborne with surprising ease. It flew down, crashing through the trees to land in a vast cloud of dust on the scree. 'You bastards!' came a cry from below.
1979 June 26	**Lord of the Flies** R Fawcett, C Gibb
	A tremendous pitch which stunned the locals. Filmed on the first ascent for a TV programme. 'Come on arms, do your stuff', the now-famous comment by Ron Fawcett on the first ascent. The climb originally finished on top of an unstable boulder, '…but that night, armed with crowbars, car jacks and brute strength, the expatriate Englishmen proved that the gentle art of trundling is not yet dead. Apparently the boulder made quite a bang, obliterating the path below The Corner, and actually causing one party to fail to reach the start of Spiral Stairs.' (Crags 20, Aug/Sept 1979). 'Christ, it's the size of an asteroid.' (an expatriate Englishman watching the boulder float 45 metres down Right Wall before it exploded on the ledge below). On a significant, subsequent ascent, 'Holy Shit' (Louise Shepherd as she peeped over the edge and saw Graham Livingstone 15 feet from the top seconding her in trainers)
	Soloed by D Thomas, summer 1990, a superb achievement.
1979 June	**Achilles, Hermes** P Wilson and party
1979 June	**Agamemnon** M Walton, P Wilson
	The honours were shared equally during the rapid first phase of development (two days) of the long neglected Esgair Maen Gwyn.
1979 June	**Artemis** G Gibson
1979 June	**Chreon** M Walton and party
1979 June	**Thermopylae, Sparta** G Gibson and party
1979 June	**Xerxes, Troy** J Walker and party
1979 Aug 18	**The Vendetta** M E Crook, M Griffiths
	Made the best of some previously climbed though unrecorded pitches.
1979 Aug 30	**Hindenburg** E Cleasby, R Matheson
	A major cleaning effort was needed. E Cleasby, I Greenwood, climbed pitch 2 on 8.7.79. The route was originally named Superskull. 'Must be at least E5.' 'How do you know, you only got three feet up it?' 'Well you didn't want to lead it.' 'True!' (an exchange from the Plas y Brenin new routes book, 1985)
1979 Sept 9	**Jacob** P Martin, K Martin
1979 Oct	**Quantum Jump** R Fawcett
	An often tried, ferocious route. Originally graded E2 5c, as Fawcett had found it quite easy. 'I couldn't understand why it hadn't been repeated.' (C Gore on the second ascent in 1982). ' … the nemesis of many a "pub-hero".' (P Williams, 1987)
1979	**Pus, Pus in Boots** S Haston, I Johnson
	'Both have claimed several notable scalps.' (S Haston, 1982). The Right-Hand Finish to Pus in Boots was climbed in 1982 by S Haston, L K McGinley. On one occasion, below a packed-out

Grochan, a cliff on which he had climbed all the routes, an incensed Haston shouted up 'You lot. Get off my cliff!' much to the mortification of his partners.

1979	**Pus 4** S Haston
1980 Jan 13	**Precious** R Fawcett

Another powerful route. Done in a spell of freak sunny weather. The belayer, C Thomas, had never met Fawcett until he was asked to hold the ropes. The original way traversed in from Right Wall. The Direct Start (now the described way) was climbed by J M Redhead in 1980: only a few feet of new climbing, but probably the technical crux.
'Precious, the best route on the Cromlech because there's a bolt in it.' (M Pretty, referring to the old bolts left from the MacInnes artificial attempt in the 50s)

1980 April 11   **Atomic Hot Rod**   R Fawcett, P Williams
One of the first three Welsh routes to be given a technical grade of 7a - it still warrants a 6b rating. 'Ron landed on top after an almighty struggle with the roof, involving a long heel-hook out left, all his gear had dropped out save for a MOAC under the roof, and a Friend, which had "walked". He lay on the top gasping for breath. "That's the hardest crack I've done, makes Crimson Cringe look easy", he said. Now I'd heard of Crimson Cringe, and knew that it was 5.12. My mouth suddenly went dry and my hands started sweating – fear; an adrenaline-fix for the climbing junkie. "If you can take in, just a little faster than the speed at which I'm seconding, it would be appreciated".' (P Williams)

1980 April 11   **Hall of Warriors**   R Fawcett, P Williams
'Some strenuous and technical moves lead to an impasse at 80 feet, where upward progress is made by utilising "the dreaded flying leap".'

1980 April 12   **J R**   R Fawcett, P Williams, C Shorter
'It would have eight bolts in it in France, and it would be twice as good.' (M Atkinson, 1985)

1980 April 18   **Ivory Madonna**   R Fawcett, P Williams
'It was a superb day. The sun had come out, beating down on the walls with an almost tropical intensity. The wet streaks running down Lord of the Flies were rapidly drying up. The crux involved an exceptionally fingery 20-foot section to reach the sanctuary of The Corner. We wondered if it was a "Desmond Decker" for a leader to slip off from the last move into it…' A climber fell off this self same move in 1982 and missed the ground by five feet before his swing took him on an airborne inspection of Cemetery Gates. '… good 6a at Pex.' (J Healey, commenting on the crux sequence during the second ascent)

1980 April 19   **Nice Chimney**   P Martin, K Martin
1980 April 19   **True Grip**   R Fawcett, P Williams
On a very cold morning, Fawcett climbed and reversed a shallow ramp three times before he worked out the crux move into Left Wall. Done with freezing fingers and a long way above protection, the route name well reflects the leader's feelings on the first ascent.

1980 May 9   **Sea Panther**   D J Roscoe, B M Roscoe
The reappearance of a familiar face after a long absence.

1980 May 18	**Ghosts, Silent Spring** P Littlejohn, S Lewis
	All in an afternoon's work; Silent Spring was another major addition to a much neglected cliff – a fine finale to a busy day.
1980 May 23	**Venturi Effect** R Fawcett, P Williams
	'It was an extremely windy evening, and on the painfully wide bridging move, the updraft was so fierce that it whistled up our shorts, chilling certain parts of the anatomy that aren't mentioned in polite circles – hence the name.'
1980 June	**Wang** M Boysen, J Brown, D Potts, S Haston
	Put up by a team of 'golden oldies' and a 'young rooster'.
1980 Aug 25	**Cockblock** J M Redhead, C Shorter, K Robertson
	The arête had been fancied for years. A brilliant effort from an inspired climber. 'The misogyny comes from within those who choose to interpret the names to their own offence.' (J M Redhead, On the Edge, 1998) Soloed by P Davidson in 1984. 'You've got to be off your rocker to solo that.' (R Fawcett on hearing the news)
1980	**King Kipper** A Williams
	Re-discovered and named by S Howe, T Birks 11.10.86.
1980	*Y Glocsyn, a prominent erratic boulder behind Pen y Pass, was trundled, apparently by two visiting Americans. This act aroused the anger of conservationists throughout Wales. Despite a £100 reward for information, the culprits were never caught.*
1981 March 26	**The Grim Jim** S Haston, P Williams (AL)
	Direct Start by J M Redhead 27.3.81.
1981 April	**Divertimento** C Shorter, J M Redhead (AL)
1981 April	**The Red Ring** S Haston, L K McGinley (AL)
	Originally climbed as The Grinder by M Boysen, W Birch, J Jordan in 9.66 (VL, HVS & A3). Five poor pegs were used to cross the roof.
	The free ascent was a magnificent achievement. 'Man, it's just the wildest.' (S Haston). 'It was recently reported that the last of the big aid routes in the Pass had fallen to siege tactics by Steve Haston and Leigh McGinley. From its old A2 grade it was to become Grind Her. The name Desecration Crack was also suggested. Eventually both names were discarded in favour of a punk anagram. We are rapidly getting to the stage where naming the routes takes longer than the actual climbing.' (The Climbers' Club Journal 1981)
1981 May 9	**Rolling Stone** P Simkiss, J Pitts
1981 May 9	**The Black Pig** C Shorter, P WIlliams (VL)
1981 May 9	**Wounded Knee** J Pitts, P Simkiss
1981 May 10	**Blackhead** C Shorter, P Williams (VL)
	'Brute force and technique are an advantage.' (P Williams, 1987)
1981 June 1	**Sphagnum** C Jones, W Parker (AL)
1981 June 27	**F B Madonna** J M Redhead, C Shorter
	A desperate start. The original name for the climb was Foreskin Bunk Madonna, which was abbreviated to its current name in the 1987 guidebook.
1981 June 27	**Simulid** W Parker, N Raeside
	The first new route on Clogwyn y Ddysgyl for ten years.

1981   **Llanberis Pass** by **G Milburn**
An updated version of the 1978 guide, which included Fawcett's routes on the walls of the Cromlech and chronicled the success of the 'Free the Pass' campaign. The first Welsh guide to have E-grades in the route descriptions.

1982 April 25   **A New Austerlitz**   G Gibson, N Harvey
A great find which has some of the best climbing on the East Wing.

1982 May 9   **Scarab**   W Parker, S Reid
1982 June 7   **Spaghetti Western**   K Martin, P Martin
The right arête of the Nose, certainly done before.

1982 June   **Sheepslayer**   S Haston, M E Crook
'A pinnacle came right out from the rock with Haston hanging on to it. He belayed, brought up Crook, and together they trundled the rocky spear. It floated down the hillside like an Exocet missile, colliding with an unfortunate sheep'.

1982 June   **Wimpey Pa**   K Martin, P Martin
1982 July 21   **Jupiter**   C Jones, S Reid (VL)
A bold and overlooked quality route.

1982 July 23   **The Scapegoat**   S Reid, W Parker (AL)
1982 Aug 7   **Fear and Loathing**   C Jones, W Parker (AL)
1982 Aug 7   **The Despicable Act**   C Jones, W Parker (1 pt aid)
Aptly named – the first aid to be used on a first ascent in the Pass for many years.
Honour was restored on the first free ascent by M E Crook, A D Newton, S Haston, P Norton on 21.6.83.

1982 Aug 20   **Dill**   W Parker, J Gibson (AL)
1982 Aug   **Spectrological Arête**   S Lewis, R Williams
1982   **Gizzard Puke**   M E Crook, S Haston
1982   **Wardance**   R Potter, B Moon
A similar line, Wet Behind the Ears (HVS), was climbed by H Moss, M Saunders around the same time.

1983 April 30   **Hornets Attack Victor Mature**   P Waters, G Griffiths
Named after a Los Angeles punk band.
The harder version of the route through the overhangs was climbed by G Gibson, A Popp on 21.6.83, who thought it was a new route, which they called Slab and Arête.
A similar line, White Lightning (4 pts aid) had been done by D Keeling, B Moore, M Carter in autumn 1970.

1983 June 5   **Rootorooni**   M Lynden, J Silvester (AL)
1983 June 16   **Reid's Route**   S Reid, S Martin
1983 June 21   **What a Jump, Hit the Basement**   C J Phillips (solo)
What a Jump had mostly been climbed before.

1983 June 30   **Silent Thunder**   S M Cathcart, P Waters
A surprising find.

1983 July 4   **Twisted Sister**   M E Crook, D Towse
1983 July 10   **Gorty's Triangle, Stalling Out**   S M Cathcart, D Gale
Together with Silent Thunder, these completed a trio of excellent routes on a small but impressive buttress.

1983 July   **China Girl**   Ms E Masson, P Gomersall (AL)
1983 Aug 8   **New Era, Steel Appeal**   S M Cathcart, D Hale
Three bolts were placed. A rather wretched event in the development of the Pass.

1983 Aug 13	**Hooded Crow** A Sharp, J Harwood

A typo in the last guide had the first pitch of this route in at 5a, which would have been a real shock to any HVS leader as the pitch is hard even for the grade now given.

1983 Aug 19	**Cunning Stunts** P Gomersall, Ms E Masson
1983 Aug 29	**Sidewinder** J Brown, C E Davies, P Nunn

Joe's first route in the Pass for over a decade.

1983 Nov 17	**Dracula Spectacula** A Brown (solo)
1984 May 9	**Sacred Idol** M E Crook, P Norton

Originally climbed as Pi by T Panther, R Stephens in 8.66 (VS & A3) and the Direct Finish by T Panther, N Bradburn (AL) in 8.76 (VS & A2). Both were transformed into a fine free climb.

1984 May	**Little Groover** R Fawcett (solo)

Probably done before.

1984 June 16	**Demi Sec Dame** J Silvester, M Lynden
1984 June 17	**Spitting Image** F A P Trower, K Toms

Originally named Splitting Image.

1984 June 23	**Zyklon 'B'** J Moran, J Sonczak

A fearsome roof problem.

1984 June 23	**Sombrero Fallout** M E Crook, A D Newton
1984 June	**Thumbling with My Wicklows** A Williams (solo)
1984 July 3	**Felony** H Stuart, W McKee, C Guest

Finished direct (a grade harder) by J Dawes in 8.85.

1984 Aug 19	**Hexagonal Phase, Bad Moon Risin'** A Sharp, J Harwood

A fine double on a neglected crag.

1984 Oct	**Featherlight, Barnstormer, Left-Hand Crack, New Form, Right-Hand Crack, Unison** W Todd, Ms S Clark

All of these were probably climbed before.

1985 March 10	**The Three Cliffs** M E Crook, C J Phillips
1985 March	**Tom's Plums, Bell Fruit** J M Redhead, M E Crook, A D Newton
1985 April 26	**Overhanging Deckchair** W Todd, B Evans
1985 April	**Telegram Sam** R Griffiths, M Roberts
1985 May 2	**Mabinogion** W Todd, J Silvester

A classy little problem.

1985 May 3	**Masochist's Mambo** W Todd, J Silvester
1985 May 3	**Tombstone Wall** J Silvester (solo)
1985 June 20	**Shadow of Youth** R Wood, L Hardy

'A very good route on a small buttress that had been climbed on for over 60 years.'

1985 June 20	**The Boys of Summer** R Drury, P Thomas, M Thomas

A bold and technical micro-route by a team of young hotshots.

1985 June	**Dried Voices** J M Redhead, R Drury

'A couple of small wires were placed from Cockblock to protect the initial section.'

1985 June	**Stumpy the Dragonslayer** S Quentin, N Craine
1985 July 1	**Long Kesh** S Boydon, S Cardy

A brilliant and major discovery; one of the most exposed routes in the Pass.

1985 July 7	**Ryley Bosvil** J M Redhead

Still one of the hardest technical problems in the Pass taking several days to accomplish. Flashed on-sight by N Dixon. 'The rock in Wales doesn't lend itself to any technical move harder than 5c.' (P Mitchell, c.1979). 'A classic product of the 80s, and a

> 'Stickman's' delight.' (P Williams. Llanberis, 1987). 'I've always been on the edge of the Llanberis scene, always played to my own perimeters.' (J M Redhead, 1998)

1985 July 19	**Body Rock** R Drury	

Once the ultimate in 'one move wonders'.

1985 Sept	**Drury's Drama** J Dawes, R Drury (both solo)
1986 May 30	**Slab and Groove** (Craig Ddu) A Legg, A Milburn (AL)
1986 June 5	**Pretty Girls Make Graves** C Smith, I Jones

This hidden gem provided a fearsome fight and pointed the way for future development in the Cwm Glas Bach area.

1986 June 18	**Rumblefish** C Smith

A 'lonely and vicious' lead, very technical and serious – a long-outstanding problem solved at last.

1986 June 21	**Grand** N Dixon

Dismissed by some as 'impossible', this was a fine achievement but slightly tarnished by the placing of an in-situ wire – an unsavoury ethic on so traditional a crag.

1986 June 25	**Marlene on the Wall** T Hodgson, J Dawes

A long-standing problem solved on sight.

1986 June 25	**The Nectarine Run** J De Montjoye, Ms H Sharp

One of the classic hard Llanberis routes.

1986 Aug 6	**Awesome** N Dixon, J Dawes

A RURP was pre-placed for the ascent.

1986 Sept 10	**Melancholony** N Dixon, S Britain

The second really hard route to be added to the Cwm Glas Bach crags.

1986 Sept 11	**Spanking for Beginners** A Popp, S Britain
1986 Sept 11	**The Dolemen** S Britain, A Popp
1986 Sept 29	**Felix the Crack** M E Crook, A D Newton
1986 Oct 4	**Killerkranky** M E Crook, N Thomas

Done on a tip-off from Paul Williams, this route triggered a new wave of interest which was to transform Scimitar Ridge into a major crag for hard climbing.

1986 Oct 11	**Never a Dull Moment** S Howe, T Birks
1986 Oct 13	**P F Putrid** C J Phillips, N Thomas
1986 Oct 13	**Watts the Crack?** M E Crook, N Thomas, C J Phillips
1987 Feb 17	**Eggmeat Arête** P Pritchard (solo)
1987 Feb 21	**Pork Trout** N Harms (solo)
1987 Feb 24	**Ringsnack** N Harms, P Pritchard
1987 Feb 28	**Milk Cow** P Pritchard, N Harms
1987 April 21	**Sheepcat** P Pritchard
1987 April 23	**Animal Locomotion** P Pritchard, N Harms

The above few routes set a trend for micro-development.

1987 April 24	**Birdseye** P Pritchard (solo)
1987 April 24	**Language, Truth, and Logic** T Hodgson, M Wragg
1987 April 25	**The Mild Very Hard Hand Jam Crack, Yr Hwntw Bach** E Jones, I A Jones
1987 April 26	**Jargon Speaker Creature** G Smith, P Hawkins

Paul Williams in full flow.

1987 April 27	**Satsumo Wrestler** J Dawes, A Popp
1987 April 28	**Black Mike** P Harrison, M Snell
1987 April 29	**Black Letter Day** P Harrison, M Snell
1987 April 29	**The Bog of the Eternal Stench** P Pritchard

1987 April	**Espasmos** I A Jones, R Griffiths
	The variation start Crook's Direct: M E Crook (solo) in 1987.
1987 April	**Return to Melancholony** N Dixon, J Dawes
1987 April	**Ribble Wobble** A Popp (solo)
1987 April	**Rim with a View** J Dawes, N Dixon
1987 May 19	**The Bat Passage** F Hall, A George
1987 May 20	**God Help the Sailors on a Night Like This!** A Popp, P Pritchard
1987 May 20	**Truncheon Meat** P Pritchard
1987 May 20	**You're Not in Poland Now** P Pritchard
1987 May 22	**Fear of Infection** G Smith, D O'Dowd
	A classic off-width crack. One early attempt at a repeat was made without the use of six-inch Tubes or Titons, instead some bits of '2 by 4' were sawn up into shape and 'larks-footed' with slings.
1987 May 24	**Hat Shoe, Boot Coat, Aesthete's Foot, Quantum Dump, Surprisingly Goute** J Dawes (solo)
1987 May 24	**Tufty Club Rebellion** A Popp, M McGowan
	'I climbed carefully and reversed several times – there is something intimidating about these routes, because the steep fall away of the gully, climbing leftwards and up for 20 feet puts you 50 feet above the ground; a sudden shock when you glance down.' (G Huxter, On the Edge, 2001)
1987 May 26	**El Guide** A George, I A Jones
	In memory of local activist John Pitts.
1987 May 26	**Libel, Smears and Slander** P Barbier, N Harms
	Climbed direct by G Hughes, A Popp, 1988.
1987 May 27	**Surgical Lust** P Pritchard, I Jones
	Due to its overhanging nature, much of the route was cleaned and brushed on lead.
1987 May	**Chopping Block** S Long, P Hawkins, M Raine
1987 May	**Hogia Tyn'Llan, Er Cof, Iachad** I A Jones, E Roberts
1987 May	**Mini Ha Ha** J Dawes (solo)
1987 May	**Play Safe, Be First** P Hawkins, M Raine, S Long
1987 May	**Rim at the Top** A Popp (solo)
1987 May	**Rimsky-Korsakov** J Dawes
1987 May	**Rumblecock** P Hawkins, I A Jones
1987 May	**Wagner's Ring** J Dawes, A Popp
1987 June 16	**Kitten versus Pig** A Popp, C Waddy
1987 June 16	**The Bells, The Bells, The Bells** C Waddy, A Popp
1987 June 18	**King Wad** P Pritchard
	'As physically hard as Indecent Exposure.' (J Dawes). 'Tim said I had to do King Wad – "there's this huge move, a complete dyno up the arête, but", he said (and I completely missed this), "you don't really have to do that".' (G Huxter, 2001)
1987 June	**Friday Night Beaver** A Wells, R Lyon
1987 June	**My Mum's Slabby Arête** P Pritchard (solo)
1987 June	**Romany Soup** C Waddy, A Popp
	A similar line, Hot Worm, was climbed by A Hughes on 23.4.91. The description 'One of the more amenable hard routes – good, varied and sustained.' was a bit of a sandbag.
1987 June	**The Moose's Toothpaste** M Thomas (solo)
1987 June	**The Stain** T Thomas, F Hall
1987 June	**Weasels Rip My Flesh** S Howe, I A Jones
	A Frank Zappa Album.

1987 July 4	**Fred** A Wells, G Turner
1987 July 6	**What a Difference a Day Makes** S Howe, I A Jones

A local activist once ascended a route after a 24-hour yo-yo.

1987 July 16	**Lasagne Verdi** P Pritchard, N Dixon
1987 July 16	**Melon Transplant** N Dixon, P Pritchard
1987 July	**Unleashing the Wild Physique** D Holmes
1987 Aug 16	**Mutiny on the Mouse Organ** A Popp, C Waddy
1987 Aug 17	**Buoux in a Tin (Without a Tin-opener)** P Pritchard (solo)

*Saussuave, the Direct Start: soloed by J Dawes on the second
ascent on 17.8.87.*

1987 Aug 17	**Health and Efficiency** J Dawes (solo)

*Claimed as Dragon the Stumpie Slayer by P Johnstone and party
22.5.88.*

1987 Aug 17	**The 39 Slaps** J Dawes

Climbed peg to peg and then 'redpointed' on the first ascent.

1987 Aug 29	**The Revenge** C Devonshire, G Pearce
1987 Aug	**Nick's Sexual Problem** N Dixon (solo)
1987 Aug	**The Kicker Conspiracy** C Waddy, S Chesslett
1987 Oct 4	**Beavering in Obscurity** I A Jones, S Howe
1987	**The Fun before the Storm** S Andrews (solo)
1987	**The Real Scoop** A Shepherd and party
1987	**Plato's Cave** H Drasdo, D Boston (1 pt aid)

*Supersedes Promises, Promises (which made a long rightward
traverse below the cave to finish up Pastoral), climbed by
H Drasdo, Ms A Cornwall on 1.10.72.*

c.1987	**Cornel Celyn** D Lampard or J Brown

Neither remembers their date of ascent!

1987   **Llanberis** by **P Williams**

*What started out as an update of Milburn's 1981 book turned into
a massive undertaking with the inclusion of Slate, which was the
subject of major developments. Williams also made a point of
researching and describing many of the earlier routes that had
been left out of previous guidebooks. The net result was an
additional 475 climbs, an increase of 90% on the previous edition.
'A few weeks after Llanberis was published, a letter dropped
through the door of my cottage signed "From the author of the
First Bumper Fun Book to the author of the second…".'
(P Williams, 1993)*

1988 April 10	**Beasts of the Field** S Howe, D Blenkinsop
1988 April 14	**Noah's Ark** S Howe, P Hawkins
1988 April 18	**Over the Beach** S Howe, G Hughes
1988 April 26	**Stuff the Stoat** D Lampard, R Lampard, I A Jones
1988 April	**Pererindod** I A Jones, T Mitchell

*The name means 'wanderings'. They also climbed Lleu Llanber, 'a
poor Hard Severe line in the same vicinity'. The details have been
lost – by the author!*

1988 May 12	**Flicker of Hope** P Littlejohn, J de Montjoye
1988 May 13	**Hairway to Steven** I A Jones, E Roberts
1988 May 14	**Chunder's Revenge** I A Jones, T Mitchell
1988 May 14	**Sheik Yerbooties** I A Jones T Mitchell

*A similar line was previously climbed by J Brown, C E Davies
c.1986 but not recorded.*

1988 May 16	**Rembrandt Pussy Horse**	G Hughes, A Wells, A Amos
1988 May 25	**Nappy Brown and the Red Hot Pokers**	P Hawkins

Climbed with the Direct Start by P A Targett, C Davies as Maxines at the Bistro, 21.2.90.

1988 May	**Belv-Eddie-Ere?**	I A Jones, G Griffiths
1988 June 1	**Fists of Fury**	P Jenkinson, E Stone

Possibly climbed in the 50s.

1988 June 1	**Rediscovered**	N Dixon, E Stone, P Jenkinson (all solo)
1988 June 9	**Alchemy**	P Littlejohn, J de Montjoye

One of the best lines in the Pass.

1988 June 9	**Big Brother is Belaying Me!**	D Hawkins

Big Brother, Perry, made the second ascent straight after. Also rope-soloed around this time by N Dixon as The Old Lemon Squeezer Strikes Back.

1988 June 10	**Accept for Access**	W McKee (solo)
1988 June 22	**Outspan**	A George, P George
1988 June 24	**Crack and Slab** (Twll Tin)	P Johnstone, P Jenkinson
1988 June 24	**The Damp Squib**	P Jenkinson
1988 June 24	**Whiplash Smile**	S Howe, P Baxter
1988 June 30	**Red Giant**	S Howe, P Baxter
1988 July 1	**Times Laughin' Stocks**	P Jenkinson (solo)
1988 July 18	**Eager Submission, Doleful**	S Howe, P Baxter
1988 Aug 8	**Alex in Wonderland**	P George, A Krolick
1988 Aug 8	**Buck and the Noise Boys**	I A Jones, A George
1988 Aug 8	**Clingstone**	A George, P George, I A Jones, S Andrews, A Krolick
1988 Sept 5	**King of Rumpy**	A Popp (solo)
1988 Sept	**Vlad the Arête**	N Dixon, A Brown

Very short! Very powerful! Very technical!

1988 Oct 21	**Bang Utot**	A Leech, C Vegoda
1988 Oct 22	**Corridors of Power**	D Atchison-Jones, Ms F Butler

Little original climbing, but another way of enjoying the left arête of Cenotaph Corner. 'Cenotaph Corner, Corridors of Power, Left Wall, Right Wall and Cemetery Gates are the classics and are brilliant routes. There are plenty of routes filling in the gaps. The experience of soloing any of these routes in the corner is unforgettable and thrilling and I can fully recommend it.'
(D Atchison-Jones, The Crag Guide to England and Wales, 1989)

1988 Oct	**Queer**	M E Crook

A strange route.

1988	**Bunghole Buster**	D Holmes, M E Crook
1988	**Famous Grouse**	M E Crook, J Tombs
1988	**Into the Groove**	G Smith
1988	**'Sgwd'**	I A Jones, E Roberts
1988	**Y Gornel**	I A Jones, R Wightman
1989 Jan 1	**Honking by the Pool**	M Turner, R Rust

The team had just left a party at Joe Brown's house, where a local climber was sprawled across a picnic table vomiting into the ornamental fish pond.

1989 May 21	**Cyfrifiadurwyr**	J Brown, C E Davies

Rediscovered and named by I A Jones, K W Robertson on 7.8.90.

1989 May 27	**Far from the Madding Throng**	J Brown C E Davies

Arête variation by I A Jones.

1989 May 27	**Scroll** P Greening (solo)
	Certainly done before but not recorded.
1989 May 28	**Tafod y Gors, Thema, Beta** J Brown, C E Davies
	The first route name means Tongue of the Marsh, i.e. Butterwort, but was originally called Gamma.
1989 May 29	**Back to Trivia** N Dixon
	The name refers to the fact that Dixon had climbed the very hard and bold route, Face Mecca, on Cloggy the day before.
1989 June 17	**The Smodge** D Lampard, A George (AL), I A Jones
	Pitch 2 previously climbed by L K McGinley in the same year. 'Dai and Al told me not to go up to the right and to try the arête direct. I couldn't and gave the ropes to Al; he then tried, failed and went up exactly where I was going to go!' (I A Jones)
1989 June 18	**Slab and Groove** (Craig Cwm Glas Bach)**, Runner Up, Pan Alley** J Brown, C E Davies
1989 June 18	**The Edge of Time** D Lampard et al
	Pitches 1 – 3 D Lampard, N Bonnett (AL), D Gleeson, climbed on 10.6.89. Pitch 4 by D Lampard, A George, B Brewer, 18.6.89. All the pitches were led on sight, to produce a big, bold expedition, with some mind-blowing situations. 'I climbed Edge of Time with Mick Pointon last year and there has been a hold chipped/improved substantially on pitch 4. There were certainly no runner placements on the top arête until you reached the traverse on Overhanging Arête. I am sure you can draw your own conclusions, but don't equate any "excessive cleaning" with our ascent. On a lighter note, on the first ascent Bob Brewer climbed the route clad only in a pair of shorts and two carrier bags that we had for our sandwiches. He hadn't heeded our warning that the crag did get very cold!' (D Lampard, 2002)
1989 June 24	**Toots Direction** S Holmes, P Knight
1989 June	**Ecover** D Green, I A Jones, F Hall
1989 June	**The House of God** P Pritchard
	Named by G Farquahar who thought it to be new, during an abortive attempt on what was to become Nightmayer, a line that Pritchard also tried.
1989 June	**Indoor Bowling Here I Come!** M E Crook, J Irvine
1989 June	**Mr Stiff** D Lampard, A George
1989 June	**The Stebbing, The Booze Brothers** I A Jones, T Mitchell
	The first name is an Essex village, and also, 'the erection you cannot conceal because you are not wearing a jacket or jumper' according to the Meaning of Lif.
1989 July 13	**Perplexus** D Lampard, M Turner
	The fourth visit by Lampard, when all five pitches were climbed. Pitch 1 by I A Jones, D Lampard, A George, in 6.89. Pitch 2 by D Lampard, I A Jones, A George. Pitch 3: D Lampard, D Green. A worthy companion to The Red Ring.
1989 July	**Y Lon Wen** I A Jones, F Hall
	The White Road or Shining Path.
1989 Aug 4	**Owain's Arête** O Jones
	The result of weeks of effort. If the small wire is not in situ the route is probably E7, a long reach will also make the route feel easier. '… is the largest feature among the craglets and arêtes above Carreg Wastad.' (On the Edge, 1996, sic)

1989 Aug 7	**Tess of the d'Urbevilles** P Jenkinson

1989 Aug 7 **Tess of the d'Urbevilles**   P Jenkinson
The first true ascent, accompanied by numerous supporters, witnesses, hecklers, and loafers.
A route with an infamous and controversial past. It was originally claimed by D Atchison-Jones, G Mclelland on 29.7.81. According to eye witnesses (closely questioned by the guidebook writer at the time) 'the first ascensionists did not follow the line which they subsequently recorded…' although the description was included in the 1987 guide with a suitable warning. 'There are over a dozen fine extremes here, plus one V Diff … and …Tess….' (both P Williams, Llanberis, 1987)

1989 Aug 7 **The Bastard Practice**   A Wainwright
After top-rope inspection. Rather fiercely cleaned in the mid 80s, the line was protected by three pegs and a glued bolt sheath – the latter was not used during the ascent.

1989 Aug 20 **Bog-trotting**   P Reilly
1989 Aug 20 **Grochanspiel**   M E Crook
1989 Aug 20 **The Yuppification of Deiniolen**   D Holmes
You have to walk along the village's main street on a sunny afternoon to really appreciate the problem. Filofaxes are 'neither use nor ornament' here; but a stiff gin and tonic may help calm the nerves, after an ascent.

1989 Aug 30 **The Glass Flipper**   I A Jones, T Mitchell
1989 Sept 30 **Skidmaster**   T Mitchell, I A Jones
1989 Oct 1 **Crampon Route**   G Steele, R N H McMillan
1989 Nov 19 **Slipstone Slab**   A Green, B Preston
1989 Dec 10 **Berlin Philharmonic**   S Davies, C Davies
1989 Dec 10 **Codswallop Flobalobalobalob**   C Davies, S Davies
The above two routes had been climbed before on several occasions.

1989 Dec **The Berlin Wall**   C Davies, M Wells, S Davies
1989 **El Guide Direct**   A Popp, G Hughes
1989 **Tales from the Riverbank**   D Lampard, A George (AL)
A major new route climbed on sight.

1990 Feb 21 **Four Horsemen of the Apocalypse**   P A Targett, C Davies
Possibly done earlier.

1990 Feb 22 **Too Late to Hesitate**   C Davies, P A Targett
1990 April 1 **Loves-a-Scent**   A Brown, P Jefferson
1990 April 4 **Cinderella Penguin**   I A Jones, P Logan, T Glynne
1990 April 27 **Anturiaethau Dic Preifat**   I A Jones, A George (AL)
1990 April 27 **The Wrath of Grapes**   A George, I A Jones (AL)
1990 April **Al Fresco**   E Stone, M Turner
Climbed on sight.

1990 May 23 **Zimmer Frame-up, Chilli Willie and the Red Hot Peppers**   I A Jones, J Green
1990 May **Punk Puffins on Rock**   M Turner, C Goodey
1990 Aug 7 **The Roc-Nest Monster**   E Stone, G McMahon, D Goodey
Cleaned and equipped by G Hughes in 1988.

1990 **B Series, Master Blaster**   I A Jones, T Mitchell
1990 **Drain Surgeon, Pooper Scooper**   T Mitchell, I A Jones
1990 **Piggy's Arête**   O Jones, P Reilly
1990 **Skid Pan**   J Brown, C Davies
1991 April 27 **Samson Too**   C Davies, G Davies, C Jex
1991 July 4 **My Best Friend**   P Baxter, M Neil

1991 July	**Back in the Fold, Peter Panic, Buhlermaniac, Strap Me to a Nubile, The Gas Man Cometh, Zirhalee, New Model Arm** I A Jones (solo)
	Back in the Fold may have been done before.
1991 Sept 5	**Celynen** I A Jones, B Hughes
1991 Sept 8	**A Touch of Class** R Newcombe, C Becker
	A classy find, surprisingly overlooked by the previous generation.
1991 Sept 12	**Vampire Butterfly, Allegrophobia** I A Jones, B Hughes, C Cartwright
	The leader had written off two Allegros in 12 months.
1991 Sept 13	**Bjorn Again** I A Jones, C Cartwright, B Hughes
1991	**Aratnerphobia** I A Jones, I McNeill
	Commemorates G Ratner's 'crap jewellery' remark.
	The variation Substance: T Shelmerdine, N Clacher in 1997.
1991	**No More Queensway Sales** A Hughes (solo)
1991	**Of Mice and Men** R Wightman, J Harrison, I A Jones
1991	**Penal Colony** A Hughes, O Jones
1991	**Second Wind** M Turner, R Wills
1991	**Stand Prow'd** O Jones
1991	**The Wrath of Grapes II, Raging Thesaurus** I A Jones, J Green
	Obviously the grapes were working their wrath to full effect on someone's brain cells as the name had been used a year before.
	The second route name describes Neil Kinnock in full flow.
1991	**Llysiau'r Gwlith** I A Jones, R Wightman
1992 April 20	**Sound as a Trout** P A Targett (solo)
	Previously inspected on abseil.
1992 May 5	**Outside Left** J Brown, C E Davies
1992 May	**Freefallin'** I Lloyd-Jones, C Stephenson
1992 June 10	**The Trumpet Blowers** A Wainwright
	Outstandingly bold and technical. George Smith generously gave Adam some pegs to protect the crux of the route, but only one at a time. It took five visits of slogging up the heathery flanks of the Pass and tedious abbing down before Adam could climb the route.
1992 June 16	**Nightmayer** S Mayers, G Lovick
	Top-roped prior to the ascent. Several accomplished climbers who were put off by the technical, strenuous, and committing run-out up the final headwall had previously looked at the line of the biggest plum left in the Pass.
1992 June 23	**Satsuma Special** P A Targett, C Greatwich
1992 June 26	**Outside Right** J Brown, C E Davies
1992 June	**Lore and Hors d'œuvre** I A Jones, D Ferguson
1992 June	**Overlord** S Mayers
	A much fancied and improbable-looking arête.
1992 June	**The Bed of Nails** I A Jones, R Wightman
	A local activist was once kept out of his home by a wife who had nailed the front door shut – he was, however, as 'Drunk as a Skunk' and very late back from the pub.
1992 July 31	**The Green Beam** P A Targett, C Davies
1992 July	**Ring Ouzel 2** G Smith, M Thomas
1992 Aug 1	**The Play-away Flake** I Lloyd-Jones (solo)
1992 Aug 5	**Melondrama** N Dixon, T Dixon, C Dixon
	The ascent was a family affair.
1992 Sept	**Autumn Acorns** P A Targett

1992 **Freudian Slits, The Amazing** C Davies, B Davies
Unfortunately the compilers of the guide could not decipher the full name for The Amazing as entered in the new routes book!

1993 May **Raiders of the Lost Sac** M Crook, G Smith

1993 June 3 **Beginner's Mind** N Dixon, D Crilley
According to one website, this route did not make it in to the last guidebook, yet the website praised its index. Perhaps they should have looked at the index.

1993 June 6 **Catflea Massacre** S Wood, I A Jones

1993 July 14 **God Told Me to Do It** G Farquhar, S Cameron
Named following a tip off from a local activist.

1993 July 27 **Ring My Bell** A Popp, N Dixon

1993 July 28 **6B Melonoma** N Dixon

1993 August 28 **Cut Back Crack, Going over the Falls, Totally Tubular**
I A Jones, P Croxford, G Sutherland, N Horwood, T Poltronetti, S Egerton, A J Stephenson, K Looker (various combinations)

1993 August 28 **Salem's Slab** I A Jones, G Sutherland

1993 Sept 4 **Bryn Rhedyn** N Dixon, A Popp

1993 **99 Flake** A Wainwright

1993 **Llanberis Pass** by **P Williams** and **I A Jones**
Slate was now the subject of a guidebook on its own. This loss was partly compensated for by the major developments that had taken place in Cwm Glas Bach, and Williams enlisted this area's most prolific pioneer to co-author the guide.

1994 April 27 **School's Out** I A Jones, R Wightman

1994 May 19 **The Leurve Shack** D Ferguson, I A Jones

1994 May **Someone's Pinched My Winkles** D Ferguson, A Ekins

1994 June 11 **Animal House Blues, The Locum Agency** D Lampard, P Jenkinson

1994 June 11 **Sâm Tan and the Pet Man** P Jenkinson, D Lampard

1994 June 28 **Pokey Little Puppy** J Dawes, R Patteson, M Hundleby

1994 June 29 **Lime Street** N Clacher, C Stephenson

1994 June 30 **Grin's Twins** N Gresham

1994 July 1 **Sunday School Outing** D Lampard, I MacNeill
The completion of a climb that had been started on the previous day. Pitch 2 had been climbed by D Lampard, A George in 1989, and was described in the 1993 guide with an inferior line. 'The rotting peg runners on pitch 3 had been placed on an earlier attempt by another party and are not necessary as other good protection exists, but we still used them!' (D Lampard)

1994 July 17 **Basking, Revision** D Ferguson, I A Jones

1994 July 17 **Tiny Is as Tiny Do, Central Scrutinizer, Nunatak**
I A Jones, D Ferguson

1994 July 18 **Elmer** I A Jones, J Green

1994 July 18 **Henri the Fiat, Hambon, Huw Pobdim, Hell Hull**
J Green, I A Jones

1994 July 19 **Profound Lichen** I A Jones, J Green

1994 July 21 **The Gorse Course** D Ferguson, B Wright

1994 July 25 **Ugly Girls Make Slaves** D Ferguson, B Wright
Named following a particularly drunken night in the Heights, which the leader rightly lived to regret.

1994 July	**Heinous Hone** M Crook
	Not yet flashed, but very nearly soloed by Johnny Dawes during one epic ascent.
1994 Aug 8	**No Fixed Abode, First of the Ninth** J Tombs, D Holmes
1994 Aug 8	**Strangling the Turtle** D Holmes, J Tombs
1994 Aug 19	**California Raisins** P A Targett, B Davies
1994	**Are You Having It about the Mammoths** G Smith, N Craine
1994	**Mr Kipling's Groove** M Crook
1994	**Some Routes Are Smaller than Others** A Wainwright
1995 May	**Little Foos** G Smith, P Pritchard, C Bull
1995 June 28	**Pocketful of Kryptonite** M Turner, L Thomas
1995 June	**Nos-mo-king, Easy Rhaeadr** J Harrison, M Smith (both led)
1995 Aug 2	**Jem** O Jones
1995 Aug 20	**Microtrauma, Ethel the Aardvark Goes Quantity Surveying** R Mirfin, W Watkins
1995 Aug 21	**Dinas in the Dog** T Dilger, M Forrest (AL), Z Leppert
1995 Aug 23	**Melons Rip My Flesh, Kermit** R Mirfin, T Emmett
1995 Aug 23	**Stanage Comes to Llanberis** T Emmett, R Mirfin
1995 Aug	**Rock Oil, The Famine Road** J Harrison, D Middleton
1995 Sept	**Havago** O Jones, E Hill, M Gronow
1996 March 7	**The Laughing Buddah** A Wainwright, A Walker
1996 March 10	**Gram -ve** T Emmett
	A fine start to a number of new routes in the area; setting the tone of what was to come.
1996 June 22	**Black Power** P Pritchard, S Smith
1996 July 19	**Persons Unknown** A Wainwright, Z Leppert, P Pritchard
	An unknown party had sieged the line over 3 or 4 days using four points of aid, and trundling a monstrous block in the process.
1996 July 25	**'Totally Wired 9'** T Emmett
1996 Aug 5	**Vital Balance** T Keep, J Bertalot
1997 Feb 3	**Wind in the Hollows** J Stephenson, J Playdell
1997 May 1	**Polling** D Ferguson, I A Jones
1997 May 1	**Up Your Hacienda Jimmy, Election Flight** I A Jones, D Ferguson
1997 May 25	**Elegant Inevitability** T Keep, S MacCartney
1997 June 15	**Grave Diggers** N Gresham, P Hammond (both led)
	All gear placed on lead, top-roped first. 'Big-Air potential.'
1997 June 16	**Down on My Knee** T Emmett, L Houlding
	All gear placed on lead, top-roped first. Tim's first lead in 1997 after a rather unfortunate accident.
1997 June 16	**The Cushion** L Houlding
1997 July 9	**Two Dogs** T Shelmerdine
1997 July 10	**Rupert's Rib** J Stephenson, T Badcock
1997 July 11	**Grazer** T Shelmerdine
1997 July	**That's Life** M Jones
1997 Aug 25	**Mas Gato Negro** P Pritchard, A Gridley, S Smith
1997 Sept	**Dead Presidents** M Crook, J Tombs
1997	**A Break from the Norm** N Clacher, T Shelmerdine
1997	**Ari Lichenas** R Hughes, T Shelmerdine
1997	**La Hain, Get a Grip** T Shelmerdine
1997	**Spice of Life** T Shelmerdine, N Clacher, S Goodey.
1997	**Sugar and Spice** T Shelmerdine, N Clacher
1997	**The Grassy Knoll** R Hughes, G Loveridge

1997	**Whoooh!** T Shelmerdine, R Hughes
1998 March 28	**Agua Caliente** M Katz
	'Top-roped first, listed gear preplaced on first ascent.'
1998 May 22	**Poket-Lips Now** T Neill, N Bullock
1998 June 22	**A Sweet Encounter** L Houlding
	Top-roped prior to lead, first protection on the first ascent placed at 11 metres.
1998	**Basil's Baby** D Lampard, I A Jones
1998	**A Pointy Reckoning** M Katz
1999 May 14	**Llwch** E Jones, I A Jones (AL)
	A surprisingly clean and dry line considering its location.
1999 June	**The Dark Side** C Klemmow
1999 June	**Trauma** L Houlding
	The crack was originally pegged by Adam Wainwright. 'Leo top-roped it prior to his first ascent. On an early attempt Leo snapped the peg while only resting on it, falling 40 feet to the slab below. His next attempts had him failing to reach the top groove and taking four long falls onto a Rock 2. Returning the next day with Noel, Leo sent it first go.' (M Reeves, who must have been a rather traumatised belayer on that first day)
1999 July	**Soupa Mario** P Hawkins, C Parkin
1999	**Ghost Dog** M Crook, Ms K Troy Davies
2000 June 18	**Eden** D Green, I A Jones, D Lampard
2000 June 18	**Rubble and Strife** I A Jones, D Lampard
2000	**The Silver Backed Gorilla** M Crook, K T Davies
2000	**Willy Two Goes** W Perrin
2001 July 3	**Summer Groove** M Jones, L Kathenes
	May have been done before.
2001 July 7	**Wyatt Earp** M Katz
2001 July	**Wholly Mammoth** I A Jones, D Powell
2001 Aug	**Barry Bush** P Robins, E Parry
2001 Aug	**One Inch Punch** P Hammond
	Pitch 1 had been climbed by D Lampard, I A Jones c.1995. They tried pitch 2 but soon backed off.
2001	**My Favourite Route in the World, Ever** P Hammond
2002 April 23	**Overhanging Buttress** P Littlejohn, T Jepson
2002 Spring	**Dinas Bach Crack** N Dixon
2002 July 7	**Byd Bach, Caseg Fraith, Roam if You Want To, Roam around the World, Without Wings, Without Wheels** I A Jones (solo)
2002 July 13	**Niche, Over the Edge, The Good Book** D Lampard, I A Jones
	Jones was thwarted on a lead of Over the Edge owing to devious misinformation and a lack of climbing strength.
2002 July 13	**Scoopy Doo** I A Jones, D Lampard
2002 July 15	**Hidden Treasure** S Crowe, Ms K Magog
2002 July 17	**Heilyn** I A Jones, M Richards
2002 July 17	**Mia** M Richards, I A Jones
2002 July 18	**Repellant** M Hedge, G Logan (both led)
2002 July 24	**Spiritwalker** M Hedge, A Richards
2002 July 25	**Days of Speed** M Hedge
2002 July 26	**Big Ben, Candice Marie** D Carroll, S Dutchman
	Candice Marie may have been climbed before.
2002 July 27	**Gochell** D Lampard, I A Jones (AL)

2002 July 27	**Warlock** D Lampard, I A Jones
2002 July 27	**Cae Perthi** I A Jones, D Lampard
2002 July 27	**The Uphill Gardener** M Hedge
2002 July 28	**Kick Back, Clinical Ground** D Lampard, R Kay
2002 July 28	**Lazy Ray's** R Kay, D Lampard
2002 July	**The Rib Route** D Lampard, D Green (both solo)
2002 July	**The Worst Route I've Ever Done** D Lampard, D Green

'Probably the worst route I've ever done in my life. I honestly thought that the top overhang was going to come off with me on it.'

2002 July	**Rogue Trooper** M Crook, Ms K Troy Davies
2002 Aug 3	**Triple Treat** I A Jones (solo)

All lines were climbed.

2002 Aug 5	**Esgairgeiliog** I A Jones, C Powell
2002 Aug 10	**Cwm Glas, Esgeiriau, Mur Mawr, Cadlas, Coed Gwydir, Chwarae Poced, Yr Hollt** I A Jones, C Powell

However, this area has been climbed on for many years, one route having been done over 30 years ago; perhaps some of the variations were new.

2002 Aug 13	**Triple A** I A Jones (solo)

Pitch 1 had been climbed by I A Jones, D lampard on 13.7.02.

2002 Aug 16	**Field of Molten Flowers** I A Jones (solo)
2002 Aug 17	**Gully Slab** D Lampard, I A Jones
2002 Aug 17	**Bad Altitude** I A Jones, D Lampard (AL)
2002 Aug 25	**Still Smiling** D Carroll, D Viggers, A Saxby
2002 Sept 1	**The Golden Pillar of Cwm Hetiau** D Lampard, D Green, I A Jones
2002 Sept 2	**Bryn Fforch** I A Jones
2002 Sept 11	**Ground Zero** D Carroll, D Viggers
2002 Sept 14	**Dave's Route** (Carreg Wastad Fach) D Carroll, D Viggers, R Watson
2002 Sept 14	**Ground Pepper** D Carroll, D Viggers
2002 Sept 15	**Geriatricks** D Carroll, D Viggers, R Watson
2002 Sept 15	**Josh, Joe** D Carroll, D Viggers (AL)
2002 Sept 15	**Claude** R Watson, D Vigers (AL), D Carroll
2002 Sept 16	**Bogus Mountain Journey, Lonely Corner** D Carroll, R Watson
2002 Sept 24	**Days of the Weak** D Carroll, Ms P Watson
2002 Sept 25	**Drama Queen** Ms P Watson, D Carroll
2002 Sept 25	**Control Freak** D Carroll, Ms P Watson
2003 Feb 19	**Prince of Deifio Muff** M Hedge, G Logan
2003 March 30	**Feeding Station** D Lampard, I A Jones (AL)
2003 May 4	**Root Canal** D Lampard, D Green
2003 July 3	**Tosspot, Franco/Russian/Anglo/Welsh Pact** J Green, Ms E Roberts
2003 July 14	**Weed It and Reap, Uchelgeilliol** I A Jones, J Green
2003 July 14	**Under Pressure, Too Much Pressure** J Green, I A Jones
2003 July 17	**War Drum** I A Jones, J Green
2003 Aug 8	**Ghost Dance, Pokeyhuntas** D Lampard, I A Jones

Ghost Dance was not climbed in one pitch on the first ascent. Jones failed on his hoped-for line; Lampard then took over and was also rebuffed but then went his own way.

Index

New Climbs

Dinas Mot: Plexus Buttress Area

Ten metres right of *Hornets Attack Victor Mature* is a broken buttress of flakes and rowan trees. To the right of this, a tongue of slab sweeps down.

The Shining Path   55 meteres   E5   (26.8.03)

A powerful initial section leads to a bold pitch in a stunning position following the lip of a prominent diagonal overhang. Start down and right of the lowest rowan tree, at some flakes 7 metres below an overlap.

1 30m. 6b. Move up right onto the slab via a triangular hold and head straight up to the break in the overlap. Pull through this and climb the crack above to a rib (seemingly innocuous); step up right and swing left onto the slab, moving left to a shallow scoop leading diagonally left to a heathery ledge. Belay below the groove down and left of the big corner.

2 25m. 6b. Climb up into the groove; then reach up for a flake and swing left onto the slab, reaching a diagonal crack running up left. Move back down right and make a committing stride onto footholds on the very lip of the slab, and keep going out on small but positive holds to reach two 'sawn-off' pegs. Another difficult move allows you to gain a rounded scoop, before initiating irreversible moves up the rounded arête to reach the finishing-jug on the right.

Clogwyn Llo

Forty Years On   42 metres   Very Severe   (14.8.03)

Start as for *Foxglove*.

1 32m. 4c. Climb the steep rib and slabs above to reach a steep wall. Continue, using the twin cracks just right of *Aratnerphobia*.

2 10m. 4c. *Aratnerphobia* pitch 2.

First Ascents

2003 Aug 14	**Forty Years On** J Brown, C Davies, P Turnbull	

The name commemorates Brown's and Davies's new-routeing partnership of over 40 years in North Wales (37 years in the Pass). The ascent also follows 52 years after Joe's first ascent in the Pass, that of Hangover!

2003 Aug 26	**The Shining Path** D Lampard, I A Jones	

Pitch 1. Pitch 2 was climbed the next day and had been top-roped proir to the protection pegs being placed and the route being cleaned on abseil. Both pegs are stainless steel and ringers, but the first is only 4cm. long while the second is 5cm.

Accident Procedure

First Aid

If spinal or head injuries are suspected, do not move the patient without skilled help, except to maintain breathing or if this is essential for further protection.

If breathing has stopped, clear the airways and start artificial respiration. Do not stop until the patient recovers or expert opinion has diagnosed death.

Summon help as quickly as is compatible with safety. Do not hesitate or delay.

Rescue

In the event of an accident where further assistance is required, dial 999 and ask for the Police. The Police are responsible for co-ordinating all rescues and will contact other services as necessary.

- State that you require cliff rescue and report the exact location (six-figure grid reference if possible) and details of the accident.
- Be prepared to give your own name and home address if asked.
- Follow any further instructions or requests issued.

Helicopter

In the event of a helicopter evacuation, all climbers on or off the cliff should take heed. A helicopter flying close to the cliff will make verbal communication very difficult and small stones will be dislodged by the rotor downdraught. All loose equipment should be secured and climbers in precarious positions should try to make themselves safe.

The people with the injured person should try to identify their location. **No** attempt should be made to throw a rope at the helicopter, but assistance should be given to the helicopter crew if requested. Do not approach until directions are given by the crew. In particular, keep well clear of the main rotor, the tail rotor, and the engine exhaust.

Follow-up

After an accident, a report has to be compiled. Normally the details will be collated at the scene by the Police or rescue team, who will then pass the information to the Mountain Rescue Council Statistics Officer.

If unreasonable equipment failure is suspected then the British Mountaineering Council's technical committee may wish to investigate; contact the BMC at 177-179 Burton Road, West Didsbury, Manchester, M20 2BB. In the event of a serious accident, any equipment used by the casualty may be impounded.

Local Hospitals

The nearest Accident and Emergency unit is at Ysbytty Gwynedd, Bangor.

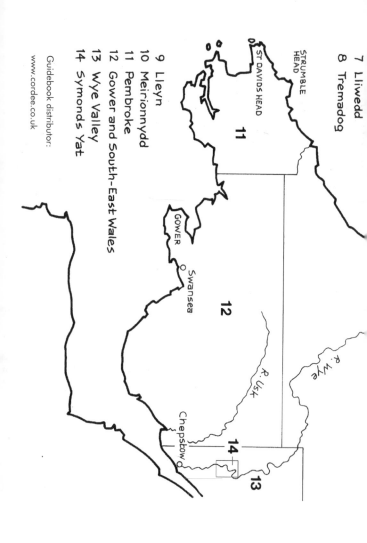

7 Lliwedd
8 Tremadog

9 Lleyn
10 Meirionnydd
11 Pembroke
12 Gower and South-East Wales
13 Wye Valley
14 Symonds Yat

STRUMBLE HEAD
ST DAVIDS HEAD
GOWER
Swansea
R. USK
R. Wye
Chepstow

11
12
14
13

Guidebook distributor:
www.cordee.co.uk